VMware vSAN 7.0 U3 Deep Dive

VMware vSAN 7.0 Update 3 Deep Dive

Copyright © 2022 by Cormac Hogan and Duncan Epping.

All rights reserved. No part of this book shall be reproduced, stored in a retrieval system, or transmitted by any means, electronic, mechanical, or otherwise, without written permission from the publisher. No patent liability is assumed on the use of the information contained herein. Although every precaution has been taken in the preparation of this book, the publisher and authors assume no responsibility for errors or omissions. Neither is any liability assumed for damages resulting from the use of the information contained herein. This book contains references to the word *master*. We recognize this as an exclusionary word. The word is used in this book for consistency because it appears, at the time of writing, in the output of CLI commands, and the log files.

International Standard Book Number: 9798426658486

All terms mentioned in this book that are known to be trademarks or service marks have been appropriately capitalized.

The use of a term in this book should not be regarded as affecting the validity of any trademark or service mark. Cover design by Aaron Epping (AaronEpping.nl)

Version: 1.0

About the authors

Cormac Hogan is a Chief Technologist in the Office of the CTO in the Cloud Infrastructure Business Group at VMware, focusing predominantly on Kubernetes platforms running on vSphere. Cormac has previously held roles in VMware's Technical Marketing, Integration Engineering and Support organizations. Cormac is the owner of CormacHogan.com, a blog site dedicated to storage, virtualization and container orchestration. He can be followed on Twitter @CormacJHogan.

Duncan Epping is a Chief Technologist working for VMware in the Office of CTO of the Cloud Infrastructure Business Group. Duncan is responsible for ensuring VMware's future innovations align with essential customer needs, translating customer problems to opportunities and functioning as the global lead evangelist for Cloud Infrastructure. Duncan is the owner of VMware Virtualization blog Yellow-Bricks.com and has various books on the topic of VMware including the "vSphere Clustering Deep Dive" series. He can be followed on Twitter @DuncanYB.

Index

- Preface 8
- Dedication 10
- Foreword 11

Introduction to VMware vSAN 13
- Software-Defined Datacenter 13
- Software-Defined Storage 14
- Hyper-Converged/Server SAN Solutions 14
- Introducing VMware vSAN 16
- What is vSAN? 17
- What does vSAN look like to an administrator? 22
- Summary 26

vSAN Prerequisites and Requirements 27
- VMware vSphere 27
- ESXi 27
- Cache and capacity devices 28
- ESXi boot considerations 29
- VMware Hardware Compatibility Guide 29
- vSAN ReadyNode 30
- A note about NVMe 30
- Storage controllers 31
- Disk Controller RAID-0 32
- Performance and RAID Caching 33
- Mixing SAS and SATA 34
- Disk Groups 34
- Disk Group Availability 35
- Disk Group Performance 36
- Capacity Tier Devices 36
- Cache Tier Devices 37
- Network Requirements 38
- Network Interface Cards 38
- Supported Virtual Switch Types 39
- NSX-T Interoperability 39
- Layer 2 or Layer 3 39
- VMkernel Network 40
- vSAN Network Traffic 40
- Jumbo Frames 41
- NIC Teaming 41
- Network I/O Control 42
- Firewall Ports 42
- vSAN Stretched Cluster 42
- vSAN Requirements 43
- Summary 44

vSAN Installation and Configuration 45
- Cluster Quickstart 45
- Cluster Quickstart Wizard 45
- Networking 52

VMkernel Network for vSAN..53
   Network Configuration Issues..56
   vSphere High Availability...65
   Summary..75

Architectural Details 77
   Distributed RAID..77
   Objects and Components..80
   Component Limits..82
   Virtual Machine Storage Objects 83
   Witnesses and Replicas 86
   Performance Stats DB Object 87
   Object Layout..87
   vSAN Software Components...88
   Component Management..89
   Data Paths for Objects 89
   Placement and Migration for Objects..90
   Cluster Monitoring, Membership, and Directory Services 91
   Host Roles...92
   Reliable Datagram Transport 92
   On-Disk Formats and Disk Format Changes (DFC)..93
   vSAN I/O Flow...94
   Deduplication and Compression 100
   Compression only 102
   Data Integrity through Checksum 103
   vSAN Encryption 104
   Data Locality...106
   Recovery from Failure...108
   Degraded Device Handling (DDH) 112
   iSCSI Targets and LUNs 112
   vSAN File Service..114
   vSAN HCI Mesh...117
   Summary..119

VM Storage Policies and VM Provisioning 121
   Introducing Storage Policy-Based Management in a vSAN Environment.........................121
   Failures to tolerate..126
   Number of Disk Stripes Per Object 131
   IOPS Limit for Object 147
   Flash Read Cache Reservation 147
   Object Space Reservation...148
   Force Provisioning 149
   Disable Object Checksum...150
   VM Home Namespace Revisited 151
   VM Swap Revisited..152
   Clone Caveat...154
   VASA Vendor Provider 156
   Virtual Machine Provisioning 159
   Changing VM Storage Policy On-the-Fly..180
   Summary..184

vSAN Operations 185
Skyline Health 185
Performance Service 193
Performance Diagnostics 195
Network Diagnostics 197
vSAN IOInsight.. 197
I/O Trip Analyzer 201
Host Management 202
Disk Management 216
vSAN Capacity Monitoring and Management 225
vCenter Management 233
vSAN Storage Services 234
vSAN iSCSI Target Service 234
vSAN File Service 239
vSAN HCI Mesh / Remote vSAN Datastores 252
Failure Scenarios 256
Summary 267

Stretched Cluster Use Case 269
What is a Stretched Cluster?... 269
Requirements and Constraints 271
Networking and Latency Requirements 272
New Concepts in vSAN Stretched Cluster 273
Configuration of a Stretched Cluster.. 277
Failures To Tolerate Policies 288
Site Disaster Tolerance Failure Scenarios 289
vSAN File Service 303
Operating a Stretched Cluster 307
Summary 309

Two Host vSAN Cluster Use Case 311
Configuration of a two-host cluster 312
vSAN Direct Connect 316
Support statements, requirements, and constraints.. 316
Summary 319

Cloud-Native Applications Use Case.. 321
What is a container? 321
Why Kubernetes? 322
Kubernetes Storage Constructs 322
Storage Class.. 322
Persistent Volumes 324
Persistent Volume Claim 324
Pod 325
vSphere CSI in action – block volume 327
Cloud-Native Storage (CNS) for vSphere Administrators – block volume........... 329
vSphere CSI in action – file volume 331
Cloud-Native Storage (CNS) for vSphere Administrators – file volume............... 334
vSphere CNS CSI architecture 335
vSphere with Tanzu Considerations 337

Data Persistence platform (DPp) 340
DPp Requirements 341
DPp deployment changes 341
vSAN Stretched Cluster support 342
Other CSI driver features 343
Summary 343

Command Line Tools 345
CLI vSAN Cluster Commands 345
esxcli vsan datastore 346
esxcli vsan debug 347
esxcli vsan faultdomain 349
esxcli vsan health 349
esxcli vsan iscsi 350
esxcli vsan maintenancemode 352
esxcli vsan network 352
esxcli vsan policy 353
esxcli vsan resync 356
esxcli vsan storage 356
esxcli vsan trace 358
Ruby vSphere Console (RVC) Commands 363
Summary 368
The End 369

Preface

When talking about virtualization and the underlying infrastructure that it runs on, one component that always comes up in conversation is storage. The reason for this is simple: In many environments, storage is a pain point. Although the storage landscape has changed with the introduction of flash technologies that mitigate many of the traditional storage issues, the pain of managing storage platforms has unfortunately not disappeared.

Storage challenges range from the operational effort, or complexity, to performance problems, or even availability constraints. The majority of these problems stem from the same fundamental problem: legacy architecture. The reason is that most storage platform architectures were developed long before virtualization existed, and virtualization changed the way these shared storage platforms are used.

In a way, you could say that virtualization forced the storage industry to look for new ways of building storage systems. Instead of having a single server connected to a single storage device (also known as a logical unit or LUN for short), virtualization typically entails having one (or many) physical server(s) running many virtual machines connecting to one or multiple storage devices. This did not only increase the load on these storage systems, but it also changed the workload patterns, increased the total capacity required, and added much complexity.

As you can imagine, for most storage administrators, this required a major shift in thinking. What should the size of my LUN be? What are my performance requirements, and how many spindles will be necessary? What kind of data services are required on these LUNs, and where will virtual machines be stored? Not only did it require a major shift in thinking, but it also required working in tandem with other IT teams. In the past server admins and network and storage admins could all live in their own isolated worlds, they now needed to communicate and work together to ensure availability of the platform they were building. Whereas in the past a mistake, such as a misconfiguration or under-provisioning, would only impact a single server, it could now impact many virtual machines.

There was a fundamental shift in how we collectively thought about how to operate and architect IT infrastructures when virtualization was introduced. Now another collective shift is happening all over again. This time it is due to the introduction of software-defined networking and software-defined storage. But let's not let history repeat itself, and let's avoid the mistakes we all made when virtualization first arrived. Let's all have frank and open discussions with our fellow datacenter administrators as we all aim to revolutionize datacenter architecture and operations!

You, the reader

This book is targeted at IT professionals who are involved in the care and feeding of a VMware vSphere environment. Ideally, you have been working with VMware vSphere for some time and perhaps you have attended an authorized course in vSphere, such as the "Install, Configure, and Manage" class. This book is not a starters guide, it is a deep dive, there should be enough in the book for administrators and architects of all levels.

Dedication

"Deafening silence reigns
As twilight fills the sky
Eventual supremacy
Daylight waits to die
Darkness always calls my name
A pawn in this recurring game
Humanity going insane"

"Skeletons of Society" by Slayer.

Foreword

It has been eight years since we first released vSAN in 2014. At the time, hyperconverged infrastructure (HCI) was a brand new concept surrounded by some amount of uncertainty and even doubt. The storage industry had always been dominated by purpose-built hardware and specialized appliances, but trends in flash as a new storage medium plus continued growth in computing and networking performance were opening the opportunity for new architectures and new business models to disrupt the industry.

Meanwhile, cloud was just taking off. Developers were eager for a better experience with more self-service and automation. As IT organizations looked to meet that demand and build their own cloud operations, "software-defined" became the next big idea, promising to replace traditional purpose-built appliances with software-based services. The goal was a cloud operating model in the data center, with lower costs thanks to scale out, x86 economics and reduced operational overhead. This in turn provided an opening for HCI, to be that architecture that delivered on the promise of software-defined and that delivered better economics, greater simplicity, and superior scalability.

Since that time, the category has seen explosive growth. vSAN has become the most widely deployed HCI software in the market with more than 30,000 customers. vSAN has become the building block for many customers' private clouds with deployments ranging from a couple of servers to thousands of nodes spread across multiple sites and hosting petabytes of data. The workloads on vSAN themselves have matured to include business critical, high-performance databases and applications. In short, HCI has become mainstream. Along the way, customer requirements and expectations have expanded. HCI has evolved from "hyperconverged infrastructure" to "hybrid cloud infrastructure" with requirements for full-stack networking and management, multi-cloud deployments and support for modern application architectures.

The vSAN team has embraced these opportunities by investing in deep integration with the rest of the VMware technology stack to deliver a complete cloud platform powered by vSphere, vSAN and NSX. That cloud platform has become the common infrastructure layer across multiple cloud environments, including partnerships with Amazon, Google, Microsoft, and hundreds of cloud provider partners to deliver a multi-cloud infrastructure-as-a-service. Meanwhile, vSAN continues to deliver new innovations like HCI Mesh, vSAN File Services, and the Data Persistence platform while embracing containers and Kubernetes through the investment in the Cloud Native Storage control plane and CSI driver.

Given all these changes, it is crucial that technology thought leaders like Cormac and Duncan provide the deeper insight and guidance to aid practitioners in leveraging these capabilities. These two are not only great technologists but great communicators that can provide the key information and insights required to get the most out of vSAN.
Thank you for your interest in VMware vSAN, and I know that it can be a fundamental building

block for your own multi-cloud infrastructure.

John Gilmartin
Senior Vice President and General Manager, Cloud Storage and Data
Cloud Infrastructure Business Group, VMware

01

Introduction to VMware vSAN

This chapter introduces you to the world of the software-defined datacenter, but with a focus on the storage aspect. The chapter covers the premise of the software-defined datacenter and then delves deeper to cover the concept of software-defined storage and associated solutions such as *hyperconverged infrastructure* (HCI) solutions.

Software-Defined Datacenter

VMworld, the VMware annual conferencing event, introduced VMware's vision for the *software-defined datacenter* (SDDC) in 2012. The SDDC is VMware's architecture for the public and private clouds where all pillars of the datacenter—computing, storage, and networking (and the associated services)—are virtualized. Virtualizing datacenter components enables the IT team to be more flexible. If you lower the operational complexity and cost while increasing availability and agility, you will lower the time to market for new services.

To achieve all of that, virtualization of components by itself is not sufficient. The platform used must be capable of being installed and configured in a fully automated fashion. More importantly, the platform should enable you to manage and monitor your infrastructure in a smart and less operationally intense manner. That is what the SDDC is all about! Raghu Raghuram (Chief Executive Officer, VMware) captured it in a single sentence: The essence of the software-defined datacenter is "abstract, pool, and automate."

Abstraction, pooling, and automation are all achieved by introducing an additional layer on top of the physical resources. This layer is usually referred to as a *virtualization layer.* Everyone reading this book should be familiar with the leading product for compute virtualization, VMware vSphere. By now, most people are probably also familiar with network virtualization, sometimes referred to as *software-defined network* (SDN) solutions. VMware offers a solution named NSX to virtualize networking and security functionality. NSX does for networking what vSphere does for compute. These layers do not just virtualize the physical resources but also allow you to abstract resources, pool them, and provide you with an API that enables you to automate all operational aspects.

Automation is not just about scripting, however. A significant part of the automation of *virtual machine* (VM) provisioning is achieved through policy-based management. Predefined policies allow you to provision VMs in a quick, easy, consistent, and repeatable manner. The resource characteristics specified on a resource pool or a vApp container exemplify a compute policy. These characteristics enable you to quantify resource policies for compute in terms of reservation, limit, and priority. Network policies can range from security to *quality of service* (QoS). Storage policies enable you to specify availability, performance, and recoverability characteristics.

This book examines the storage component of VMware's SDDC. More specifically, the book covers how a product called *VMware vSAN* (vSAN), fits into this vision. You will learn how it has been implemented and integrated within the current platform and how you can leverage its capabilities and the book expands on the lower-level implementation details. Before going further, though, you want to have a generic understanding of where vSAN fits into the bigger software-defined storage picture.

Software-Defined Storage

Software-defined storage (SDS) is a term that has been used, and abused, by many vendors. Because software-defined storage is currently defined in so many different ways, consider the following quote from VMware:

> **"Software-Defined Storage is the automation and pooling of storage through a software control plane, and the ability to provide storage from industry-standard servers. This offers a significant simplification to the way storage is provisioned and managed, and also paves the way for storage on industry-standard servers at a fraction of the cost."**

A software defined storage product is a solution that abstracts the hardware and allows you to easily pool all resources and provide them to the consumer using a user-friendly *user interface (*UI) and *application programming interface* (API). A software-defined storage solution allows you to both scale up and scale out, without increasing the operational effort.

Many industry experts feel that software-defined storage is about moving functionality from the traditional storage devices to the host. This trend was started by virtualized versions of storage solutions such as HP's StoreVirtual VSA and evolved into solutions that were built to run on many different hardware platforms. One example of such a solution is Nexenta. These solutions were the start of a new era.

Hyper-Converged/Server SAN Solutions

Over recent years there have been many debates around what hyperconverged is versus a Server SAN solution. In our opinion, the big difference between these two is the level of integration with the platform it is running on and the delivery model. When it comes to the delivery mode there are two distinct flavors:
- Appliance based
- Software only

An appliance-based solution is one where the hardware and the software are sold and delivered as a single bundle. It will come preinstalled with a hypervisor and usually requires little to no effort to configure. There also is deep integration with the platform it sits on (or in) typically. This can range from using the provided storage APIs to providing extensive data services to being embedded in the hypervisor.

In all of these cases local storage is aggregated into a large, shared pool by leveraging a virtual storage appliance or a kernel-based storage stack. The best example of an appliance-based solution today would be Dell VxRail. Other companies which used this model are Nutanix and HPE SimpliVity. When one would have asked the general audience a couple of years ago what a typical "hyperconverged appliance" looked like the answer would have been: a 2U form factor with four hosts. However, hyper-convergence is not about a form factor in our opinion, and most vendors have moved on from this concept. Yes, some still offer this form factor, but they offer it alongside various other form factors like 1U, 2U, 1U two hosts, 2U two hosts, and even blade and composable infrastructure solutions.

It is not about the form factor; it is about combining different components into a single solution. This solution needs to be easy to install, configure, manage, and monitor.

You might ask, "If these are generic x86 servers with hypervisors installed and a virtual storage appliance or a kernel-based storage stack, what are the benefits over a traditional storage system?" The benefits of a hyperconverged platform are as follows:

- Time to market is short, less than 1 hour to install, and configure
- Ease of management and level of integration
- Ability to scale out and scale up, both capacity and performance-wise
- Lower total costs of acquisition compared to traditional environments
- Lower upfront investment required

As mentioned, many of these solutions are sold as a single *stock keeping unit* (SKU), and typically a single point of contact for support is provided. This can make support discussions much easier. However, a hurdle for many companies is the fact that these solutions are tied to hardware and specific configurations. The hardware used by (appliance-based) hyperconverged vendors is often not the same as the preferred hardware supplier you may already have. This can lead to operational challenges when it comes to updating/patching or even cabling and racking. In addition, a trust issue exists. Some people swear by server vendor X and would never want to touch any other brand, whereas others won't come close to server vendor X. Fortunately, most hyperconverged vendors these days offer the ability to buy their solution through different server hardware vendors. If that does not provide sufficient flexibility, then this is where the software-based storage solutions come into play.

Software-only storage solutions come in two flavors. The most common solution today amongst HCI vendors is the virtual storage appliance (VSA). VSA solutions are deployed as a VM on top of a hypervisor installed on physical hardware. VSAs allow you to pool underlying physical resources into a shared storage device. An example of a VSA would for instance be Nutanix. The advantage of software-only solutions is that you typically can leverage existing hardware if it is on the *hardware compatibility list* (HCL). In most cases, the HCL is comparable to what the underlying hypervisor supports, except for key components like disk controllers and flash devices.

vSAN is also a software-only solution, but vSAN differs significantly from a VSAs. vSAN sits in a different layer and is not a VSA-based solution. On top of that, vSAN is typically combined with hardware by a vendor of your choice. Hence, VMware refers to vSAN as a hyperconverged software solution as it is the enabler of many hyperconverged offerings. An example of an HCI offering based on vSAN would be Dell EMC's product called VxRail.

Introducing VMware vSAN

VMware's strategy for software-defined storage is to focus on a set of VMware initiatives related to local storage, shared storage, and storage/data services. In essence, VMware wants to make vSphere a platform for storage services.

Historically, storage was configured and deployed at the start of a project and was not changed during its life cycle. If there was a need to change some characteristics or features of a LUN or volume that were being leveraged by VMs, in many cases the original LUN or volume was deleted and a new volume with the required features or characteristics was created. This was a very intrusive, risky, and time-consuming operation due to the requirement to migrate workloads between LUNs or volumes, which may have taken weeks to coordinate.

With software-defined storage, VM storage requirements can be dynamically instantiated. There is no need to repurpose LUNs or volumes. VM workloads and requirements may change over time, and the underlying storage can be adapted to the workload at any time. vSAN aims to provide storage services and service-level agreement *automation* through a software layer on the hosts that *integrates* with, *abstracts*, and *pools* the underlying hardware.

A key factor for software-defined storage is, in our opinion, *storage policy-based management* (SPBM). SPBM is a critical component of how VMware is implementing software-defined storage.

Using SPBM and vSphere APIs, the underlying storage technology surfaces an abstracted pool of storage capacity with various capabilities that are presented to vSphere administrators for VM provisioning. The capabilities can relate to performance, availability, or storage services such as thin provisioning, compression, replication, and more. A vSphere administrator can then create a *VM storage policy* using a subset of the capabilities that are required by the application running in the VM. At provisioning time, the vSphere administrator selects a VM storage policy. SPBM then ensures that the VM is always instantiated on the appropriate underlying storage, based on the requirements placed in the VM storage policy, and that the VM is provisioned with the right amount of resources, the required services from the abstracted pool of storage resources.

Should the VM's workload, availability requirement, or I/O pattern change over time, it is simply a matter of applying a new VM storage policy with requirements and characteristics that reflect the new workload to that specific VM, or even virtual disk, after which the policy will be seamlessly applied without any manual intervention from the administrator (in contrast to many legacy storage systems, where a manual migration of VMs or virtual disks to a different datastore would be required). vSAN has been developed to seamlessly integrate with vSphere and the SPBM functionality it offers.

What is vSAN?

vSAN is a storage solution from VMware, released as a beta in 2013, made generally available to the public in March 2014, and reached version 7.0 Update 3 in October of 2021. vSAN is fully integrated with vSphere. It is an object-based storage system that aims to simplify VM storage placement decisions for vSphere administrators by leveraging storage policy-based management. It fully supports and is integrated with core vSphere features such as vSphere High Availability (HA), vSphere Distributed Resource Scheduler (DRS), and vMotion. vSAN and vSphere go hand in hand as illustrated below.

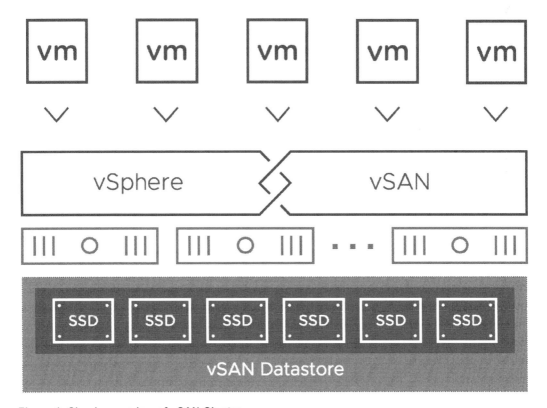

Figure 1: Simple overview of vSAN Cluster

vSAN's goal is to provide both resilience and scale-out storage functionality. It can also be thought of in the context of QoS in so far as VM storage policies can be created that define the level of performance and availability required on a per-VM, or even virtual disk, basis.

vSAN is a software-based distributed storage solution that is built directly into the hypervisor. Although not a virtual appliance like many of the other solutions out there, vSAN can best be thought of as a kernel-based solution that is included with the hypervisor. Technically, however, this is not completely accurate because components critical for performance and responsiveness such as the data path and clustering are in the kernel, while other components that collectively can be considered part of the "control plane" are implemented as native user-space agents. Nevertheless, with vSAN, there is no need to install anything other than the software you are already familiar with: VMware vSphere.

vSAN is about simplicity, and when we say *simplicity*, we do mean simplicity. Want to try out vSAN? Within a few easy steps, you have your environment up and running. Of course, there are certain recommendations and requirements to optimize your experience, we will discuss these in further detail in chapter 2.

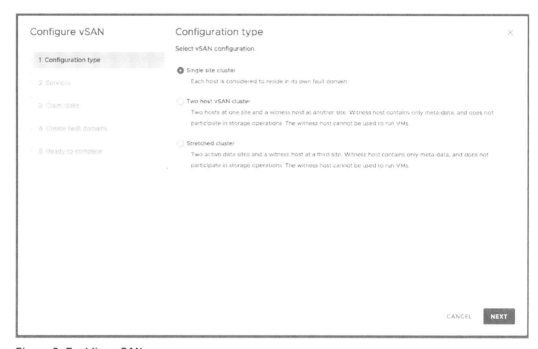

Figure 2: Enabling vSAN

Now that you know it is easy to use and simple to configure, what are the benefits of a solution like vSAN? What are the key selling points?

- **Software-defined:** Use industry-standard hardware
- **Flexible:** Scale as needed and when needed, both scale-up and scale-out
- **Simple:** Easy to configure, manage and operate
- **Automated:** Per-VM or per-disk policy-based management
- **Hyperconverged:** Repeatable building-block

That sounds compelling, doesn't it? Where does vSAN fit you may ask, what are the use cases and are there situations where it doesn't fit today? Today the use cases are as follows:

- **Business critical apps:** Stable storage platform with all data services required to run business critical workloads, whether that is Microsoft Exchange, SQL, Oracle etc.
- **Virtual desktops:** Scale-out model using predictive and repeatable infrastructure blocks lowers costs and simplifies operations.
- **Test and dev:** Avoid acquisition of expensive storage (lowers *total cost of ownership* [TCO]), fast time to provision.
- **Cloud-Native Applications:** Provides the storage infrastructure needed for running your cloud-native apps and persisting your associated data.
- **Management or DMZ infrastructure:** Fully isolated resulting in increased security and no dependencies on the resources it is potentially managing.
- **Disaster recovery target:** Inexpensive disaster recovery solution, enabled through a feature like vSphere replication that allows you to replicate to any storage platform.
- **Remote office/branch office (ROBO):** With the ability to start with as little as two hosts, centrally managed, vSAN is the ideal fit for ROBO environments.
- **Stretched cluster:** Providing very high availability across remote sites for a wide range of potential workloads.

Now that you know what vSAN is and that it is ready for any type of workload, let's have a brief look at what was introduced in terms of functionality with each release.

- **vSAN 1.0: March 2014**
  Initial release
- **vSAN 6.0: March 2015**
  All-flash configurations
  64 host cluster scalability
  2x performance increase for hybrid configurations
  New snapshot mechanism
  Enhanced cloning mechanism
  Fault domain/rack awareness
- **vSAN 6.1: September 2015**
  Stretched clustering across a max of 5 ms RTT (milliseconds)
  2-node vSAN for remote office, branch office (ROBO) solutions
  vRealize Operations management pack
  vSphere replication—5 minutes RPO
  Health monitoring
- **vSAN 6.2: March 2016**
  RAID 5 and 6 over the network (erasure coding)
  Space efficiency (deduplication and compression)
  QoS—IOPS limits
  Software checksums

- IPv6 support
- Performance monitoring
- **vSAN 6.5: November 2016**
  - vSAN iSCSI Service
  - vSAN 2-node Direct Connect
  - 512e device support
  - Cloud-Native Application support
- **vSAN 6.6: April 2017**
  - Local Protection for Stretched Clusters
  - Removal of Multicast
  - ESXi Host Client (HTML-5) management and monitoring functionality
  - Enhanced rebalancing, repairs, and resyncs
  - Resync throttling
  - Maintenance Mode Pre-Check
  - Stretched Cluster Witness Replacement UI
  - vSAN Support Insight
  - vSAN Easy Install
  - vSAN Config Assist / Firmware Update
  - Enhanced Performance and Health Monitoring
- **vSAN 6.6.1: November 2017**
  - Update Manager Integration
  - Performance Diagnostics added to Cloud Analytics
  - Storage Device Serviceability
  - New Licensing for ROBO and VDI
- **vSAN 6.7: April 2018**
  - HTML-5 User Interface support
  - Native vRealize Operations dashboards in the HTML-5 client
  - Support for Microsoft WSFC using vSAN iSCSI
  - Fast Network Failovers
  - Optimization: Adaptive Resync
  - Optimization: Witness Traffic Separation for Stretched Clusters
  - Optimization: Preferred Site Override for Stretched Clusters
  - Optimization: Efficient Resync for Stretched Clusters
  - Optimization: Enhanced Diagnostic Partition
  - Optimization: Efficient Decommissioning
  - Optimization: Efficient and consistent storage policies
  - 4K Native Device Support
  - FIPS 140-2 Level 1 validation
- **vSAN 6.7 U1: October 2018**
  - Trim/Unmap
  - Cluster Quickstart Wizard
  - Mixed MTU Support
  - Historical Capacity Reporting
  - Additional vR Ops Dashboards

Enhanced support experience
  Secondary FTT for Racks
- **vSAN 6.7 U3: August 2019**
  Cloud-Native Storage
  Native SCSI-3 PGR for Windows Server Failover Cluster (WSFC) support
  Improved Capacity Usage views (including block container volumes)
  Improved Resync insights – ability to see queued but not yet active resyncs
  Maintenance Mode/Data Migration pre-checks
  Online iSCSI LUN Resize
  Improved destage performance with LSOM enhancements
  Parallel resync operations
  vsantop command line tool for performance monitoring
- **vSAN 7.0: April 2020**
  Integrated Native File Services (NFS File Shares)
  Read-Write-Many Persistent Volumes via CSI-CNS and vSAN 7
  vSAN Memory performance metric now displayed
  Shared disks with multi-writer flag no longer need to be Easy Zero Thick on vSAN 7
  Support for larger 1PB Logical capacity when deduplication and compression enabled
  Objects immediately repaired when Witness Appliance replaced
  NVMe hot-plug support
- **vSAN 7.0 U1: October 2020**
  vSAN File Services now supports the SMB protocol – more details
  vSAN File Services now supports Kerberos and Active Directory
  vSAN File Services Scale Increase from 8 to 32
  HCI Mesh introduced for mounting remote vSAN datastore
  A new Compression Only Data Service
  vSAN "Shared" Witness Appliance
  vSAN Data Persistence platform for cloud-native applications in vSphere with Tanzu
  Increased usable capacity with new capacity management features
- **vSAN 7.0 U2: March 2021**
  HCI Mesh now allows remote mounting of vSAN datastore from non-vSAN clusters
  HCI Mesh, vSAN datastores can support up to 128 remote host mounts
  vSAN Stretched Cluster now supports 20+20+1 configurations
  vSAN Stretched Cluster has deeper integrations with DRS for object sync and fail-back
  vSAN File Services now works on vSAN Stretched Cluster and 2-node vSAN
  vSAN File Services Scale Increase from 32 to 100 shares
  vSAN now supports vSphere Proactive HA
  vSAN supports the new vSphere Native Key Provider
  vSAN over RDMA
  Skyline Health Check History

- **vSAN 7.0 U3: October 2021**
  Stretched cluster site/witness failure resiliency
  Nested fault domains for two-node deployments
  vSAN File Services - Access Based Enumeration
  vSAN cluster shutdown and restart
  Enhanced network monitoring and anomaly detection
  vSAN health check correlation
  VM I/O trip analyzer
  Stretched Cluster support for vanilla Kubernetes
  vSAN Data Persistence Platform now supports asynchronous installation and upgrades
  CNS platform has improved performance, scale, and resiliency

Hopefully, that gives a quick overview of all the capabilities introduced and available in each of the releases. Even though there are many items listed this list is still not complete. This, however, does not mean vSAN is complex to configure, manage, and monitor. Let's take a look from an administrator perspective; what does vSAN look like?

What does vSAN look like to an administrator?

When vSAN is enabled, by default a single shared datastore is presented to all hosts that are part of the vSAN-enabled cluster. Just like any other storage solution out there, this datastore can be used as a destination for VMs and all associated components, such as virtual disks, swap files, and VM configuration files. When you deploy a new VM, you will see the familiar interface and a list of available datastores, including your vSAN-based datastore, as shown in the following screenshot.

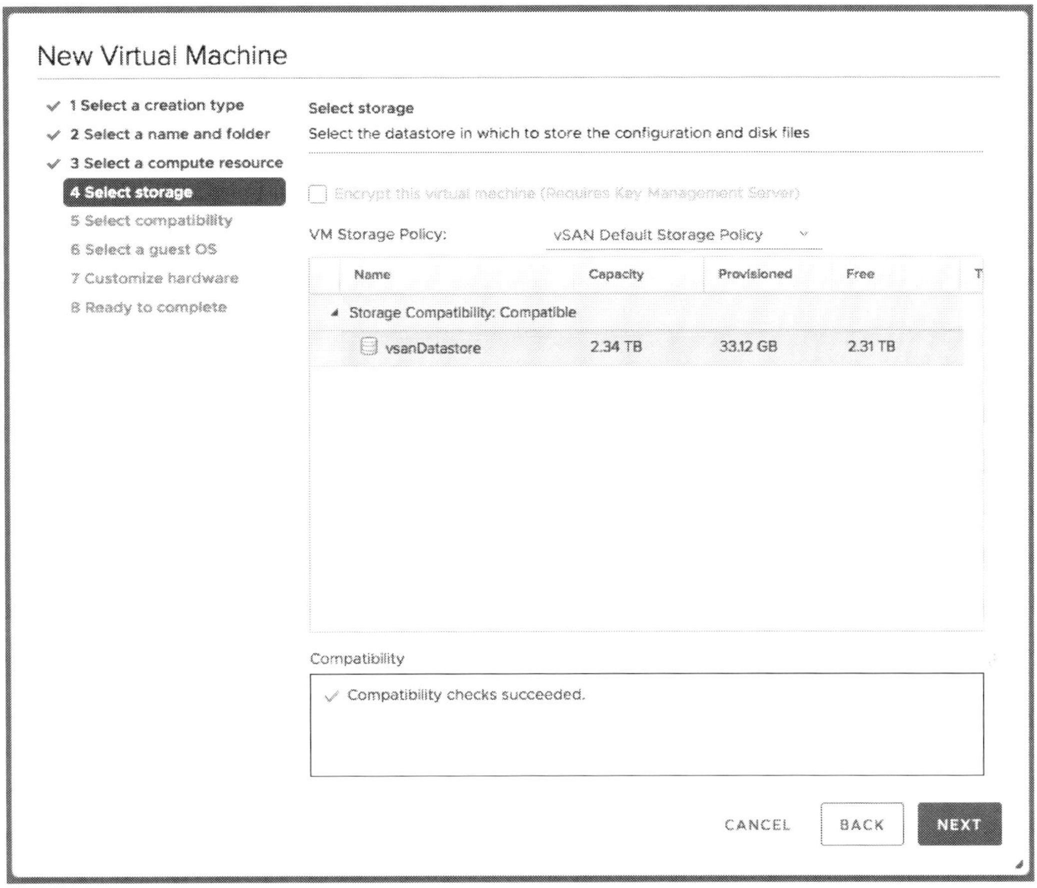

01 // Introduction to VMware vSAN

Figure 3: Enabling vSAN

This vSAN datastore is formed out of host local storage resources. Typically, all hosts within a vSAN-enabled cluster will contribute performance (flash) and capacity (magnetic disks or flash) to this shared datastore. This means that when your cluster grows, your datastore will grow with it. vSAN is what is called a scale-out storage system (adding hosts to a cluster), but also allows scaling up (adding devices to a host).

Each host contributing storage capacity to the vSAN cluster will require at least one flash device and one capacity device (magnetic disk or flash). Note that the capacity tier is either all-flash or all magnetic disks; they cannot be mixed in the same vSAN cluster. Thus, we have 2 flavors of vSAN. We have the all-flash version, where the cache and capacity are comprised entirely of flash devices. And we have the hybrid model, where flash devices are used for the cache layer, and magnetic disks are used for the capacity tier. At a minimum, vSAN requires three hosts in your cluster to contribute storage (or two hosts if you decide to use a witness host, which is a common configuration for ROBO, this is discussed in chapter 8); other hosts in your cluster could leverage these storage resources without contributing storage resources to the cluster itself, although this is not common. The diagram below shows a cluster that has four hosts, of which three (esxi-01, esxi-02, and esxi-03) contribute storage and a fourth does not contribute but only consumes storage resources. Although it is technically possible to have a non-uniform cluster and have a host not contributing storage, VMware highly recommends creating a uniform cluster and having all hosts contribute storage for overall better utilization, performance, and availability.

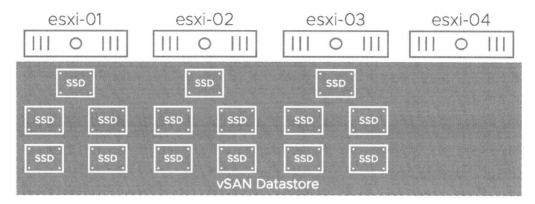

Figure 4: non-uniform vSAN cluster example

The typical boundary for vSAN in terms of both size and connectivity is a vSphere cluster. Although vSAN is now also capable of sharing storage to regular vSphere clusters, we are not going to discuss this functionality (HCI Mesh) at this stage. This means that vSAN supports single clusters/datastores of up to 64 hosts, but of course a single vCenter Server instance can manage many 64 host clusters. It is a common practice for most customers however to limit their clusters to around 24 hosts. This is for operational considerations like the time it takes to update a full cluster. Each host can run a supported maximum of 200 VMs, up to a total of 6,400 VMs within a 64-host vSAN cluster. As you can imagine with a storage system at this scale, performance and responsiveness are of the utmost importance. vSAN is designed to take advantage of flash to provide the experience users expect in today's world. Flash resources are used for all writes and, depending on the type of hardware configuration used (all-flash or hybrid), reads will typically also be served from flash.

To ensure VMs can be deployed with certain characteristics, vSAN enables you to set policies on a per-virtual disk or a per-VM basis. These policies help you meet the defined *service level objectives* (SLOs) for your workload. These can be performance-related characteristics such as read caching or disk striping but can also be availability-related characteristics that ensure strategic replica placement of your VM's disks (and other important files) across racks or even locations.

If you have worked with VM storage policies in the past, you might now wonder whether all VMs stored on the same vSAN datastore will need to have the same VM storage policy assigned. The answer is no. vSAN allows you to have different policies for VMs provisioned to the same datastore and even different policies for disks from the same VM.

As stated earlier, by leveraging policies, the level of resilience can be configured on a per-virtual disk granular level. How many hosts and disks a mirror copy will reside on depends on the selected policy. Because vSAN can use mirror copies (RAID-1) or erasure coding (RAID-5/6) defined by policy to provide resiliency, it does not require a host local RAID configuration. RAID stands for Redundant Array of Inexpensive Disks. In other words, hosts contributing to vSAN storage capacity should simply provide a set of disks to vSAN.

Whether you have defined a policy to tolerate a single host failure or a policy that will tolerate up to three hosts failing, vSAN will ensure that enough replicas of your objects are created. The following example illustrates how this is an important aspect of vSAN and one of the major differentiators between vSAN and most other virtual storage solutions out there.

Example: We have configured a policy that can tolerate one failure and created a new virtual disk. We have chosen to go with failures to tolerate = 1, which in this case results in a RAID-1 configuration. This means that vSAN will create two identical storage objects and a witness. The witness is a component tied to the VM that allows vSAN to determine who should win ownership in the case of a failure. If you are familiar with clustering technologies, think of the witness component as a quorum object that will arbitrate ownership in the event of a failure. The diagram below may help clarify these sometimes difficult-to-understand concepts. This figure illustrates what it would look like on a high level for a VM with a virtual disk that can tolerate one failure. This can be the failure of a host, NICs, disk controller, disk, or flash device, for instance.

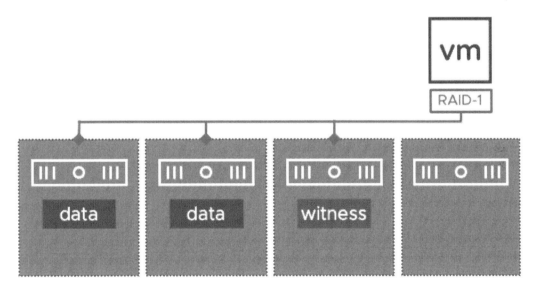

Figure 5: vSAN Failures to tolerate

In the diagram above, the VM's compute resides on the fourth host and its virtual disks reside on the other hosts in the cluster. In this scenario, the vSAN network is used for storage I/O, allowing for the VM to freely move around the cluster without the need for storage components to be migrated along with the compute. This does, however, result in the first requirement when implementing vSAN. vSAN requires at a minimum one dedicated 1 GbE NIC port for small scale hybrid configurations, but VMware recommends 10 GbE for the vSAN network. 10 GbE is a requirement for all-flash vSAN configurations, which are the most common configurations deployed by vSAN customers today.

Yes, this might still sound complex, but in all fairness, vSAN masks away all the complexity, as you will learn as you progress through the various chapters in this book.

VxRail – vSAN Inside

We have mentioned the VxRail product from Dell EMC several times already in this introduction. It is probably worth calling out that this HCI appliance is based on VMware vSphere and VMware vSAN, and that the contents of this book are also directly applicable to this product. Of course, there may be some operational differences from the deployment and configuration perspective which are some of the benefits of the VxRail model. However, administrators and architects of VxRail systems should also get benefit from the content found in this book.

VMware Cloud on AWS, Azure, Google, and VMware vSAN

VMware vSAN is not only the storage of choice in the VMware Cloud on AWS offering but is also the storage platform of choice for the Microsoft Azure VMware Solution and the Google Cloud VMware Engine. Although we do not directly discuss these public cloud offerings in this book, we would like to ensure that you, the reader, know about this offering. These public cloud services by AWS, Azure, and Google are the fastest and easiest way to deploy and consume a VMware based SDDC, or to get familiar with products like VMware vSAN and VMware NSX. Do note, the infrastructure provided as part of these offerings is managed by the public cloud provider, as such some functionality that we will discuss in the book may be restricted from configurational changes.

Summary

To conclude, VMware vSAN is a market-leading, hypervisor-based distributed storage platform that enables convergence of compute and storage resources, typically referred to as hyperconverged infrastructure. It enables you to define VM-level granular service level objectives through policy-based management. It allows you to control availability and performance in a way never seen before, simple, and efficient.

This chapter just scratched the surface. Now it's time to take it to the next level. Chapter 2 describes the requirements for installing and configuring vSAN.

02

vSAN Prerequisites and Requirements

Before delving into the installation and configuration of vSAN, it's necessary to discuss the requirements and the prerequisites. VMware vSphere is the foundation of every vSAN-based virtual infrastructure.

VMware vSphere

vSAN was first released with VMware vSphere 5.5 U1 way back in 2014. Additional versions of vSAN have since been released, the most recent release being vSphere 7.0U3 which was released towards the latter part of 2021. Each of the releases included additional vSAN features, which will be discussed at various stages of this book, and were listed in Chapter 1, "Introduction to vSAN."

VMware vSphere consists of two major components: the vCenter Server management tool and the ESXi hypervisor. To install and configure vSAN, both vCenter Server and ESXi are required.

VMware vCenter Server provides a centralized management platform for VMware vSphere environments. It is the solution used to provision new VMs, configure hosts, and perform many other operational tasks associated with managing a virtualized infrastructure.

To run a fully supported vSAN environment, VMware strongly recommends using the latest version of vSphere where possible. vSAN is configured and monitored via the vSphere client. Starting with vSphere 6.7, the vSphere HTML-5 client introduced full support for managing and monitoring vSAN. vSAN can also be fully configured and managed through the *command-line interface* (CLI) and the vSphere API for those wanting to automate some (or all) of the aspects of vSAN configuration, monitoring, or management. Although a single cluster can contain only one "local" vSAN datastore, a vCenter server can manage multiple vSAN and compute clusters.

ESXi

VMware vSphere ESXi is an enterprise-grade virtualization hypervisor product that allows you to run multiple instances of an operating system in a fully isolated fashion on a single server. It is a bare-metal solution, meaning that it does not require a guest-OS and has an extremely thin footprint. ESXi is the foundation for the large majority of virtualized environments worldwide.

For standard datacenter deployments, vSAN requires a minimum of three ESXi hosts (where each host has local storage and is contributing this storage to the vSAN datastore) to form a *supported* vSAN cluster. This is to allow the cluster to meet the minimum availability requirements of tolerating at least one host failure. There is of course the option of deploying a 2-node vSAN configuration along with a witness appliance, but this is aimed primarily are remote office/branch office type environments and not datacenters. There are some additional considerations around the use of a 2-node vSAN cluster which will be discussed in more detail in Chapter 8, "Two Node Use Case." The role of the witness appliance, and indeed the witness components will be discussed in detail throughout this book, so don't worry about those for the moment.

As of vSAN 6.0, a maximum of 64 ESXi hosts in a cluster is supported. The ESXi hosts and vCenter server must be running version 6.0 at a minimum to support 64 hosts, we however recommend using vSphere 7.0 U3 at a minimum.

From a CPU usage perspective, the important factor to keep in mind is that the ESXi CPU is now performing storage tasks, alongside virtualization tasks, when vSAN is configured. As storage device density increases, the more VMs we may be able to provision to a vSAN cluster. This in turn means increased CPU consumption as we are running more and more workloads. All this needs to be considered when sizing a vSAN cluster. One helpful fact is that the latest generations of CPUs are much more efficient when it comes to offloading certain operations, for example *Advanced Encryption Standard – New Instructions* (AES-NI) for encryption and Intel CRC32/CRC32C for checksum calculations which makes the processing extremely fast and efficient.

vSAN memory consumption depends on the number and configuration of storage devices. Therefore, the amount of memory needed per ESXi host is completely dependent on the number of devices in each host and how they are configured. *VMware knowledgebase article 2113954* assists vSAN customers in determining the correct memory configuration for your vSAN deployments. vSAN does not consume all this memory, but it is required to implement the correct configuration. In all cases, we recommend that each host is configured with at least 64 GB per host to ensure that your workloads, vSAN and the hypervisor have sufficient resources to ensure an optimal user experience. vSAN scales back on its memory usage when hosts have less than 32 GB of memory which may impact overall vSAN performance.

One last point on memory – vSAN allocates 0.4% of memory per host, up to a maximum of 1GB, for its client cache. Client cache is a low latency host local read cache. This is an in-memory cache which caches the data of a VM on the same host where the VM is located. This local client-side cache will be discussed in further detail in the vSAN Architecture chapter.

Cache and capacity devices

There are two models of vSAN: the all-flash model and the hybrid model. A hybrid configuration is where the cache tier is made up of flash-based devices and the capacity tier is made up of magnetic disks. (Magnetic disks may also be referred to as *Hard Disk Drives*, or HDDs throughout this book). In the all-flash version, both the cache tier and capacity tier are made up of flash devices. The flash devices of the cache and capacity tier are typically different grades of flash device in terms of performance and endurance. This allows you, under certain circumstances, to create all-flash configurations at close to the cost of SAS-based magnetic disk configurations.

ESXi boot considerations

When it comes to installing an ESXi host for vSAN-based infrastructure, there are various options to consider regarding where to place the ESXi image. ESXi can be installed on a local magnetic disk, USB flash drive, SD card or SATADOM devices. At the time of writing (vSAN 7.0U3), stateless booting of ESXi (auto-deploy) is not supported.

Pre vSphere 7.0 the preferred method of deploying ESXi was to a USB flash device or SD card. This provided the advantage of not consuming a magnetic disk or flash device for the boot image. However, there are some drawbacks to this approach, such as a lack of space for storing log files and vSAN trace files, as well as endurance considerations. Hence starting with vSphere 7.0 VMware changed this recommendation. Details can be found in KB 85685.

We highly recommend using local persistent devices for the installation of ESXi. This will provide the ability to not only store log files and trace files locally, but it will also provide the added benefit that memory dumps, in the case of a host failure, can be stored persistently.

There is a large variety of devices supported for the installation of ESXi, and we have seen customers using solutions ranging from HDDs in a RAID-1 configuration, to an M.2 flash device or a SATADOM device. We recommend a reliable device that provides at minimum 128GB of capacity. This should provide a future proof (ESXi 8.0 and beyond) solution.

VMware Hardware Compatibility Guide

Before installing and configuring ESXi, please validate that your configuration is on the official VMware compatibility guide for vSAN, which you can find at the following website for ready node configurations http://vmwa.re/vsanhcl or the following website if you want to validate individual components: http://vmwa.re/vsanhclc. Please note, vSAN Skyline Health has a health check which will validate your hardware configuration in combination with the firmware and drivers regularly as combinations of support may change over time because of discovered issues or introduced enhancements.

vSAN has strict requirements around driver and firmware versions when it comes to disks, flash devices, and disk controllers. With all the various options, configuring the perfect vSAN host using a *Do-It-Yourself* (DIY) approach can be a complex exercise. Before reading about all the different components that you need to manually validate via the DIY approach, you will want to learn about an excellent alternative: vSAN ReadyNode Configurations.

vSAN ReadyNode

vSAN ReadyNode configurations are a great alternative to manually selecting components. ReadyNodes are also the preferred way of building a vSAN configuration. Various vendors have gone through the exercise for you and created configurations that are called *vSAN ReadyNodes*. These nodes consist of tested and certified hardware only and, in our opinion, provide an additional guarantee that the hardware components, along with the driver and firmware versions, have been validated for use with vSAN. It is important to note that even with vSAN ReadyNodes, the configurations can be modified and tweaked to use different hardware components, and your configuration will still be fully supported. Further information is available in the compatibility guide which provides a list of supported ReadyNodes, as shown in the figure below.

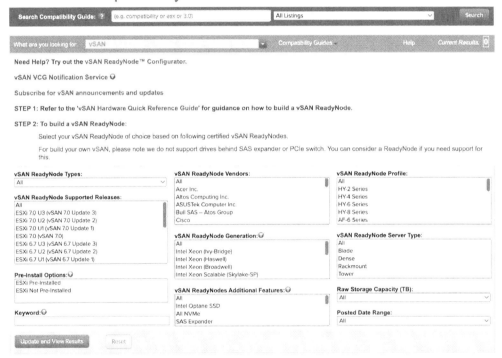

Figure 6: vSAN ReadyNode compatibility guide

For the more adventurous types, or those who prefer a particular server model or vendor that is not currently listed in the *vSAN ReadyNode* compatibility guide, some specifics for the various components, such as storage controllers and disk drives, must be called out. The sections that follow highlight these considerations in more detail.

A note about NVMe

Although many current customers of vSAN still leverage SAS and SATA, NVMe devices are becoming more prevalent every day and have been supported by vSAN since 2015. NVMe devices are not only used by vSAN for the caching tier, but we also have many customers already leveraging these for their capacity tier. NVMe provides various benefits to vSAN, with performance and endurance being the most important characteristics. Performance is driven by the fact that many supported NVMe devices for vSAN included higher class flash, but the bottleneck of the limited queue depth of the average disk controller is also avoided by having a deep queue dedicated to not only a single device. On top of that, endurance in many cases is also much better for NVMe based flash devices, whereas with SAS and SATA devices 10 drive writes per day (DWPD) or less was very common, for NVMe based flash devices, like Intel Optane, 30 drive writes per day (DWPD) is normal.

As a result, VMware typically recommends customers explore the ability to adopt an all-NVMe based architecture.

Storage controllers

As mentioned, many customers still use storage controllers in their vSAN environment today and may even consider it for future deployments simply as there's no performance or endurance requirement that would require purchasing NVMe devices. In this scenario, it is recommended that this disk controller run in what is commonly referred to as *pass-through mode*, *HBA mode*, or *JBOD mode*. (JBOD stands for Just a Bunch Of Disks.) In other words, the disk controller should provide the capability to pass through to the underlying magnetic disks and/or flash devices such as solid-state disks (SSDs) as individual disk drives without a layer of RAID sitting on top. The result of this is that ESXi can perform operations directly on the disk without those operations being intercepted and interpreted by the storage controller. As we will see in the vSAN architecture chapter, vSAN will take care of any RAID configuration in software when policy attributes such as availability and performance for virtual machines are defined. The vSAN compatibility guide will call out the disk controllers that have successfully passed testing.

Every server vendor has many different disk controllers that can be selected when configuring a new server. It is also important to review the footnotes with each controller, as this can reveal information such as whether the controller is supported with internal only disk devices, or whether it can be used with *just a bunch of disks* (JBODs) external devices, as well as whether the controller supports SAS Expanders, which seems to be a commonly asked question.

In some scenarios, hardware may have already been acquired or the disk controllers that are available do not support pass-through mode. In other words, the devices behind these controllers are not directly visible to the ESXi host. In those scenarios, administrators must place each individual drive in a RAID-0 volume configuration and then the devices become visible to the ESXi host. The important thing to note here is that each physical device is placed in its own RAID-0 configuration – no other hardware RAID configurations that may be created on the controller are supported by vSAN. You must ensure that this is a valid configuration for the controller. Once again, the compatibility guide will list whether a controller is supported in pass-through mode,

RAID-0 mode, or indeed whether the controller supports both modes. Make sure to validate the compatibility guide before configuring your disk controller in a specific way. Also, note that the compatibility guide lists both the supported firmware and the driver for each individual disk controller. Validate these versions and upgrade if needed before deploying any virtual machines. After initial deployment, it is strongly recommended that vSAN Skyline Health be referenced to verify that the health checks for the storage controller, driver, and firmware all pass.

Sharing the storage controller with vSAN and non-vSAN devices

Before vSAN 6.7, the recommendation was not to use the same storage controller for vSAN devices and non-vSAN devices, for example, the ESXi boot disk. The reason for this was errors in vSAN could have a secondary effect on the non-vSAN devices and vice versa. The symptoms vary, but extreme cases have been known to lock up the storage controller, leading to a reboot of the ESXi host to clear the issue. *VMware KB 2129050* has greater detail on what can be shared with what when it comes to the storage controller. Starting with vSAN 6.7, storage controllers are now checked to see if they can run vSAN and non-vSAN workloads concurrently. If they can, this will be explicitly listed against the controller on the compatibility guide. If it is not listed, it would be best to dedicate the selected controller to vSAN workload or non-vSAN workloads, and not mix them on the same controller.

Disk Controller RAID-0

For disk controllers that do not support pass-through/HBA/JBOD mode, vSAN supports disk drives presented via a RAID-0 configuration. The physical disk devices can be used by vSAN if they are created as volumes using a RAID-0 configuration. These RAID-0 volumes must only contain a single drive. This needs to be done for both the magnetic disks and/or the flash devices. This configuration of RAID-0 can be done using the disk controller software/firmware. Administrators need to understand, however, that when *Solid State Disks* (SSDs) are exposed to a vSAN leveraging a RAID-0 configuration, in many cases the drive is not recognized as a flash device because these characteristics are masked by the RAID-0 configuration. If this occurs, you will need to mark the drive as a flash device. This can be done via the vSphere client. Simply select the device in question and click on the appropriate disk services icon to toggle a device between SSD and HDD.

There is also an example that shows how to address another common device presentation issue: how to mark a device as local. In some environments, devices can be recognized as shared volumes even though they are local to the ESXi host. This is because some SAS controllers allow devices to be accessed from more than one host. In this case, the devices, although local, are shown as shared (not local). When they are marked like this, vSAN will not consume them. These devices will need to be marked as local in the vSphere client.

If you wish to mark a device as a flash device or mark a device as local, this is possible via the vSphere client as shown in the screenshot below. Depending on the type of device and how it is currently marked, the menu and the icons will change accordingly. In the screenshot below, the device is marked as a flash device and is already local. Therefore, the icons are displayed so that an administrator can mark the device as an HDD and mark it as remote.

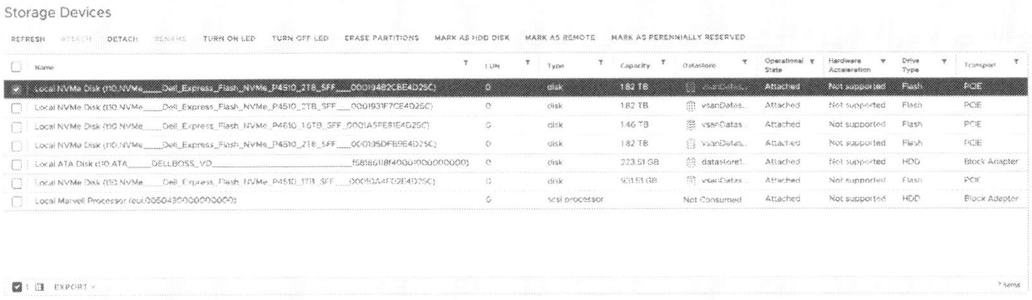

Figure 7: Marking Storage Devices

When using RAID-0 instead of pass-through, administrators must take into consideration certain operational impacts. When pass-through is used, drives are (in most scenarios) instantly recognized, and there is no need to configure the drives as a local device or as a flash device/SSD within ESXi. As well as that, when a RAID-0 is used, the physical drive is bound to that RAID-0 configuration. This means that the RAID-0 configuration has a 1:1 relationship with a given drive. If this drive fails and needs to be replaced with a new drive, this relationship is broken and a new RAID-0 configuration with the new replacement drive must be manually created by the administrator. The effort involved will differ per RAID controller used, whereas with a disk controller in pass-through mode, replacing the drive is a matter of removing the old device and inserting the replacement device. Of course, this is assuming the hot plug of the device is supported, and this can be checked on the device compatibility listings.

Depending on the RAID controller, vendor specific tools might be required to make the device "active" once more after replacement/repair has been completed. The original RAID-0 configuration may need to be removed completely and a brand-new RAID-0 volume may have to be created to allow vSAN to consume the replacement device. From a day 2 operation perspective, this is not desirable. Ideally, on drive failure, you simply want to identify the bad drive and eject it from the host. Then replace it with a new drive, and let vSAN consume it as quickly as possible, all with minimal human interaction. Therefore, we would **strongly recommend** storage controllers that **support JBOD/HBA/pass-through mode** over those storage controllers that require RAID-0 volumes to be created. If you want to further simplify your configuration from a hardware point of view, we recommend considering NVMe devices. NVMe uses its own embedded storage controllers, which takes the shared disk controller out of the equation, leading to fewer components to manage.

Performance and RAID Caching

VMware has carried out many performance tests using various types of disk controllers and RAID controllers. In most cases, the performance difference between pass-through and RAID-0 configurations was negligible.

However, one point to note when utilizing RAID-0 configurations is that the storage controllers write cache should be disabled. The main reason for this is because vSAN has its own caching mechanism and we want to ensure that any IOs which are acknowledged back to the guest operating system running in the VM has been stored on persistent storage (write buffer) rather than stored on a disk controller cache which is outside of what vSAN controls. When the storage controller cache cannot be completely disabled in a RAID-0 configuration, you should configure the storage controller cache as a 100% read cache, effectively disabling the write cache.

Mixing SAS and SATA

VMware does not make any specific recommendations around mixing SAS and SATA devices on vSAN. If the controller supports it, one could even mix SAS and SATA devices in the same disk group behind the same controller. However, customers need to be aware that the overall performance of any VM workload may well be reduced to the slowest hardware since VMs on vSAN can be distributed across multiple hosts and thus multiple devices.

Disk Groups

vSAN's architecture includes a caching tier and a capacity tier. At this point, you will be aware that vSAN comes in two flavors – all-flash and hybrid. In a hybrid configuration, we use a flash device for the cache tier and one or more HDDs for the capacity tier. In all-flash vSAN, as the name implies, we once again have a flash device for the cache tier and one or more flash devices for the capacity tier.

To build a relationship between the capacity tier and its cache device, vSAN has the concept of disk groups. Disk groups contain at most one cache device and up to seven capacity devices. Any I/O destined to the capacity tier of that disk group will have its I/O cached on the flash devices that are part of the same disk group. A detailed description of the I/O path, including where data services such as deduplication, encryption, and checksum are performed, will be covered in the architecture chapter. For the moment, it is enough to understand the concept of a disk group, and how it binds capacity devices to a single cache device.

At most, a vSAN host can have five disk groups, each containing seven capacity devices, resulting in a maximum of 35 capacity devices. The configuration of this is extremely simple, we will go through the exact steps in chapter 3, nevertheless, the below screenshot shows the screen used to configure all disk groups in a single step. One thing to point out, the screenshot also mentions vSAN Direct, we will discuss this feature in chapter 9.

Figure 8: Configuring Disk Groups

Disk Group Availability

When designing vSAN, you will typically want to know if there is a recommendation on a minimum number of disk groups. What you will notice from the vSAN ReadyNodes listings, most of the ReadyNodes are configured with two disk groups. The reason for this is quite simple – it enables a reduced failure domain. The following example should help explain it.

Consider a configuration where there is a host with a single disk group. In that disk group, there is one cache device and six capacity devices. Now let's envision a situation where the cache device suffers a failure in that disk group. This means that the whole disk group goes offline, and vSAN now must rebuild the failed content of those VMs elsewhere in the cluster. As vSAN can no longer store any VM data on this host, we may also end up in a situation where the remaining hosts may begin to come under capacity pressure.

Now let's consider a configuration where instead of a single disk group with six capacity devices, I have two disk groups with one cache device and three capacity devices. Now if one of the cache devices fails, I have a smaller failure domain. The failure this time has only impacted three capacity devices. This likely means that I have impacted fewer VMs, I have fewer data to build, and I can continue to make use of the healthy disk group on that host.

Now of course, if both disk groups are sitting behind the same storage controller and it is the controller that has a failure, then multiple disk groups do not help you in this case. For additional availability, you could consider adding an additional storage controller, and place each disk group (cache and capacity devices) behind its own controller. This will then mean that if there is a controller failure, you continue to have the smaller failure domains, which means that after the failure you still have a complete disk group available. Another option to consider would be NVMe based devices, this removes the potential single-point-of-failure (disk controller) from the configuration.

In a nutshell, more disk groups of smaller capacity are more desirable than fewer disk groups of larger capacity. Of course, the cost of a second controller and a second flash device for the second disk group need to be weighed up against the availability gains.

Disk Group Performance

Let's take the previous example where we discussed a host with two disk groups, each disk group sitting behind a different controller. While this is very advantageous from an availability perspective, it is also very advantageous from a performance perspective. Testing has revealed that moving disk groups to their own controller can significantly boost the performance of your vSAN environment. Of course, just like the availability discussion, the cost of a second controller and a second flash device for the second disk group need to be weighed up against the performance gains.

Capacity Tier Devices

VMware strongly recommends a uniform configuration for all hosts participating in a vSAN cluster. This includes having a similar number of capacity tier devices per host, where possible. Having said that, VMware understands that over time, original devices used in the cluster design may be no longer available and so in many cases, newer devices may have to be used to not just scale up the vSAN cluster, but also newer devices may have to be used to replace older, original devices which have failed. VMware supports such configurations, so don't worry if you find your cluster getting into a non-uniform state over time.

Each ESXi host that is participating in a vSAN cluster and contributing storage to the vSAN datastore must have at least one capacity device. Additional capacity devices will increase the capacity of the vSAN datastore, and may also increase performance as VM storage objects can be striped across multiple capacity devices, and on many occasions, multiple disk groups. This means that a single VM object could utilize multiple caching devices.

A higher number of capacity devices will also lead to a larger number of capacity balancing options when the reactive or proactive rebalancing threshold is reached. From a reactive perspective, when a disk has reached 80% of its capacity vSAN will automatically try to move components on that disk to other disks or disk groups in the same host, or disks on other hosts, to prevent that disk from running out of capacity. The same applies to proactive rebalancing, but in this case, vSAN constantly monitors all devices and takes action when a device has reached a delta of 30% or greater capacity usage than any other device and then triggers the rebalance to create a balanced environment from a capacity point of view across all devices.

vSAN supports various types of HDDs, ranging from SATA 7200 RPM up to SAS 15K RPM, and these are listed in the compatibility guide. A large portion of VM storage I/O performance will be met by flash devices in the cache tier but note that any I/O that needs to be serviced from the capacity tier (i.e., a read cache miss) will be bound by the performance characteristics of those devices. A 7200 RPM SATA magnetic disk will provide a different experience than a high-performance flash device, but usually will also come at a different price point, depending on the hardware vendor used. However, with the inclusion of RAID-5, RAID-6, Deduplication & Compression, or Compression Only, all-flash configurations are in many cases roughly the same cost as hybrid configurations. Note, starting with vSAN 7.0 the supported logical capacity of each device has been extended to 1PB when deduplication and compression is enabled. Do note, selecting devices of this capacity may have an impact on things like rebuild times when a device has failed.

Cache Tier Devices

Each ESXi host, whether it is in a hybrid configuration or an all-flash configuration, must have at least one flash device when that host is contributing capacity to a vSAN cluster. This flash device, in hybrid configurations, is utilized by vSAN as both a write buffer and a read cache, split 70% read and 30% write. In an all-flash configuration, the flash device is dedicating 100% as a write cache. This is simply because the overhead involved in servicing a read from the capacity tier on all-flash is minimal since the capacity tier in all-flash is also comprised of flash devices. The main difference between the device used for the cache tier and the device(s) used for the capacity tier in all-flash is that the cache tier device tends to have a much higher endurance specification than the capacity tier flash devices.

The flash cache device in vSAN sits in front of a group of capacity devices. Each disk group requires one flash device. Because vSAN can have a maximum of five disk groups per host, the maximum number of flash devices per host used for the cache tier is also five. The larger the cache device in a host, the greater the performance will be because more I/O can be cached/buffered. For devices larger than 600 GB, capacity above 600 GB is used to extend the lifespan of the device (endurance).

For the best vSAN performance, choose a high specification flash device. VMware has published a list of supported PCIe flash devices, SSDs, and NVMe devices in the VMware compatibility guide. Before procuring new equipment, review the VMware compatibility guide to ensure that your configuration is a supported configuration.

The designated flash device performance classes specified within the VMware vSAN Hardware Quick Reference Guide are as follows:

- **Class B**: 5,000–9999 writes per second
- **Class C**: 10,000–19,999 writes per second

- **Class D**: 20,000–29,999 writes per second
- **Class E**: 30,000–99,999 writes per second
- **Class F**: 100,000–349,999 writes per second
- **Class G**: 350,000+ writes per second

This question often arises: "Can I use a consumer-grade SSD and will vSAN work?" From a technical point of view, vSAN works perfectly fine with a consumer-grade SSD; however, in most cases, consumer-grade SSDs have much lower endurance guarantees, lack any type of power loss protection capabilities, have different (lower) performance characteristics, and may experience unpredictable latency spikes ranging from milliseconds to seconds. This is the main reason why Class A devices have been removed from the compatibility guide. Although it might be attractive from a price point to use a consumer-grade SSD, when this drive fails, it will impact the disk group to which this SSD is bound. When a cache device fails, the disk group to which it is bound is marked as unhealthy. This brings us to the second important column on the compatibility guide page, which is the flash device endurance class, which is as follows:

- **Class A**: >= 365 TBW
- **Class B**: >= 1825 TBW
- **Class C**: >= 3650 TBW
- **Class D**: >= 7300 TBW

The higher the class, the more reliable and longer the lifetime of the average device in this case. For those who are not aware, TBW stands for "terabytes written" and is the guaranteed total amount of data that can be written to the device measured in Terabytes.

After having looked at the various SSDs, PCIe flash devices, and NVMe devices, we have concluded that it is almost impossible to recommend a brand or type of flash to use. This decision should be driven by the budgetary constraints, server platform vendor support and more importantly the requirements of the applications that you plan to deploy in your VMs running on vSAN.

Network Requirements

This section covers the requirements and prerequisites from a networking perspective for vSAN. vSAN is a distributed storage solution and therefore heavily depends on the network for intra-host communication. Consistency and reliability are the keys. Therefore, it is critical that the network interconnect between the hosts is of high quality and has no underlying issues. It is strongly recommended that the network health is monitored just as closely as the vSAN health.

Network Interface Cards

Each ESXi host must have at least one 1GbE *network interface card* (NIC) dedicated to vSAN hybrid configurations at a minimum. For all-flash configurations, 10GbE NICs are required. However, as a best practice, VMware and the authors of this book are recommending a minimum of 10GbE NICs for all configurations! For redundancy, you can configure a team of NICs on a per-host basis. We consider this a best practice, but it is not necessary to build a fully functional vSAN cluster.

We are also seeing faster devices appearing in customer environments, 25 GbE is the new 10GbE. Also, 40 GbE and higher are fully supported, and can even bring the benefit of lower latency for I/O. Starting with vSAN 7.0 Update 2 support for RDMA (RoCE v2) has also been introduced, which will help lower the latency even more.

One recommendation, however – care should be taken to validate the NIC, its driver, and firmware versions. At the time of writing, this was not included in the vSAN health check, so customers are advised to use the VMware Compatibility Guide – IO Devices section to verify that their NIC is indeed supported and at the correct versions. (http://vmwa.re/28h) There have been numerous support issues caused by misbehaving networks cards, which are a critical component of distributed systems like vSAN.

Supported Virtual Switch Types

vSAN is supported on both VMware *vSphere distributed switches* (VDS) and VMware *vSphere standard switches* (VSS). There are some advantages to using a Distributed Switch that will be covered in Chapter 3, "vSAN Installation and Configuration." No other virtual switch types have been explicitly tested with vSAN. A license for the use of VDS is included with vSAN, irrespective of the vSphere edition used.

NSX-T Interoperability

NSX is VMware's network virtualization platform. At the time of writing, VMware does not support running vSAN traffic on NSX-T, or as is stated more specifically in the VMware NSX documentation: "NSX-T does not support the configuration of the vSAN data network over an NSX-managed VXLAN or Geneve overlay." Do note, vSAN File Services can be configured on an NSX-T based environment, but more details about that when we discuss vSAN File Services.

Layer 2 or Layer 3

vSAN is supported over layer 2 (L2/switched) or layer 3 (L3/routed) networks. Do note that vSAN, prior to version 6.6, relies on the availability of multicast traffic. This means that in versions of vSAN prior to version 6.6, both cases (L2 and L3) must allow multicast traffic and, in the case of L3, the multicast traffic must also be routed between the networks. These typically involved technologies like Internet Group Management Protocol (IGMP) and Protocol-Independent Multicast (PIM). We have noticed during the many conversations we have had with customers that multicast traffic is usually not allowed on their network by default and required long conversations with the networking team before vSAN could be successfully configured. This was a major contributing factor toward the removal of the multicast requirement on vSAN traffic in version 6.6 and later.

VMkernel Network

On each ESXi host that wants to participate in a vSAN cluster, a VMkernel port for vSAN communication must be created. The VMkernel port is labeled vSAN traffic and is used for intra-cluster node communication. It is also used for reads and writes when one of the ESXi hosts in the cluster runs a particular VM but the actual data blocks making up the VM files are located on a different ESXi host in the cluster. In this case, I/O will need to traverse the network configured between the hosts in the cluster, as depicted in the diagram below, where VMkernel interface vmk2 is used for vSAN traffic by all the hosts in the vSAN cluster. The VM residing on the first host does all of its reads and writes leveraging the vSAN network as all components of that VM are stored elsewhere.

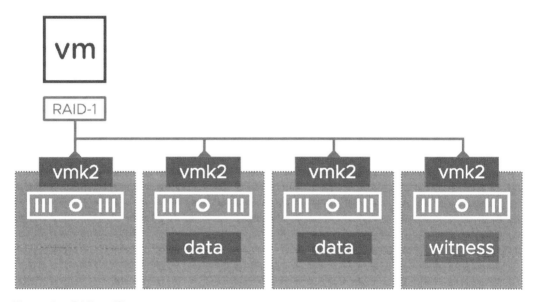

Figure 9: vSAN traffic

vSAN Network Traffic

For inter-cluster host communication, vSAN uses a proprietary protocol called RDT, the *Reliable Datagram Transport*. VMware has not published a specification of the protocol. This is similar to the approach taken for other VMware products and features such as vMotion, Fault Tolerance, and vSphere Replication. The vSAN network may be used for three different traffic types. It is important to know these because they introduce a requirement for your physical network switch configuration:

- **Multicast heartbeats:** In vSAN versions prior to v6.6, these are used to discover all participating vSAN hosts in the cluster, as well as to determine the state of a host. Compared to other traffic types, multicast heartbeats generate very few packets. With vSAN 6.6 and later, these are no longer used.
- Multicast and unicast packets from the clustering service (CMMDS): This traffic does

metadata updates like object placement and statistics. These generate more network traffic than the heartbeats, but it's still a very small percentage. As of vSAN version 6.6, all CMMDS updates are sent unicast.
- Storage traffic (e.g., reads, writes): This is most of the network traffic. Any host within the cluster communicates to any other host over unicast.

Jumbo Frames

Jumbo frames are supported on the vSAN network. We believe that every vSAN deployment is different, both from a server hardware perspective and from a network hardware perspective. Therefore, it is difficult to recommend for or against the use of jumbo frames. In addition, there is an operational impact in implementing jumbo frames on non-greenfield sites. When jumbo frames are not consistently configured end to end, network problems may occur.

Tests have been conducted to test the benefits of jumbo frames, and the major improvement observed with jumbo frames is with CPU usage. The data can fit in a smaller number of packets (sometimes into a single frame when the packet is 8KB or less in size) when jumbo frames are enabled, and thus no fragmentation/defragmentation operations are needed to send and receive these packets. However, no noticeable improvement in performance (i.e. IOPS or throughput) has been observed with jumbo frames.

In an operationally mature environment where a consistent implementation can be guaranteed, the use of jumbo frames is left to the administrator's discretion.

NIC Teaming

Another potential way of optimizing network performance is teaming of NICs. NIC teaming in ESXi is transparent to vSAN. You can use any of the NIC teaming options available in vSphere on the vSAN network. For the most part, NIC teaming offers availability rather than any performance gain. The only drawback with NIC teaming is that it adds complexity to the networking configuration of vSAN. Chapter 3 covers the configuration options, details, and various parameters in more detail.

NIC Teaming - Performance vs. Availability

As mentioned previously, there is no guarantee that NIC Teaming will give you a performance improvement. This is because most of the NIC teaming algorithms are not able to utilize the full bandwidth of multiple physical NICs at the same time. Various factors play a part, including the size of the cluster, the number of NICs, and the number of different IP addresses used. In our testing, *Link Aggregation Control Protocol* (LACP) offers the best chance of balancing vSAN traffic across multiple vSAN networks using *Link Aggregation Groups* (LAG). Thus, if performance is your key goal, then LACP is the best option for network configuration, with the downside of added complexity as you will also need to make configuration changes on the physical network switch. If availability is your key goal, then any of the other supported NIC teaming policies should suffice.

Network I/O Control

Although it is recommended to use 10 GbE NICs minimum, there is no requirement to solely dedicate these cards to the vSAN network. NICs can be shared with other traffic types. However, you should consider using *Network I/O Control* (NIOC) to ensure that the vSAN traffic is guaranteed a certain amount of bandwidth over the network in the case where contention for bandwidth of the network arises. This is especially true if a 10 GbE NIC is shared with (for instance) vMotion traffic, which is infamous for utilizing all available bandwidth when possible. NIOC requires the creation of a distributed switch because NIOC is not available with standard switches. Luckily, the distributed switch is included with the vSAN license.

Chapter 3 provides various examples of how NIOC can be configured for the various types of network configurations.

Firewall Ports

When you are enabling vSAN, several ESXi firewall ports are automatically opened (both ingoing and outgoing) on each ESXi host that participates in the vSAN cluster. The ports are used for inter-cluster host communication and communication with the storage provider on the ESXi hosts. The table below provides a list of the most used vSAN-specific network ports. Most of the traffic in a vSAN cluster (98% or more) will be RDT traffic on port 2233. More extensive details can be found in KB 52959.

NAME	PORT	PROTOCOL
CMMDS	12345, 23451, 12321	UDP
RDT	2233	TCP
VSANVP	8080	TCP
Health	443	TCP
Witness Host	2233	TCP
Witness Host	12321	UDP
KMS Server	Vendor specific	Vendor specific

Table 1: ESXi ports and protocols Opened by vSAN

vSAN Stretched Cluster

vSAN stretched cluster allows VMs to be deployed across sites in different datacenters, and if one site or datacenter fails, VMs can be restarted on the surviving site, utilizing vSphere HA. There are several items to consider for vSAN Stretched Cluster configurations, including latency and bandwidth, not only between the datacenter sites but also to the witness site. These will be covered in greater detail in the *vSAN Stretched Cluster* section, later in this book (Chapter 7), but we will list some of the basic guidelines here for your convenience:

- Maximum of 5 ms RTT latency between data sites (requirement)
- Maximum of 200 ms RTT between data sites and the witness site (requirement)

- 10 Gbps between data sites
- 100 Mbps from data sites to witness site

vSAN 2-Node Remote Office/Branch Office (ROBO)

In much the same way as there are specific network requirements for vSAN stretched cluster, there are also network requirements around latency and bandwidth for 2-node ROBO deployments. For 2-node configurations the following general guidelines apply:

- 500ms RTT max between 2-node/ROBO location and central witness (requirement)
- 1 Mbps from 2-node/ROBO location to central witness

VMware vSAN supports back-to-back cabling of the network between the 2-nodes at a remote office/branch office. Where previously, there was a requirement to have a 1 GbE network switch to provide connectivity between the vSAN nodes at the ROBO location. This provides the added benefit that at a relatively low cost, 10GbE can be introduced in a 2-node configuration without the need for a 10GbE physical switch infrastructure.

vSAN Requirements

Before enabling vSAN, it is highly recommended that the vSphere administrator validate that the environment meets all the prerequisites and requirements. To enhance resilience, this list also includes recommendations from an infrastructure perspective:

- Minimum of three ESXi hosts for standard datacenter deployments. Minimum of two ESXi hosts and a witness host for the smallest deployment, for example, remote office/branch office.
- VMware vCenter Server. Recommended is 7.0 U3 at the time of writing, but the latest is preferred. vCenter version needs to be equal to, or newer than, the ESXi version. Remember that vCenter contains a great deal of management and monitoring functionality for vSAN.
- At least one device for the capacity tier. One magnetic disk for hosts contributing storage to the vSAN datastore in a hybrid configuration; one flash device for hosts contributing storage to vSAN datastore in an all-flash configuration.
- At least one flash device for the cache tier for hosts contributing storage to vSAN datastore, whether hybrid or all-flash.
- One boot device to install ESXi. Boot device should meet the requirements outlined in *VMware knowledgebase article* 85685.
- At least one disk controller. Pass-through/JBOD mode capable disk controller preferred.
- Dedicated network port for vSAN—VMkernel interface. A dual 10GbE configuration is preferred, but 1GbE is supported for smaller hybrid configurations. With 10GbE, the adapter does not need to be dedicated to vSAN traffic, but can be shared with other traffic types, such as management traffic, vMotion traffic, etc.
- Minimum memory per host to install ESXi, as per *VMware knowledgebase article 2113954*.

Summary

Although configuring vSAN takes a couple of clicks, it is important to take the time to ensure that all requirements are met and to ensure that all prerequisites are in place. A stable storage platform starts at the foundation, the infrastructure on which it is enabled. Before moving on to Chapter 3, you should run through the requirements above.

We have also discussed additional recommendations, which are not requirements for a fully functional vSAN, but which might be desirable from a production standpoint such as networking redundancy, jumbo frames, and network IO control.

03

vSAN Installation and Configuration

This chapter describes in detail the installation and configuration process, as well as all initial preparation steps that you might need to consider before proceeding with a vSAN cluster deployment. You will find information on how to correctly set up network and storage devices, as well as some helpful tips and tricks on how to deploy the most optimal vSAN configuration.

Cluster Quickstart

Prior to vSAN 6.7 Update 1, there were various steps and workflows involved to get a vSAN cluster fully configured. The first step would normally be adding hosts to a vCenter Server instance. After having added the hosts, you would normally configure these, unless of course, you had fully automated the installation and configuration. Configuration, for the most part, means setting up all the required VMkernel interfaces (vSAN, Management, and vMotion networks) and vSwitch port groups (or distributed port groups for that matter). After the configuration of the network, a cluster could be created, and the hosts could be added to the cluster.

Although not overly complicated, it would require the administrator to go from one UI workflow to the other, some of which were in a completely different section of the vSphere Client. With the introduction of the vSphere HTML-5 Client, or vSphere Client for short, a new UI was also developed for the creation of a vSAN cluster. This workflow, named the Cluster Quickstart wizard, combines all the different workflows and steps needed to form a vSAN cluster into a single workflow.

Cluster Quickstart Wizard

When creating a vSAN cluster in a greenfield deployment the steps that you need to go through are all part of the Cluster Quickstart wizard. When vCenter Server has been deployed the first thing you will need to do is create a cluster. When you create a cluster, you have the option to enable vSphere HA, vSphere DRS, and vSAN. When the cluster is created, the vSphere Client will automatically continue with the Cluster Quickstart workflow, regardless of whether vSAN is enabled or not.

Let's look at this process a bit more in-depth. The first thing to do is to create a cluster. You can do this by right-clicking in the vSphere Client on the virtual datacenter object. Next you select "New Cluster". You provide the cluster with a name, and then select the cluster services you would like to have enabled. In our case, this will be vSphere HA, vSphere DRS, and VMware vSAN.

Figure 10: Creation of a cluster

After you have clicked "Next" and "Finish" you are now taken to the section in the UI called Cluster Quickstart. The next step will be to click "ADD", and add new, or existing hosts into your newly created vSAN cluster.

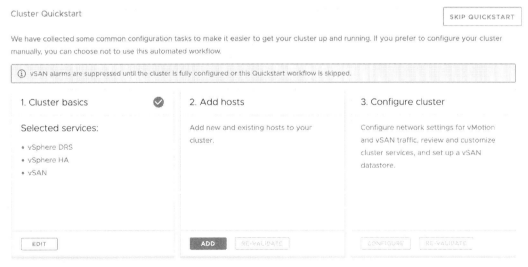

Figure 11: Cluster Quickstart wizard

In our case, we already had three stand-alone hosts added to vCenter Server, which means that we

03 // vSAN Installation and Configuration

will click on "Existing hosts" and add all three at the same time by simply clicking the top tick box. Before the hosts are added to the cluster, a host summary is provided with relevant information. In this summary, for instance, it is called out when the host(s) you are adding have any powered-on VMs.

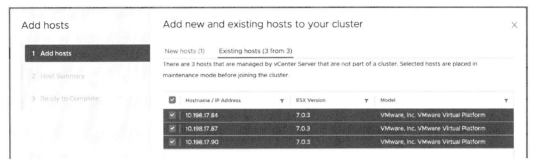

Figure 12: Select the hosts to be added to the cluster.

When you click finish, the hosts will be added to the cluster and all cluster services will be configured. What is useful to know is that the hosts are added to the cluster in "maintenance mode". This is to prevent any workloads from using a host which may not be fully configured yet. Another feature as part of this workflow is the fact that after adding the host to the cluster the hosts are validated against various Skyline Health checks. This is to ensure that the hosts are healthy and compatible with our compatibility guide. If a disk controller driver is not certified, for instance, then this will be called out. This will then allow you to install the correct driver, or firmware, before enabling vSAN and deploying workloads.

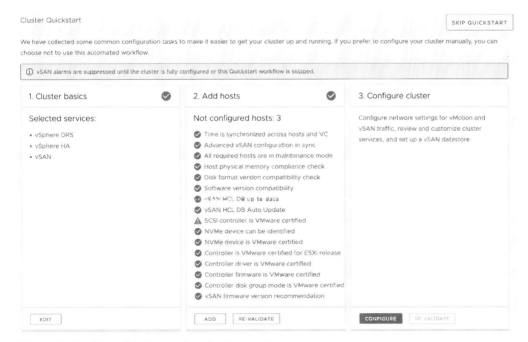

Figure 13: Health validation during cluster creation

After verifying the health of the hosts, and potentially correcting issues, the last step can be taken. In this step required networking settings for vMotion and vSAN traffic will be configured, as well as clustering services.

The Quickstart wizard assumes that a distributed switch is used. It will configure the distributed switch as recommended by the *VMware Validated Designs* (VVD). You can, when preferred, configure the network settings after this workflow has been completed. We would, however, recommend doing it as part of the workflow.

In our case, we are going to add the first physical adapters to the distributed switch as shown in the next screenshot.

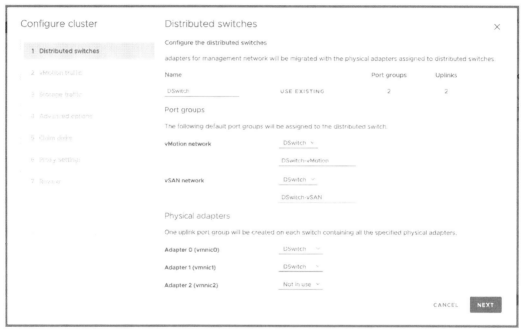

Figure 14: Configuration of the Distributed Switch

After the configuration of the distributed switch, the VMkernel interfaces for both vMotion and vSAN traffic will need to be configured. The interface allows you to specify static IP addresses or use DHCP. Note that in a single window you can provide all the needed IP details for all hosts in the cluster.

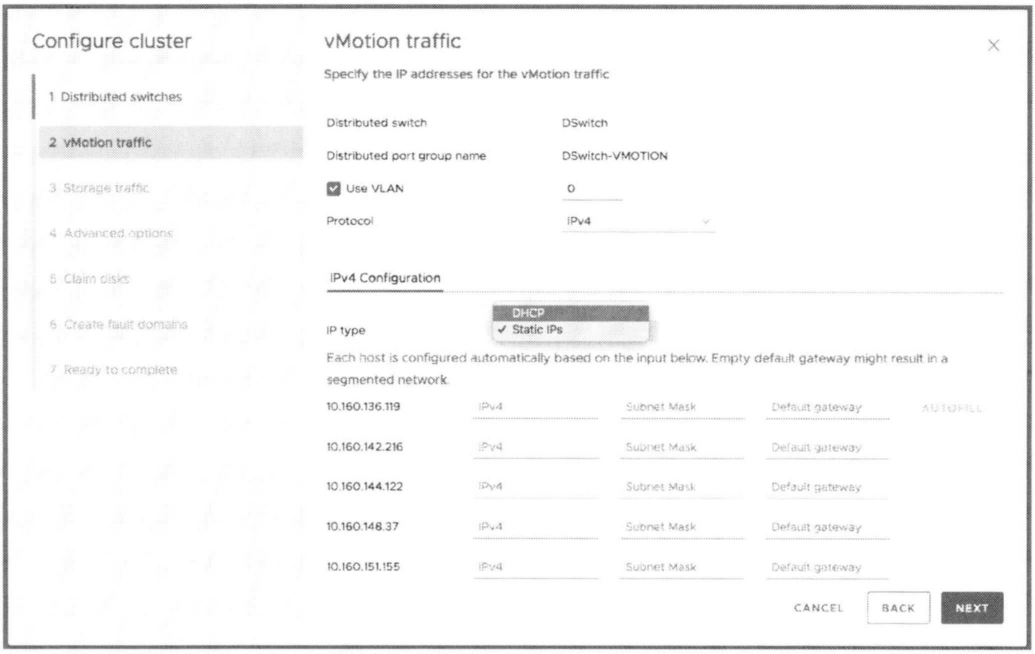

03 // vSAN Installation and Configuration

Figure 15: Configuration of the VMkernel interfaces

Next, it is possible to configure various advanced configuration aspects of vSphere HA and vSphere DRS. Configuration options continue with advanced vSAN functionality like Deduplication and Compression, Compression Only, Fault Domains, Data-At-Rest and In-Transit encryption, and even Stretched Clusters. We will discuss each of these features and their functionality in later chapters.

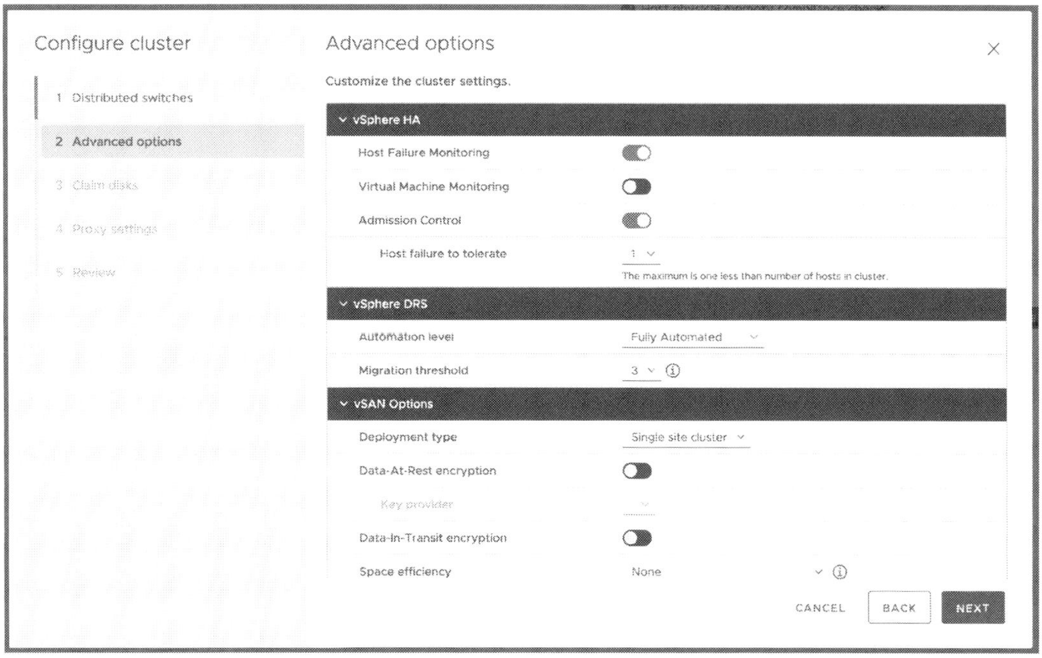

Figure 16: Configuration of cluster level services

In the next step, all the host local storage devices that need to be part of the vSAN Datastore can be claimed. Note that vSAN will group the devices based on their disk model. This allows you to quickly claim all devices of a specific type for either cache or capacity as shown in the screenshot below.

Figure 17: Claim vSAN devices

Depending on which services have been selected, next you will have the ability to configure either fault domains or configure your stretched cluster. If you are configuring a stretched cluster then two additional steps are presented, namely the selection of the Witness Host and claiming the disks of the witness host. The function of the witness components and witness host will be covered in greater detail in the architecture chapter, for the moment it is enough to understand that it plays a role in the configuration of stretched clusters. In this example we have a single location with three racks, so we will create three fault domains and add the hosts to each fault domain accordingly to the physical placement of the host.

03 // vSAN Installation and Configuration

Figure 18: Creation of Fault Domains

Fault domains and how they work is something we will discuss in-depth in Chapter 4. For now, it is sufficient to know that these can be configured from the same workflow end-to-end.

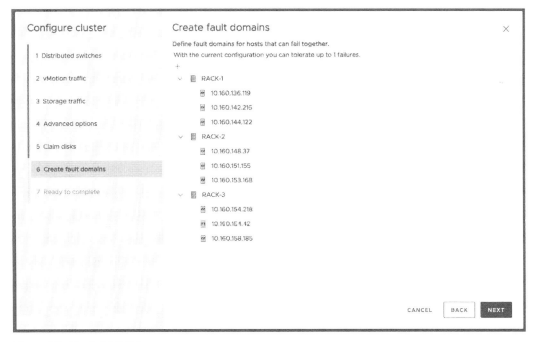

Figure 19: Fault domains

This completes the configuration of the cluster with a summary of all settings that have been configured. Note that if anything is misconfigured, you can step back through the wizard and make the required changes.

Figure 20: Summary

Now when you click finish the cluster will be fully configured end-to-end. This will, depending on which services are enabled, take several minutes. In some cases, for instance, when vSAN Data-At-Rest encryption is enabled, disk groups will need to be configured with a new on-disk format, which can be time-consuming. Nevertheless, regardless of functionality being enabled or disabled, we believe that this workflow is a big step forward compared to previous vSphere versions.

After the configuration of the hosts has been completed, each of them will be taken out of maintenance mode and will be ready to host workloads. Of course, there are a couple of other things to consider when it comes to installing and configuring a vSAN infrastructure end to end.

Networking

Network connectivity is the heart of any vSAN cluster. vSAN cluster hosts use the network for virtual machine (VM) I/O and communicate their state with one another. Consistent and correct network configuration is key to a successful vSAN deployment. Because the majority of disk I/O will either come from a remote host or will need to go to a remote host, VMware recommends leveraging a minimum 10 GbE network infrastructure. Note that although 1 GbE is fully supported in hybrid configurations, it could become a bottleneck in large-scale deployments.

As mentioned in the previous chapter, VMware vSphere provides two different types of virtual switches, both of which are fully supported with vSAN.

Although we recommend using the vSphere Distributed Switch, it is fully supported to use the VMware standard Virtual Switch. Note that when using the Cluster Quickstart wizard, by default the vSphere Distributed Switch is used. This however is for a good reason, as the VDS provides you with the ability to enable Network I/O Control. This in turn allows you to prioritize traffic streams when the environment is under contention. Before we dive into NIOC, let's discuss some of the basic aspects of vSAN networking, and some of the design decisions around it.

VMkernel Network for vSAN

All ESXi hosts participating in a vSAN network need to communicate with one another. As such, a vSAN cluster will not successfully form until a vSAN VMkernel port is available on multiple ESXi hosts participating in the vSAN cluster. The vSphere administrator can create a vSAN VMkernel port manually on each ESXi host in the cluster before the vSAN cluster forms or can have the VMkernel port created as part of the Cluster Quickstart wizard.

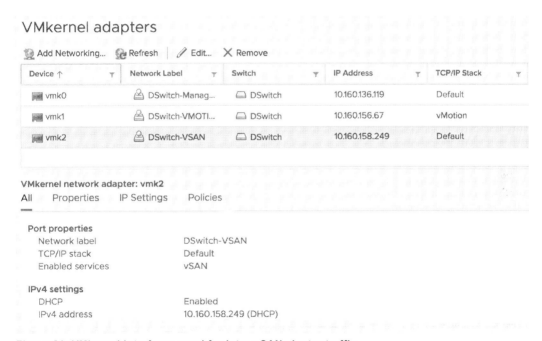

Figure 21: VMkernel interfaces used for intra-vSAN cluster traffic

Without a VMkernel network for vSAN, the cluster will not form successfully. If communication is not possible between the ESXi hosts in the vSAN cluster, only one ESXi host will join the vSAN cluster. Other ESXi hosts will not be able to join. This will still result in a single vSAN datastore, but each host can only see itself as part of that datastore. A warning message will display when there are communication difficulties between ESXi hosts in the cluster. If the cluster is created before the VMkernel ports are created, a warning message is also displayed regarding communication difficulties between the ESXi hosts. Once the VMkernel ports are created and communication is established, the cluster will form successfully.

VSS vSAN Network Configuration

With a VSS, creating a port group for vSAN network traffic is straightforward. By virtue of installing an ESXi host, a VSS is automatically created to carry ESXi network management traffic and VM traffic. You can use an already-existing standard switch and its associated uplinks to external networks to create a new VMkernel port for vSAN traffic. Alternatively, you may choose to create a new standard switch for the vSAN network traffic VMkernel port by selecting unused uplinks for the new standard switch. Of course, the steps to create a VMkernel interface will have to be repeated for every ESXi host in the vSAN cluster. Each time you scale out by adding a new host to the cluster, you must ensure that the VSS configuration is identical on the new host, this leads to unnecessary operational overhead and complexity. This is the big advantage of the vSphere Distributed Switch.

VDS vSAN Network Configuration

In the case of a VDS, a distributed port group needs to be configured to carry the vSAN traffic. Once the distributed port group is created, VMkernel interfaces on the individual ESXi hosts can then be created to use that distributed port group.

Although the official VMware documentation makes no distinction regarding which versions of Distributed Switch you should be using, the authors recommend using the latest version of the Distributed Switch with vSAN. Note that all ESXi hosts attaching to this Distributed Switch must be running the same version of ESXi when a given distributed switch version has been selected, preferably the version of the selected Distributed Switch should be the same as the ESXi/vSphere version. Earlier versions of ESXi will not be able to utilize newer versions of the Distributed Switch when added to the cluster.

One of the steps when creating a Distributed Switch is to select whether NIOC is enabled or disabled. We recommend leaving this at the default option of enabled. Later on, we discuss the value of NIOC in a vSAN environment.

Port Group Port Allocations

One important consideration with the creation of port groups is the port allocation settings and the number of ports associated with the port group. Note that the default number of ports is eight and that the allocation setting is elastic by default. This means that when all ports are assigned, a new set of eight ports is created. A port group with an allocation type of elastic can automatically increase the number of ports as more devices are allocated. With the port binding set to static, a port is assigned to the VMkernel port when it connects to the distributed port group. If you plan to have a 16-host or larger vSAN cluster, you could consider configuring a greater number of ports for the port group instead of the default of eight. This means that in times of maintenance and outages, the ports always stay available for the host until it is ready to rejoin the cluster, and it means that the switch doesn't incur any overhead by having to delete and re-add the ports.

When creating a distributed switch and distributed port groups, there are a lot of additional options to choose from, such as port binding type. These options are well documented in the official VMware vSphere documentation, and although we discussed port allocation in a little detail here, most of the settings are beyond the scope of this book. Readers who are unfamiliar with these options can find explanations in the official VMware vSphere documentation. However, you can simply leave these Distributed Switch and port groups at the default settings and vSAN will deploy just fine with those settings.

TCP/IP Stack

One thing we would like to discuss however is the TCP/IP stack. We often get questions about this. The common question is whether vSAN can use a custom TCP/IP stack, or does vSAN have its own TCP/IP stack? Neither is the case, unfortunately. At the time of writing, vSAN only supports the use of the default TCP/IP stack for the vSAN network. The TCP/IP provisioning stack can only be used for provisioning traffic and the vMotion TCP/IP stack can only be used for vMotion. You will not be able to select these stacks for vSAN traffic. Options for configuring different network stacks may be found in official VMware documentation and are beyond the scope of this book but suffice to say that different network stacks can be configured on the ESXi host and have different properties such as default gateways associated with each network stack.

In normal vSAN configurations, not having a custom TCP/IP stack is not an issue. However, when a stretched cluster is implemented additional network configuration steps may need to be taken into account for each of the hosts in the cluster, but also in the case of an L3 (routed network) implementation for the vSAN network. There is of course the ability to override the default gateway when creating the vSAN VMkernel interface, this is supported for vSAN starting vSAN 7.0 U1. An alternative to using the "override default gateway" option would be to configure static routes using the CLI. We will talk about these network considerations and configuration in more detail, and how ESXi hosts in a stretched vSAN cluster can communicate over L3 networks in Chapter 7.

IPv4 and IPv6

Another decision that will need to be made when manually configuring the vSAN network stack is the use of IPv4 versus that of IPv6 and of course the use of DHCP versus static configured IP addresses. VMware vSAN supports both the use of IPv4 and IPv6, the choice is up to you as an administrator or the network administrator. When it comes to the allocation of IP addresses we prefer statically assigned. Although DHCP is fully supported it will make troubleshooting more complex. One definite recommendation around the use of DHCP-allocated IP addresses is to make sure that the range of IP addresses is reserved for vSAN use, which will prevent other devices from consuming them should a host be offline for an extended period.

Network Configuration Issues

If the vSAN VMkernel is not properly configured, a warning will be displayed in the vSAN > Skyline Health section on the monitor tab of your vSAN cluster object. If you click the warning for the particular tests that have failed, further details related to the network status of all hosts in the cluster will display. In this scenario a single host in a twelve-host cluster is part of a different IP subnet, causing connectivity issues as expected. You can also see that the cluster has a partition, with 11 hosts in partition number 1 and the misconfigured host in its own partition, partition number 2

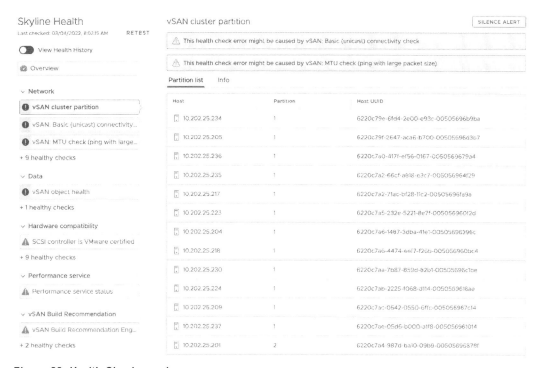

Figure 22: Health Check warning

On top of that, in the Disk Management section it shows the network partition groups. This is displayed in this section of the UI, as lack of network connectivity will impact vSAN capacity.

03 // vSAN Installation and Configuration

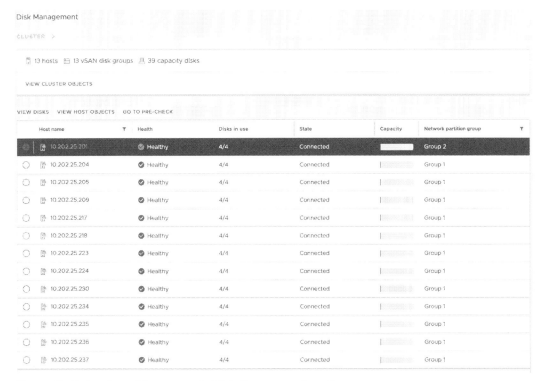

Figure 23: Network partition group in Disk Management section

Network I/O Control Configuration Example

As previously mentioned, NIOC can be used to guarantee bandwidth for vSAN cluster communication and I/O. NIOC is available only on VDS, not on VSS. Indeed, VDS is only available with some of the higher vSphere editions; however, as mentioned earlier vSAN includes VDS irrespective of the vSphere edition used.

If you are using an earlier version of a Distributed Switch prior to your vSphere version, although not explicitly called out in the vSphere documentation, we recommend upgrading to the most recent version of the Distributed Switch if you plan to use it with vSAN. This is simply a cautionary recommendation as we did all our vSAN testing with the most recent version (7.0.3) of the Distributed Switch.

Network I/O Control

NIOC has a traffic type called *vSAN traffic,* and thus provides QoS on vSAN traffic. Although this QoS configuration might not be necessary for most vSAN cluster environments, it is a good feature to have available if vSAN traffic appears to be impacted by other traffic types sharing the same 10 GbE (or higher) network interface card. An example of a traffic type that could impact vSAN is *vMotion.* By its very nature, vMotion traffic is "bursty" and might claim the full available bandwidth on a NIC port, impacting other traffic types sharing the NIC, including vSAN traffic. Leveraging

57

NIOC in those situations will avoid a self-imposed *denial-of-service* (DoS) attack during for instance maintenance mode, where many VMs are migrated concurrently.

Setting up NIOC is quite straightforward, and once configured it will guarantee a certain bandwidth for the vSAN traffic between all hosts. NIOC is enabled by default when a VDS is created. If the feature was disabled during the initial creation of the Distributed Switch, it may be enabled once again by editing the Distributed Switch properties via the vSphere Client. To begin with, use the vSphere Client to select the VDS in the network section. From there, select the VDS and navigate to the configure tab and select the resource allocation view. This displays the NIOC configuration options.

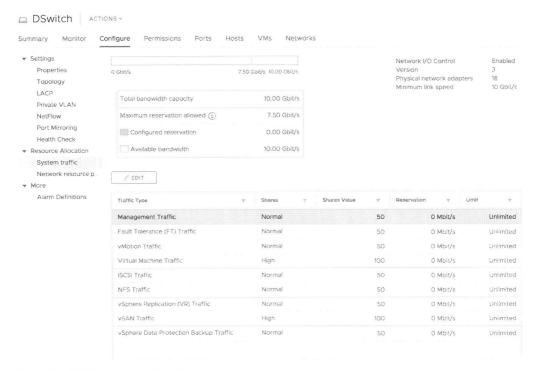

Figure 24: NIOC resource allocation

To change the resource allocation for the vSAN traffic in NIOC, simply edit the properties of the vSAN traffic type. The next screenshot shows the modifiable configuration options for each traffic stream.

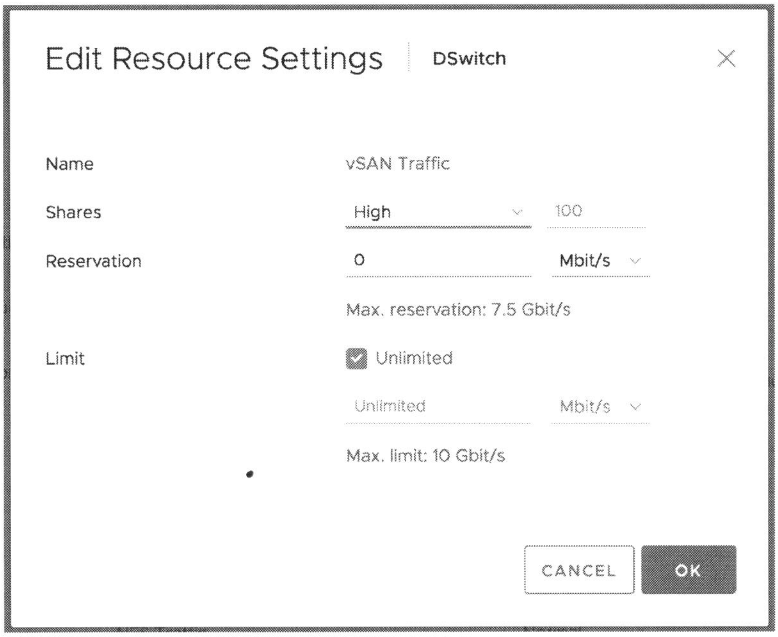

Figure 25: NIOC configuration

By default, the limit is set to unlimited, physical adapter shares are set to 100, and there is no reservation. The unlimited value means that vSAN network traffic is allowed to consume all the network bandwidth when there is no congestion. We do not recommend setting a limit on the vSAN traffic. The reason for this is because a limit is a "hard" setting. In other words, if a 2 Gbps limit is configured on vSAN traffic, the traffic will be limited even when additional bandwidth is available. Therefore, you should not use limits because of this behavior.

With a reservation, you can configure the minimum bandwidth that needs to be available for a particular traffic stream. This must not exceed 75% of available bandwidth. The reason for not using reservations is because unused reserved bandwidth cannot be allocated to other traffic like for instance VM traffic. We recommend leaving this untouched and instead using the shares mechanism.

With the share mechanism, if network contention arises, the physical adapter shares will be used by NIOC for traffic management. These shares are compared with the share values assigned to other traffic types to determine which traffic type gets priority. You can use shares to "artificially limit" your traffic types based on actual resource usage and demand.

With vSAN deployments, VMware is recommending a 10 GbE network infrastructure at a minimum. In these deployments, two 10 GbE network ports are usually used and are connected to two physical 10 GbE capable switches to provide availability. The various types of traffic will need to share this network capacity, and this is where NIOC can prove invaluable.

Design Considerations: Distributed Switch and Network I/O Control

To provide QoS and performance predictability, vSAN and NIOC should go hand in hand. Before discussing the configuration options, the following types of networks are being considered:

- Management network
- vMotion network
- vSAN network
- VM network

This design consideration assumes 10 GbE redundant networking links and a redundant switch pair for availability. Two scenarios will be described. These scenarios are based on the type of network switch used:

1. Redundant 10 GbE switch setup *without* "link aggregation" capability
2. Redundant 10 GbE switch setup *with* "link aggregation" capability

Note: Link aggregation (IEEE 802.3ad) allows users to use more than one connection between network devices. It combines multiple physical connections into one logical connection and provides a level of redundancy and bandwidth improvement.

In both configurations, recommended practice dictates that you create the following port groups and VMkernel interfaces:

- 1 × Management network VMkernel interface
- 1 × vMotion VMkernel interface (with all interfaces in the same subnet)
- 1 × vSAN VMkernel interface
- 1 × VM port group

To simplify the configuration, you should have a single vSAN and vMotion VMkernel interface per host.

To ensure traffic types are separated on different physical ports, we will leverage standard Distributed Switch capabilities. We will also show how to use shares to avoid noisy neighbor scenarios.

Scenario 1: Redundant 10 GbE Switch Without "Link Aggregation" Capability

In this configuration, two individual 10 GbE uplinks are available. It is recommended to separate traffic and designate a single 10 GbE uplink to vSAN for simplicity reasons. We often are asked how much bandwidth each traffic type requires; we recommend monitoring current bandwidth consumption and making design decisions based on facts. However, for this exercise, we will make assumptions based on our experience and commonly used configurations by our customers. The recommended minimum amount of bandwidth to dynamically keep available per traffic type is as follows:

- **Management network**: 1 GbE
- **vMotion VMkernel interface**: 5 GbE
- **VM network**: 2 GbE
- **vSAN VMkernel interface**: 10 GbE

Note that various traffic types will share the same uplink. The management network, VM network, and vMotion network traffic are configured to share uplink 1, and vSAN traffic is configured to use uplink 2. With the network configuration done this way, sufficient bandwidth exists for all the various types of traffic when the vSAN cluster is in a normal operating state.

To make sure that no single traffic type can impact other traffic types during times of contention, NIOC is configured, and the shares mechanism is deployed. When defining traffic type network shares, this scenario works under the assumption that there is only one physical port available and that all traffic types share that same physical port for this exercise.

This scenario also considers a worst-case scenario approach. This will guarantee performance even when a failure has occurred. By taking this approach, we can ensure that vSAN always has 50% of the bandwidth at its disposal while leaving the remaining traffic types with sufficient bandwidth to avoid a potential self-inflicted DoS.

The following table outlines the recommendations for configuring shares for the different traffic types. Note that in the table we have only outlined the most used traffic types. In our scenario, we have divided the total amount of shares across the different traffic types based on the expected minimum bandwidth requirements per traffic type.

TRAFFIC TYPE	SHARES	LIMIT
Management Network	20	N/A
vMotion VMkernel Interface	50	N/A
VM Port Group	30	N/A
vSAN VMkernel Interface	100	N/A

Table 2: Recommended share configuration per traffic type

Explicit Failover Order

When selecting the uplinks used for the various types of traffic, you should separate traffic types to provide predictability and avoid noisy neighbor scenarios. The following configuration is our recommendation:

- Management network VMkernel interface
  Explicit failover order = Uplink 1 active/Uplink 2 standby
- vMotion VMkernel interface
  Explicit failover order = Uplink 1 active/Uplink 2 standby

- VM port group
  Explicit failover order = Uplink 1 active/Uplink 2 standby
- vSAN VMkernel interface
  Explicit failover order = Uplink 2 active/Uplink 1 standby

Setting an explicit failover order in the teaming and failover section of the port groups is recommended for predictability. The explicit failover order always uses the highest-order uplink from the list of active adapters that passes failover detection criteria.

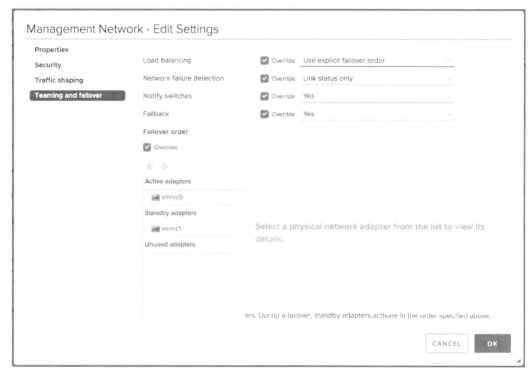

Figure 26: Using Explicit Failover Order

Separating traffic types allows for optimal storage performance while also providing sufficient bandwidth for the vMotion and VM traffic. Although this could also be achieved by using the *load-based teaming* (LBT) mechanism, note that the LBT load balancing period is 30 seconds, potentially causing a short period of contention when "bursty" traffic share the same uplinks. Also note that when troubleshooting network issues, it might be difficult to keep track of the relationship between the physical NIC port and VMkernel interface.

While this configuration provides a level of availability, it doesn't offer any sort of balancing for the vSAN traffic. It is either using one link or the other link. Thus, one disadvantage of this approach is that the vSAN traffic will never be able to use more than the bandwidth of a single NIC port. In the next section, we will discuss a network configuration that provides availability as well as load-balancing across uplinks, allowing vSAN to consume available bandwidth on multiple uplinks.

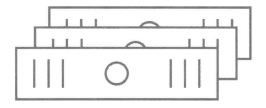

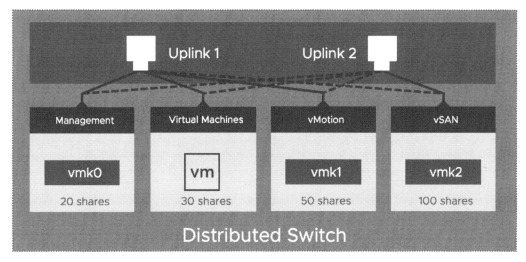

Figure 27: Using Explicit Failover Order

Scenario 2: Redundant 10 GbE Switch with Link Aggregation Capability

In this next scenario, there are two 10 GbE uplinks set up in a teamed configuration (often referred to as EtherChannel or link aggregation). Because of the physical switch capabilities, the configuration of the virtual layer will be extremely simple. We will consider the previous recommended minimum bandwidth requirements for the design:

- **Management network**: 1 GbE
- **vMotion VMkernel**: 5 GbE
- **VM port group**: 2 GbE
- **vSAN VMkernel interface**: 10 GbE

When the physical uplinks are teamed (link aggregation), the Distributed Switch load-balancing mechanism is required to be configured with one of the following configuration options:

- IP-Hash
- Link aggregation control protocol (LACP)

IP-Hash is a load-balancing option available to VMkernel interfaces that are connected to multiple uplinks on an ESXi host. An uplink is chosen based on a hash of the source and destination IP addresses of each packet. For non-IP packets, whatever is located at those IP address offsets in the packet is used to compute the hash. Again, this may not work well with vSAN since there may be only a single vSAN IP address per host.

LACP allows you to connect ESXi hosts to physical switches by employing dynamic link aggregation. LAGs (link aggregation groups) are created on the Distributed Switch to aggregate the bandwidth of the physical NICs on the ESXi hosts that are in turn connected to LACP port channels.

The official vSphere networking guide has much more detail on IP-hash and LACP support and should be referenced for additional details. Also, the vSAN Network Design documentation discusses LACP extensively. (https://vmwa.re/vsannetwork)

> **Although IP-Hash and LACP aggregate physical NICs (and/or ports), the algorithm used selects which physical NIC port to use for a particular data stream. A data stream with the same source and destination address will, as a result, only use a single physical NIC port and thus not use the aggregate bandwidth.**

It is recommended to configure all port groups and VMkernel interfaces to use either LACP or IP-Hash depending on the type of physical switch being used:

- Management network VMkernel interface = LACP/IP-Hash
- vMotion VMkernel interface = LACP/IP-Hash
- VM port group = LACP/IP-Hash
- vSAN VMkernel interface = LACP/IP-Hash

Because various traffic types will share the same uplinks, you also want to make sure that no traffic type can affect other types of traffic during times of contention. For that, the NIOC shared mechanism is used.

Working under the same assumptions as before that there is only one physical port available and that all traffic types share the same physical port, we once again take a worst-case scenario approach into consideration. This approach will guarantee performance even in a failure scenario. By taking this approach, we can ensure that vSAN always has 50% of the bandwidth at its disposal while giving the other traffic types sufficient bandwidth to avoid a potential self-inflicted DoS situation arising.

When both uplinks are available, this will equate to 10 GbE for vSAN traffic. When only one uplink is available (due to NIC failure or maintenance reasons), the bandwidth is also cut in half, giving a 5 GbE bandwidth. Table 2 in the previous example outlines the recommendations for configuring shares for the traffic types.

The next diagram depicts this configuration scenario.

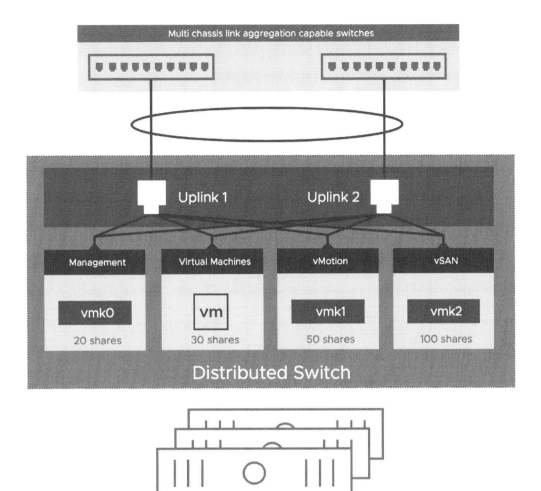

Figure 28: Distributed switch configuration for link aggregation

Either of the scenarios discussed here should provide an optimal network configuration for your vSAN cluster. However, once again we do want to highlight that whilst all these configurations provide availability, the one that we have found to provide the best load-balancing across uplinks, and thus the best-aggregated performance is the LACP configuration. This has to be weighed up against the added complexity of configuring Link Aggregation on the physical switch. Lastly, we do want to note that vSAN over RDMA is explicitly not supported at the time of writing in combination with LACP.

vSphere High Availability

vSphere *High Availability* (HA) is fully supported on a vSAN cluster to provide additional availability to VMs deployed in the cluster; however, several significant changes have been made to vSphere HA to ensure correct interoperability with vSAN. These changes are important to understand as they will impact the way you configure vSphere HA.

vSphere HA Communication Network

In non-vSAN deployments, communication of vSphere HA agents takes place over the management network. In a vSAN environment, vSphere HA agents communicate over the vSAN network. The reasoning behind this is that in the event of a network failure we want vSphere HA and vSAN to be part of the same network partition. This avoids possible conflicts when vSphere HA and vSAN observe different partitions when a failure occurs, with different partitions holding subsets of the storage components and objects. As such vSAN always needs to be configured before vSphere HA is enabled. If vSAN is configured after vSphere HA is configured, then a warning will inform you to temporarily disable HA first before continuing with the configuration of vSAN.

> **vSAN always needs to be configured before vSphere HA is enabled. If vSphere HA is already enabled, it needs to be disabled temporarily!**

vSphere HA in vSAN environments, by default, continues to use the management network's default gateway for isolation detection. We suspect that most vSAN environments will have the management network and the vSAN network sharing the same physical infrastructure (especially in 10 GbE environments), but logically separate them using VLANs. If the vSAN and management networks are on a different physical or logical network, it is required to change the default vSphere HA isolation address from the management network to the vSAN network. The reason for this is that in the event of a vSAN network issue that leads to a host being isolated from a vSAN perspective, vSphere HA won't take any action since the isolation response IP address is set on the management network, so it is still able to ping the isolated host.

By default, the isolation address is the default gateway of the management network as previously mentioned. VMware's recommendation when using vSphere HA with vSAN is to use an IP address on the vSAN network as an isolation address. To prevent vSphere HA from using the default gateway, and to use an IP address on the vSAN network, the following settings must be changed at a minimum in the advanced options for vSphere HA:

- das.useDefaultIsolationAddress=false
- das.isolationAddress0=<ip address on vSAN network>

In some cases, there may not be a suitable isolation address on the vSAN network. However, most network switches can create a so-called Switch Virtual Interface. Discuss this with your network administrator as this may be a viable alternative. We have seen customers who configured the isolation address to use one, or multiple, IP addresses of their vSAN VMkernel interfaces, this however is not recommended. In a scenario where the host is isolated of which the IP address is used as the isolation address, it will be impossible to declare the host isolated as the host will always be able to ping its own interface.

vSphere HA Heartbeat Datastores

Another noticeable difference with vSphere HA on vSAN is that the vSAN datastore cannot be used for datastore heartbeats. These heartbeats play a significant role in determining VM ownership in the event of a vSphere HA cluster partition with traditional SAN or NAS datastores. vSphere HA does not use the vSAN datastore for heart-beating and won't let a user designate it as a heartbeat datastore. If no heartbeat datastores can be configured vSphere HA will display a warning, this warning can be disabled by configuring the advanced setting "das.ignoreInsufficientHbDatastore = true".

> Note: If ESXi hosts participating in a vSAN cluster also have access to shared storage, either **VMFS (Virtual Machine File System)** or **NFS (Network File System)**, these traditional datastores may be used for vSphere HA heartbeats.

vSphere HA Admission Control

There is another consideration to discuss regarding vSphere HA and vSAN interoperability. When configuring vSphere HA, one of the decisions that need to be made is about admission control. Admission control ensures that vSphere HA has sufficient resources at its disposal to restart VMs after a failure. It does this by setting aside resources.

Starting with vSAN 7.0 U1, there now also is a mechanism to automatically set aside storage capacity resources for vSAN to ensure that objects which are impacted by a failure can be rebuilt. This functionality is called "Host rebuild reserve" and needs to be enabled for vSAN separately. Although it provides similar functionality as vSphere HA Admission Control does, it is not the same. If a failure occurs, vSAN will try to use the reserved capacity on the remaining nodes in the cluster to bring the VMs to a compliant state by rebuilding any missing or failed components.

vSphere HA Isolation Response

When a host isolation event occurs in a vSAN cluster with vSphere HA enabled, vSphere HA will apply the configured isolation response. With vSphere HA, you can select four different types of responses to an isolation event to specify what action to take on virtual machines that are on the isolated host:

- Disabled (Default)
- Power off and restart VMs (vSAN Recommended)
- Shut down and restart VMs

The recommendation is to have vSphere HA automatically power off the VMs running on that host when a host isolation event occurs. Therefore, the "isolation response" should be set to "**power off and restart VMs**" and not the default setting that is "Disabled".

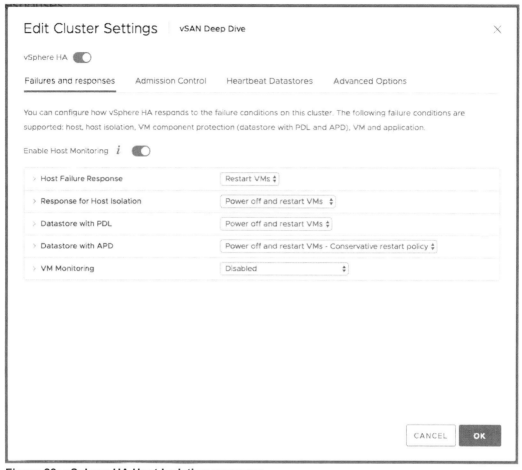

Figure 29: vSphere HA Host Isolation response

Note that "Power off and restart VMs" is like pulling the power cable from a physical host. The VM process is killed. *This is not a clean shutdown!* In the case of an isolation event, however, it is unlikely that vSAN can write to the disks on the isolated host and as such powering off is recommended. If the ESXi host is partitioned, it is also unlikely that any VM on the isolated host will be able to access a quorum of components of the storage object.

Proactive HA support

A feature of vSphere HA which was not supported previously is Proactive HA. Proactive HA enables vSphere to migrate VMs from a degraded host to a healthy host. Starting with vSAN 7.0 U2 support has been introduced for Proactive HA. You may wonder why Proactive HA wasn't supported pre-7.0 U2, and the answer is straightforward, vSAN was not aware of the state of a host from a Proactive HA perspective. Meaning that if Proactive HA would mark a host as degraded and place it in quarantine, vSAN would still consider the host for placing data and would not proactively migrate data from the host. This indeed changed with 7.0 U2.

Figure 30: Configure Proactive HA

When Proactive HA is configured, and please note that you need server vendor plugins to configure it (Providers), vSAN will consider the state of a host when placing data and will also proactively move data from a host when a host is degraded.

If your server vendor of choice supports Proactive HA, we would recommend considering enabling it with the automation level set to "Automated" and the remediation level set to "Mixed mode". In the case of "Mixed mode" Proactive HA will decide, based on the type of failure that has occurred, whether to place the host into maintenance mode or to place it into quarantine mode.

vSphere HA Component Protection

In a traditional SAN and NAS environment it is possible to configure a response to an *all paths down* (APD) scenario *and permanent device loss* (PDL) scenario within HA. This capability is part of a feature called VM Component Protection. At the time of writing this is not supported for vSAN and as such a response to APD and/or PDL does not have to be configured for vSphere HA in a vSAN only cluster. However, it can be configured when traditional datastores are available in your environment, or when you are leveraging vSAN HCI Mesh to mount remote vSAN datastores.

The question then remains, would it be beneficial to configure heartbeat datastores when available in a vSAN environment. The following table describes the different failure scenarios we have tested with a logically separated vSAN and Management network, with and without the availability of heartbeat datastores and a correctly and incorrectly configured isolation address.

ISOLATION ADDRESS	DATASTORE HEARTBEATS	OBSERVED BEHAVIOR
IP on vSAN Network	Not configured	The isolated host cannot ping the isolation address, isolation is declared, VMs killed and VMs restarted
IP on Management Network	Not configured	Can ping the isolation address, isolation is not declared, yet rest of the cluster restarts the VMs even though they are still running on the isolated hosts
IP on vSAN Network	Configured	The isolated host cannot ping the isolation address, isolation is declared, VMs killed and VMs restarted
IP on Management Network	Configured	VMs are not powered-off and not restarted as the "isolated host" can still ping the management network and the datastore heartbeat mechanism is used to inform the master about the state. The master knows HA network is not working, but the VMs are not powered off.

Table 3: Recommended share configuration per traffic type

Key Takeaways

- Always use an isolation address that is in the same network as vSAN when the management network and the vSAN network is logically or physically separated. By doing so, during an isolation, the isolation is validated using the vSAN VMkernel interface.
- Always set the isolation response to power-off, this would avoid the scenario of a duplicate MAC address or IP address on the network when VMs are restarted when you have a single network being isolated for a specific host.
- Last but not least, if you have traditional storage, then you can enable heartbeat datastores. It doesn't add much in terms of availability, but still, it will allow vSphere HA to communicate state through the datastore.

Now that we know what has changed for vSphere HA, let's take a look at some core constructs of vSAN.

Cache Device to Capacity Device Sizing Ratio

When designing your vSAN environment from a hardware perspective, realize that vSAN heavily relies on your caching device for performance. With previous releases of vSAN, it was recommended to have a 10% cache capacity ratio. Meaning that 5000GB (or to write it another way, 5TB) of capacity would require 500GB of cache. In 2018 this recommendation was changed, and VMware released a blog article (https://vmwa.re/flashcache) that included a new recommendation. This new recommendation however applies to all-flash environments only. For hybrid environments, VMware still recommends the 10% rule of thumb and we will discuss that in greater depth below. For all-flash environments, the new caching guidelines focus on the read/write profile of the workloads and the type of I/O. The next table describes it best.

READ/WRITE PROFILE	WORKLOAD TYPES	AF-8 80K IOPS	AF-6 50K IOPS	AF-4 25K IOPS
70/30 Read/Write Random	Read intensive, standard workloads	800 GB	400 GB	200 GB
>30% Write Random	Medium writes, mixed workloads	1.2 TB	800 GB	400 GB
100% Write Sequential	Heavy writes, sequential workloads	1.6 TB	1.2 TB	600 GB

Table 4: Caching Guidelines

Note that the above guidelines are implemented through the vSAN ReadyNode program. If you decide to build your own configuration, you will need to take the above recommendations into consideration to ensure performance and endurance.

On the VMware Compatibility Guide for vSAN details can be found for the recommended cache size of each of the vSAN ReadyNode profiles and configurations: http://vmwa.re/vsanhcl.

Cache in a Hybrid environment

As mentioned, as a of thumb, VMware recommends 10% cache capacity of the expected consumed total virtual disk capacity before "failures to tolerate" has been accounted for hybrid configurations. VMware also supports lower ratios. Larger ratios may improve the performance of VMs by more I/O can be cached. It should be noted however that the maximum logical size of the write cache partition is 600GB. Since write cache on hybrid configurations is 30% of all cache, with the remaining 70% dedicated to read cache, a 2 TB cache device would be fully utilized. If larger SSDs are used, then the additional capacity will be used for write endurance purposes.

Flash will function as read cache and write buffer capacity for VMs in vSAN. For the moment, it is sufficient to understand that in a hybrid vSAN cluster 70% of your caching device will be used as a read cache and 30% as a write buffer.

The 10% value assumes that most working data sets are about 10%. Using this rule of thumb (and it is just a rule of thumb) to cover most workloads means that live data from the application running in your VM should be in flash.

For example, assume that we have 100 VMs. Each VM has a 100 GB virtual disk, of which anticipated usage is 50 GB on average. In this scenario, this would result in the following:
10% of (100 × 50 GB) = 500 GB

This total amount of cache capacity should be divided by the number of ESXi hosts in the vSAN cluster. If you have five hosts, in this example that would lead to 100 GB of cache capacity recommended per host.

A useful way to determine the working set size is to take a snapshot of the VM and monitor the size of the snapshot over time. Another way would be to examine the incremental backup size of a particular VM. These will give you a good idea of how much data is changing in that VM.

Add Devices to vSAN Disk Groups

Automatic versus manual mode of adding disks to a disk group used to be a topic of hot debate. This discussion however has been put to rest by the vSAN team when the "automatic mode" was deprecated in vSAN 6.6. This was the result of direct feedback from our customers. They wanted to control where and when devices were added to a disk group, and as such VMware decided to deprecate the automated mode.

Disk Group Creation Example

Manual disk group creation is necessary only when additional disk groups need to be added after the initial creation of the cluster. The mechanism to create a disk group is quite straightforward. You need to remember some restrictions, however, as mentioned previously:

- At most, there can be one caching device per disk group.
- At most, there can be seven capacity devices per disk group.

Multiple disk groups may be created if a host has more than seven capacity devices and/or more than one caching device. Navigate to the disk management section under vSAN in the configuration section of the vSphere Client on your cluster object. From here, you select a host in the cluster and click "View disks", this will then show you all current disk groups and currently unclaimed disks. Next, you can click "Create disk group" to create a new disk group. This will then display all eligible devices (SSD and magnetic disks) in the host.

03 // vSAN Installation and Configuration

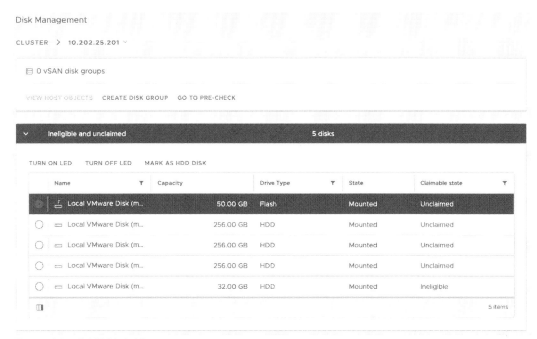

Figure 31: vSAN Disk Management

At this point, vSphere administrators have several options available. They can decide to claim all disks from all hosts if they want, or they can individually build disk groups one host at a time. The first option is useful if disks show up as not local, such as disks that may be behind a SAS controller, as discussed in chapter 2. For more granular control, however, administrators may like to set up disk groups one host at a time.

When you decide to configure disk groups manually, the vSphere Client provides a very intuitive user interface (UI) to do this. From the UI, you can select the capacity devices and flash devices that form the disk group in a single step.

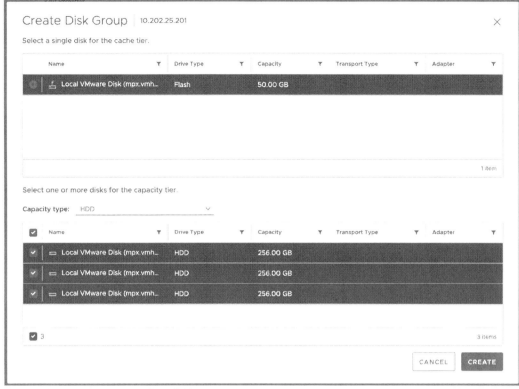

Figure 32: Claiming disks for vSAN

After the disk groups have been created for each host, the vSAN datastore is created. This vSAN datastore can now be used for the deployment of VMs or other types of vSAN objects like iSCSI volumes, vSAN File Services file shares, etc.

vSAN Datastore Properties

The raw size of a vSAN datastore is governed by the number of capacity devices per ESXi host and the number of ESXi hosts in the cluster. Cache devices do not contribute to the capacity of the vSAN datastore. There is some metadata overhead to also consider. For example, if a host has seven × 2 TB flash capacity devices in the cluster, and there are eight hosts in the cluster, the raw capacity is as follows:

```
7 x 2 TB x 8 = 112 TB raw capacity
```

Now that we know how to calculate how much raw capacity, we will have available. But how do we know much effective capacity we will have? Well, this depends on various factors, but it all begins with the hardware configuration, all-flash or hybrid. When creating your vSAN cluster, if your vSAN cluster is an all-flash configuration, you have the option to enable Deduplication and Compression or Compression Only. These space efficiency features play a big factor in the available capacity for an all-flash configuration. Note that these data services are not available in a hybrid configuration. We will discuss space efficiency features in more detail in Chapter 4.

But it is not just deduplication and compression (or compression only) that can provide space-saving on the vSAN datastore or can change the amount of available effective capacity. There is also the number of replica copies configured if the VM is using a RAID-1 policy. This is enabled through the policy-based management framework. Conversely, you may decide to use erasure coding policies such as RAID-5 and RAID-6 (but note that this space efficiency feature is only available on all-flash vSAN). On top of that, there's also the ability to reserve capacity for vSAN operations and host failures. Enabling these reservation options will directly impact how many VMs can be deployed on the datastore.

After creating the disk groups, your vSAN is configured. Once the vSAN datastore is formed, a number of datastore capabilities are surfaced up into vCenter Server. These capabilities will be used to create the appropriate VM storage policies for VMs, and their associated virtual machine disk (VMDK) storage objects deployed on the vSAN datastore. These include stripe width, number of failures to tolerate, force provisioning, and provisioned capacity. If the VM availability mechanism needs to be optimized for performance, use RAID-1. If it needs to be optimized for capacity, use RAID-5 or RAID-6. Before deploying VMs, however, you first need to understand how to create appropriate VM storage policies that meet the requirements of the application running in the VM.

VM storage policies and vSAN capabilities will be discussed in greater detail later in Chapter 5, "VM Storage Policies on vSAN," but suffice it to know for now that these capabilities form the VM policy requirements. These allow a vSphere administrator to specify requirements based on performance, availability, and data services when it comes to VM provisioning. Chapter 5 discusses VM storage policies in the context of vSAN and how to correctly deploy a VM using vSAN capabilities.

Summary

If everything is configured and working as designed, vSAN can be configured in just a few clicks. However, it is vitally important that the infrastructure is ready in advance. Identifying appropriate magnetic disk drives or flash devices for capacity, sizing your flash resources for caching performance, and verifying that your networking is configured to provide the best availability and performance are all tasks that must be configured and designed up front.

Now the vSAN cluster is up and running, let's look at some of the architectural components of vSAN in the next chapter.

04

Architectural Details

This chapter examines some of the underlying architectural details of vSAN. We have already touched on a number of these aspects, including the use of flash devices for caching I/O, witness disks, the desire for pass-through storage controllers, and so on.

This chapter covers these features in detail, in addition to the new architectural concepts and terminology that are introduced by vSAN. Although most vSphere administrators will never see many of these low-level constructs, it will be useful to have a generic understanding of the services that make up vSAN when designing and sizing vSAN deployments, as well troubleshooting or when analyzing log files. Before examining some of the lower-level details, here is one concept that we need to discuss first as it is the core of vSAN: distributed RAID (Redundant Array of Inexpensive Disks).

Distributed RAID

vSAN can provide highly available and high-performing VMs using distributed RAID, or put another way, RAID over the network. From an availability perspective, distributed RAID simply implies that the vSAN environment can withstand the failure of one or more ESXi hosts (or components in that host, such as a disk drive or network interface card) and continue to provide complete functionality for all your VMs. To ensure that VMs perform optimally, vSAN distributed RAID provides the ability to divide the constituent parts of a virtual machine, including virtual disks, across multiple physical disks and hosts.

A point to note, however, is that VM availability and performance are now defined on a per-VM basis using storage policies. To be more accurate, it is defined on a per-object basis. When we talk about VMs or virtual disks, it is good to realize that this applies to all types of objects, including for instance vSAN File Service file shares or iSCSI LUNs. We will however often use VM or virtual disk in our examples as it makes it easier to comprehend.

Using a storage policy, administrators can define how many host or disk failures an object can tolerate in a vSAN cluster and across how many hosts and devices, an object is deployed. If you explicitly choose not to set an availability requirement in the storage policy by setting the number of *failures to tolerate* equal to zero, a host or disk failure can certainly impact your object's availability. More detailed information on policy settings will be discussed in chapter 5.

In the earlier releases, vSAN used RAID-1 (synchronous mirroring) exclusively across hosts to meet the availability and reliability requirement of storage objects deployed on the system. The number of mirror copies (replicas) of the VM storage objects depended on the storage policy, in particular, the number of *failures to tolerate* requirement. The ability to select more than one failure depended on the available resources in the cluster, such as hosts and disks. Depending on the VM storage policy, you could have up to three replica objects of a VM's disk (VMDK) object across a vSAN cluster for availability, assuming there were enough hosts in the cluster to accommodate this. By default, vSAN always deploys VMs with *failures to tolerate* equal to 1; this means that there is always a replica copy of the VM storage objects for every VM deployed on the vSAN datastore. This is the default policy associated with vSAN datastores. This can be changed based on the policy selected during VM provisioning, or by changing the default policy associated with the vSAN datastore.

vSAN includes two other RAID types, RAID-5 and RAID-6. These are commonly referred to as *erasure coding*. In earlier vSAN versions, objects with these policies were created when the *failure tolerance method* capability setting was set to *capacity* rather than *performance* in the VM storage policy. The mechanism for selecting RAID-5 and RAID-6 has changed in later versions of vSAN, where the setting is embedded into the *failures to tolerate* setting. While this has already been mentioned, it is important to repeat once more that this erasure coding feature is only available on all-flash vSAN configurations. It is not available on hybrid vSAN.

The purpose of introducing these additional distributed RAID types is to save on capacity usage. Both RAID-5 and RAID-6 use a distributed parity mechanism rather than mirrors to protect the data. With RAID-5, the data is distributed across three capacity devices on three ESXi hosts, and then the parity of this data is calculated and stored on a fourth capacity device on a fourth ESXi host. Thus, a minimum of 4 hosts are required in a vSAN cluster to implement a RAID-5 object on vSAN. The parity is not always stored on the same disk or the same host. It is distributed, as shown below.

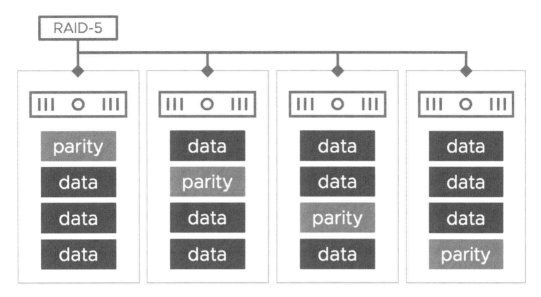

Figure 33: RAID-5 deployment with distributed parity

A RAID-5 configuration can tolerate only one host failure. RAID-6 is designed to tolerate two host failures. In a RAID-6 configuration, data is distributed across four capacity devices on four ESXi hosts, and when the parity is calculated, it is stored on two additional capacity devices on two additional ESXi hosts. Therefore, if you wish to utilize a RAID-6 configuration, a total of six ESXi hosts are required. Once again, the parity is distributed, as shown in the next diagram.

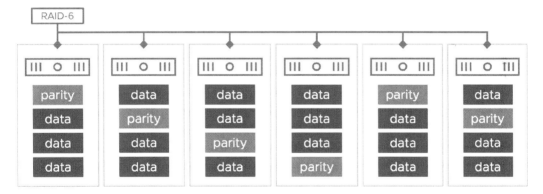

Figure 34: RAID-6 deployment with distributed parity

The space savings can be calculated as follows. If you deploy a 100GB VMDK object and wish to tolerate one failure using a RAID-1 configuration, a total of 200GB of capacity would be consumed on the vSAN datastore. Similarly, if you deploy the same 100GB VMDK object and wish to tolerate two failures using a RAID-1 configuration, a total of 300 GB of capacity would be consumed on the vSAN datastore. With RAID-5, a total of 133.33 GB would be consumed to tolerate one failure (3 data + 1 parity). With RAID-6, a total of 150 GB would be consumed to tolerate two failures (4 data + 2 parity).

Using VM Storage Policies on vSAN, administrators can now choose between performance and capacity. If performance is the absolute end goal for administrators, then RAID-1 (Mirroring), which is still the default, is what should be used. If administrators do not need maximum performance, and are more concerned with space-saving on capacity, then RAID-5/6 (Erasure Coding) may be used.

Depending on the *number of disk stripes per object* policy setting (configurable through Advanced Policy Rules), a VM disk object may be "striped" across several capacity tier devices to achieve improved performance. However, a stripe configuration does not always necessitate a performance improvement. The section "Stripe Width Policy Setting," which can be found in chapter 5, explains the reasons for this as well as when it is useful to increase the stripe width in the policy of a VMDK object.

Objects and Components

Now that we have explained how VMs are protected, it is important to understand the concept that the vSAN datastore is an *object storage system* and that VMs are now made up of a few different storage objects. This is a new concept for vSphere administrators as traditionally a VM has been made up of a set of files on a LUN or volume.

We have not spoken in detail about objects and components so far, so before we go into detail about the various types of objects, let's start with the definition and concepts of an object and component on vSAN.

An *object* is an individual storage block device, compatible with SCSI semantics that resides on the vSAN datastore. It may be created on-demand and at any size, though some object sizes are limited. For example, VMDKs follow the vSphere capacity limitation of 62TB.

Objects are the main unit of storage on vSAN. In vSAN, the objects that make up a virtual machine are VMDKs, the VM home namespace, and when the VM is powered on, a VM swap object is also created. A namespace object can be thought of as a directory-like object, where files can be stored.

If a snapshot is taken of the virtual machine during its lifespan, then a delta disk object is created. If the snapshot includes the memory of the virtual machine, this is also instantiated as an object, so a snapshot could be made up of either one or two objects, depending on the snapshot type.

In case a failure has occurred, you may also see a special object called a durability component. This component is used by vSAN to temporarily store new writes and is very similar to a regular VMDK component, but we will discuss this in more depth at a later stage.

Other object types include iSCSI targets and LUNs, file shares, and a performance stats object used for storing vSAN performance metrics. iSCSI targets are like VM home namespaces, and iSCSI LUNs and file shares are like VMDKs. The performance stats database is also akin to a namespace object. One other item to note is that if you plan to store files on the vSAN datastore, for example, ISO images, then this also creates a namespace type object to facilitate the storing of the file or files.

Each "object" in vSAN has its own RAID tree that turns the requirements placed in the policy into an actual layout on physical devices. When a VM storage policy is selected during VM deployment, the requirements around availability and performance in the policy are applied to the VM's objects, thus these have a direct relationship to the layout of the object.

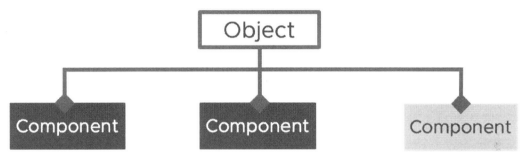

Figure 35: Sample RAID tree

Components are leaves of the object's RAID tree—that is, a "piece" of an object that is stored on a particular "cache device + capacity device" combination in a disk group. A component gets transparent caching/buffering from the cache device (which is always flash), with its data "at rest" on a capacity device (which could be flash in all-flash vSAN configurations or magnetic disk in hybrid vSAN configurations).

We stated previously that a VM can have five different types of objects on a vSAN datastore as follows, keeping in mind that each VM may have multiples of some of these objects associated with it:

- The VM home or "namespace directory"
- A swap object (if the VM is powered on)
- Virtual disks/VMDKs
- Delta disks (each is a unique object) created for snapshots
- Snapshot memory (each is a unique object) optionally created for snapshots

Of the five objects, the VM home namespace may need a little further explanation. Every VM gets its own unique home namespace object. All VM files, excluding VMDKs, deltas (snapshots), memory (snapshots), durability component, and swap, reside in this *VM home namespace* object on the vSAN datastore. The typical files found in the VM home namespace are the ".vmx", the ".log" files, ".vmdk" descriptor files, snapshot deltas descriptors files, and everything else one would expect to find in a VM home directory.

Each storage object is deployed on vSAN as a RAID tree, and each leaf of the tree is said to be a component. For instance, if I choose to deploy a VMDK with a stripe width of 2 but did not wish to tolerate any failures (for whatever reason), a RAID-0 stripe would be configured across a minimum of two disks for this VMDK. The VMDK would be the object, and each of the stripes would be a component of that object.

Similarly, if I specified that my VMDK should be able to tolerate at least one failure in the cluster (host, disk, or network) by selecting a RAID-1 policy, a mirror of the VMDK object would be created with one replica component on one host and another replica component on another host in my vSAN cluster. We require one other component in this object, referred to as a witness component, to give us quorum in the event of failure or split-brain/cluster partition scenarios. The witness component is very important and special but is not used for storing any data belonging to a VM. It holds only metadata. We will return to the witness component shortly, but for the moment let's concentrate on VM storage objects. Hopefully, you understand the concept of the RAID tree at this point. The object layout and placement decisions will be covered extensively in chapter 5.

Finally, if my policy included a requirement for both striping and availability with RAID-1, my striped components would be mirrored across hosts, giving me a RAID 0+1 configuration. This would result in four components making up my single object, two striped components in each replica.

Note also that delta disks are created when a snapshot is taken of a VM. A delta disk inherits the same policy as the parent disk (RAID settings, stripe width, replicas, and so on).

Component Limits

One major limit applies to components in vSAN. It is important to understand this because it is a hard limit and limits the number of VMs you can run on a single host and in your cluster.

- **Maximum number of components per host limit: 9,000**

Components per host include components from powered-off VMs, unregistered VMs, and templates. vSAN distributes components across the various hosts in the cluster and will always try to achieve an even distribution of components for balance. However, some hosts may have more components than others, which is why VMware recommends, as a best practice, that hosts participating in a vSAN cluster be similarly or identically configured. Components are a significant sizing consideration when designing and deploying vSAN clusters. If hosts participating in a vSAN cluster are uniformly configured, vSAN will try to evenly distribute components across all hosts and disk groups.

The vSphere client enables administrators to interrogate objects and components of a VM. The next screenshot provides an example of one such layout. The VM has a single hard disk. From the list of object components, you can see that the objects (Hard disk 1 and VM Home) are mirrored across two different hosts with the witness placed on a third host. This is visible in the "hosts"

04 // Architecture Details

column, where it shows the host location of the components.

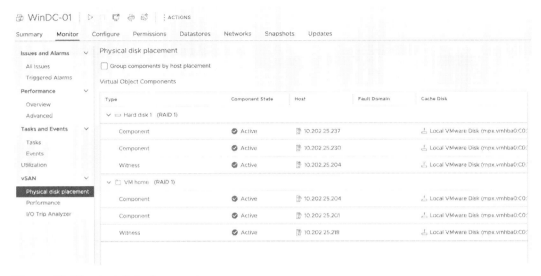

Figure 36: Physical disk placement

Virtual Machine Storage Objects

As stated earlier, the five storage objects are VM home namespace, VM Swap, VMDK, delta disks, and snapshot memory as illustrated in the diagram below.

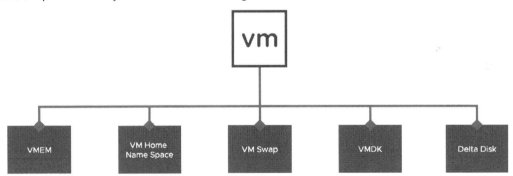

Figure 37: VM storage objects

We will now look at how characteristics defined in the VM storage policy impact these storage objects.

Namespace Object

Virtual machines use the namespace object as their VM home and use it to store all of the virtual machine files that are not dedicated objects in their own right. So, for example, this includes, but is not limited to, the following:

- The ".vmx", ".vmdk" (the descriptor portion), ".log" files that the VMX uses.
- Digest files for *content-based read cache* (CBRC) for VMware Horizon View. This feature is referred to as the View Storage Accelerator. *Virtual desktop infrastructure* (VDI) is a significant use case for vSAN.
- vSphere Replication and Site Recovery Manager files.
- Guest customization files.
- Files created by other solutions.

These VM home namespace objects are not shared between VMs; there is one per VM. vSAN leverages VMFS as the file system within the namespace object to store all the files of the VM. This is a fully fleshed VMFS that includes cluster capabilities to support all the solutions that require locks on VMFS (e.g., vMotion, vSphere HA). This appears as an auto-mounted subdirectory when you examine the ESXi hosts' file systems.

For the VM home namespace, a special VM storage policy is used. For the most part, the VM home storage object does not inherit all the same policy requirements as the VMDKs. If you think about it, why would you want to give something like the VM home namespace a percentage of flash read cache on vSAN hybrid systems or even a stripe width? You wouldn't, which is why the VM home namespace does not have these settings applied even when they are in the policy associated with the virtual machine. The VM home namespace does, however, inherit the *failures to tolerate* setting. This allows the VM to survive multiple hardware failures in the cluster. It also means that the VM home namespace could be deployed as a RAID-5 or RAID-6 configuration, not just a RAID-1 configuration as was the case in prior versions of vSAN.

Since high performance is not a major requirement for the VM home namespace storage object, vSAN overwrites the inherited policy settings so that stripe width is always set to 1 and read cache reservation (on hybrid) is always set to 0%. It also has object space reservation set to 0% so that it is always thinly provisioned, even if the policy is set to 'thick'. This avoids the VM home namespace object consuming unnecessary capacity, i.e., 255GB of capacity, mirrored, and makes this disk space available to other objects that might need them, such as VMDKs. However, as files within the VM home namespace grow over time, logs, etc., the VM home namespace will grow accordingly.

One other important note is that if the option force provisioning is set in the policy, the VM home namespace object also inherits that, meaning that a VM will be deployed even if the full complement of resources is not available. You will learn more about this in the next chapter when policies are covered in detail. However, suffice to say that a VM Home Namespace could be deployed as a RAID-0 rather than a RAID-1 if there are not enough resources in the cluster.

Note that the namespace object has other uses other than the VM's home namespace. The iSCSI on vSAN feature uses the namespace object for the iSCSI target. This is used to track iSCSI LUNs available through this target. The vSAN Performance stats database is also held in the namespace object. And finally, any files that might be uploaded to the vSAN datastore, such as ISO images, will be stored in a namespace object as well.

Virtual Machine Swap Object

Several changes have taken place around the VM swap object over the last number of releases. Since vSAN 6.7, the VM swap object now inherits the *failures to tolerate* setting in the VM Storage Policy, which means that swap can now be configured as RAID-1, RAID-5, or RAID-6. This is a change from previous versions of vSAN where the VM swap object was always provisioned with RAID-1, and *failures to tolerate* set to 1. The thought process behind this earlier RAID-1 configuration is that swap does not need to persist when a virtual machine is restarted. Therefore, if vSphere HA restarts the virtual machine on another host elsewhere in the cluster, a new swap object is created. Thus, there is no need to add additional protection above tolerating one failure. However, it is possible that if all of the other objects are deployed to tolerate additional failures with policies such as *2 failures - RAID-1(mirroring)*, or indeed *2 failures - RAID-6 (erasure coding)* then it would make sense to have VM swap to also tolerate 2 failures and avoid unnecessary VM outages.

Note that swap does not inherit the stripe width policy setting. It is always provisioned with a *number of disk stripes per object* setting of 1.

By default, swap objects are provisioned 'thin' since vSAN 6.7. Prior to this, swap objects were always provisioned 'thick' upfront, without the need to set object space reservation to 100% in the policy. This means, in terms of admission control, vSAN would not deploy the VM unless there is enough disk space to accommodate the full size of the VM swap object. Since vSAN 6.2, customers can use an advanced host option called *SwapThickProvisionDisabled* to allow the VM swap to be provisioned as a thin object. If this advanced setting is set to true, the VM swap objects will be thinly provisioned in previous versions of vSAN.

VMDKs and Delta Disk Objects

As you have just read, VM home namespace and VM swap have their own default policies when a VM is deployed and do not adhere to all of the capabilities set in the policy. Therefore, it is only the VMDKs and snapshot files (delta disks) of these disk files that obey all the capabilities that are set in the VM storage policies. Delta disks created as the result of a VM snapshot use the vSANSparse format, a special on-disk format that is only available to delta disks created on the vSAN datastore.

Because vSAN objects may be made up of multiple components, each VMDK and delta has its own RAID tree configuration when deployed on vSAN.

Note that full clones, linked clones, instant clones, and vSANSparse delta disks all create VMDK objects on the vSAN datastore. To determine what type of VMDK a disk object is, the VMDK descriptor file in the VM Home Namespace object can be referenced.

Witnesses and Replicas

As part of the RAID-1 tree, each object has at least 2 replicas which can be made up of one or more components. We mentioned that when we create VM objects, one or more witness components *may* also get created. Witnesses are components that may make up a leaf of the RAID-1 tree, but they contain only metadata. They are there to act as tiebreakers and are only used for quorum determination in the event of failures in the vSAN cluster. They do not store any VM-specific data.

A common question is whether the witness consumes any space on the vSAN datastore. With the current on-disk format a witness consumes about 16 MB of space for metadata on the vSAN datastore. Although insignificant to most, it could be something to consider when running through the design, sizing, and scaling exercises when planning to deploy many VMs with many VMDKs and many delta snapshots on vSAN. Witness do however contribute towards the overall component count in a vSAN cluster.

Let's take the easiest case to explain their purpose: Suppose, for example, that we have deployed a VM that has *number of disk stripes per object* setting of 1 and it also has number of *failures to tolerate* setting of 1. We wish to use RAID-1 for the VM for performance. In this case, two replica copies of the VM need to be created. Effectively, this is a RAID-1 with two replicas; however, with two replicas, there is no way to differentiate between a network partition and a host failure. Therefore, a third entity called the witness is added to the configuration.

For an object on vSAN to be available, two conditions must be met:

- For a RAID-1 configuration, at least one full replica needs to be intact for the object to be available. For a RAID-0 configuration, all stripes need to be intact. For RAID-5 configurations, three out of four RAID-5 components must be intact for the object to be available, and for RAID-6, four out of the six RAID-6 components must be intact.
- The second rule is that there must be more than 50% of all votes associated with components available.

In the preceding example, only when there is access to one replica copy and a witness, or indeed two replica copies (and no witness), would you be able to access the object. That way, at most only one part of the partitioned cluster can ever access an object in the event of a network partition.

Performance Stats DB Object

vSAN provides a performance service for monitoring vSAN, both from a VM (front-end) perspective, vSAN (back-end) perspective and iSCSI perspective. This service aggregates performance information from all the ESXi hosts in the cluster and stores the metrics in a stats database on the vSAN datastore. As previously mentioned, the object in which the "stats DB" is stored is also a namespace object. Therefore, the use of namespace objects is not limited to VMs, although this is the most common use. Administrators can choose bespoke policies for the Performance Stats object when enabling the Performance Service. In the screenshot below, the default storage policy is chosen but it can be changed by clicking on the down arrow to the right of the storage policy listed and selecting a different policy.

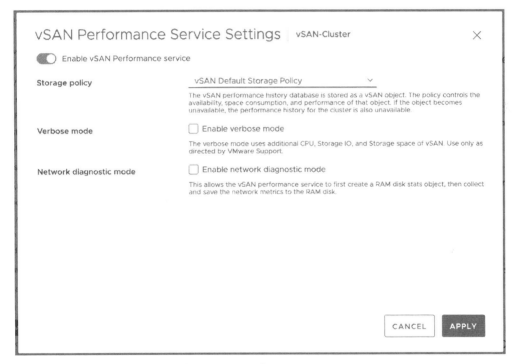

Figure 38: Policy setting for Performance Service

Object Layout

The next question people usually ask is how objects are laid out in a vSAN environment. vSAN takes care of object placement to meet the *failure to tolerate* requirements and while an administrator should not worry about these placement decisions, we understand that with a new solution you may have the desire to have a better understanding of the physical placement of components and objects. VMware expected that administrators would have this desire; therefore, the vSphere user interface enables vSphere administrators to interrogate the layout of a VM object and see where each component (stripes, replicas, witnesses) that make up a storage object resides.

> vSAN will never let components of different replicas (mirrors) share the same host for availability purposes.

The visibility into all objects has improved significantly in recent versions of vSAN. Both the VM swap objects and snapshot deltas are now visible via the vSphere Client. While the views might be slightly different in each of the subsequent versions of vSAN, administrators can navigate to the vSAN Cluster, then the Monitor tab, then vSAN followed by Virtual Objects, and select either the VM or an individual object and then click View Placement Details. The physical disk placement of the objects will be listed there. One can also group components belonging to a VM on a per host basis, as shown in the screenshot.

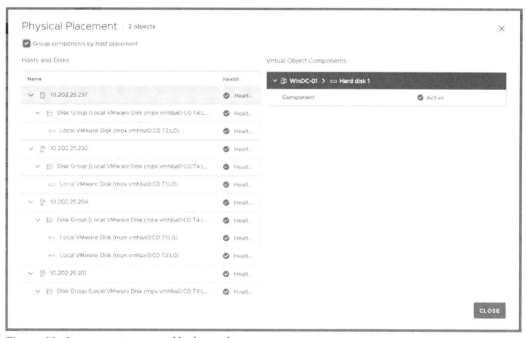

Figure 39: Components grouped by host placement

vSAN Software Components

This section briefly outlines some of the software components that make up the distributed software layer.

Much of this information will not be of particular use to vSphere administrators on a day-to-day basis. All this complexity is hidden away in how VMware has implemented the installation, configuration, and management of vSAN. However, we do want to highlight some of the major components behind the scenes for you because you may see messages from time to time related to these components appearing in the vSphere UI and the VMkernel logs. We want to provide you with some background on what the function is of these components, which may help in troubleshooting scenarios.

04 // Architecture Details

The vSAN architecture consists of four major components, as illustrated in the diagram below and described in more depth in the sections that follow.

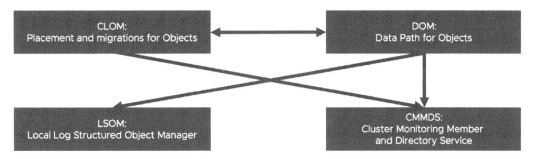

Figure 40: vSAN software components

Component Management

The vSAN local *log structured object manager* (LSOM) works at the physical disk level. LSOM is responsible for providing persistence of storage for the vSAN cluster. By this, we mean that it stores the components that makeup VM storage objects as well as any configuration information. It will also determine if a block is in cache, or if we need to go to the capacity tier to retrieve it.

LSOM is the layer at which checksum verification is performed on vSAN. LSOM also reports events for devices. For example, if a device has become unhealthy, it is LSOM that is responsible for retrying I/O if transient device errors occur.

LSOM also aids in the recovery of objects. On every ESXi host boot, LSOM performs an SSD log recovery by reading the entire log to ensure that the in-memory state is up to date and correct. This means that a reboot of an ESXi host that is participating in a vSAN cluster can take longer than an ESXi host that is not participating in a vSAN cluster. However, this was mitigated by the introduction of the ESXi quick boot functionality introduced in vSphere 6.7, and further improved in vSAN 7.0 U1 where we save the in-memory metadata table to disk during host restarts.

Data Paths for Objects

The *distributed object manager* (DOM) provides distributed data access paths to objects built from local (LSOM) components. The DOM is responsible for the creation of reliable, fault-tolerant storage objects from local components across multiple ESXi hosts in the vSAN cluster. It does this by implementing distributed RAID types for objects.

DOM is also responsible for handling different types of failures such as I/O failing from a device and being unable to contact a host. In the event of an unexpected host failure, during recovery DOM must resynchronize all the components that make up every object. Components publish a *bytesToSync* value periodically to show the progress of a synchronization operation. This can be monitored via the vSphere web client UI when recovery operations are taking place. DOM is also the vSAN software component that calculates checksums, which are later checked on-disk by the LSOM software component.

Object Ownership

For every storage object in the cluster, vSAN elects an owner for the object, typically referred to as the DOM owner, short for distributed object manager owner. The DOM owner can be considered the storage head responsible for coordinating (internally within vSAN) who can do I/O to the object. We briefly discussed owners when we spoke about vSAN iSCSI earlier in this chapter. The owner is the entity that ensures consistent data on the distributed object by performing a transaction for every operation that modifies the data/metadata of the object.

One thing we do want to point out is that with the introduction of HCI Mesh in vSAN 7.0 U1 a change has also been introduced to DOM. Starting with 7.0 U1 DOM has been split up into multiple components, enabling vSAN to establish a "DOM client – DOM owner" relationship to allow for remote mounting of vSAN datastores, both from other vSAN clusters as well as from a vanilla vSphere cluster. We will discuss HCI Mesh in detail in chapter 6 where we discuss vSAN Operations.

As an analogy, in NFS configurations, consider the concept of NFS server and NFS client. Only certain DOM clients can communicate successfully with the server. In this case, the object owner can be considered along the same lines as an NFS server, determining which clients can do I/O and which clients cannot.

The final part of object ownership is the concept of a component manager. The component manager can be thought of as the network front end of LSOM (in other words, how a storage object in vSAN can be accessed).

An object owner communicates to the component manager to find the leaves on the RAID tree that contain the components of the storage object. Typically, only one client is accessing the object. However, in the case of a vMotion operation, multiple clients may be accessing the same object as the DOM object is being moved between hosts.

In most cases, the DOM owner and the DOM client co-reside on the same node in the vSAN cluster. In the case of RAID-1 replicas, reads are balanced across replicas for cache efficiency reasons. The DOM owner chooses which replica to read from, based on the *Logical Block Address* (LBA). This request is then sent on to LSOM.

Placement and Migration for Objects

The *cluster level object manager* (CLOM) is responsible for ensuring that an object has a configuration that matches its policy (i.e., the requested stripe width is implemented or that there are enough mirrors/replicas in place to meet the availability requirement of the VM). Effectively, CLOM takes the policy assigned to an object and applies a variety of heuristics to find a configuration in the current cluster that will meet that policy. It does this while also load balancing the resource utilization across all the nodes in the vSAN cluster.

DOM then applies a configuration as dictated by CLOM. CLOM distributes components across the various ESXi hosts in the cluster. CLOM tries to create some sort of balance, but it is not unusual for some hosts to have more components, capacity used/reserved, or flash read cache used/reserved than others.

Each node in a vSAN cluster runs an instance of *CLOM, called clomd*. Each instance of CLOM is responsible for the configurations and policy compliance of the objects owned by the DOM on the ESXi host where it runs. Therefore, it needs to communicate with *cluster monitoring, membership, and directory service* (CMMDS) to be aware of ownership transitions.

> **CLOM only communicates with entities on the node where it runs. It does not use the network.**

Cluster Monitoring, Membership, and Directory Services

The purpose of *cluster monitoring, membership, and directory services* (CMMDS) is to discover, establish, and maintain a cluster of networked node members. It manages the physical cluster resources inventory of items such as hosts, devices, and networks and stores object metadata information such as policies, distributed RAID configuration, and so on in an in-memory database. The object metadata is always also persisted on disk. It is also responsible for the detection of failures in nodes and network paths.

Other software components browse the directory and subscribe to updates to learn of changes in cluster topology and object configuration. For instance, DOM can use the content of the directory to determine which nodes are storing which components of an object, and the paths by which those nodes are reachable.

CMMDS is used to elect "owners" for objects. The owner of an object will manage which clients can do I/O to a particular object, as discussed earlier.

Note that prior to vSAN 6.6, CMMDS would only form a cluster and elect a master if there was multicast network connectivity between all the ESXi hosts in the vSAN cluster. This requirement has since been relaxed, and CMMDS now uses unicast traffic. It no longer requires multicast configured on the vSAN network.

Host Roles

When a vSAN cluster is formed, you may notice through *esxcli* commands that each ESXi host in a vSAN cluster has a particular role. These roles are for the vSAN clustering service *only*. The clustering service (CMMDS) is responsible for maintaining an updated directory of disks, disk groups, and objects that resides on each ESXi host in the vSAN cluster. This has nothing to do with managing objects in the cluster or doing I/O to an object by the way; this is simply to allow nodes in the cluster to keep track of one another. The **clustering service** is based on a master (with a backup) and agents, where all nodes send updates to the master and the master then redistributes them to the agents.

Roles are applied during a cluster discovery, at which time the ESXi hosts participating in the vSAN cluster elect the master. A vSphere administrator has no control over which role a cluster member takes.

A common question is why a backup role is needed. The reason for this is that if the ESXi host that is currently in the master role suffers a catastrophic failure and there is no backup, all ESXi hosts must reconcile their entire view of the directory with the newly elected master. This would mean that all the nodes in the cluster might be sending all their directory contents from their respective view of the cluster to the new master. Having a backup negates the requirement to send all of this information over the network, and thus speeds up the process of electing a new master node.

In the case of vSAN stretched clusters, which allows nodes in a vSAN cluster to be geographically dispersed across different sites, the master node will reside on one site whilst the backup node will reside on the other site.

An important point to make is that, to a user or even a vSphere administrator, the ESXi node that is elected to the role of a master has no special features or other visible differences. Because the master is automatically elected, even on failures, and given that the node has no user-visible difference in abilities, doing operations (create VM, clone VM, delete VM, etc.) on a master node versus any other node makes no difference.

Reliable Datagram Transport

The *reliable datagram transport* (RDT) is the communication mechanism within vSAN. It uses *Transmission Control Protocol* (TCP) at the transport layer. When an operation needs to be performed on a vSAN object, DOM uses RDT to talk to the owner of the vSAN object. Because the RDT promises reliable delivery, users of the RDT can rely on it to retry requests after path or node failures, which may result in a change of object ownership and hence a new path to the owner of the object. RDT creates and tears down TCP connections (sockets) on demand.

RDT is built on top of the vSAN clustering service. The CMMDS uses heartbeats to determine link state. If a link failure is detected, RDT will drop connections on the path and choose a different healthy path where possible. Thus, CMMDS and RDT are responsible for handling path failures and timeouts.

Note that RDT is also used by HCI Mesh for communications. We want to point this out as this subsequently means that only ESXi hosts can directly connect to a vSAN datastore. Even though vSAN iSCSI and vSAN File Service storage services exist, these do not allow you to directly mount a datastore, they will provide access to an object on vSAN through iSCSI, NFS, or SMB respectively.

On-Disk Formats and Disk Format Changes (DFC)

Before looking at the various I/O-related flows, let's briefly discuss the on-disk formats used by vSAN.

Cache Devices

VMware uses its own proprietary on-disk format for the flash devices used in the cache layer by vSAN. In hybrid configurations, which have both a read cache and a write buffer, the read cache portion of the flash device has its own on-disk format, and there is also a log-structured format for the write buffer portion of the flash device. In the case of all-flash configurations, there is only a write buffer; there is no read cache. Both formats are specially designed to boost the endurance of the flash device beyond the basic functionality provided by the flash device firmware.

Capacity Devices

It may come as a surprise to some, but in the original vSAN 5.5 release, VMware used the *Virtual Machine File System* (VMFS) as the on-disk format for vSAN. However, this was not the traditional VMFS. Instead, it used a new format unique to vSAN called *VMFS local* (VMFS-L). VMFS-L was the on-disk file system format of the local storage on each ESXi host in vSAN. The standard VMFS file system is specifically designed to work in clustered environments where many hosts are sharing a datastore. It was not designed with single host/local disk environments in mind, and certainly not distributed datastores. VMFS-L was introduced for use cases like distributed storage. Primarily, the clustered on-disk locking and associated heartbeats on VMFS were removed. These are necessary only when many hosts share the file system. They are unnecessary when only a single host is using them. Now instead of placing a SCSI reservation on the volume to place a lock on the metadata, a new lock manager is implemented that avoided using SCSI reservations completely. VMFS-L did not require on-disk heart beating either. It simply updated an in-memory copy of the heartbeat (because no other host needs to know about the lock). Tests showed that VMFS-L provisioned disks in about half the time of standard VMFS with these changes incorporated.

All versions of vSAN since 6.0 use a new on-disk format called vSANFS. This new format was based on the VirstoFS, a high-performance, sparse filesystem from a company called Virsto that VMware acquired many years ago. This new vSANFS on-disk format improved the performance of snapshots (through a new vsanSparse format) as well as cloning operations. Customers upgrading from vSAN 5.5 to vSAN 6.x could upgrade from VMFS-L (v1) to vSANFS (v2) through a seamless rolling upgrade process, where the content of each host's disk group was evacuated elsewhere in the cluster. The disk group on the host was then removed and recreated with the new v2 on-disk format, and this process was repeated until all disk groups were upgraded. This continues to be the case today, where any changes needed to the on-disk format are handled through a rolling upgrade process.

Throughout the various releases, newer versions of the on-disk format have been introduced to accommodate new features and functionality such as unmap, deduplication and compression, compression, encryption, and checksumming.

Note that not all on-disk format changes require a rolling upgrade. Some of the changes are simply metadata updates and do not require the evacuation of disk groups to make the version change. Also note that unless you leverage a particular data service, e.g., turning on encryption, a rolling upgrade will not be needed until you turn on the feature. In the case of encryption, the *disk format change* (DFC) is necessary to write the new *disk encryption keys* (DEK) from the *key management server* (KMS) down to the disk. Once complete, all subsequent writes to the disk are encrypted. Encryption will be covered in more detail later.

vSAN I/O Flow

In this section, we will trace the I/O flow on both a read and a write operation from an application within a guest OS when the VM is deployed on a vSAN datastore. We will look at a read operation when the stripe width value is set to 2, and we will look at a write operation when the number of failures to tolerate is set to 1 using RAID-1. This will give you an understanding of the underlying I/O flow, and this can be leveraged to get an understanding of the I/O flows when other capability values are specified. We will also discuss the destaging to the capacity layer, as this is where deduplication, compression, and checksum come into play. We will also include encryption, as this takes place at both the caching tier and the capacity tier.

Before we do, let's first look at the role of flash in the I/O path.

Caching Algorithms

There are different caching algorithms in place for the hybrid configurations and the all-flash configurations. In a nutshell, the caching algorithm on hybrid configurations is concerned with optimally destaging blocks from the cache tier to the capacity tier, whilst the caching algorithm on all-flash configurations is concerned with ensuring that hot blocks (data that is live) are held in the caching tier while cold blocks (data that is not being accessed) are held in the capacity tier.

The Role of the Cache Layer

As mentioned in the previous section, flash devices have two cache-related purposes in vSAN. When they are used in the caching layer on hybrid configurations, they act as both a read cache and a write buffer. This dramatically improves the performance of the I/O, at the same time providing the ability to scale out capacity based on low-cost SATA or SAS magnetic disk drives.

There is no read cache in all-flash vSAN configurations; the caching tier acts as a write buffer only.

Purpose of Read Cache

The purpose of the read cache in hybrid configurations is to maintain a list of commonly accessed disk blocks by VMs. This reduces the I/O read latency in the event of a cache hit; that is, the disk block is in cache and does not have to be retrieved from magnetic disk. The actual block that is being read by the application running in the VM may not be on the same ESXi host where the VM is running. In this case, DOM picks a mirror for a given read (based on offset) and sends it to the correct component of the object. This is then sent to LSOM to determine if the block is in the cache. If there is a cache miss, the block is retrieved directly from magnetic disk in the capacity tier, but of course, this will incur a latency penalty and could also impact the number of *input/output operations per second* (IOPS) achievable by vSAN. This is the purpose of having a read cache on hybrid vSAN configurations, as it reduces the number of IOPS that need to be sent to magnetic disks. The goal is to have a minimum read cache hit rate of 90%. vSAN also has a read-ahead cache optimization where 1 MB of data around the data block being read is also brought into cache in the logical assumption that the next read will be local to the last read, and thus it will now be cached.

vSAN balances read requests across multiple mirrors of the same object. vSAN always tries to make sure that it sends a given read request to the same mirror so that the block only gets cached once in the cluster. In other words, the block is cached only on one cache device in the cluster (on the ESXi host that contains the mirror where the read requests are sent). Because cache space is relatively expensive, this mechanism optimizes how much cache you require for vSAN. Correctly sizing the vSAN cache has a very significant impact on performance in a steady state.

Read cache for All-Flash vSAN configurations?

In all-flash vSAN configurations, since the capacity layer is also flash if a read cache miss occurs, fetching the data block from the capacity tier is not as expensive as fetching a data block from the capacity tier in a hybrid solution. Instead, it is a very quick (typically sub-millisecond) operation. Therefore, it is not necessary to have a flash-based read cache in all-flash vSAN configurations since the capacity tier can handle reads effectively. By not implementing a read cache, we also free up the cache tier for more writes, boosting overall performance.

Purpose of Write Cache

The write cache behaves as a write-back buffer in both all-flash and hybrid vSAN configurations. Writes are acknowledged when they enter the flash device used in the cache tier. The fact that we can use flash devices for writes in hybrid configurations significantly reduces the latency for write operations since the writes do not have to be destaged to the capacity tier before they are acknowledged.

Because the writes go to the cache tier flash devices, we must ensure that there is a copy of the data block elsewhere in the vSAN cluster. All VMs deployed to vSAN have an availability policy setting that ensures at least one additional copy of virtual machine data is available, (unless of course administrators explicitly override the default policy and choose a *failure to tolerate* setting of 0). This availability policy includes the write cache contents. Once a write is initiated by the application running inside of the guest OS, the write is sent to all replicas in parallel. Writes are buffered in the cache tier flash devices associated with the disk groups where the components of the VMDK storage object reside.

This means that in the event of a host failure, we also have a copy of the in-cache data and so no corruption will happen to the data; the virtual machine will simply reuse the replicated copy of the cache as well as the replicated disk data.

Note that all-flash vSAN configurations continue to use the cache tier as a write buffer, and all virtual machine writes land first on this cache device, same as in hybrid configurations. The major algorithm change here is how the write cache is used. The write cache is now used to hold "hot" blocks of data (data that is in a state of change). Only when the blocks become "cold" (no longer updated/written) they are moved to the capacity tier.

Anatomy of a vSAN Read on Hybrid vSAN

For an object placed on a vSAN datastore, when using a RAID-1 configuration, there may be multiple replicas when the *failures to tolerate* value is set to a value greater than 0 in the VM storage policy. Reads may now be spread across the replicas. Different reads may be sent to different replicas according to their *logical block address* (LBA) on disk. This is to ensure that vSAN does not necessarily consume more read cache than necessary and avoids caching the same data in multiple locations.

Taking the example of an application issuing a read request, the cluster service (CMMDS) is first consulted to determine the DOM owner of the data. The DOM owner, using the LBA, determines which component will service the request. In the case of the object having multiple replicas, a replica is chosen for the read request based on the LBA, as mentioned above. The request is then sent to the correct replica. The request next goes to LSOM to determine if the block is in read cache. If the block is present in read cache, the read is serviced from that read cache. If a read cache miss occurs, and the block is not in cache, the next step is to read the data from the capacity tier, and on hybrid vSAN configurations, the capacity tier will be made up of magnetic disks.

In many cases, the data may have to be transferred over the network if the data is on the capacity tier of a different ESXi host. Once the data is retrieved, it is returned to the requesting ESXi host and the read is served up to the VM.

The next diagram gives an idea of the steps involved in a read operation on hybrid vSAN. In this particular example, the stripe width setting is 2, and the VM's storage object is striped across disks that reside on different hosts. (Each stripe is therefore a component, to use the correct vSAN terminology.) Note that Stripe-1a and Stripe-1b reside on the same host, while Stripe-2a and Stripe-2b reside on different hosts. In this scenario, our read needs to come from Stripe-2b. If the owner does not have the block that the application within the VM wants to read, the read will go over the network to retrieve the data block.

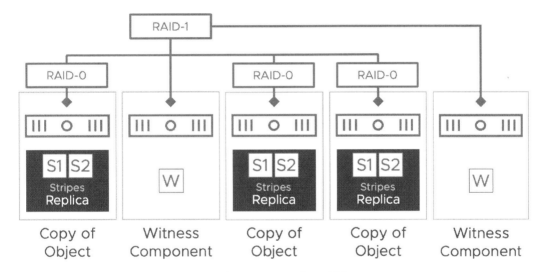

Figure 41: vSAN I/O flow: Failures to tolerate = 1 + stripe width = 2

Anatomy of a vSAN Read on All-Flash vSAN

Since there is no read cache in all-flash vSAN clusters, the I/O flow is different when compared to a read operation on hybrid configurations. On an all-flash vSAN, when a read is issued, the write buffer is first checked to see if the block is present (i.e., is it a hot block?). The same is done on hybrid. If the block being read is in the write buffer, it will be fetched from there. If the requested block is not in the write buffer, the block is fetched from the capacity tier. This may come as a surprise since we explicitly state that there is no dedicated read cache for all-flash vSAN. But note that in all-flash vSAN data can still be read from the cache tier as long as it isn't destaged (hot) yet. In essence, there is no separate read cache area defined on a cache device but read operations from the cache tier are still possible.

Remember that the capacity tier is also flash in an all-flash vSAN, so the latency overhead in first checking the cache tier, and then having to retrieve the block from the capacity tier is minimal. This is the reason why we have not implemented a read cache for all-flash vSAN configurations, and the cache tier is totally dedicated as a write buffer. By not implementing a read cache, as mentioned earlier, we free up the cache tier for more writes, boosting overall IOPS performance.

Anatomy of a vSAN Write on Hybrid vSAN

Now that we know how a read works, let's take a look at a write operation. When a new VM is deployed, its components are stored on multiple hosts. vSAN will not use data locality unless this is explicitly stated in the policy, and as such it could be possible that your VM runs on ESXi-01 from a CPU and memory perspective, while the components of the VM are stored on both ESXi-02 and ESXi-03, as shown in the diagram below

Figure 42: vSAN I/O flow: Write acknowledgment

We are keeping this as a very simple write operation since hybrid systems do not support many of the data services that are supported on all-flash systems. For example, all-flash systems support erasure coding (RAID-5/RAID-6) object configurations, as well as deduplication and compression, and Compression Only. These data services are not supported with hybrid vSAN. Shortly, we will look at the impact of these data services on the I/O path when we look at the anatomy of a vSAN write on all-flash. Both checksum and encryption are supported on both hybrid and all-flash configurations, we will also look at where checksum and encryption occur in the I/O path when we look at the all-flash configuration.

In this example, when an application within a VM issues a write operation, the owner of the object clones the write operation. The write is sent to cache on ESXi-02 and to the cache on ESXi-03 in *parallel*. The write is acknowledged when the write reaches the cache. At this point, the data has arrived on the device, but may not have been stored in its final location. However, there is no risk to the data because the device has indeed received the data. The owner waits for an acknowledgment that the write has been successful from *both* hosts and completes the I/O. Later, the write data will be destaged as part of a batch commit to magnetic disk. Note that ESXi-02 may destage writes at a different time than ESXi-03. This is not coordinated because it depends on various things such as how fast the write buffer is filling up, how much capacity is left, and where data are stored on magnetic disks.

Retiring Writes to Capacity tier on Hybrid vSAN

Writes across virtual disks from applications and the guest OS running inside a VM deployed on vSAN accumulates in the cache tier over time. On hybrid vSAN configuration, vSAN has an elevator algorithm implemented that periodically flushes the data in the write buffer in cache to magnetic disk in address order. The write buffer of the flash device is split into several "buckets." Data blocks, as they are written, are assigned to buckets in increasing LBA order. When destaging occurs, perhaps due to resource constraints, or when the write buffer cache reaches 30% capacity, the data in the oldest bucket is destaged first. Therefore, it is important to run tests long enough, and create sufficient IO flow, during a proof-of-concept to cause destaging. This is what will happen when vSAN is in production, so you certainly want to simulate this behavior during POCs as well to capture steady-state performance statistics from your vSAN deployment.

As mentioned earlier, when destaging writes, vSAN considers the location of the I/O. The data accumulated on a per bucket basis provides a sequential (proximal) workload for the magnetic disk. In other words, the LBAs near one another on the magnetic disk should be destaged together for improved performance. This proximal mechanism also provides improved throughput on the capacity tier flash devices for all-flash vSAN configurations.

The proximal mechanism considers many parameters such as the rate of incoming I/O, queues, disk utilization, and optimal batching. This is a self-tuning algorithm that decides how often writes on the cache tier destage to the capacity tier.

Anatomy of a vSAN Write on all-flash vSAN

A write operation on an all-flash vSAN is very similar to how writes are done in hybrid vSAN configurations. In hybrid configurations, only 30% of the cache tier is dedicated to the write buffer, and the other 70% is assigned to the read cache. Since there is no read cache in all-flash configurations, the full 100% of the cache tier is assigned to the write buffer (up to a maximum of 600 GB in the current version of vSAN). However, larger devices are supported and vSAN will use the whole capacity, increasing the lifespan of the cache device. 600 GB is the maximum cache that can be used at any one time, regardless of the physical capacity of the device. However, this 600 GB can use each block of the device to reduce wear of the cells. Thus, the bigger the device, the fewer times the cache device uses the same cells, increasing the lifespan of the device due to the maximum number of writes.

The role of the cache tier is also different between hybrid and all-flash. As we have seen, the write buffer in hybrid vSAN improves performance since writes do not need to go directly to the capacity tier made up of magnetic disks, thus improving latency. In all-flash vSAN, the purpose of the write buffer is endurance. A design goal of all-flash vSAN is to place high endurance flash devices in the cache tier so that they can handle the most amounts of I/O. This allows the capacity tier to use a lower specification flash device, as they do not need to handle the same number of writes as the cache tier.

Having said that, write operations for all-flash are still very similar to hybrid. It is only when the block being written is in the write buffer of all the replicas that the write is acknowledged.

In the previous section, we mentioned that there are additional data services available to all-flash systems when compared with hybrid systems. Notably, all-flash allows customers to use RAID-5/RAID-6 erasure coding policies for space saving initiatives, as well as Deduplication and Compression or Compression Only. In this anatomy of a write I/O on all-flash, let's assume that vSAN has checksums, deduplication and compression and encryption enabled, and what impact that has on the I/O. Let's first describe those data services.

Deduplication and Compression

Alongside erasure coding, vSAN has two additional data reduction features, deduplication, and compression. When enabled on a cluster level, vSAN will aim to deduplicate each block (store unique blocks of data only). If a new block arrives and it is already stored on the vSAN datastore, rather than storing the same block again, a small hash entry is created to the already existing block. If the same block of data occurs many times, significant space savings are achieved.

Deduplication on vSAN uses the SHA-1 hashing algorithm, creating a "fingerprint" for every data block. This hashing algorithm ensures that no two 4KB blocks of data result in the same hash, so that all blocks of data are uniquely hashed. When a new block arrives in, it is hashed and then compared to the existing table of hashes. If it already exists, then there is no need to store this new block. vSAN simply adds a new reference to it. If it does not already exist, a new hash entry is created, and the block is persisted.

vSAN uses the LZ4 compression mechanism. If, after deduplication, a new block is found to be unique, it also goes through compression. If the LZ4 compression manages to reduce the size of a 4 KB block to less than or equal to 2 KB, then the compressed version of the block is persisted to the capacity tier. If compression cannot reduce the size to less than 2 KB, then the full-sized block is persisted. It is done this way (deduplication followed by compression) because if the block already exists, then we don't have to pay the compression penalty for that block.

These features are only available for all-flash vSAN. Compression and deduplication cannot be enabled separately when vSAN is deployed on-premises; they are either disabled or enabled together. Deduplication and compression work on a disk group level. In other words, only objects deployed on the same disk group can contribute toward space savings. If components from different but identical VMs are deployed to different disk groups, there will not be any deduplication of identical blocks of data.

However, deduplication and compression are a cluster wide feature—they are either on or off. You cannot choose which virtual machines, or which disk groups, to enable it on.

For components deployed on the same disk group that have deduplication and compression enabled, deduplication will be done on a 4 KB block level. A disk group will only use one copy of that 4 KB block and all duplicate blocks will be eliminated as shown below.

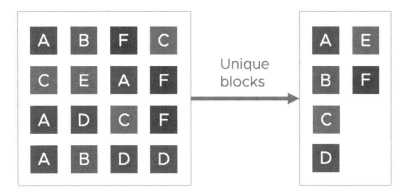

Figure 43: vSAN I/O flow: Write acknowledgment

The process of deduplication is done when the block is being destaged from the cache tier to the capacity tier. This is what we commonly refer to as near-line deduplication. To track the deduplicated blocks, hash tables are used. The deduplicated data and hash table metadata are spread across the capacity devices that make up the disk group.

Deduplication does not differentiate between the components in the disk group. It may deduplicate blocks in the VM home namespace, VM swap, VMDK object, or snapshot delta object.

If a disk group begins to fill up capacity-wise, vSAN examines the footprint of the deduplicated components and balances the ones which will make the most significant difference to the capacity used in the disk group.

Please note however that if deduplication and compression are enabled on a disk group, a single device failure will make the entire disk group appear unhealthy.

The deduplication and compression process is shown below. In step 1 the VM writes data to vSAN that lands on the caching tier. When the data becomes cold and needs to be destaged, vSAN reads the block into memory (step 2). It will compute the hashes, eliminate the duplicates, and compress the remaining blocks before writing them to the capacity tier (step 3). These operations occur "asynchronous" to the I/O operations of the Guest OS. They do not create additional latency for Guest OS I/O.

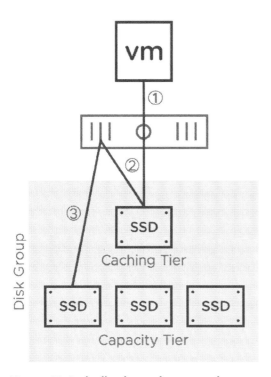

Figure 44: Deduplication and compression process

Compression only

As stated above, vSAN uses the LZ4 compression mechanism. In the case of Deduplication and Compression, after deduplication, a new block is found to be unique, it also goes through compression. However, in the case of Compression only no deduplication effort occurs. This not only removes the overhead that the deduplication process introduces, but also increases the availability of the cluster. You may ask yourself why it would change the availability levels of the cluster. The answer is simple. When Deduplication and Compression is enabled all devices in a disk group hold metadata for the disk group. If a flash device fails within a disk group, this impacts the full disk group as a portion of the required **metadata** could be missing. As a result, when a single device fails within a disk group that has Deduplication and Compression enabled, the full disk group will be marked as inaccessible. Fortunately, this is not the case for Compression only. Compression only does not introduce changes to the metadata structure of a disk group, and as a result a failure of a capacity device would not automatically render the full disk group to be inaccessible.

Now, let's get back to the compression process. Again, if the LZ4 compression manages to reduce the size of a 4 KB block to less than or equal to 2 KB, then the compressed version of the block is persisted to the capacity tier. If compression cannot reduce the size to less than 2 KB, then the full-sized block is persisted as the cost of compression at this point would be higher than the savings.

You may ask yourself at this point, when should I use Compression only and when should I use Deduplication and Compression? The answer to that is "it depends". Of course, there are guidelines provided by VMware, and these guidelines are based on how applications are expected to behave from an IO stance, results may vary however depending on your workload. In general, though, the below list gives an indication of which setting to use for which kinds of applications.

- OLTP databases – Compression only
- Mixed workloads – Compression only
- Full clone based VDI – Deduplication and compression
- Linked or instance clone based VDI – Compression only
- General virtualized workloads with a common Guest OS – Deduplication and compression

Data Integrity through Checksum

vSAN provides checksum functionality, which is enabled by default. Checksum verifies that any written data is the same at the source and destination of the data. Checksum functionality is available on both hybrid configurations and all-flash configurations. The checksum mechanism is implemented using the very common *cyclic redundancy check* (CRC-32C) (Castagnoli) for best performance, utilizing special CPU instructions on Intel processors (Intel c2c32c) that makes the process extremely fast.

For each 4 KB block of data, a 5-byte checksum is created and is stored separately from the data. This occurs before any data are written to persistent storage. In other words, the checksum is calculated before writing the block to the caching layer. The checksum data goes all the way through the vSAN I/O stack. The checksum is persisted with the data.

If a checksum error is discovered in the I/O path, the checksum error is automatically repaired. A message stating that a checksum error has been detected and corrected is logged in the VMkernel log.

The checksum functionality also includes a data scrubber mechanism, which validates the data and checksums up to 36 times per year. This will protect your vSAN environment for instance against data corruption because of bit rot. This number is defined through the advanced setting called *VSAN.ObjectScrubsPerYearBase*.

Figure 45: Scrub advanced setting

Administrators can configure checksum to be enabled or disabled on a per vSAN object basis if they so wish. This feature should only be disabled if an application can provide its own checksumming functionality, for example, in the case of Hadoop HDFS. We would recommend leaving it at the default setting of enabled for the vast majority of vSAN workloads. Such a policy setting is shown below.

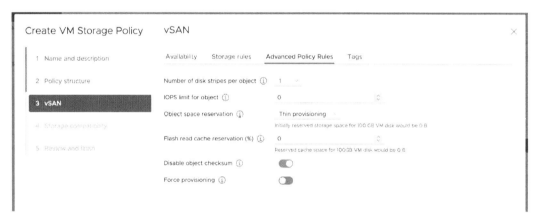

Figure 46: Checksum policy setting

vSAN Encryption

vSAN provides both data-at-rest and data-in-transit encryption. These features are enabled cluster-wide, once enabled, apply to all vSAN objects. The encryption feature is hardware agnostic and does not require any special encryption devices such as *self-encrypting drives* (SEDs). The encryption cipher used is the Advanced Encryption Standard XTS-AES 256.

As stated, vSAN supports both data-at-rest, as well as data-in-transit encryption. vSAN data-at-rest encryption encrypts the data in the cache tier and the capacity tier. Therefore, vSAN encrypts the data when it comes into cache, but when it is time to destage this data to the capacity tier, vSAN decrypts (or un-encrypts) the data as it leaves the cache tier, then runs the deduplication and compression algorithms, and finally encrypts the data once more. This ensures that even when the caching tier devices are decommissioned for whatever reason, the data in the cache is still encrypted.

vSAN data-in-transit encryption can be enabled independently of, or together with, vSAN data-at-rest encryption and was introduced in vSAN 7.0 U1. Data-in-transit encryption increases security as it ensures that all traffic is encrypted over the network. It uses the same cryptographic module that vSAN data-at-rest encryption uses, it does however not require need for a key management server as it has its own automated key rotation mechanism.

vSAN Encryption vs vSphere VM Encryption

One common question is why we have vSAN Encryption mechanisms as well as a per-VM encryption mechanism available in vSphere? The reason for this is that VM encryption does not lend itself to deduplication or compression because of where the encryption of data occurs in the IO path. With vSAN encryption, the actual encryption of the data takes place after the deduplication and compression algorithms when the data hits the capacity tier. This means that vSAN encryption allows deduplication and compression to do their data reduction before we encrypt the persisted data. This gives us the ability to achieve decent data reduction compared to the VM encrypt mechanism.

If you plan to use vSAN encryption, or even the VM encryption mechanism for that matter, please be aware that VMware does not provide a full *key manager server* (KMS), however, starting with vSAN 7.0 U2 there is the option to use the Native Key Provider which is included with vCenter Server. You may wonder why anyone would want to use a 3rd party vendor when a native key provider is included. The Native Key Provider does not provide the same functionality as a key management server. For instance, the Native Key Provider can only be used for vSphere and vSAN at the time of writing. Also, the Native Key Provider does not have support for the Key Management Interop Protocol (KMIP) and it also doesn't come with the resiliency or availability features a full KMS typically comes with. If those before mentioned features are required, we recommend selecting a KMS from one of our supported partners. Details of supported KMS partners can be found on the official VMware vSAN compatibility website.

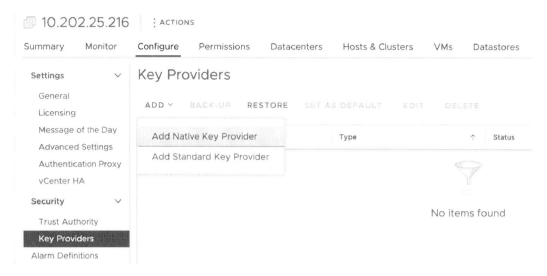

Figure 47: Native Key Provider

The KMS solution provides the *key encryption key* (KEK) and *data encryption keys* (DEK). The KEK is used to encrypt the DEKs. The DEK does the on-disk encryption. The DEKs created by the KMS are transferred to vSAN **hosts** using the *key management interoperability protocol* (KMIP). You might think that if the keys are stored on the host, isn't this somewhat insecure? This is the reason why the KEK is used to encrypt the DEKs, i.e., the keys are themselves encrypted. Unless you have access to the KEK, you cannot decrypt the DEK, and thus you cannot decrypt the data on disk.

The vSAN encryption feature relies heavily on *Advanced Encryption Standard Native Instruction (AESNI)*. This is available on all modern CPUs. There are also health checks which ensure that the KMS is still accessible and that all the hosts in the vSAN cluster support AESNI.

vSAN encryption is supported on both hybrid and all-flash models of vSAN. Note that although implementation is using a third-party KMS, encryption is performed natively within vSphere/vSAN, using modules that are native to the VMkernel.

Data Locality

A question that usually comes now is this: What about data locality? Is cache (for instance) kept local to the VM? Do the VM cache and the VMDK storage object need to travel with the VM each time vSphere *distributed resource scheduler* (DRS) migrates a VM due to a compute imbalance?

In general, the answer is no – vSAN is designed to deploy VMs and their respective objects with no data locality. There are some exceptions which we will come to shortly. However, vSAN has been designed with core vSphere features in mind. In other words, one should be able to do vMotion and/or enable DRS without worrying about a decrease in performance when a VM is migrated to a new host. Similarly, we did not want to have every vMotion operation turn into a Storage vMotion operation and move all of its data every time that you move a VM's compute. This is especially true when you consider the fact that by default vSphere DRS runs once every 5 minutes at a minimum which can result in VMs being migrated to a different host every 5 minutes. For these reasons, vSAN may deploy a VM's compute and a VM's storage on completely different hosts in the cluster.

However, note that there is a layer of small in-memory read cache dedicated to client-side caching. Small in this case means 0.4% of a host's memory capacity, up to a max of 1 GB per host. This in-memory cache means that blocks of a VM are cached in memory on the host where the VM is located. When the VM migrates, the cache is invalidated and will need to be warmed up again on the destination host. Note that in most cases hot data already resides in the flash read cache or the write cache layer and as such the performance impact of a migration on a VM is low.

Content Based Read Cache

If there is a specific requirement to provide an additional form of data locality, however, it is good to know that vSAN integrates with *content based read cache* (CBRC), mostly seen when used as an in-memory read cache for VMware Horizon View. This can be enabled without the need to make any changes to your vSAN configuration. Note that CBRC does not need a specific object or component created on the vSAN datastore; the CBRC digests are stored in the VM home namespace object.

Data Locality in vSAN Stretched Clusters

We mentioned that there are some caveats to this treatment of data locality. One such caveat arises when considering a vSAN stretched cluster deployment. vSAN stretched clusters allow hosts in a vSAN cluster to be deployed at different, geographically dispersed sites. In a vSAN stretched cluster, one mirror of the data is located at site 1 and the other mirror is located at site 2. vSAN stretched cluster supports RAID-1 protection across sites. Should it be a requirement, administrators can implement a *secondary failure to tolerate* setting at each site if they wish.

Previously we mentioned that vSAN implements a sort of round-robin policy when it comes to reading from mirrors, based on the LBA offset. This would not be suitable for vSAN stretched clusters as 50% of the reads would need to traverse the link to the remote site. Since VMware supports latency of up to 5ms between the sites, this would have an adverse effect on the performance of the VM.

Rather than continuing to read in a round-robin, block offset fashion, vSAN now has the smarts to figure out in which site a VM is running in a stretched cluster configuration and change its read algorithm to do 100% of the reads from the mirror/replica at the local site. This means that there are no reads done across the link during steady-state operations. It also means that all the caching is done on the local site, or even on the local host using the in-memory cache. This avoids incurring any additional latency, as reads do not have to traverse the inter-site link.

Note that this is **not read locality** on a per-host basis. It is **read locality on a per VM and per-site** basis. On the same site, the VM's compute could be on any of the ESXi hosts while its local data object could be on any other ESXi host within the site.

Data Locality in Shared Nothing applications

vSAN continues to expand on the use-cases and applications that it can support. One of the applications that is gaining momentum on vSAN are what might be termed next-gen applications, and a common next-gen application is Hadoop/Big-Data. We have worked closely with some of the leading Hadoop partners on creating reference architecture for running Hadoop on vSAN. One of the initial requirements was to have data locality – in other words, a VM's compute and storage should run on the same host. We should caveat that this is an optional requirement. However, if the application has built-in replication and its service is provided by multiple VMs, administrators need to ensure the data of the VMs are placed on different hosts. If 2 replica copies ended up on the same host, and if that host suffered a failure, then this would render the application inaccessible.

For example, with an application like *Hadoop distributed file system* (HDFS) which has a built-in replication factor, we can provision HDFS with several VMs, and with vSAN data locality and DRS anti-affinity rules, we can ensure that each VMs compute and storage are placed on the same vSAN nodes. Thus, a failure of a single node would not impact the availability of the application's data, since it is being replicated to other VMs which also have host affinity and data locality.

In this case, we would not even need vSAN to protect the VMs as the application has built-in protection, so the VMs could be deployed with FTT=0.

Note that this feature was only available under special request in vSAN 6.7 and higher at the time of writing. At the time of writing, today this policy is primarily used by the agent VMs in vSAN File Service. This topic will be discussed in greater detail later in the book.

Recovery from Failure

When a failure has been detected, vSAN will determine which objects had components on the failed device. These failing components will then get marked as either *degraded* or *absent*, but the point is that I/O flow is renewed instantaneously to the remaining components in the object.

Depending on the type of failure, vSAN will take immediate action or wait for some period of time before it starts the resync process. This is called the CLOM repair delay timer and it is 60 minutes by default. The distinction here is if vSAN knows what has happened to a device. For instance, when a host fails, vSAN typically does not know why this happened, or even what has happened exactly. Is it a host failure, a network failure, or is it transient or permanent? It may be something as simple as a reboot of the host in question. Should this occur, the affected components are said to be in an "*absent*" state and the repair delay timer starts counting. If a device such as a disk or SSD reports a permanent error, it is marked as *"degraded"* and it is re-protected immediately by vSAN (replacement components are built and synchronized).

vSAN leverages durability components to increase the availability of impacted objects starting with vSAN 7.0 U2 when a component is marked Absent. This could be in the case a host has failed. Durability components will be created to ensure we still maintain the specified availability level specified within the policy. The benefit of this approach is that if a second host fails in an FTT=1 scenario you can recover the first failed host, as we can still merge the data with the first failed host with the durability component. The reason for this is that the durability component holds all writes since the failure of the first host. Not only are these durability components great for improving the resync times, but they also provide a higher level of availability to vSAN.

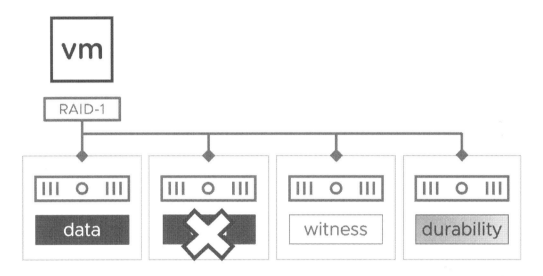

Figure 48: Durability component

Let's take an example where we have suffered a permanent host failure.
As soon as vSAN realizes the component is absent, a timer of 60 minutes will start. As in this scenario, the component is marked absent, and a durability component is created. If the absent component comes back within those 60 minutes, vSAN will synchronize the replicas, or rebuild data/parity segments in the case of RAID-5/RAID-6. If the component doesn't come back, vSAN will create a new replica, and resync the existing and the durability component to this new replica.

Note that, prior to vSAN release 6.7U1, administrators were able to decrease this time-out value by changing the advanced setting called *vSAN.ClomRepairDelay* on each of your ESXi hosts in the Advanced Settings section. Caution should be exercised, however, because if it is set to a value that is too low, and you do a simple maintenance task such as rebooting a host, you may find that vSAN starts rebuilding new components before the host has completed its reboot cycle. This adds unnecessary overhead to vSAN and could have an impact on the overall performance of the cluster. If you want to change this advanced setting, we highly recommend ensuring consistency across all ESXi hosts in the cluster.

In the latest version of vSAN, the advanced parameter is now available in the vSphere client. As shown below, this can be found under Cluster > Configure > vSAN > Services > Advanced options.

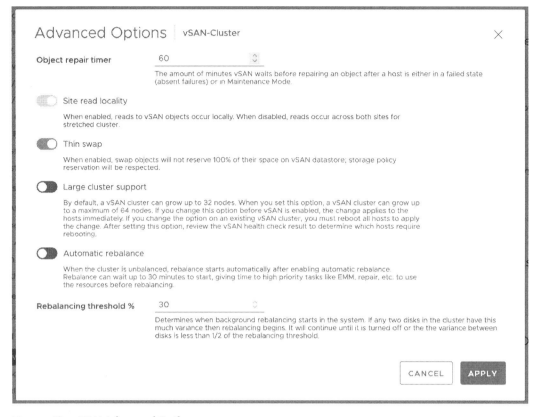

Figure 49: vSAN Advanced Options

As mentioned, in some scenarios vSAN responds to a failure immediately. This depends on the type of failure and a good example is a magnetic disk or flash device failure. In many cases, the controller or device itself will be able to indicate what has happened and will essentially inform vSAN that it is unlikely that the device will return within a reasonable amount of time. vSAN will then respond by marking all impacted components as "*degraded*," and vSAN immediately creates a new replica and starts the resynchronization of that new replica. It should be noted that in this scenario vSAN does not create a durability component.

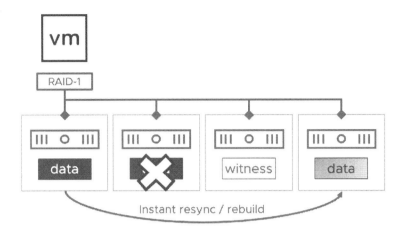

Figure 50: Disk failure: Instant mirror copy

Of course, before it will create this mirror vSAN will validate whether sufficient resources exist to store this new copy.

If recovery occurs before the 60 minutes have elapsed or before the creation of the replica has been completed, vSAN will decide which method will be faster to complete (continue to create a new replica or update replica that just came back up online), and then pursues only that method to regain compliance. Once it regains compliance obsolete components are discarded.

vSAN never "discards" absent components. However, if we rebuild an absent component somewhere else then when the absent component comes back, vSAN will conclude it is no longer relevant and will discard the component.

Reconfiguration can take place on vSAN for a few reasons. First, a user might choose to change an object's policy and the current configuration might not conform to the new policy, so a new configuration must be computed and applied to the object. Second, a disk or node in the cluster might fail. If an object loses one of the components in its configuration, it may no longer comply with its policy.

Reconfiguration is probably the most resource-intensive task because a lot of data will need to be transferred in most scenarios. To ensure that regular VM I/O is not impacted by reconfiguration tasks, vSAN can throttle the reconfiguration task to the extent that it does not impact the performance of VMs. Much effort has gone into ensuring that resync traffic does not negatively impact the VM I/O. In times of network contention, vSAN may automatically throttle any resync IO to 20% of available bandwidth, giving VM I/O most of the available network bandwidth. When there is no contention for network bandwidth, then resync traffic can consume all the available bandwidth.

Degraded Device Handling (DDH)

vSAN has a feature called *degraded device handling* (DDH). The driving factor behind such a feature is to deal with situations where either an SSD or a magnetic disk drive is misbehaving. VSAN needed a way to handle a drive that is constantly reporting transient errors, but not failing. Of course, in situations like this, the drive may introduce poor performance to the cluster overall. The objective of this new feature is to have a mechanism that monitors these misbehaving storage devices and isolates them so that they do not impact the overall cluster.

The feature is monitoring vSAN, looking for patterns of significant latency on the capacity drives. If a sustained period of high latency is observed, then vSAN will unmount the disk group on which the disk resides. The components in the disk group will be marked as a permanent error and the components will be rebuilt elsewhere in the cluster. What this means is that the performance of the virtual machines can be consistent and will not be impacted by this one misbehaving drive.

Enhancements continue to be made to this feature. For example, there are regular attempts to remount disks marked under permanent error. This will only succeed if the condition that caused the initial failure is no longer present. If successful, the physical disk does not need to be replaced, although the components must be resynced. If unsuccessful, the disk continues to be marked as a permanent error. This will be visible in the vSphere UI under Disk Management.

The feature also checks to see whether there are any available replicas available before unmounting. If this is the last available replica, DDH will not unmount it but will continue to make it available since it is the last available replica. Unmounting it in this case would result in complete object unavailability.

vSAN Storage Services

vSAN is mostly known as a platform that provides block storage capacity for VMs running on top of vSphere. However, starting with vSAN 6.5 the first storage service was introduced that did not target the vSphere platform but was intended to be used by (guest) Operating Systems and Applications directly. This feature was the vSAN iSCSI Target Service. In vSAN 7.0 support for vSAN File Services was introduced, which was primarily intended for cloud-native applications. Starting with vSAN 7.0 U1 support for remote mounting of vSAN datastores was also included. Let us look at these features individually.

iSCSI Targets and LUNs

vSAN has the ability to create iSCSI targets and LUNs using vSAN objects and present the LUNs to external iSCSI initiators. This involves the enabling of the vSAN iSCSI Target Service, which at the same time creates an iSCSI Target namespace object. As per the vSphere client when enabling the vSAN iSCSI Target Service, vSAN creates a namespace object that stores metadata for an iSCSI target service, like the VM Home namespace object of a virtual machine. The storage policy for the iSCSI Target namespace object should have a *failure to tolerate* of 1. Once again, administrators can choose their own specific policy for the iSCSI Target namespace when enabling the iSCSI Target Service. In the next screenshot, we can see where the storage policy for the iSCSI Target home object can be selected.

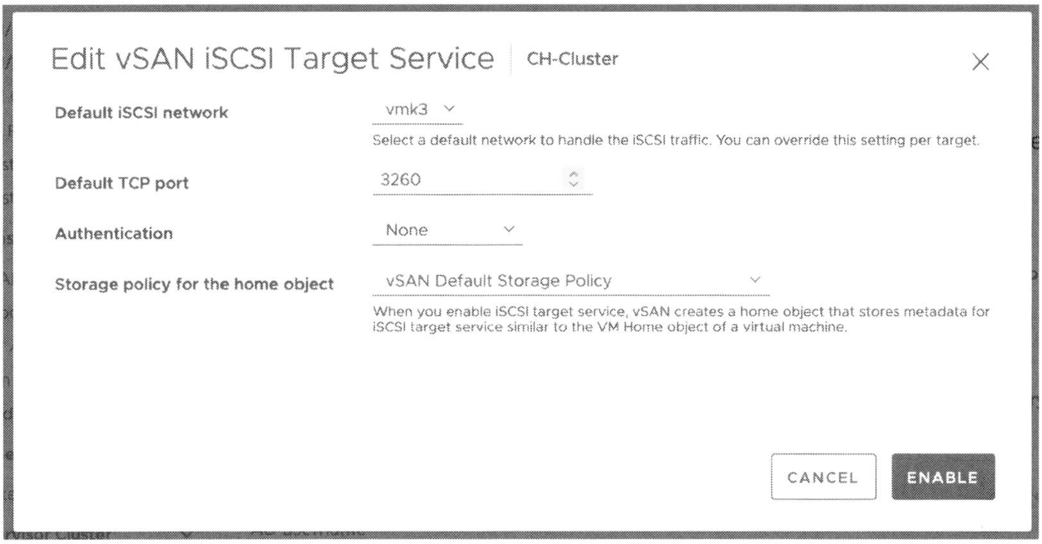

Figure 51: Policy setting for iSCSI Target

As you proceed to create iSCSI Targets and iSCSI LUNs on vSAN, these can be assigned their own different policy as well.

One item to note is that support for transparent failover is supported starting vSAN 6.7. Support for Windows Server Failover Cluster (WSFC) using node majority or file share quorum was always available on vSAN. Now that vSAN iSCSI supports transparent failure, it enables support for features like WSFC using shared-disk mode.

Let's add a little more detail around how iSCSI on vSAN is architected. With the iSCSI implementation on vSAN, there is the concept of a Target I/O owner for vSAN iSCSI. The Target I/O owner (or just I/O owner) is responsible for coordinating who can do I/O to an object and is basically what an iSCSI initiator connects to, i.e., whoever wants to consume the storage, most likely a virtual machine elsewhere in the datacenter. However, the I/O owner may be on a completely different vSAN node/host to the actual iSCSI LUN backed by a vSAN VMDK object. This is not a problem for vSAN deployments, as this can be considered akin to a VM's compute residing on one vSAN host and the VM's storage residing on a completely different vSAN host. This 'non-locality' feature of vSAN allows us to do operations like maintenance mode, vMotion, capacity balancing, and so on without impacting the performance of the VM. The same is true for the vSAN iSCSI implementation - the I/O owner should be able to move to a different host, and even the iSCSI LUNs should be able to migrate to different hosts while not impacting our iSCSI availability or performance. This enables the vSAN iSCSI implementation to be unaffected by operations such as maintenance mode, balancing tasks, and of course any failures in the cluster.

With iSCSI LUNs on a vSAN stretched cluster, a scenario could arise where the I/O owner is residing on one site in the stretched cluster, whilst the actual vSAN object backing the iSCSI LUN could be on the other site. In that case, all the traffic between the iSCSI initiator and the iSCSI target would have to traverse the inter-site link. But remember that this is already true for writes since write data is written to both sites anyway in a vSAN stretched cluster (RAID-1). When it comes to read workloads, we do have the ability to read data from the local site for both iSCSI and VM workloads, and not traverse the inter-site link. This means that it doesn't matter which site has the I/O owner resides.

But there is one caveat when it comes to supporting iSCSI on vSAN stretched clusters. The key issue is the location of the iSCSI initiator. If the initiator is somewhere on site A, and the target I/O owner is on site B, then, in this case, the iSCSI traffic (as well as any vSAN traffic) would need to **traverse the inter-site link**. In a nutshell, such a configuration could end up adding an additional inter-site trip for iSCSI traffic. For this reason, starting with vSAN 7.0 U1, the ability to specify site affinity was introduced in the UI when creating an iSCSI Target as shown in the screenshot below.

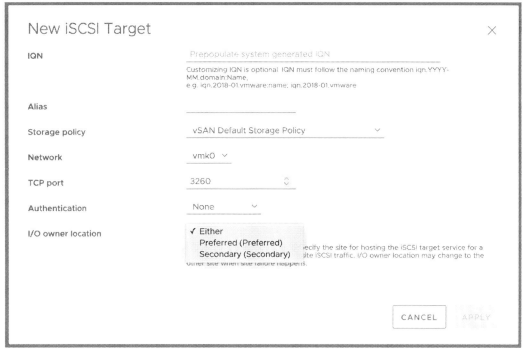

Figure 52: iSCSI Target in a stretched cluster

vSAN File Service

One of the most requested features since the initial release of vSAN has been native file services. Starting with vSAN 7.0 support for the creation of file shares natively was added. Initially, vSAN File Service with 7.0 only introduced support for NFS, but with 7.0 U1 support for SMB was also introduced, alongside support for authentication using Kerberos (NFS) or Active Directory (SMB).

04 // Architecture Details

From an architectural point of view, vSAN File Service was implemented in a different way than you may expect and that is why we want to discuss it in this chapter.

When you enable File Service, vSAN will deploy "agent VMs" and these VMs/appliances are fully managed by vSAN and ESX Agent Manager (EAM). These agent VMs also referred to as "FS VMs", run Photon OS and have the file service capabilities enabled through docker/container technology. After these File Service Agent VMs have been deployed, and the docker container instances have been instantiated and configured, vSAN File Service will be up and running and available for use.

We realize that without having a vSAN environment in front of you with vSAN File Service enabled it may be difficult to understand what the implementation exactly looks like. Let's look at the next diagram and then step by step walkthrough of the communication path of vSAN File Service and the different components involved.

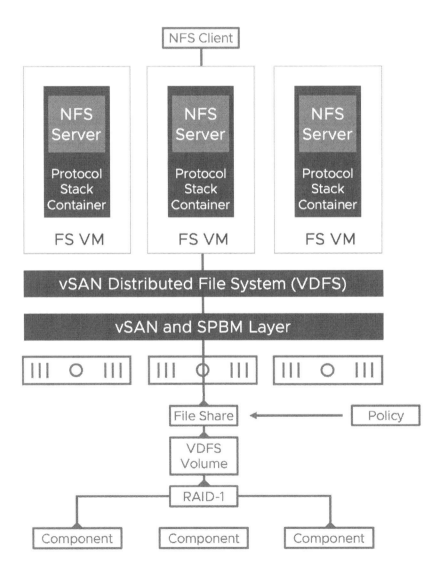

115

Figure 53: vSAN File Service Architecture

Let's look at the communication, top to bottom:
- An NFS client connects to the vSAN File Services NFS Server
- The NFS Server runs within the protocol stack container, the IP addresses and DNS names provided during the configuration are assigned to the protocol stack container
- The FS VM has no IP address assigned
- The FS VM has a VMCI device (vSocket interface), which is used to communicate with the ESXi host securely
- The ESXi host has VDFS kernel modules
- VDFS communicates with the vSAN layer and SPBM
- vSAN is responsible for the lifecycle management of the storage objects (file shares)
- A file share has a 1:1 relationship with a VDFS volume and is formed out of vSAN objects
- Each file share / VDFS volume has a policy assigned, and the layout of the vSAN objects is determined by this policy by vSAN
- Objects are formatted with the VDFS file system and presented as a single VDFS volume using the selected protocol (NFS or SMB)

FS VMs allow for communication to the kernel using the vSocket library through the VMCI device. The VDFS layer leverages vSAN and SPBM for the lifecycle management of the objects that form a file share. What is this VDFS layer then? Well, VDFS is the layer that exposes a (distributed) file system that resides within the vSAN object(s) and allows the protocol stack container to share it as NFS v3, NFS v4.1, or SMB. As mentioned, the objects are presented as a single volume.

Even though vSAN File Services uses a VM to ultimately allow a client to connect to a share, the important part here is that the VM is only used to host the protocol stack container. All the distributed file system logic lives within the vSphere layer.

One thing which is key to understand about the implementation is the fact that the containers are assigned the IP addresses and the DNS name, which are provided during the configuration. The container instances have a unique MAC Address assigned. During the configuration also a port group, or NSX-T segment, needs to be selected for network access. This port group, or segment, is connected to each VM and each container will connect to that network. As the MAC Address used to communicate is not the same as the MAC Address of the interface of the VM, it is necessary to enable MAC Learning on the NSX-T segment or Forged Transmits and Promiscuous Mode on the port group.

At this point, you may wonder how many agent VMs and containers will be provisioned in your cluster. This will depend on the version of vSAN you are running and how many hosts you have within a cluster. With vSAN 7.0 U2 and higher, a maximum of 64 active VMs and containers will be provisioned, simply said one VM and one container per host in the cluster on which you enable vSAN File Service.

This brings up the next question, what happens with the agent VMs and the container when you place a host into maintenance mode, or power off a host for that matter. Let's take maintenance mode as an example. When you go into maintenance mode the protocol stack container is restarted on a different agent VM, so you end up in a situation where you will have 2 (or more even) protocol stack containers running within VM. Of course, vSAN File Service will rebalance the protocol stack containers when the host exits maintenance mode, and the cluster returns to normal.

The last thing we want to discuss is support for vSAN Stretched Cluster. Like vSAN iSCSI, vSAN File Service provides support for stretched vSAN configurations (and 2-node). In 7.0 U2, you can specify during the configuration of vSAN File Services to which site certain IP addresses belong. In other words, you can specify "site affinity" of your File Service protocol stack containers, and the IP addresses associated with them. On top of that, when creating file shares, you can specify per file share affinity to a site. We do want to point out that in this case affinity can be considered a soft affinity rule. Meaning that if hosts, or VMs, fail on which these file service containers are running it could be that the protocol stack container, with its IP address, is restarted in the opposite location. We will discuss how you can configure vSAN File Services in a stretched cluster configuration in chapter 7.

vSAN HCI Mesh

What is HCI Mesh? HCI Mesh provides the ability to cross-mount vSAN datastores. In other words, you can go to a vSAN based cluster and mount a vSAN datastore from another vSAN Cluster. Or you could go to a vSphere cluster and mount a vSAN datastore, both are supported starting with vSAN 7.0 U2.

You may ask yourself, why would you want to do this? It could be that you are running out of disk space on your local vSAN datastore, or maybe you do not have any local storage or SAN-attached even. HCI Mesh enables you to run VMs "locally" (from a compute perspective) while having the storage objects be stored remotely. Of course, it means that an administrator will need to mount the remote datastore, and the decision will need to be made to use that remote datastore from a storage point of view. But when this has been done you can even move the VM between clusters by simply doing a compute-only vMotion. One thing to note is that we leverage the native vSAN protocol, and the datastore is not exposed through standard NFS or iSCSI, etc.

As mentioned earlier in this chapter, the way we have implemented this is by separating certain processes that normally would run on a single host. In this case, we are referring to the DOM components, specifically the DOM Client and the DOM Owner. On top of that, a CMMDS Client has been developed, which connects to CMMDS directly. The relationship between the various processes is shown in the diagram below.

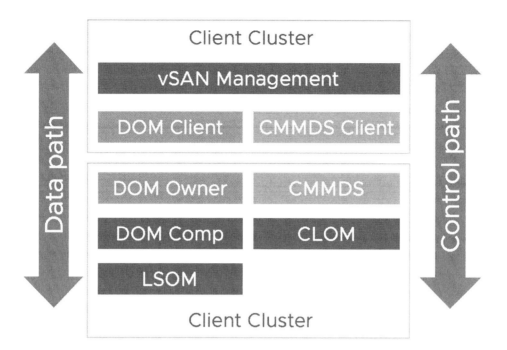

Figure 54: vSAN HCI Mesh components

When HCI Mesh, or Datastore Sharing as it is called in the vSphere Client, is enabled on a cluster which does not have vSAN enabled, the DOM Client and the CMMDS client are loaded on each host of the cluster. The DOM Client and the CMMDS Client then connect with the DOM Owner and CMMDS to provide the ability to provision workloads on the remote datastore. Note that a remote datastore can only be mounted when the "Server Cluster" is managed by the same vCenter Server instance as the "Client Cluster". There are various operational considerations, but we will discuss these in chapter 6 where we are discussing various operational aspects of vSAN.

One thing we do want to bring up is vSphere HA. From an architectural perspective, the implementation of vSAN with HCI Mesh is different, it also means that there's an additional consideration when it comes to availability. To ensure VMs are protected by vSphere HA in the situation anything happens between a "client" host and the "server" cluster, it is recommended to enable the APD response. This is very straightforward. You simply go to the HA cluster settings and set the "Datastore with APD" setting to either "Power off and restart VMs – Conservative" or "Power off and restart VMs – Aggressive". The difference between conservative and aggressive is that with conservative HA will only kill the VMs when it knows for sure the VMs can be restarted. With aggressive, it will also kill the VMs on a host impacted by an APD while it isn't sure it can restart the VMs. VMware recommends using the "Conservative Restart Policy".

Summary

vSAN has a unique architecture that is future-proof but at the same time extensible. It is designed to handle extreme I/O load and cope with different failure scenarios. However, to consume some of these key features, a VM needs to have an appropriate policy associated with it. Your decision-making during the creation of policies will determine how flexible, performant, and resilient your workloads will be.

In the next chapter, we will look at VM Storage Policies, and how to use them to make your VMs resilient to failures on vSAN.

05

VM Storage Policies and VM Provisioning

VM storage policies and storage policy-based management (SPBM) build on earlier vSphere functionality which tried to match the storage requirements of a VM to a particular vSphere datastore. This was known as profile driven storage, and all VMs residing on the same datastore inherited the capabilities of the datastore. With vSAN, the storage quality of service no longer resides with the datastore; instead, it resides with the VM and is enforced by a VM storage policy associated with the VM and its VMDKs. Once the policy is pushed down to the storage layer, in this case vSAN, the underlying storage is then responsible for creating and placing components for the VM to meet the requirements configured in the policy.

Introducing Storage Policy-Based Management in a vSAN Environment

vSAN leverages a policy-based approach for VM deployment, using a method called *storage policy-based management* (SPBM). All VMs deployed to a vSAN datastore must use a VM storage policy, and if one is not specified at deployment time, a default one that is associated with the datastore is assigned to the VM. The VM storage policy may contain one or more vSAN capabilities. This chapter will describe the vSAN capabilities and how the components for each object that makes up a VM are distributed according to the capabilities configured in the VM's policy.

After the vSAN cluster has been configured and the vSAN datastore has been created, vSAN presents a set of capabilities to vCenter Server. These capabilities are surfaced by the *vSphere APIs for Storage Awareness* (VASA) storage provider (more on this shortly) when the vSAN cluster is successfully configured. These capabilities are used to set the availability, capacity, and performance policies on a per-VM (and per-VMDK) basis when that VM is deployed on the vSAN datastore.

Through SPBM, administrators create a policy defining the storage requirements for the VM, and this policy is pushed out to the storage, which in turn instantiates per-VM (and per-VMDK) storage for virtual machines. In vSphere 6.0, VMware introduced *Virtual Volumes* (VVols). SPBM for VMs using VVols is very similar to SPBM for VMs deployed on vSAN. In other words, administrators no longer need to carve up LUNs or volumes for virtual machine storage. Instead, the underlying storage infrastructure instantiates virtual machine storage based on the contents of the policy. Similarly, with the arrival of the Kubernetes platform, and the ability to run Kubernetes clusters on top of vSphere infrastructure, persistent volumes created in Kubernetes and backed by VMDKs can also leverage SPBM. Each persistent volume can, using Kubernetes Storage Classes which map to a vSphere storage policy, be instantiated with its own set of storage capabilities. The ability to use vSAN as a platform for modern, containerized applications will be discussed in detail in a later chapter.

Suffice to say that what we have now with SPBM is a mechanism whereby we can specify the requirements of the VM, and the VMDKs. These requirements are then used to create a policy. This policy is then sent to the storage layer (in the case of VVols, this is a SAN or *network-attached storage* (NAS) storage array) asking it to build a storage object for this VM that meets these policy requirements. In fact, a VM can have multiple policies associated with it, and different policies for different VMDKs.

By way of explaining capabilities and policies, capabilities are what the underlying storage can provide by way of availability, performance, and reliability. These capabilities are visible in vCenter Server. The capabilities are then used to create a VM storage policy (or just policy for short). A policy may contain one or more capabilities, and these capabilities reflect the requirements of your VM or application running in a VM.

Deploying VMs on a vSAN datastore is very different from previous approaches in vSphere. With traditional storage, an administrator presents a shared LUN or volume to a group of ESXi hosts. In the case of block storage, an administrator would then be required to partition, format, and build a VMFS datastore for storing VM files. Care had to be taken to ensure that any shared LUN was uniformly presented from the array to all ESXi hosts. Similarly, administrators had to ensure that the path policies were set identically for that LUN on all ESXi hosts. This resulted in operational complexity and overhead. In the case of *network-attached storage* (NAS), a *network file system* (NFS) volume is mounted to the ESXi hosts, and once again a VM is created on the datastore. There is no way from the ESXi host to specify, for example, a RAID-0 stripe width for these VMDKs, nor is there any way to specify a RAID-1 replica for the VMDK. VMs and VMDKs simply inherited the capabilities of the underlying LUN or share that was presented to the ESXi hosts as a datastore.

In the case of vSAN (and vVols), the approach to deploying VMs is quite different. Consideration must be given to the availability, performance, and reliability factors of the application running in the VM. Based on these requirements, an appropriate VM storage policy must be created and associated with the VM during deployment. However, it is possible to change the policy after the VM has been deployed, on-the-fly, which will be discussed later in this chapter.

05 // VM Storage Policies and VM Provisioning

Figure 55: Standard vSAN capabilities

vSAN features include the ability to implement various storage configurations, for example, administrators can create RAID-5 and RAID-6 configurations for virtual machine objects deployed on an all-flash vSAN configuration. There are also RAID-0 and RAID-1 configurations available on all vSAN models. However, with RAID-5 and RAID-6, administrators can deploy VMs that are able to tolerate one or two failures, but the amount of space consumed on the vSAN datastore is much less than a RAID-1 configuration. There is also an additional policy for software checksum. Checksum is enabled by default, but it can be disabled through policies on a per VM or per VMDK basis if an administrator wishes to disable it. Another capability relates to quality of service and provides the ability to limit the number of *input/output operations per second* (IOPS) for a particular object. We can also specify how VMs, which are part of a stretched cluster, should be protected within a site. For this RAID-1, RAID-5, or RAID-6 can be used. This is an additional level of protection within a site that works alongside the cross-site protection. A similar configuration is also available for 2-node vSAN configurations. Do note that the secondary level of resilience capability does require a minimum of 3 disk groups per host in a 2-node configuration. Each host will have a full RAID tree locally. Depending on the number of disk groups, this could be a RAID-1 or RAID-5 configuration.

Figure 56: Advanced vSAN capabilities

You can select the capabilities when a VM storage policy is created. Note that certain capabilities apply to hybrid vSAN configurations (e.g., flash read cache reservation), while other capabilities apply to all-flash vSAN configurations only (e.g., RAID-5 and/or RAID-6).

VM storage policies are essential in vSAN deployments because they define how a VM is deployed on a vSAN datastore. Using VM storage policies, you can define the capabilities that can provide the number of VMDK RAID-0 stripe components or the number of RAID-1 mirror copies of a VMDK. Let's now revisit erasure coding before learning how to configure them via policies. We have already learned that if an administrator desires a VM to tolerate one failure but does not want to consume as much capacity as a RAID-1 mirror, a RAID-5 configuration can be used. If this configuration was implemented with RAID-1, the amount of capacity consumed would be 200% the size of the VMDK due to having two copies of the data. If this is implemented with RAID-5, the amount of capacity consumed would be 133% the size of the VMDK, the extra 33% accounting for the single parity segment since RAID-5 is implemented on vSAN as 3 data segments and 1 parity segment. RAID-5 requires a minimum of four hosts in an all-flash vSAN cluster and will implement a distributed parity mechanism across the storage of all four hosts.

Similarly, if an administrator desires a VM to tolerate two failures using a RAID-1 mirroring configuration, there will need to be three copies of the VMDK, meaning the amount of capacity consumed would be 300% the size of the VMDK. When using a RAID-6 implementation instead of RAID-1, a double parity is implemented, which is also distributed across all the hosts. By this, we mean 4 data segments and 2 parity segments. For RAID-6, there must be a minimum of six hosts in an all-flash vSAN cluster. RAID-6 also allows a VM to tolerate two failures, but only consumes capacity equivalent to 150% the size of the VMDK, the overhead of the two parity segments.

The sections that follow will highlight where you should use these capabilities when creating a VM storage policy and when to tune these values to something other than the default. Remember that a VM storage policy will contain one or more capabilities.

Note: Some significant changes were made to how the layout of vSAN objects was implemented in vSAN 7.0U1. A concerted effort was made to address the requirement of keeping 25-30% of what was termed slack space on the vSAN datastore. This was a considerable overhead but was necessary due to the way vSAN implemented its recovery and resyncing mechanism. Data that was being rebuilt or resynchronized used this slack space as a staging area. The slack space needed to be this large since vSAN would attempt to rebuild as many missing or failed components as possible, so if a complete host failed, vSAN needed space to stage the rebuild of all components on this host. In vSAN 7.0U1, a new approach was envisioned. This revolved around negating the need to build whole replicas or mirrors. The decision was made to implement large objects greater than 255GB in size in a different way than objects smaller than 255GB. Now, instead of implementing a top of tree RAID-1 (mirror) with 2 x RAID-0 branches, vSAN implemented on top of tree RAID-0 (concatenation) with each of the underlying components mirrored in a RAID-1 configuration. Now when rebuild operations are required, for example when a policy change is requested, vSAN can work on each component on the concatenation as a distinct item, working on a much smaller chunk of data. Previously vSAN had to set aside slack space for the whole of the mirror. This is all preamble to some of the examples shown later, when vSAN objects with the same policy will get a different layout depending on their size.

As an administrator, you can decide which of these capabilities can be added to the policy, but this is of course dependent on the requirements of your VM. For example, what performance and availability requirements does the VM have?

The capabilities for "vSAN" storage datastore specific rules are as follows:

Availability
- Site disaster tolerance
    - None – standard cluster **(default)**
    - None – standard cluster with fault domains
    - Host mirroring – 2 node cluster
    - Site mirroring - stretched cluster
    - None – keep data on preferred (stretched cluster)
    - None – keep data on non-preferred (stretched cluster)
    - None – stretched cluster
- Failures to tolerate
    - No data redundancy
    - No data redundancy with host affinity
    - 1 failure – RAID-1 (Mirroring) **(default)**
    - 1 failure – RAID-5 (Erasure Coding)
    - 2 failures – RAID-1 (Mirroring)
    - 2 failures – RAID-6 (Erasure Coding)
    - 3 failures – RAID-1 (Mirroring)

Storage rules
- Encryption Services
    - Data-At-Rest encryption
    - No encryption
    - No preference **(default)**
- Space Efficiency
    - Deduplication and compression
    - Compression only
    - No space efficiency
    - No preference **(default)**
- Storage tier
    - All flash
    - Hybrid
    - No preference **(default)**

Advanced Policy Rules
- Number of disk stripes per object (**default** value of 1)
- IOPS limit for an object (**default** value of 0 meaning unlimited)
- Object space reservation
    - Thin provisioning **(default)**
    - 25% reservation

- 50% reservation
- 75% reservation
- Thick provisioning
- Flash read cache reservation (hybrid vSAN only) (**default** value of 0 meaning none)
- Disable object checksum (**default** off)
- Force provisioning (**default** off)

Storage rules

Whilst we have already seen what the Availability and Advanced Policy rules looked like in the vSphere UI, we have not yet seen the Storage rules. The next screenshot displays what the Storage rules look like.

Figure 57: Storage rules

These configuration settings are primarily related to HCI-Mesh, where a vSphere cluster can consume storage from both a local vSAN datastore as well as multiple remote vSAN datastores. HCI-Mesh is discussed in greater detail in the Operations chapter later in the book. The reason for having Storage rules relate to the fact that there could be a local datastore that is encrypted, or perhaps some of the remote datastores are encrypted. It could be that the local datastore has deduplication or compression enabled, or that the local datastore is from a hybrid vSAN but the remote datastores are on vSAN All-Flash clusters. By using some of the settings in this configuration screen, an administrator can create policies that will place VMs with the same availability policy on either the local vSAN datastore or one of the remote datastores, depending on these settings. By default, these are left at "No preference" meaning that none of these capabilities are considered when provisioning a VM in an HCI-Mesh environment.

The sections that follow describe the vSAN capabilities in detail.

Failures to tolerate

In this section, we are going to discuss *Failures to tolerate*, specifically **RAID-1** which is the default setting. In the next section, we will describe RAID-5 and RAID-6. *Failures to tolerate* is often shorthanded to FTT and this shorthand is used quite extensively in this book. The maximum value for FTT is 3. This is available if RAID-1 is used. The maximum for FTT is 2 when using erasure coding assuming RAID-6 is used. We will examine these limits in more detail shortly.

The *Failures to tolerate* capability sets a requirement on the vSAN storage object (e.g., VMDK) to tolerate at least *n number of failures in the cluster*. This is the number of concurrent hosts, networks, disk controllers, or storage device failures that may occur in the cluster and still ensure the availability of the object. When failures to tolerate is set to *RAID-1* the VM's storage objects are mirrored; however, the mirroring is done across different ESXi hosts, as shown below.

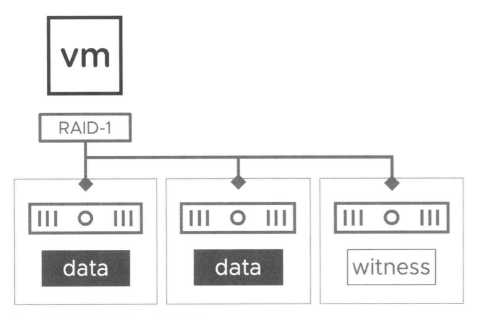

Figure 58: RAID-1 - Failures to tolerate

When this capability is set to a value of *n*, it specifies that the vSAN configuration must contain at least *n*+1 replica copies of the data; this also implies that there are 2*n*+1 hosts in the cluster.

Note that this requirement will create a configuration for the VM objects that may also contain an additional number of witness components being instantiated. The witness components are used to ensure that the VM remains available even when there are as many as *failures to tolerate* concurrent failures in the vSAN cluster. Witnesses provide a quorum when failures occur in the cluster, or if a selection decision must be made on which component(s) to keep online when a cluster partition or split-brain situation arises.

One aspect worth noting is that any disk failure on a single host is treated as a "failure" for this metric (although multiple disk failures on the same host are also treated as a single host failure). Therefore, the VM may not persist (remain accessible) if there is a disk failure on host A and a complete host failure of host B when the number of failures to tolerate is set to one.

As mentioned earlier, this is the layout when the object that is created on the vSAN datastore is less than 255GB in size. We will look at the larger size layout shortly.

NUMBER OF FAILURES TO TOLERATE	REPLICAS	WITNESS OBJECTS	MINIMUM NUMBER OF ESXI HOSTS
0	1	0	1
1	2	1	3
2	3	2	5
3	4	3	7

Table 5: Witness and hosts required to meet the number of failures to tolerate requirement

The table is true if the capability called *number of disk objects to stripe* is set to 1 and RAID-1 is used as the *Failures to tolerate* setting, which is the default. The behavior is subtly different if there is a stripe width greater than 1. Number of disk stripes per object will be discussed in more detail shortly.

If no policy is chosen when a VM is deployed, the default policy associated with the vSAN datastore is chosen which in turn, by default, sets the number of *failures to tolerate* to 1. When a new policy is created, the default value of number of *failures to tolerate* is also 1. This means that even if this capability is not explicitly specified in the policy, it is implied.

Recommended Practice for Number of Failures to Tolerate

The recommended practice (with RAID-1 configurations) for number of *failures to tolerate* is 1, unless you have a pressing concern to provide additional availability to allow VMs to tolerate more than one failure. Note that increasing the number of failures to tolerate would require additional hosts in the cluster, as well as additional disk capacity to be available for the creation of the extra mirror/replicas.

vSAN has multiple management workflows to warn/protect against accidental decommissioning of hosts that could result in vSAN being unable to meet the number of *failures to tolerate* policy of given VMs. This includes a noncompliant state being shown in the VM summary tab for the VM Storage Policy.

Then the question arises: What is the minimal number of hosts for a vSAN cluster? If we omit the 2-node configuration (more typically seen in remote office-branch office type deployments) for the moment, customers would for the most part require three ESXi hosts to deploy vSAN. However, what about scenarios where you need to do maintenance or upgrades and want to maintain the same level of availability during maintenance hours?

To comply with a policy of *failures to tolerate* = 1 using RAID-1, you need three hosts at a minimum. Even if one host fails, you can still access your data, because with three hosts and two mirror copies and a witness, you will still have more than 50% of your components (votes) available. But what happens when you place one of those hosts in maintenance mode?

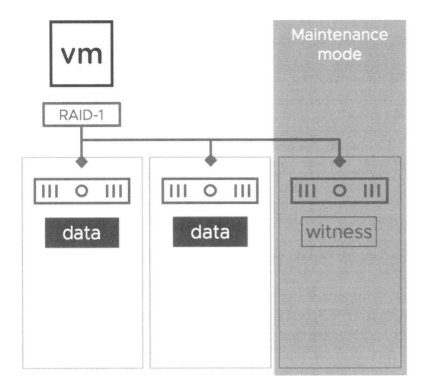

Figure 59: vSAN: Minimum number of hosts

Placing a host into maintenance mode will place all components on this host in an absent state. This host can no longer contribute capacity to the vSAN datastore when in maintenance mode. Similarly, it will not be possible to provision new VMs with an FTT=1 when one node is in maintenance mode (unless you force provision the VM, or deploy a VM with an FTT=0). If both remaining hosts keep functioning as expected, all VMs will continue to run. However, if another host fails or needs to be placed into maintenance mode, you have a challenge. At this point, the remaining host will have less than 50% of the components of your VM. As a result, VMs cannot be restarted (nor do any I/O).

RAID-5 and RAID-6

In this section, we are going to discuss *Failures to tolerate* implemented through RAID-5 and RAID-6.

These options allow administrators to choose between performance and capacity. If performance is the absolute end goal, then RAID-1 could be used. If administrators did not need maximum performance and were more concerned with capacity usage, then RAID-5/6 could be used.

The easiest way to explain the behavior is to display the various policy settings and the resulting object configuration as shown in the following table. Using the Site disaster tolerance set to "None

– standard cluster", the table below explains the type of configuration that will be provisioned and the minimum number of ESXi hosts required.

FAILURES TO TOLERATE	OBJECT CONFIGURATION	MINIMUM NUMBER OF ESXI HOSTS
No data redundancy	RAID-0	1
1 failure, RAID-5 (Erasure Coding)	RAID-5	4
1 failure, RAID-1 (Mirroring)	RAID-1	3
2 failures, RAID-6 (Erasure Coding)	RAID-6	6
2 failures, RAID-1 (mirroring)	RAID-1	5
3 failures, RAID-1 (mirroring)	RAID-1	7

Table 6: Object configuration when number of failures to tolerate and failure tolerance method set

As can be seen from the table, when RAID-5/6 is selected, the maximum number of failures that can be tolerated is 2. RAID-1 allows up to 3 failures to be tolerated in the cluster, using 4 copies of the data.

One might ask why RAID-5/6 is less performing than RAID-1. The reason lies in I/O amplification. I/O amplification is the phenomenon where the actual amount of I/O is a multiple of the logical amount intended to be read or written. In steady-state, where there are no failures in the cluster, there is no read amplification when using RAID-5/6 versus RAID-1. However, there is write amplification. This is because the parity component needs to be updated every time there is a write to the associated data components. In the case of RAID-5, we need to read the component that is going to be updated with additional write data, read the current parity, merge the new write data with the current data, write this back, calculate the new parity value, and write this back also. In essence, a single write operation can amplify into two reads and two writes. With RAID-6, which has double parity, a single write can amplify into three reads and three writes.

And indeed, when there is a failure of some component in the RAID-5 and RAID-6 objects, and data need to be determined using parity, then the I/O amplification is even higher. These are the considerations an administrator needs to evaluate when deciding on RAID-1 vs RAID-5/6.

One item to keep in mind is that even though RAID-5/6 consumes less capacity, it does require more hosts than the traditional RAID-1 approach, and it is only supported on an all-flash vSAN configuration. When using RAID-1, the rule is that to tolerate n failures, there must be a minimum of $2n+1$ hosts for the mirrors/replicas and witness components. Therefore, to tolerate one failure, there must be at least three hosts. To tolerate two failures, there must be at least five hosts. For those wondering why we need five hosts, we need to ensure that in the case of a network partition scenario we need to determine who owns the data, which will be the partition that has the most votes. To do so we need an odd number of components, and because of this requirement, we need an odd number of hosts. To tolerate three failures, there must be seven hosts in the cluster. All of the hosts must be contributing storage to the vSAN datastore.

With RAID-5, four hosts are needed to tolerate one failure and with RAID-6 six hosts are needed to tolerate two failures, even though less space is consumed on each host. The following diagram shows an example of a RAID-5 configuration for an object, deployed across four hosts with a distributed parity.

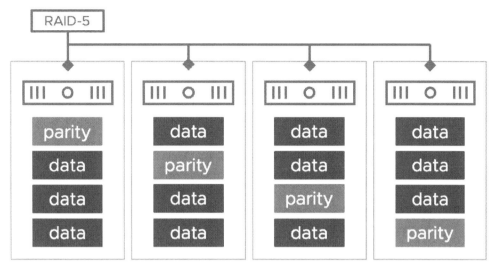

Figure 60: RAID-5 configuration

The RAID-5 or RAID-6 configurations also work with *number of disk stripes per object*. If stripe width is also specified as part of the policy along with RAID-5/6 each of the components on each host is striped in a RAID-0 configuration, and these are in turn placed in either a RAID-5 or a RAID-6 configuration. However new behaviour when using disk stripes with erasure coding was introduced in 7.0U1 which will be discussed shortly.

Number of Disk Stripes Per Object

This capability defines the number of physical disks across which each replica of a storage object (e.g., VMDK) is striped. Number of disk stripes per object is often short-handed to stripe width or even SW and this shorthand is used quite extensively in this book.

When RAID-1 is used, this policy setting can be considered in the context of a RAID-0 configuration on each RAID-1 mirror/replica where I/O traverses several physical disks. When RAID-5/6 is used, each segment of the RAID-5 or RAID-6 stripe may also be configured as a RAID-0 stripe. The next diagram shows a vSAN object if both RAID-0 and RAID-1 capabilities are used.

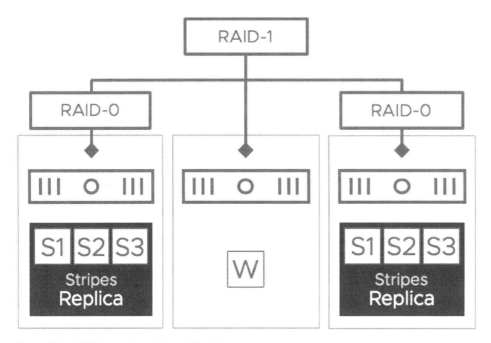

Figure 61: RAID-1 configuration with stripes

To understand the impact of stripe width, let's examine it first in the context of **write operations** and then in the context of read operations.

Because all writes go to the cache device write buffer, the value of an increased stripe width may or may not improve performance. This is because there is no guarantee that the new stripe will use a different cache device; the new stripe may be placed on a capacity device in the same disk group and thus the new stripe will use the same cache device. If the new stripe is placed in a different disk group, either on the same host or on a different host, and thus leverages a different cache device, performance might improve. However, you as the vSphere administrator have no control over this behavior. The only occasion where an increased stripe width could add value is when there is a large amount of data to destage from the cache tier to the capacity tier. In this case, having a stripe could improve destage performance as multiple capacity devices would be available to destage data to.

How can you tell whether your cache tier has lots of blocks to be destaged? This information is readily available in the vSphere Client. The next screenshot taken from the disk group on a **host** level view under *Monitor > vSAN > Performance > Disks* shows the write buffer free percentage.

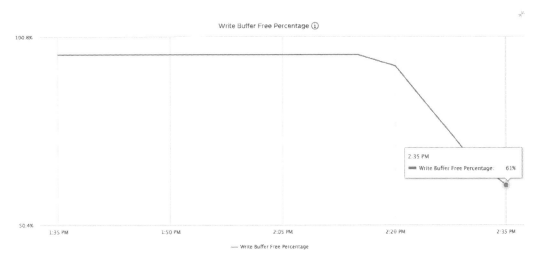

Figure 62: Write buffer free percentage

Let's summarize the above in a couple simple bullet points so that it is easier to grasp.

There are three different scenarios for stripes:
- **Striping across hosts**: Improved performance with different cache tier flash devices
- **Striping across disk groups**: Improved performance with different cache tier flash devices
- **Striping in the same disk group**: No significant performance improvement (using same cache tier flash device)

From a **read operation** perspective, an increased stripe width will help when you are experiencing many read cache misses but note that this is a consideration in hybrid configurations only. All-flash vSAN configurations do not have a read cache, and in all-flash, all read requests are serviced by flash. Consider the example of a VM deployed on a hybrid vSAN consuming 2,000 read operations per second and experiencing a hit rate of 90%. In this case, there are still 200 read operations that need to be serviced from magnetic disk in the capacity tier. If we assume that a single magnetic disk can provide 80 IOPS, then it is obvious that this single device is not able to service all of those read operations in a timely fashion. An increase in stripe width would help on this occasion to meet the VM read I/O requirements. In an all-flash vSAN that runs extremely read-intensive workloads, striping across multiple capacity flash devices can also improve performance.

How can you tell whether you have read cache misses? The vSAN Performance Services provides you with all the information needed to identify this scenario. The next screenshot shows that there is a 0% read cache hit rate. Either this is a very idle system, or it is an all-flash vSAN that does not use read cache. In fact, it is all-flash. This graph can be found on a **host** level view under *Monitor > vSAN > Performance > Disks*, note that you will need to go to a particular host first and selected the disk group you would like to have this level of detail for.

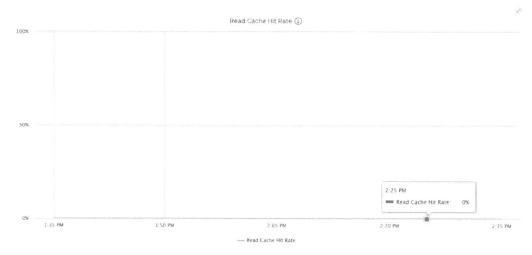

Figure 63: Read Cache Hit Rate

In general, the default stripe width of 1 should meet most, if not all VM workloads. Stripe width is a capability that should be changed only when write destaging or read cache misses are identified as a performance constraint.

RAID-0 used when no Striping is specified in the Policy

Those who have been looking at the vSphere Client regularly, where you can see the placement of components, may have noticed that vSAN appears to create a multi-component RAID-0 for your VMDK even when you did not explicitly ask it to. Or perhaps you have requested a stripe width of two in your policy and then observed what appears to be a stripe width of three (or more) being created. vSAN will split objects as it sees fit when there are space constraints. This is not striping per se, since components can end up on the same physical capacity device, which in many ways can be thought of as a concatenation. We can refer to it as chunking.

vSAN will use this chunking method on certain occasions. The first of these is when a VMDK is larger than any single chunk of free space. Essentially, vSAN hides the fact that even when there are small capacity devices on the hosts, administrators can still create very large VMDKs. Therefore, it is not uncommon to see large VMDKs split into multiple components, even when no stripe width is specified in the VM storage policy. vSAN will use this chunking method when a VMDK is larger than any capacity device.

There is another occasion where this chunking may occur. By default, an object will also be split if its size is greater than 255 GB (the maximum component size). An object might appear to be made up of multiple 255 GB RAID-0 chunks even though striping may not have been a policy requirement. It can be split even before it reaches 255 GB when free disk space makes vSAN think that there is a benefit in doing so. Note that just because there is a standard split at 255 GB, it doesn't mean all new chunks will go onto different capacity devices. In fact, since this is not striping per se, multiple chunks may be placed on the same physical capacity device. It may, or may not, depending on overall balance and free capacity.

If you use physical disks that are smaller than 255GB, then you might see errors similar to the following when you try to deploy a virtual machine:

> There is no more space for virtual disk XX. You might be able to continue this session by freeing disk space on the relevant volume and clicking retry.

As VMDKs are thin provisioned on the vSAN datastore, each component grows automatically throughout its life. Because the default component size is 255GB, the object will not be able to grow to its full size of 255GB if the physical disk is smaller than 255GB. For example, if a VMDK of 255GB is provisioned (with FTT=1 and SW=1) on a 200GB physical disk, it can't grow greater than 200GB (because of the physical disk size limit). You will get the out of space error shown above if you write more than 200GB data to the VMDK. In situations like this, one option is to modify *VSAN.ClomMaxComponentSizeGB* to a size that is approximately 80% of the physical disk size. **KB article 2080503** has instructions on how to change this setting.

> **Keep in mind that the secondary effect of this is that you are introducing more components into the system and may reach component limits If too many are created because of changing this advanced setting.**

Let's look at what some of our tests have shown. That may help clarify what will happen in certain scenarios and how the components will be distributed across the cluster. Note that the initial set of tests here are implemented on a vSAN 6.7U1 cluster. We will repeat the same set of tests in a vSAN 7.0U3 cluster to show how object layout has changed for larger sizes next.

Test 1 – vSAN 6.7U1

On an all-flash configuration, we created a 150 GB VM on a vSAN datastore that had 100 GB SSDs as its capacity devices. We also set a policy of *failures to tolerate* (FTT) = 1. We got a simple RAID-1 for our VMDK with two components, each replica having just one component (so no RAID-0). Now, this is because the VM is deployed on the vSAN datastore as thin by default (*Object Space Reservation* = 0%), so even though we created a 150 GB VM, each component can sit on a single 100 GB SSD because it is thinly provisioned, as demonstrated below.

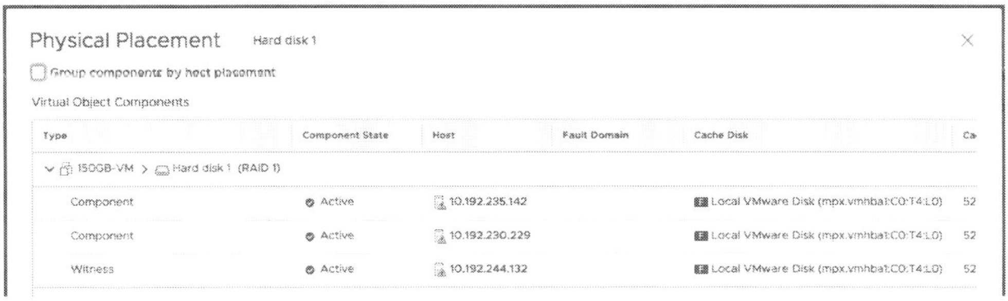

Figure 64: Physical disk placement, no striping

Test 2 – vSAN 6.7U1

On the same cluster, we created a 150 GB VM, with a policy of FTT = 1 (RAID-1) and thick provisioning enabled. Thick provisioning is the equivalent of setting *Object Space Reservation* = 100% in the policy. Now we get another RAID-1 of the VMDK, but each replica is made up of a RAID-0 with two components. Thick provisioning guarantees space reservation, and as such the VM needs to span at least two devices, and therefore a RAID-0 configuration is being used as shown in the screenshot below.

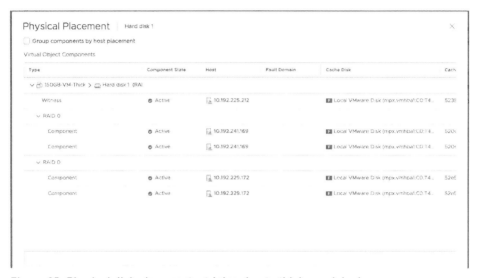

Figure 65: Physical disk placement, striping due to thick provisioning

Test 3 – vSAN 6.7U1

We created a 300 GB VM, with a policy of *failures to tolerate* = 1, *object space reservation* = thick or 100%, and *number of disk stripes per object* (SW) = 2. We got another RAID-1 of our VMDK as before, but now each replica is made up of a RAID-0 with *four* components. Here, even with a SW = 2 setting, my VMDK requirement is still too large to span two devices. A third and fourth capacity device is required in this case, as shown below.

We can conclude that multiple components in a RAID-0 configuration are used for VMDKs that are larger than a single capacity device, even if a stripe width is not specified in the policy.

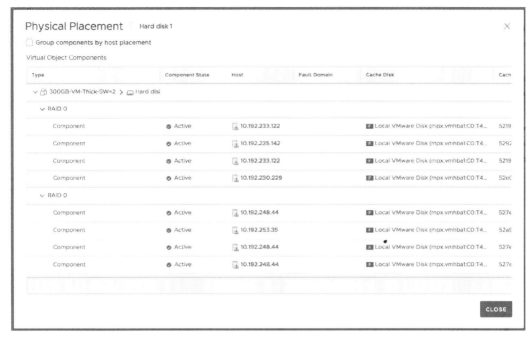

Figure 66: Complex deployment

Increasing Components to Reduce Slack Space

While the above tests held true for vSAN 6.7, major changes appeared in 7.0U1 and later around the need to reduce the recommended 25-30% slack space. This led to some significant changes in how objects were built in vSAN 7.0U1 and later. Rather than having to deal with component sizes of 255GB, a decision was taken to create many smaller components to back a VSAN object, rather than a few large components. Today, in the event of rebuilds, repairs, reconfigurations, and rebalancing, it means that smaller amounts of slack space would be consumed for these operational tasks. Thus, creating a virtual machine with a RAID-1 policy that required a disk larger than 255GB could now result in more than 1 RAID-0 component, concatenated together, on either side of the RAID-1 tree. The advantage here is that vSAN can concurrently work on multiple concatenated components simultaneously, speeding up recovery times and requiring far less slack space for internal operations.

Let's repeat the above tests and check the results, but this time we are not limited by small devices. This time we want to see the layout when objects smaller and larger than 255GB are created.

Test 4 – vSAN 7.0U3

On the same cluster, a 255 GB VM, with a policy of FTT = 1 (RAID-1) and thick provisioning enabled is created. For thick disks, Object Space Reservation is set to Thick in the Advanced Policy Rules. After deploying a VM with this policy, the object layout was examined under Cluster > Monitor > vSAN > Virtual Objects, and once the VMDK was selected, we click on the "View Placement Details" to get a detailed view of the layout. Here is the 255GB Thick provisioned VMDK layout.

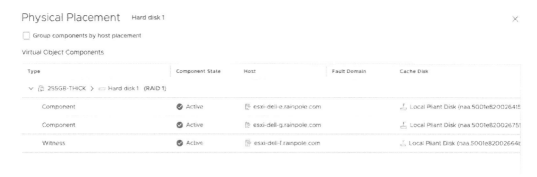

Figure 67: 255GB Thick object layout in vSAN 7.0U1 and later

As you can see, this is very much the same as what we saw in the vSAN 6.7U1 deployment. A simple RAID-1 object with an additional witness component. All components are on separate hosts.

Test 5 – vSAN 7.0U3

Let's now repeat the previous test but increase the size to 256GB. This should be enough to go beyond the threshold for large objects, and vSAN should now implement the new layout format. Object Space Reservation is once again set to Thick in the Advanced Policy Rules. After deployment, this is what the object looks like.

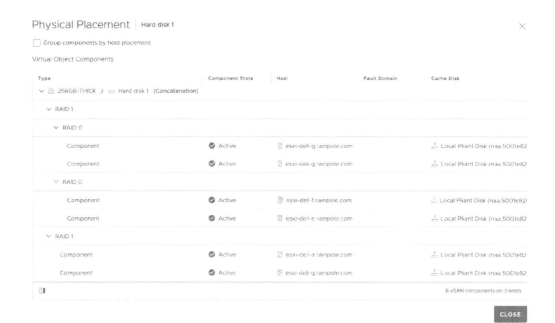

Figure 68: 256GB Thick object layout in vSAN 7.0U1 and later

Note now that the top of the object tree is a concatenation, and that the components are in their own distinct RAID-1 mirror configurations under the top-level concatenation. Perhaps an easier way to visualize this layout is as follows:

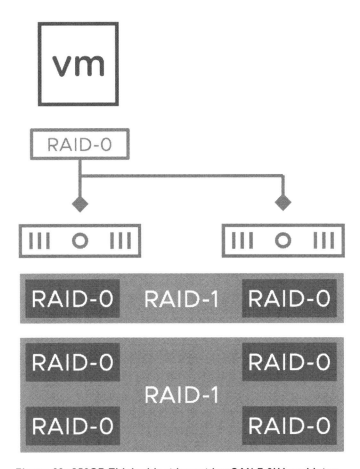

Figure 69: 256GB Thick object layout in vSAN 7.0U1 and later

This may come as a surprise to some of you who upgrade from vSAN 6 to vSAN 7. However, the purpose behind this change is to reduce the requirement for slack space, which was always an approximation anyway. With this enhancement, more of the vSAN datastore should be available for workloads rather than set aside for some internal vSAN operations, which is good news.

Stripe Width Maximum

In vSAN, the maximum stripe width that can be defined in a policy is 12. This can be striping across capacity devices in the same host, or across capacity devices, in different hosts, as mentioned earlier. I'm going to add a caveat here that, since vSAN 7.0U1, certain limits have been placed on striping for both large objects as well as RAID-5 and RAID-6 objects. The description that follows applied to vSAN versions prior to 7.0U1, as well as to objects that are 255GB or less in size. Discussions around the change in behavior for large objects in 7.0U1 and later will be covered shortly.

> Remember that when you specify a stripe width there has to be at least a stripe width (SW) × (FTT+1) number of capacity devices before vSAN can satisfy the policy requirement.

Ignoring for the moment that additional devices may be needed to host the witness component(s), this means that the larger the number of FTT and SW, the more complex the placement of object and associated components will become. The number of disk stripes per object setting in the VM storage policy means stripe across "at least" this number of capacity devices per mirror. vSAN may, when it sees fit, use additional stripes.

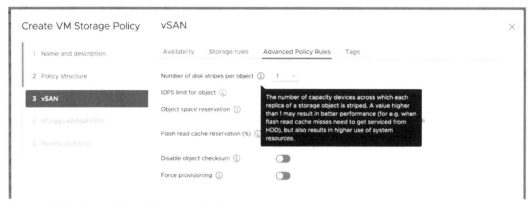

Figure 70: Number of disk stripes per object

Stripe Width Configuration Error

You may ask yourself what happens if a vSphere administrator requests the vSAN cluster to meet a stripe width policy setting that is not available or achievable, typically due to a lack of resources. During the creation of the policy, vSAN will verify if there is a datastore that is compatible with the capabilities specified in the policy. As shown in the screenshot below, where we have requested FTT=3 and SW=12, no datastore is shown as compatible with the defined policy.

Figure 71: No compatible datastore

If you would forcefully try to deploy a VM using this policy then the creation of the VM will fail. This is demonstrated in the screenshot below.

05 // VM Storage Policies and VM Provisioning

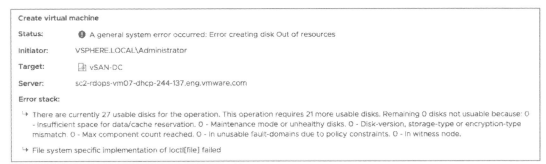

Figure 72: VM creation tasks fails

What this error message is telling us is that vSAN needs 48 disks (4 copies of the data by a stripe width of 12) to implement this policy. There are currently only 27 disks available in the cluster, so 21 more are needed to create such a policy.

Stripe Width Chunk Size

A question that then often arises after the stripe width discussion is whether there is a specific segment size. In other words, when the stripe width is defined using the VM storage policies, which increment do the components use to grow? vSAN uses a stripe segment size of 1 MB in a round-robin fashion for RAID-1 and RAID-5/6 if you striped each component. This is not configurable.

Stripe Width Best Practice

After reading this section, you should more clearly understand that increasing the stripe width could potentially complicate placement. vSAN has a lot of logic built in to handle smart placement of objects. We recommend not increasing the stripe width *unless* you have identified a pressing performance issue such as read cache misses or during destaging.

Remember that all I/O should go to the flash layer first. All writes certainly go to flash first, and in the case of hybrid configurations, are later destaged to magnetic disks. For reads, the operation is first attempted on the flash layer. If a read cache miss occurs, the block is read from magnetic disk in hybrid configurations and from flash capacity devices in all-flash configurations. Therefore, if all of your reads are being satisfied by the cache tier, there is no point in increasing the stripe width as it does not give any benefits. Doing the math correctly beforehand is much more effective, leading to proper sizing of the flash-based cache tier, rather than trying to increase the stripe width after the VM has been deployed!

Changes to Stripe Width behavior for large RAID-1 objects

Due to the previously documented concerns about the 20-30% slack space, and the decision to create multiple smaller components rather than a few larger components for vSAN objects, steps were taken to reduce the number of components on the vSAN datastore. One of these steps involved limiting the stripe width settings for objects larger than 2TB in size. These objects now have the first 2TB configured as per the stripe width policy setting, whilst the rest of the object will be limited to using a stripe width of 3. Note that this will not be visible in the UI. The only change that you will see for the larger objects in vSAN 7.0U1 and later are the top of tree concatenation as seen previously, and therefore more components in each branch of the RAID tree.

By way of example, here is a 255GB VMDK object created with a policy that has an FTT=1, a stripe width of 8, and an object space reservation of Thick. In the lower right-hand corner, you can see that there are 16 vSAN components in total, 8 on each side of the mirror representing the striped components.

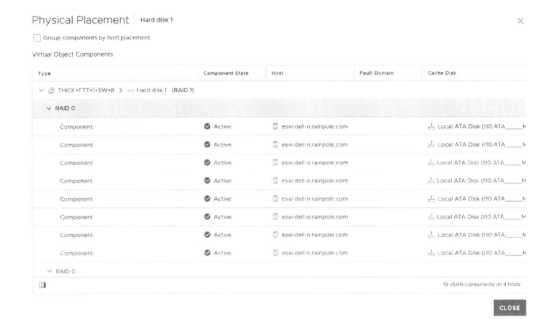

Figure 73: RAID-1, Stripe Width = 8, Object size < 255GB

The next figure shows a similar deployment, but the size has been bumped up to 256GB.

05 // VM Storage Policies and VM Provisioning

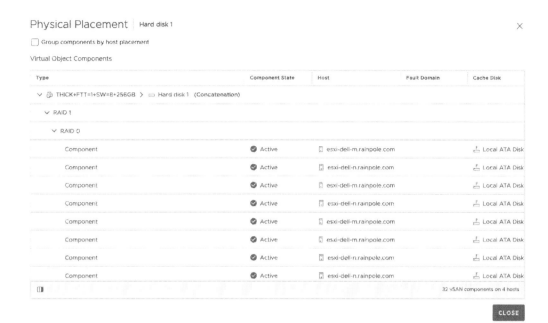

Figure 74: RAID-1, Stripe Width = 8, Object size = 256GB

Note that the top of the tree is now a concatenation, with 2 x RAID-1 configurations underneath, although the second is not visible in the screenshot. In the lower right-hand corner, the component count has now risen to 32. The components, 8 replicated to 8 in one RAID-1 configuration, and 8 more replicated to another 8 in another RAID-1 configuration, both of which are concatenated will be much smaller in size than previously, but there are more of them. This is the sort of layout change you will observe with the newer layout mechanism in vSAN 7.0U1 and later.

Changes to Stripe Width behavior for large RAID-5/6 objects

Similar considerations apply to RAID-5/RAID-6 objects created on the vSAN datastore from vSAN 7.0U1 and later. vSAN now treats the component count of an erasure coding stripe toward the stripe width. For example, a RAID-5 object will already have an effective stripe width of 4, while a RAID-6 object is considered to have an effective stripe width of 6. Therefore, the value of Stripe Width must be increased in multiples of 4 or 6 respectively to achieve an additional stripe for that given component.

Let's look at some example layouts to make things a little clearer. I'm going to use a new vSAN cluster to run this test. The new cluster has a total of 13 ESXi hosts, with a single disk group containing 4 disks – 1 cache and 3 capacity devices. This gives me a total of 39 capacity devices for this testing.

Let's begin with RAID-5. A policy is created that select FTT=1 (RAID-5) along with a Stripe Width of 4. When this object is deployed, there is no noticeable difference between it and an object that is deployed with a Stripe Width of 1. It has 4 components in total. You can think of it as a 3+1 configuration, with 3 data segments and 1 parity segment, even though the parity is striped across all components. As mentioned, a Stripe Width of 4 is already in place for RAID-5 objects. Note that the object created in this case was 255GB or smaller in size.

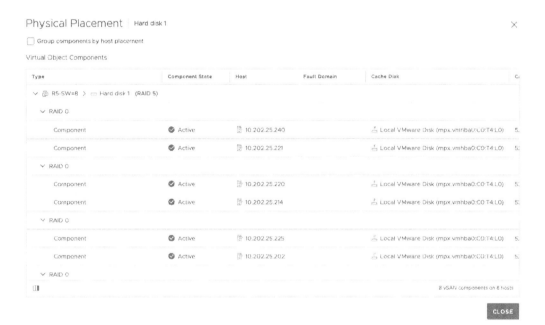

Figure 75: RAID-5, Stripe Width = 4, Object size < 255GB

You can increase the Stripe Width up to 7, and no change will be noticed in the object layout. It is only when the Stripe Width is increased to 8 that we notice a change in the object.

Figuro 76: RAID-5, Stripe Width = 8, Object size < 255GB

Now we see that each segment of the RAID-5 object has become a RAID-0 with 2 components. These components are now striped to meet the policy requirements. To continue striping the RAID-5 configuration, you would need to grow the stripe width value by a factor of 4. With the maximum stripe width limit set to 12, this implies that each RAID-5 component could have an effective stripe width of 3. Let's do another test and repeat the above test with a RAID-5 object that is larger than

255GB.

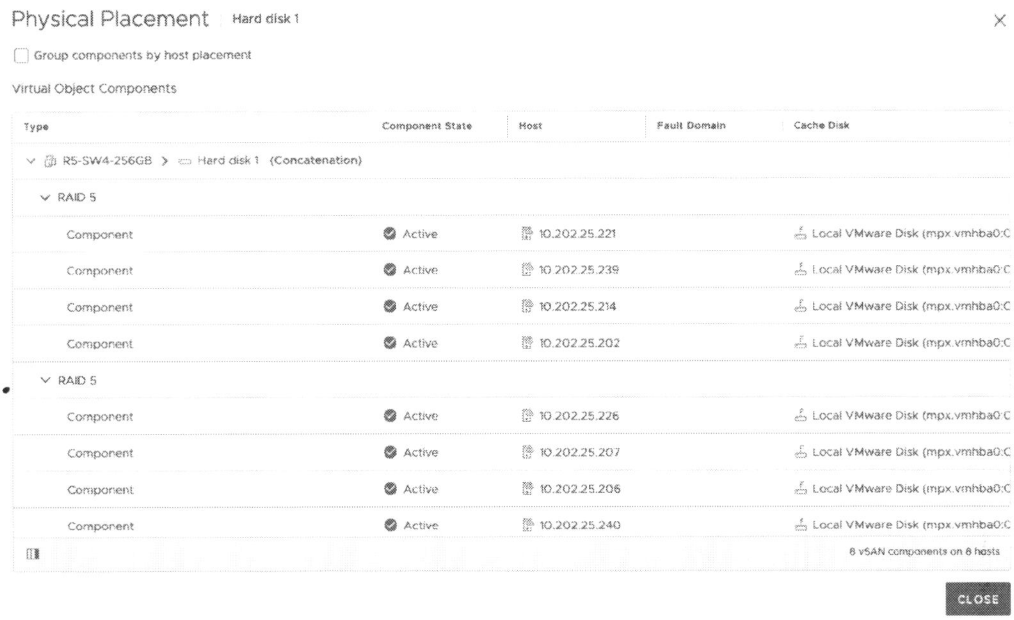

Figure 77: RAID-5, Stripe Width = 4, Object size > 255GB

This policy request requires vSAN to build the object with a concatenation at the top of the tree, as seen previously, but underneath the concatenation are two RAID-5 configurations, each with 4 components. As we've mentioned before, we now have much smaller components that can be worked on individually, in parallel, or serially, meaning that operations on vSAN segments due to failures, or policy changes, are now much more granular, and require less slack space than previously. Note that the component count has risen to 8 in the above example.

One final test, with a large RAID-5 object and a stripe width set to 8, just to observe how the components in the object get distributed. As before, if the stripe width is set to anywhere between 1 and 7, no change to the layout is observed. But when we set the stripe width to 8 (all RAID-5 segments get a second stripe), this is the observed layout.

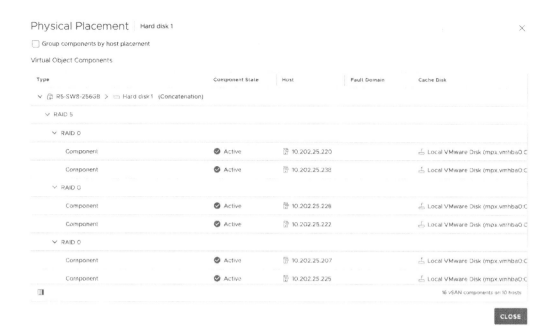

Figure 78: RAID-5, Stripe Width = 8, Object size > 255GB

Now each segment of the RAID-5 has a RAID-0 with two striped components. The component count, as observed in the lower right-hand corner has risen to 16.

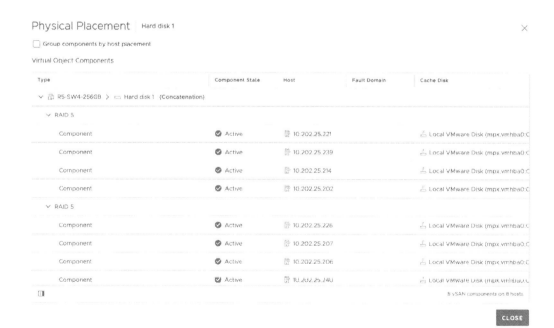

Figure 79: RAID-5, Stripe Width = 8, Object size > 255GB

You can be assured that RAID-6 behaves similarly, so there is no point in reproducing another set of screenshots for those objects. The only difference, as mentioned, is that RAID-6 has an effective stripe width of 6, a stripe width of 12 would have to be specified to increase it. As a result of the maximum stripe width of 12, RAID-6 segments can only have at most 1 additional stripe added to their segments.

IOPS Limit for Object

IOPS limit for object is a Quality of Service (QoS) capability introduced with vSAN 6.2. This allows administrators to ensure that an object, such as a VMDK, does not generate more than a predefined number of I/O operations per second. This is a great way of ensuring that a "noisy neighbor" virtual machine does not impact other virtual machine components in the same disk group by consuming more than its fair share of resources.

By default, vSAN uses a normalized I/O size of 32 KB as a base. **This means that a 64 KB I/O will therefore represent two I/O operations in the QoS calculation**. I/Os that are less than or equal to 32 KB will be considered single I/O operations. For example, 2 × 4 KB I/Os are considered two distinct I/Os. It should also be noted that both read and write IOPS are regarded as equivalent. Neither cache hit rate nor sequential I/O is considered. If the IOPS limit threshold is passed, the I/O is throttled back to bring the IOPS value back under the threshold. The default value for this capability is 0, meaning that there is no IOPS limit threshold and VMs can consume as many IOPS as they want, subject to available resources.

We do not see this capability used too often by vSAN customers. Only a small number of Service Providers use this to limit their customer's workloads.

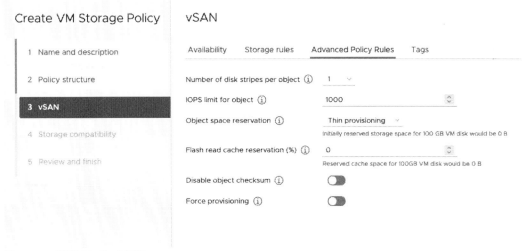

Figure 80: IOPS Limit of 1000

Flash Read Cache Reservation

This capability applies to hybrid vSAN configurations only. It is the amount of flash capacity reserved on the cache tier device as read cache for the storage object. It is specified as a percentage of the logical size of the storage object (i.e., VMDK). This is specified as a percentage value (%), with up to four decimal places. This fine granular unit size is needed so that administrators can express sub 1% units. Take the example of a 1 TB VMDK. If you limited the read cache reservation to 1% increments, this would mean cache reservations in increments of 10 GB, which in most cases is far too much for a single VM.

Note that you do not have to set a reservation to allow a storage object to use cache. All VMs equally share the read cache of cache devices. The reservation should be left unset (default) unless you are trying to solve a real performance problem and you believe dedicating read cache to a particular workload is the solution. If you add this capability to the VM storage policy and set it to a value 0 (zero), you will not have any read cache reserved for the VM that uses this policy. In the current version of vSAN, there is no proportional share mechanism for this resource when multiple VMs are consuming read cache, so every VM consuming read cache will share it equally.

Object Space Reservation

We have come across *Object Space Reservation* (OSR) when we looked at the chunking behavior earlier in the context of RAID-0. By default, all objects deployed on vSAN are thin provisioned. This means that no space is reserved at VM deployment time but rather space is consumed as the VM uses storage. The object space reservation is the amount of space to reserve specified as a percentage of the total object address space.

This is a property used for specifying a thick provisioned storage object. If object space reservation is set to Thick provisioning (or 100% in the vSphere Client), all of the storage capacity requirements of the VM are reserved upfront. This will be *lazy zeroed thick* (LZT) format and not *eager zeroed thick* (EZT). The difference between LZT and EZT is that EZT virtual disks are zeroed out at creation time; LZT virtual disks are zeroed out at first write time.

One thing to bring to the reader's attention is the special case of using object space reservation when deduplication and compression are enabled on the vSAN cluster. When deduplication and compression space-saving features are enabled, any objects that wish to use object space reservation in a policy must have it set to either Thin provisioning (0% in the vSphere Web Client) or Thick provisioning (100% in the vSphere Web Client). **Values between 1% and 99% are not allowed**, objects must be either fully thin or fully thick for deduplication and compression to work. Any existing objects that have Object Space Reservation between 1% and 99% will need to be reconfigured with thick or thin provisioning prior to enabling deduplication and compression on the cluster.

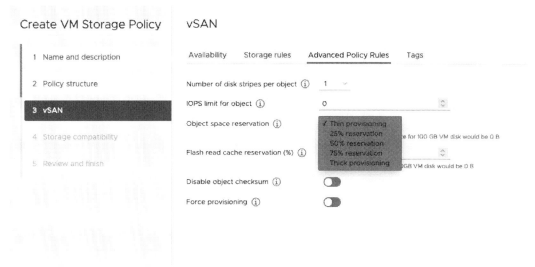

Figure 81: Object space reservation

Force Provisioning

If the force provisioning parameter is enabled, any object that has this setting in its policy will be provisioned even if the requirements specified in the VM storage policy cannot be satisfied by the vSAN datastore. The VM will be shown as noncompliant in the VM summary tab and relevant VM storage policy views in the vSphere client. If there is not enough space in the cluster to satisfy the reservation requirements of at least one replica, however, the provisioning will fail even if force provisioning is turned on. When additional resources become available in the cluster, vSAN will bring this object to a compliant state.

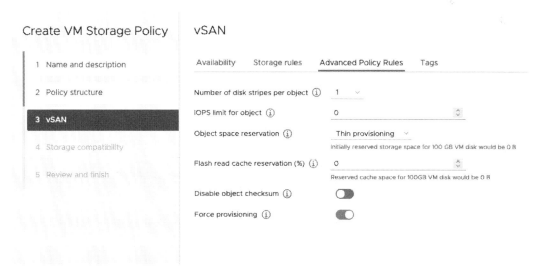

Figure 82: Force provisioning enabled

One thing that might not be well understood regarding *force provisioning* is that if a policy cannot be met, it attempts a much simpler placement with requirements that reduce *failures to tolerate* to

0, *number of disk stripes per object* to 1 and *flash read cache reservation* to 0 (on hybrid configurations). This means vSAN will attempt to create an object with just a single copy of data. Any OSR policy setting is still honored. Therefore, there is no gradual reduction in capabilities as vSAN tries to find a placement for an object. For example, if the policy contains *failures to tolerate* = 2, vSAN won't attempt an object placement using *failures to tolerate* = 1. Instead, it immediately looks to implement *failures to tolerate* = 0.

Similarly, if the requirement was *failures to tolerate* = 1, *number of disk stripes per object* = 4, but vSAN doesn't have enough capacity devices to accommodate *number of disk stripes per object* = 4, then it will fall back to *failures to tolerate* = 0, *number of disk stripes per object* = 1, even though a policy of *failures to tolerate* = 1, *number of disk stripes per object* = 2 or *failures to tolerate* = 1, *number of disk stripes per object* = 3 may have succeeded.

Caution should be exercised if this policy setting is implemented. Since this allows VMs to be provisioned with no protection, it can lead to scenarios where VMs and data are at risk.

Administrators who use this option to *force provision* virtual machines need to be aware that although virtual machine objects may be provisioned with only one replica copy (perhaps due to lack of space), once additional resources become available in the cluster, vSAN may immediately consume these resources to try to satisfy the policy settings of virtual machines. Thus, administrators may see the additional space from newly added capacity devices very quickly consumed if there are objects that are force provisioned on the cluster.

In the past, the use case for setting *force provision* was when a vSAN management cluster needed to be bootstrapped. In this scenario, you would start with a single vSAN node that would host the vCenter Server, which was then used to configure a larger vSAN cluster. vCenter would be deployed initially with *failures to tolerate* = 0 but once additional nodes were added to the cluster, it would get reconfigured with *failures to tolerate* = 1.

Another use case is the situation where a cluster is under maintenance or a failure has occurred, but there is still a need to provision new virtual machines.

> **Remember that this parameter should be used only when needed and as an exception. When used by default, this could easily lead to scenarios where VMs, and all data associated with them, are at risk due to provisioning with no FTT. Use with caution!**

Disable Object Checksum

This feature, which is enabled by default, is looking for data corruption (bit rot), and if found, automatically corrects it. Checksum is validated on the complete I/O path, which means that when writing data, the checksum is calculated and automatically stored. Upon a read, the checksum of the data is validated, and if there is a mismatch the data is repaired.

vSAN also includes a checksum scrubber mechanism. This mechanism is configured to check all data on the vSAN datastore. The frequency is controlled by advanced host settings *VSAN.ObjectScrubsPerYear* and *VSAN.ObjectScrubsPerYearBase*. The recommendation is to leave these settings configured to the default values. Note that the scrubber runs in the background and only when there is limited IO, to avoid a performance impact on the workload.

In some rare cases, you may desire to disable checksums completely. The reason for this could be performance, although the overhead is negligible, and most customers prefer data integrity over a minimal performance increase. In certain cases, the application, especially if it is a newer next-gen or cloud-native application, may already provide a checksum mechanism, or the workload does not require a checksum. If that is the case, then checksums can be disabled through the "disable object checksum" capability.

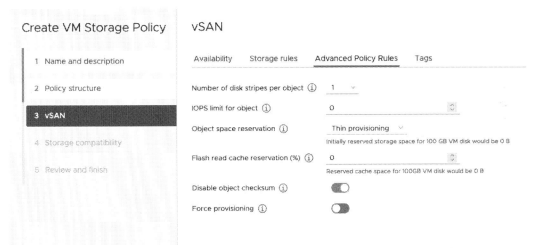

Figure 83: Object checksum disabled

> We do not recommend disabling Object Checksum. This feature was introduced as a direct request by customers and partners who have workloads that have their own checksum mechanism. Even if that is the case, we would still not recommend disabling Object Checksum. Use at your own risk!

That completes the vSAN policy capabilities overview. All above-mentioned capabilities can be specified within a policy and a policy is associated with virtual machines or virtual disks. There is however more to a virtual machine as explained in earlier chapters. Let's now look at those special objects and let's examine which policy capabilities are inherited and which are not.

VM Home Namespace Revisited

The VM namespace on vSAN is a *255 GB thin object*. A namespace is a per-VM object. As you could imagine, if policy settings were allocated to the VM home namespace, such as proportional capacity and flash read cache reservation, much of the magnetic disk and flash resources could be wasted. To that end, the VM home namespace has its own special policy, as follows:

- Number of disk stripes per object: 1
- Failures to tolerate: <as-per-policy>
    - This includes RAID-1, RAID-5, and RAID-6 configurations
- Flash read cache reservation: 0%
- Force provisioning: Off
- Object space reservation: thin
- Checksum disabled: <as-per-policy>
- IOPS limit for object: <as-per-policy>

To validate our learnings, we deployed a VM, and for this virtual machine, both disk stripes, as well as failures to tolerate, were configured to 2. As can be seen in the screenshot below, the VM Home object only has the failures to tolerate applied; stripe width is ignored. Remember RAID-1 with FTT=2 requires 5 vSAN hosts due to the additional witness components.

VM Home (RAID 1)		
Witness	Active	10.192.253.35
Witness	Active	10.192.244.132
Component	Active	10.192.230.229
Component	Active	10.192.229.172
Component	Active	10.192.235.142

Figure 84: VM Home components and FTT=2

VM Swap Revisited

The VM Swap object is only created when the VM is powered on and is deleted when the VM is powered off. The VM swap follows much the same conventions as the VM home namespace. It has the same default policy as the VM home namespace, which is 1 disk stripe, and 0% read cache reservation. Pre-vSAN 6.7, VM swap had a 100% object space reservation. Starting vSAN 6.7, VM swap is thin provisioned by default. This was done to avoid relatively high amounts of capacity needlessly being reserved for swap space.

This new behavior, if desired, can be disabled using the advanced system setting called *SwapThickProvisionDisabled*. This setting is set to 1 by default on vSAN 6.7 and higher. To disable this behavior, it needs to be configured to 0. Note that this is the same advanced system setting that was used pre-vSphere 6.7, which was set to 0 by default.

05 // VM Storage Policies and VM Provisioning

Figure 85: Changing Swap behavior

In later versions of vSAN, this configuration parameter was moved directly into the vSphere client UI, under Cluster > Configure > vSAN > Services > Advanced Options. It is enabled by default, as can be seen in the figure below. You can revert to a thick swap by toggling the button.

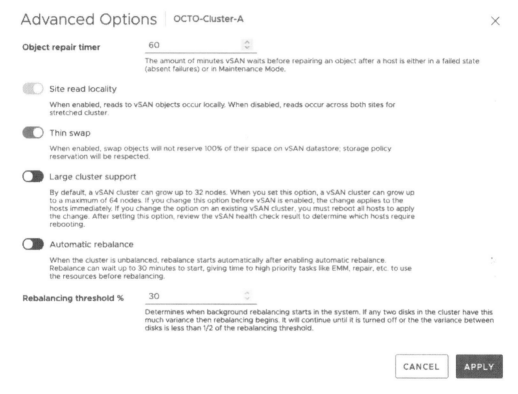

Figure 86: Thin swap

> We recommend validating if memory is overcommitted or not and how much spare capacity is available on vSAN. Free capacity needs to be available for swap when a VM wants to consume it. If new blocks can't be allocated, the VM will fail!

Pre-vSAN 6.7 VM swap did not inherit the FTT from the VM storage policy either. It only used an FTT=1, and a RAID-1 configuration. However, with vSAN 6.7 this behavior has also changed, and now VM swap, like VM Home Namespace, follows the FTT specified by the administrator in the VMs policy. This is to ensure that the swap file has the same availability characteristics as the VM itself.

- Number of disk stripes per object: 1
- Number of failures to tolerate: <as-per-policy>
- Flash read cache reservation: 0%
- Force provisioning: On
- Object space reservation: 0% (thin)
- Failure tolerance method: <as-per-policy>
- Checksum disabled: <as-per-policy>
- IOPS limit for object: <as-per-policy>

There is one additional point concerning swap, and that is that it has force provisioning set to on. This means that if some of the policy requirements cannot be met, such as *failures to tolerate*, the VM swap is still created.

To validate our learnings, we deployed a VM, and for this virtual machine both disk stripes as well as *failures to tolerate* were configured to 2. As can be seen in the screenshot below, the VM Swap object only has the *failures to tolerate* applied and the stripe width is ignored. As before, RAID-1 with FTT=2 requires 5 vSAN hosts due to the additional witness components.

Virtual Machine SWAP Object (RAID 1)		
Witness	Active	10.192.229.172
Component	Active	10.192.253.35
Component	Active	10.192.235.142
Component	Active	10.192.244.132
Witness	Active	10.192.230.229

Figure 87: VM Swap components and FTT=2

VM swap is not limited in size, in the way the VM home namespace is limited. It can grow larger than a single 255 GB thin object.

Delta Disk / Snapshot Caveat

For the most part, a delta VMDK (or snapshot, as it's often referred to) will always inherit the policy associated with the base disk. In vSAN, a vSphere administrator can also specify a VM storage policy for a linked clone. In the case of linked clones, the policy is applied just to the linked clone (top-level delta disk), not the base disk. This is not visible through the UI, however. Both VMware Horizon View and VMware vCloud Director use this capability through the vSphere API.

Clone Caveat

A clone operation always starts with a snapshot, even though you might be cloning to a new policy. Take an example that you plan to clone from a RAID-5 VM to a RAID-1 VM, but there is a failure in the cluster (perhaps 1 node out of 4 is down). Whilst the RAID-5 VMs will continue to run, you will not be able to clone it to a RAID-1, as there are not enough resources available to create the initial snapshot (which must be a RAID-5 since the policy is inherited from the base VMDK) to start the cloning process.

At this point, you should be aware that you can reserve space for objects deployed on the vSAN datastore. However, by default, virtual machine disks on the vSAN datastore are thin provisioned. Now you are probably wondering where you can find out how much space a VM consumes and how much is reserved. Let's look at how you can do that.

Verifying How Much Space Is Consumed

When you select the vSAN datastore in the UI, then the Monitor tab, and then select **vSAN** > **Capacity**, you can get a nice overview of how much space is being consumed by the different types of objects.

Figure 88: Space consumption

This view provides information on all objects that you might find on a vSAN datastore, such as VM home namespaces, VMDKs, swap objects, container volumes, iSCSI , and LUNS, and so on. It also provides a global view of how much space has been consumed, and what space savings you are getting from deduplication and compression, once enabled on the cluster. A detailed analysis for sure. We delve deeper into these metrics in the operations chapter.

Now we have discussed all policy capabilities and the impact they have on a VM (and associated objects), let's have a look at the component which surfaces up the capabilities to vCenter Server.

VASA Vendor Provider

As part of the vSAN cluster creation step, each ESXi host has a vSAN storage provider registered with vCenter. This uses the *vSphere APIs for Storage Awareness* (VASA) to surface the vSAN capabilities to vCenter Server. The capabilities can then be used to create VM storage policies for the VMs deployed on the vSAN datastore. If you are familiar with VASA and have used it with traditional storage environments, you'll find this functionality familiar; however, with traditional storage environments that leverage VASA, some configuration work needs to be done to add the storage provider for that storage. In the context of vSAN, a vSphere administrator does not need to worry about registering these; these are automatically registered when a vSAN cluster is created.

An Introduction to VASA

VASA enables storage vendors to publish the capabilities of their storage to vCenter Server, which in turn can display these capabilities in the vSphere Client. VASA may also provide information about storage health status, configuration info, capacity, thin provisioning info, and so on. VASA enables VMware to have an end-to-end story regarding storage. Traditionally, this enabled storage arrays to inform the VASA storage provider of capabilities. Then the storage provider informed vCenter Server to allow users to see storage array capabilities from the vSphere Client. Through VM storage policies, these storage capabilities are used in the vSphere Client to assist administrators in choosing the right storage in terms of space, performance, and *service level agreement* (SLA) requirements. This is true for both traditional storage arrays and vSAN.

With vSAN and vVols, the administrator defines the capabilities that they want to have for VM storage through a VM storage policy. This policy information is then pushed down to the storage layer, informing it of the requirements you have for storage. VASA will then inform the administrator whether the underlying storage (e.g., vSAN) can meet these requirements, effectively communicating compliance information on a per-storage object basis. VASA functionality is working in a bidirectional mode. Early versions of VASA for traditional storage arrays would only surface up capabilities. It not only surfaces up capabilities, but also verifies whether a VM's storage requirements are being met based on the contents of the policy.

Storage Providers

The next screenshot illustrates an example of what the storage provider section looks like. When a vSAN cluster is created, the VASA storage provider from every ESXi host in the cluster is registered to the vCenter server. In an environment where the vCenter server is managing multiple vSAN clusters (12 hosts in total), the VASA vSAN storage provider configuration would look like this. Note that there's a long list of IOFILTER Providers. These providers are needed for features like Storage IO Control and VM Encryption, or any of the 3rd party IO Filters you may have installed. IO Filters are essentially storage services that are decoupled from your storage system. They may provide storage agnostic replication services, or host local flash caching for instance.

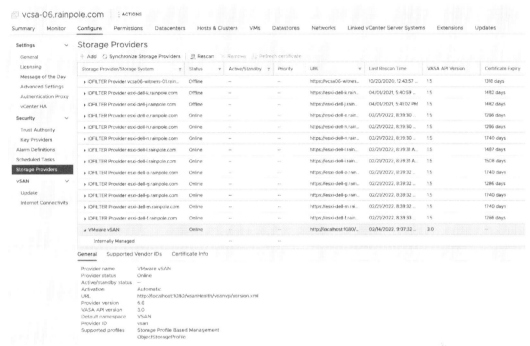

Figure 89: vSAN Storage Provider

You can always check the status of the storage providers by navigating in the vSphere Client to the vCenter Server inventory item, selecting the Configure tab, and then the Storage Providers view. The vSAN provider should always be online. Note that the vSAN storage provider is listed as "internally managed" and you will only see one listed. Internally managed means that all operational aspects are automatically handled by vSAN. In early versions of vSphere, you were able to view all hosts registered with the vSAN storage provider, but this is no longer the case.

vSAN Storage Providers: Highly Available

The vSAN storage provider is high availability. Should one ESXi host fail, another ESXi host in the cluster can take over the presentation of these vSAN capabilities. In other words, should the storage provider that is currently online go offline or fail for whatever reason (most likely because of a host failure), one of the standby providers on another ESXi host will be promoted to online.

There is very little work that a vSphere administrator needs to do with storage providers to create a vSAN cluster. This is simply for your own reference. However, if you do run into a situation where the vSAN capabilities are not surfacing up in the VM storage policies section, it is worth visiting this part of the configuration and verifying that the storage provider is online. If the storage provider is not online, you will not discover any vSAN capabilities when trying to build a VM storage policy. At this point, as a troubleshooting step, you could consider doing a resync of the storage providers by clicking on the Synchronize Storage Providers in the Storage Provider screen.

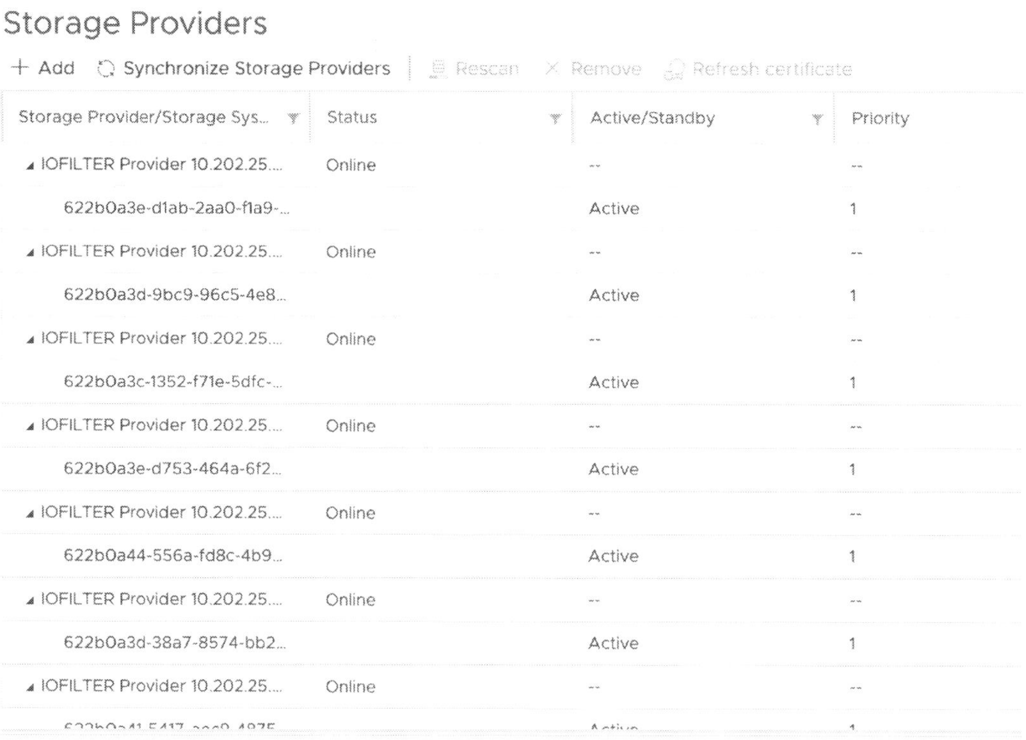

Figure 90: Synchronize storage provider

The VASA storage providers do not play any role in the data path for vSAN. If storage providers fail, this has no impact on VMs running on the vSAN datastore. The impact of not having a storage provider is a lack of visibility into the underlying capabilities, so you will not be able to create new storage policies. However, already running VMs and policies are unaffected.

Now that we have discussed both VASA and all vSAN policy capabilities, let's have a look at various examples of VMs provisioned with a specific capability enabled.

Assigning a VM Storage Policy During VM Provisioning

The assignment of a VM storage policy is done during the VM provisioning. At the point where the vSphere administrator must select a destination datastore, the appropriate policy is selected from the drop-down menu of available VM storage policies. The datastores are then separated into compatible and incompatible datastores, allowing the vSphere administrator to make the appropriate and correct choice for VM placement as shown in the screenshot below.

05 // VM Storage Policies and VM Provisioning

Figure 91: Incompatible datastore

In early versions of vSphere and vSAN, this matching of datastores did not necessarily mean that the datastore would meet the requirements in the VM storage policy. It was a little confusing because what it meant was that the datastore understood the set of requirements placed in the policy because they were vSAN requirements. But it did not mean that it could successfully provision the storage object on the vSAN datastore. Thus, it was difficult to know if a VM with a specific policy could be provisioned until you tried to provision it with the policy. Then it would either fail or succeed.

In the more recent versions of vSAN, the VM is now validated to check if it can be provisioned with the specified capabilities in the policy. In the screenshot above we have a policy with *failures to tolerate* set to 3 in a 3 node vSAN cluster. This is not possible, since we have already learned that such a configuration would require *2n + 1* hosts in the cluster, where n is the number of failures to tolerate. Thus, we would need 7 hosts in the vSAN cluster to achieve compliance with this policy. As shown, the vSAN cluster is not capable of matching those requirements, and as such, the datastore is listed as incompatible.

Virtual Machine Provisioning

You have previously learned about the various vSAN capabilities that you can add to a VM storage policy/ This policy can then be used by VMs deployed on a vSAN datastore. This section covers how to create the appropriate VM storage policy using these capabilities. It also discusses the layout of these VM storage objects as they are deployed on the vSAN datastore. Hopefully, this will give you a better understanding of the inner workings of vSAN.

159

Policy Setting: Failures to Tolerate = 1, RAID-1

Let's begin by creating a very simple VM storage policy. Then we can examine what will happen if a VM is deployed to a vSAN datastore using this policy. Let's create the first policy to have a single capability setting of number of *failures to tolerate* set to 1. We are going to use RAID-1 mirroring to implement failures to tolerate initially. Later, we shall look at RAID-5 and RAID-6 configurations for the VM objects which offer different protection mechanisms. But before we get to that, it is important to understand that this default policy *of failures to tolerate* = 1 means that any VMs deployed on the vSAN datastore with this policy will be configured with an additional mirror copy (replica) of the data. This means that if there is a single failure in the vSAN cluster, a full complement of the vSAN storage objects is still available. Let's see this in action, but before we do, let's visualize the expected results as shown in the next figure.

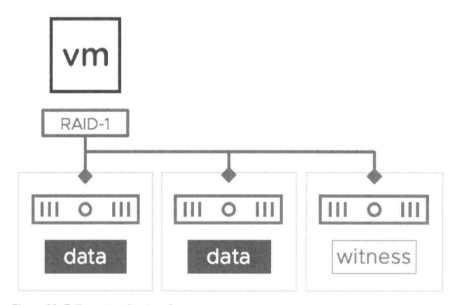

Figure 92: Failures to tolerate = 1

In this vSAN environment, there are several ESXi hosts. This is an all-flash configuration, where each ESXi host has a single disk group and a flash device for caching and multiple devices per disk group for capacity. The vSAN cluster has been enabled, vSAN networking has been configured and the ESXi hosts have formed a vSAN datastore. To this datastore, we will deploy a new VM.

We will keep this first VM storage policy simple, with just a single capability, *failures to tolerate* set to 1.

To begin, go to the Policies and Profiles section in the navigation bar on the left-hand side of the vSphere Client, and click the VM storage policies icon. Next click on CREATE. This will open the Create VM Storage Policy screen, as shown below. Make sure to provide the new policy with a proper name. In this scenario, we will name the policy **FTT=1 – RAID 1**.

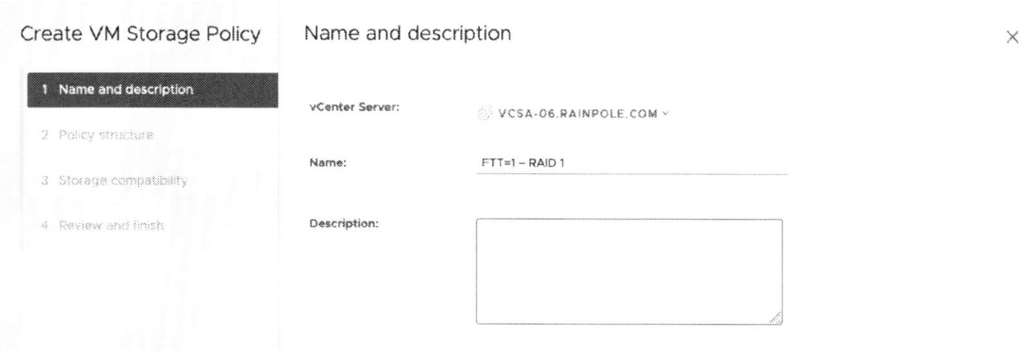

Figure 93: Create a new VM storage policy

The next screen displays information about the policy structure. This includes host-based services, vSAN rule sets, vSANDirect rule sets, and tag-based placement. The host-based services are I/O filters, in most environments limited to vSphere features called Storage I/O Control and VM Encryption. Note however that there are also 3rd party I/O filters, these can also be included in a policy. vSANDirect rules are like tag rules and are used to identify devices that are consumed by vSANDirect for the vSAN Data Persistence platform, which will be discussed in further detail when we discuss vSAN as a platform for modern applications. Tag-based placement rules are typically used in scenarios where VMs need to be deployed on datastores that are not represented by a storage provider or to differentiate between multiple datastores that offer the same capabilities, e.g., an HCI-Mesh environment, or when placement of VMs should be determined by specific categories that those VMs, or VM owners, belong to.

This was described on VMware's VirtualBlocks blog by Jason Massae as follows:

> "Many are familiar with SPBM policies when used with vSAN or VVols as they have some incredible features and functionalities. But another valuable SPBM use is with Tags and Categories. By using tags, we can create high-level generic policies or very custom and detailed policies. With tag based SPBM, you can create your own specific categories and tags based on almost anything you can envision. Performance levels or tiers, disk configurations, locations, OS type, departments, and disk types such as SAS, SATA or SSD are just a few examples. The categories and tags you can create are almost limitless!"

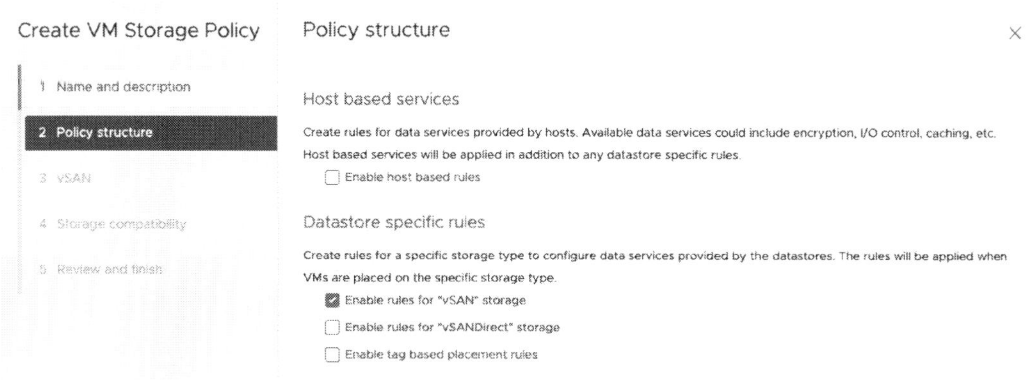

Figure 94: Enable rules for vSAN storage

On the next screen, we can begin to add requirements for vSAN. For our first policy, the capability that we want to configure is *Failures to tolerate*, and we will set this to *1 failure – RAID-1 (Mirroring)*, as shown below.

Figure 95: Failures to tolerate = 1 failure

Note that below the *Failures to tolerate* setting it now displays what the impact is on consumed storage space. It uses a 100 GB VM disk as an example, and as shown in the screenshot above, this policy setting results in 200 GB consumed. This of course is assuming that 100% of the capacity of the virtual disk is used, as vSAN disks are provision thin by default. This gives administrators a good idea of how much space will be consumed depending on the requirements placed in the policy.

Clicking Next moves the wizard onto the storage compatibility view, and at this point, all vSAN datastores managed by the vCenter server should be displayed as compatible, as below. This means that the contents of the VM storage policy (i.e., the capabilities) are understood and the requirements **can be met** by the vSAN datastore.

Figure 96: Storage compatibility

Similarly, if the INCOMPATIBLE view is selected, we should see datastores that are not compatible with the policy. In this example, NFS datastores and VMFS datastores are shown.

05 // VM Storage Policies and VM Provisioning

Figure 97: Storage incompatibility

Click Next and review your policy and click Finish to create it. Congratulations! You have created your first VM storage policy. We will now go ahead and deploy a new VM using this policy. The process for deploying a new VM is the same as before. The only difference is at the storage-selection step, here the created policy will need to be selected, as shown below. Any datastores available to the VM will be displayed, and their associated storage compatibility is also shown. In the example here, the vSAN datastore is shown as Compatible but the NFS v3 datastore is shown as Incompatible since it cannot implement the required VM storage policy. Selecting the vSAN datastore will populate the Compatibility check window with details about whether the checks were successful or not.

Figure 98: Select vSAN Storage Policy

Note that if no policy is selected the vSAN default storage policy will be applied. This policy is selected for all new VMs deployed on vSAN by default. The capabilities for the default policy are *failures to tolerate* set to 1 – RAID-1 and *number of disk stripes per object* set to 1.

Once the VM has been deployed, we can check the layout of the VM's objects. Navigate to the VM and then click Monitor > vSAN > Physical disk placement, as shown below. From here, we can see the layout of the VM's storage objects such as the VM home, VM Swap (if the virtual machine is powered on), and VM disk files (VMDKs).

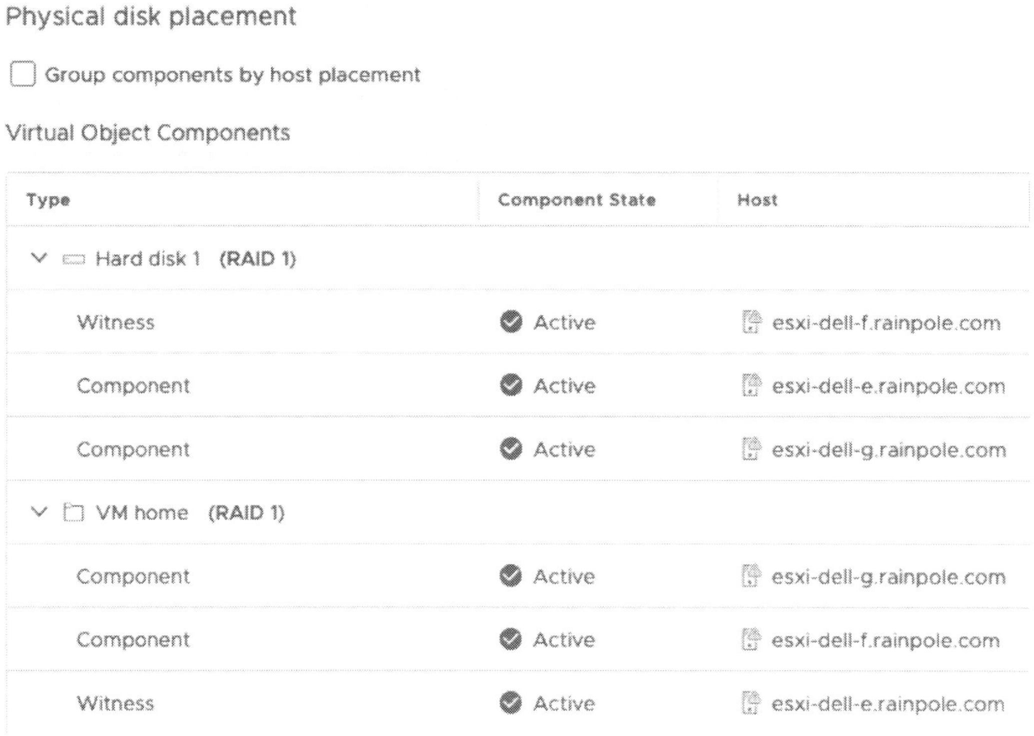

Physical disk placement

☐ Group components by host placement

Virtual Object Components

Type	Component State	Host
∨ 🖴 Hard disk 1 (RAID 1)		
Witness	✅ Active	🗎 esxi-dell-f.rainpole.com
Component	✅ Active	🗎 esxi-dell-e.rainpole.com
Component	✅ Active	🗎 esxi-dell-g.rainpole.com
∨ 🗂 VM home (RAID 1)		
Component	✅ Active	🗎 esxi-dell-g.rainpole.com
Component	✅ Active	🗎 esxi-dell-f.rainpole.com
Witness	✅ Active	🗎 esxi-dell-e.rainpole.com

Figure 99: Physical disk placement

As you can see, there is a RAID-1 (mirror) configuration around all components.

There are two components making up the RAID-1 mirrored storage object for Hard disk 1, one on the host esxi-dell-e and the other on the host esxi-dell-f. These are the mirror replicas of the data that make failure tolerance possible. There is also a witness component on the host esxi-dell-g. Remember that 50% of the components (votes) must be present for the VM object to remain available. In this example, if there was no witness and a host failed or became partitioned from the rest of the cluster, you could lose one component (50%). Even though you still had a valid replica available, more than 50% of the components (votes) would not be available. This is the reason for the witness disk; it determines who owns the object during a failure and provides a greater than 50% majority.

The witness itself is essentially a piece of metadata; it is about 16 MB in size, and so it doesn't consume a lot of space. As you create storage objects with more and more components, additional witnesses may get created. This is entirely dependent on the object configuration and how vSAN decides to place components.

Policy Setting: Failures to Tolerate = 1, Stripe Width = 2

Let's try another VM storage policy setting that adds another capability. In this case, we will use a cluster with more resources than the first example to facilitate the additional requirements. This time we will explicitly request *failures to tolerate* set to 1 and *number of disk stripes per object* set to 2. Let's build out that VM storage policy and deploy a VM with that policy and see how it affects the layout of the various VM storage objects. In this scenario, we expect a RAID-1 configuration mirrored by a RAID-0 stripe configuration, resulting in four disk components. There are two components in each RAID-0 stripe, which is in turn mirrored in a RAID-1 configuration. The below diagrams show what this may look like from a logical perspective.

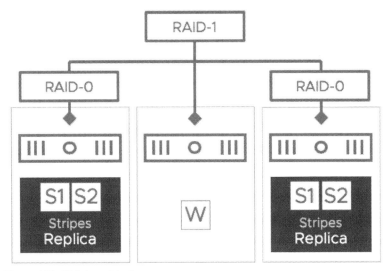

Figure 100: Striping objects

Now, let's create the VM storage policy and then provision a VM to see if the actual result matches the theory.

When creating the new policy, the steps are very similar to the first exercise, so we are not going to fully repeat this. To meet the necessary VM requirements, we select number of disk stripes per object and set this to 2. The number of disk stripes defined is a minimum number, so depending on the size of the virtual disk and the size of the capacity tier devices, a virtual disk might end up being striped across multiple disks or hosts.

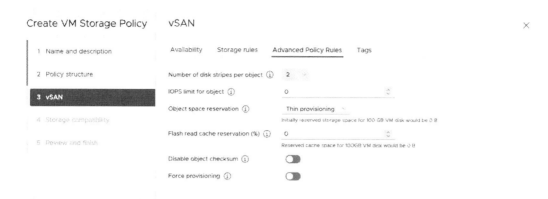

Figure 101: Number of disk stripes per object = 2

Now that we have created a new VM storage policy, let's provision a VM. During the VM provisioning process, we will select the appropriate VM Storage Policy. Again, the vSAN Datastore is displayed as being compatible with the policy as shown next.

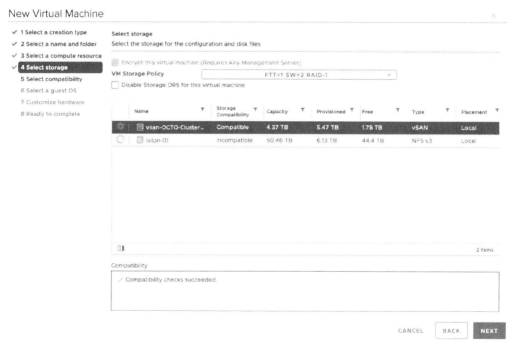

Figure 102: VM Storage Policy = 2

After we have deployed the VM, we will examine the physical disk layout again, as shown on the next page.

Physical disk placement

☐ Group components by host placement

Virtual Object Components

Type	Component State	Host	Fault Domain	Cache Disk
Hard disk 1 (RAID 1)				
RAID 0				
Component	Active	esxi-dell-g.rainpole.com		Local Pliant Disk (naa.5001e82002675164)
Component	Active	esxi-dell-g.rainpole.com		Local Pliant Disk (naa.5001e82002675164)
RAID 0				
Component	Active	esxi-dell-e.rainpole.com		Local Pliant Disk (naa.5001e82002641 5f0)
Component	Active	esxi-dell-e.rainpole.com		Local Pliant Disk (naa.5001e820026415f0)
Witness	Active	esxi-dell-f.rainpole.com		Local Pliant Disk (naa.5001e82002664b00)
VM home (RAID 1)				
Witness	Active	esxi-dell-f.rainpole.com		Local Pliant Disk (naa.5001e82002664b00)
Component	Active	esxi-dell-g.rainpole.com		Local Pliant Disk (naa.5001e82002675164)
Component	Active	esxi-dell-e.rainpole.com		Local Pliant Disk (naa.5001e820026415f0)
Virtual machine swap object (RAID 1)				
Component	Active	esxi-dell-g.rainpole.com		Local Pliant Disk (naa.5001e82002675164)
Component	Active	esxi-dell-e.rainpole.com		Local Pliant Disk (naa.5001e820026415f0)
Witness	Active	esxi-dell-f.rainpole.com		Local Pliant Disk (naa.5001e82002664b00)

Figure 103: Physical disk placement for SW = 2

As you can see in the screenshot above, a RAID-1 configuration has been created for Hard disk 1, adhering to the number of failures to tolerate requirement specified in the VM storage policy. However, now you see that additionally each replica is made up of a RAID-0 stripe configuration, and each stripe contains two components, adhering to the number of disk stripes per object requirement of 2.

In this example, we also have a witness component for the virtual disk object. It is important to point out that the number of witness components, if any, is directly related to how the components are distributed across the hosts and disks in the cluster. Depending on the size of the vSAN cluster, several witness components might have been necessary to ensure that greater than 50% of the components of this VM's objects remained available in the event of a failure, especially a host failure. In this case, the vote count would determine the winner in the case of a partition. The vote count is not visible in the UI unfortunately, but it can be examined using the command-line tool RVC, and the Ruby vSphere Console (RVC) command `vsan.vm_object_info`. Below you can see a condensed version of this output which will give you an idea of how votes work. We will learn more about RVC in chapter 10.

```
DOM Object: c133bf5b-c8ae-df22-c11e-02003a542fc6
      RAID_1
        RAID_0
          Component: c133bf5b-8457-8023-aa44-02003a542fc6
          host: esxi-dell-g.rainpole.com
             votes: 2, usage: 0.0 GB, proxy component: false)
          Component: c133bf5b-b8d3-8123-c51a-02003a542fc6
          host: esxi-dell-g.rainpole.com
             votes: 1, usage: 0.0 GB, proxy component: false)
        RAID_0
```

```
        Component: c133bf5b-d86a-8223-86a6-02003a542fc6
          host: esxi-dell-e.rainpole.com
             votes: 1, usage: 0.0 GB, proxy component: false)
        Component: c133bf5b-60f4-8223-14d5-02003a542fc6
          host: esxi-dell-e.rainpole.com
             votes: 1, usage: 0.0 GB, proxy component: false)
    Witness: 1ec22962-a6cd-242a-cc31-246e962f4854
          host: esxi-dell-f.rainpole.com
             votes: 2, usage: 0.0 GB, proxy component: false)
```

As shown above, this RAID-1 configuration has two RAID-0 configurations underneath. Each component of the RAID-0 configuration has 1 vote, except for one component, which has 2 votes. This is to ensure that when a host is isolated it can't achieve majority by itself.

An interesting point to note is that the VM home namespace and the swap, as shown in the screenshot above, do not implement the *number of disk stripes per object* requirement. The VM home namespace and the VM swap only implement the *failures to tolerate* requirement, as highlighted earlier in the book.

Policy Setting: Failures to Tolerate = 2, Stripe Width = 2

In this next example, we create another VM storage policy that has the *number of disk stripes per object* set to 2 but this time we also set *failures to tolerate* to 2. This implies that any VM deployed with this policy on the vSAN cluster should be able to tolerate up to two different failures, be it host, network, or disk failures. Considering the "two-host failure" capability specified and the number of disk stripes of 2, the expected disk layout is as shown in the diagram below.

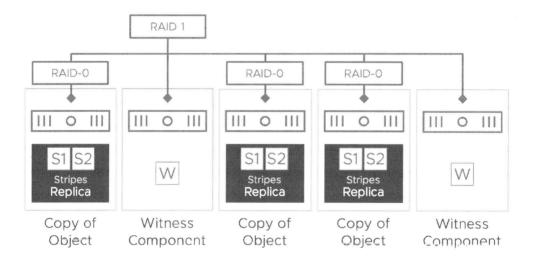

Figure 104: Logical placement FTT = 2 and SW = 2

There are a few considerations with regard to this configuration. Because we are continuing with a RAID-1 mirroring configuration to tolerate failures, there need to be $n+1$ copies of the data and $2n+1$ hosts in the cluster to tolerate n failures. Therefore, to tolerate two failures, there will be three copies of the data, and there must be a minimum of five hosts in the cluster to also store the witness components.

A new cluster is used to test this scenario. After we have provisioned a VM, the physical disk placement can be examined to see how the VM storage objects have been laid out across hosts and disks.

Virtual Object Components

Type	Component State	Host	Fault Domain
∨ Virtual Machine SWAP Object (RAID 1)			
Witness	Active	10.192.235.142	
Component	Active	10.192.253.35	
Component	Active	10.192.230.229	
Component	Active	10.192.248.44	
Witness	Active	10.192.233.122	
∨ Hard disk 1 (RAID 1)			
∨ RAID 0			
Component	Active	10.192.235.142	
Component	Active	10.192.235.142	
∨ RAID 0			
Component	Active	10.192.230.229	
Component	Active	10.192.230.229	
∨ RAID 0			
Component	Active	10.192.233.122	
Component	Active	10.192.233.122	
Witness	Active	10.192.225.212	
Witness	Active	10.192.241.169	
∨ VM Home (RAID 1)			
Witness	Active	10.192.253.35	
Component	Active	10.192.248.44	
Component	Active	10.192.233.122	
Component	Active	10.192.235.142	
Witness	Active	10.192.230.229	

Figure 105: Physical placement FTT = 2 and SW = 2

Looking at the physical placement of the VM provisioned with the FTT = 2 and SW = 2 we can conclude that the placement of components becomes rather complex when both the SW and FTT values are increased to 2.

We see that for the virtual disk of this VM, vSAN has implemented three RAID-0 stripe configurations. For RAID-0 stripe configurations, all components in at least one of the RAID-0 stripe configurations must remain intact. That is why a third RAID-0 stripe configuration has been created. You might assume that if the first component in the first RAID-0 stripe configuration was lost, and the second component of the second RAID-0 stripe configuration was lost, vSAN might be able to use the remaining components, one from each stripe, to keep the storage object intact. This is not the case. Therefore, to tolerate two failures in the cluster, a third RAID-0 stripe configuration is necessary because two failures might take out the other two RAID-0 stripe configurations. This is also why all these RAID-0 configurations are mirrored in a RAID-1 configuration. The bottom line with this policy setting is that any two hosts are allowed to fail in the cluster, and vSAN will guarantee that the VM's data remains accessible due to the way the object has been distributed around the cluster. Also, note that the components are stored on five different ESXi hosts in this nine-node vSAN cluster.

Next, let's examine the VM home namespace and VM swap. As we have mentioned before, these objects do not implement the *number of disk stripes per object policy* setting but do implement the *failures to tolerate*. As demonstrated. there is no RAID-0 configuration on these objects, but we can see that there are now three replicas in the RAID-1 mirror configuration to meet the *failures to tolerate* set to 2 in the VM storage policy. What can also be observed here is an increase in the number of witness disks. Not to labor the point, but once again keep in mind that greater than 50% of the components of the VM home namespace object (or 50% of the votes depending on the quorum mechanism used) must be available for this object to remain online. Therefore, if two replicas were lost, there would still be one replica (i.e., a copy of the VM home namespace data) available and two witness components; therefore, greater than 50% of the components would still be available if two failures took out two replicas of the VM home namespace object or swap object.

Policy Setting: RAID-5

Let us now look at a policy where we leverage erasure coding, more commonly referred to as RAID-5 or RAID-6. The big advantage of leveraging erasure coding over mirroring is that it requires less disk capacity to protect against a single failure (FTT=1). For a 100 GB VMDK, this only consumes 133.33 GB, which is 33% above the actual size of the VMDK. The additional 33.33 GB is used for parity. Previously when we created a policy to protect against a single failure using RAID-1, because of the mirror copies, an additional 100% of capacity was consumed. In the event of a data component failure in a RAID-5 configuration, a single component's data can be reconstructed using the remaining 2 data components along with the parity component.

When an Erasure Coding policy is created, administrators need to be aware that these are only available on All-flash vSAN configurations. When failures to tolerate is set to wither RAID-5 or RAID-6 Erasure Coding, a warning is displayed to highlight this requirement.

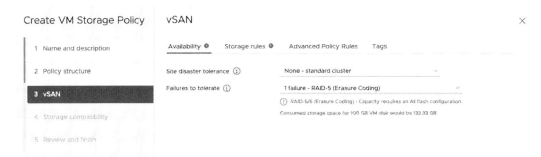

Figure 106: Erasure Coding warning in Availability

Note that a warning has also been added to Storage rules. If we examine the Storage rules, we can see why.

Figure 107: Erasure Coding warning in Storage rules

The warning is against the storage tier. This, if you recall, is a section primarily used for HCI-Mesh. Since we can remotely mount vSAN datastores to this vSphere cluster, which are both hybrid and All-flash, this setting will prevent a RAID-5 policy from showing remote vSAN datastore as compatible, if they are not an All-flash vSAN configuration. Thus, even if you do not plan to use HCI-Mesh, set the Storage tier to All-flash for Erasure Coding policies. This will toggle the warning message.

After creating the RAID-5 FTT=1 policy, deploy a VM with it. The physical disk placement can be examined as before, and we should now observe a RAID-5 layout across four disks and four hosts. The below screenshot shows the physical disk placement view, and as described, we see a RAID-5 configuration for the objects, each having 4 components. This is a so-called 3+1 configuration, meaning 3 data and 1 parity segment.

VMware vSAN Deep Dive

Physical disk placement

☐ Group components by host placement

Virtual Object Components

Type	Component State	Host	Fault Domain	Cache Disk
∨ ⌐ Hard disk 1 (RAID 5)				
Component	✓ Active	esxi-dell-o.rainpole.com		Local ATA Disk (t10.ATA_____Micron_P420m2DMTFDGAR1T4MAX_____
Component	✓ Active	esxi-dell-n.rainpole.com		Local ATA Disk (t10.ATA_____Micron_P420m2DMTFDGAR1T4MAX_____
Component	✓ Active	esxi-dell-p.rainpole.com		Local ATA Disk (t10.ATA_____Micron_P420m2DMTFDGAR1T4MAX_____
Component	✓ Active	esxi-dell-m.rainpole.com		Local ATA Disk (t10.ATA_____Micron_P420m2DMTFDGAR1T4MAX_____
∨ ⌐ VM home (RAID 5)				
Component	✓ Active	esxi-dell-o.rainpole.com		Local ATA Disk (t10.ATA_____Micron_P420m2DMTFDGAR1T4MAX_____
Component	✓ Active	esxi-dell-n.rainpole.com		Local ATA Disk (t10.ATA_____Micron_P420m2DMTFDGAR1T4MAX_____
Component	✓ Active	esxi-dell-m.rainpole.com		Local ATA Disk (t10.ATA_____Micron_P420m2DMTFDGAR1T4MAX_____
Component	✓ Active	esxi-dell-p.rainpole.com		Local ATA Disk (t10.ATA_____Micron_P420m2DMTFDGAR1T4MAX_____
∨ Virtual machine swap object (RAID 5)				
Component	✓ Active	esxi-dell-n.rainpole.com		Local ATA Disk (t10.ATA_____Micron_P420m2DMTFDGAR1T4MAX_____
Component	✓ Active	esxi-dell-m.rainpole.com		Local ATA Disk (t10.ATA_____Micron_P420m2DMTFDGAR1T4MAX_____
Component	✓ Active	esxi-dell-p.rainpole.com		Local ATA Disk (t10.ATA_____Micron_P420m2DMTFDGAR1T4MAX_____
Component	✓ Active	esxi-dell-o.rainpole.com		Local ATA Disk (t10.ATA_____Micron_P420m2DMTFDGAR1T4MAX_____

Figure 108: Physical placement RAID-5

Note that the VM home namespace and VM Swap objects also inherit the RAID-5 configuration.

Policy Setting: RAID-6

Besides RAID-5, the option to tolerate two failures in a capacity-efficient manner is also available via erasure coding and is called RAID-6. To configure a RAID-6 object, select *2 failures – RAID-6* for the *Failures to tolerate* policy setting. Note the storage consumption model. For a 100 GB VMDK, this only consumes 150 GB, which is 50% above the actual size of the VMDK. The additional 50 GB is used by the two parity blocks of the RAID-6 object, 25GB each in the 100 GB VMDK example. Previously when we created a policy for RAID-1 objects with failures to tolerate set to 2, because of the mirror copies, an additional 200% of capacity was consumed. This means that a 100 GB VMDK required 300 GB of disk capacity at the backend. RAID-6 consumes half that amount of capacity to provide the same level of availability.

Virtual Object Components

Type	Component State	Host	Fault Domain
∨ VM Home (RAID 6)			
Component	Active	10.192.248.44	
Component	Active	10.192.244.132	
Component	Active	10.192.235.142	
Component	Active	10.192.229.172	
Component	Active	10.192.253.35	
Component	Active	10.192.225.212	
∨ Hard disk 1 (RAID 6)			
Component	Active	10.192.225.212	
Component	Active	10.192.235.142	
Component	Active	10.192.253.35	
Component	Active	10.192.248.44	
Component	Active	10.192.244.132	
Component	Active	10.192.229.172	
∨ Virtual Machine SWAP Object (RAID 6)			
Component	Active	10.192.248.44	
Component	Active	10.192.235.142	
Component	Active	10.192.253.35	
Component	Active	10.192.229.172	
Component	Active	10.192.225.212	
Component	Active	10.192.244.132	

Figure 109: Physical placement RAID-6

When a VM is deployed with this policy, the physical disk placement can be examined as before, and as demonstrated in the screenshot above, a RAID-6 layout is observed across six disks and six hosts. Note that again the VM Swap and VM home namespace objects also inherit the RAID-6 configuration.

Policy Setting: RAID-5/6 and Stripe Width

Prior to vSAN 7.0U1, it was possible to use RAID-5/6 with the use of a stripe width in the policy. Each part of a RAID-5/6 object was striped with the number of stripe width components in a RAID-0 configuration. In this example, a VM was deployed on a vSAN 6.7U1 vSAN with a RAID-6 configuration as per the previous example, but the policy included 2 disk stripes per object. This led to the following object configuration in the physical disk placement view.

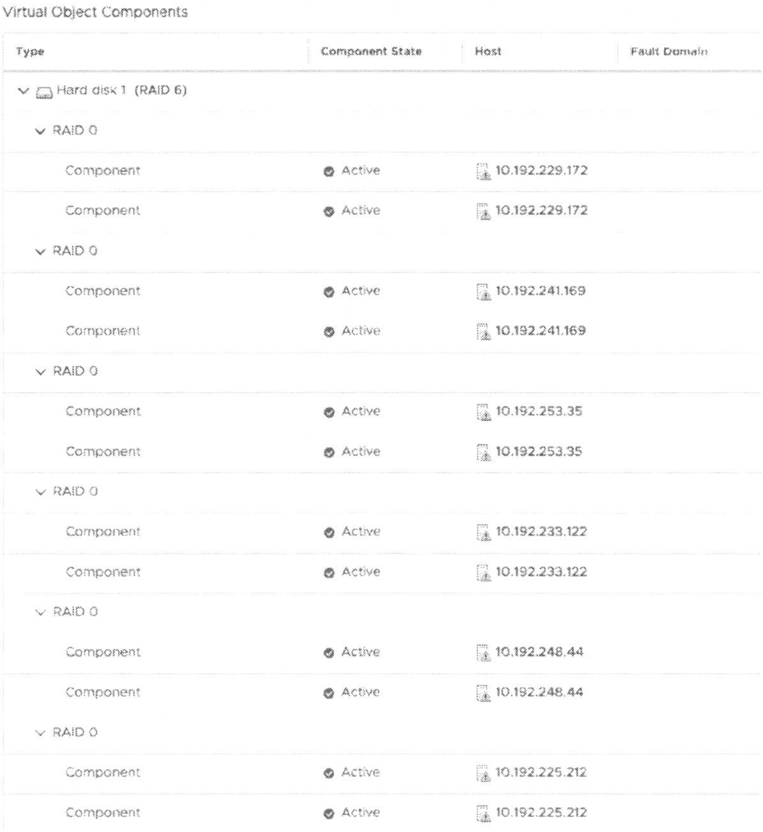

Virtual Object Components

Type	Component State	Host	Fault Domain
∨ Hard disk 1 (RAID 6)			
∨ RAID 0			
Component	● Active	10.192.229.172	
Component	● Active	10.192.229.172	
∨ RAID 0			
Component	● Active	10.192.241.169	
Component	● Active	10.192.241.169	
∨ RAID 0			
Component	● Active	10.192.253.35	
Component	● Active	10.192.253.35	
∨ RAID 0			
Component	● Active	10.192.233.122	
Component	● Active	10.192.233.122	
∨ RAID 0			
Component	● Active	10.192.248.44	
Component	● Active	10.192.248.44	
∨ RAID 0			
Component	● Active	10.192.225.212	
Component	● Active	10.192.225.212	

Figure 110: Physical placement RAID-6 – SW = 2

The VM home namespace and the VM Swap objects do not implement the stripe width, so they continue to have a RAID-6 configuration without any striping as per the previous example. Note that this configuration requires a minimum of 6 hosts in the vSAN cluster.

Virtual Object Components

Type	Component State	Host	Fault Domain
> Hard disk 1 (RAID 6)			
∨ VM Home (RAID 6)			
Component	Active	10.192.225.212	
Component	Active	10.192.229.172	
Component	Active	10.192.233.122	
Component	Active	10.192.241.169	
Component	Active	10.192.253.35	
Component	Active	10.192.248.44	
∨ Virtual Machine SWAP Object (RAID 6)			
Component	Active	10.192.241.169	
Component	Active	10.192.248.44	
Component	Active	10.192.229.172	
Component	Active	10.192.253.35	
Component	Active	10.192.233.122	
Component	Active	10.192.225.212	

Figure 111: Physical placement RAID-6 – SW = 2 for VM Swap and Home

Although in the above example we showed how this works with a RAID-6 configuration, the same principles apply to a RAID-5 configuration prior to the release of vSAN 7.0U1. However, the configuration of erasure coding policies with stripe width changed considerably in vSAN 7.0U1. This has already been mentioned earlier in this chapter, but it is worth repeating here again. To handle large objects whilst reducing the number of components, vSAN will now treat the component count of an erasure coding segment toward the stripe width. For example, a RAID-5 object will have an effective stripe width of 4, while a RAID-6 object is considered to have an effective stripe width of 6. Therefore, the value of Stripe Width must be increased in multiples of 4 or 6 respectively to achieve an additional stripe for that given component.

Default Policy

As mentioned earlier, vSAN has a default policy. This means that if no policy is chosen for a VM deployed on the vSAN datastore, a default policy that is automatically associated with the vSAN datastore is used.

The default policy contains the following capabilities:

- Number of failures to tolerate = 1
- Number of disk stripes per object = 1
- Flash read cache reservation = 0%
- Object space reservation = Thin Provisioning
- Force provisioning = disabled

- Checksum = enabled
- IOPS Limit = 0 (unlimited)

Note that this default policy for the vSAN datastore, called the vSAN default storage policy, can be edited. If you wish to change the default policy, you can simply edit the capability values of the policy from the vSphere Client by selecting the policy and clicking Edit Settings.

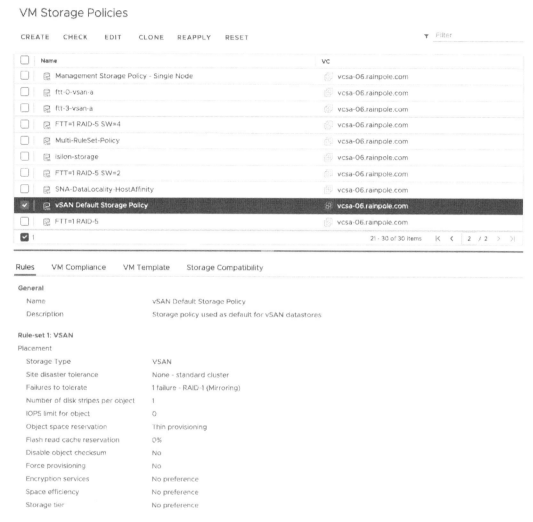

Figure 112: Default vSAN policy

An alternative to editing the default policy is to create a new policy with the desired capabilities and associate this new policy with the vSAN datastore. This would be the preferred way of changing the default policy inherited by VMs that are deployed on the vSAN datastore.

If you are managing multiple vSAN deployments with a single vCenter server, different default policies can be associated with different vSAN datastores. Therefore, if you have a "test-and-dev" cluster and a "production" cluster, there can be different default policies associated with the different vSAN datastores. To change the default policy of the vSAN datastore you need to go to the Storage view in the vSphere Client and select the vSAN datastore then click Configure > General followed by clicking Edit on Default Storage Policy. Now you can simply associate a different policy with the datastore you selected as demonstrated in the screenshot below.

Figure 113: Change default vSAN policy

Witnesses and Replicas: Failure Scenarios

Failure scenarios are often a hot topic of discussion when it comes to vSAN. What should one configure, and how do we expect vSAN to respond? This section runs through some simple scenarios to demonstrate what you can expect of vSAN in certain situations.

The following examples use a four-host vSAN cluster and use a RAID-1 mirroring configuration. We will examine various *failures to tolerate* and *stripe width* settings and discuss the behavior in the event of a host failure. You should understand that the examples shown here are for illustrative purposes only. These are simply to explain some of the decisions that vSAN *might* make when it comes to object placement. vSAN may choose any configuration if it satisfies the customer requirements (i.e., failures to tolerate and stripe width). For example, with higher numbers of failures to tolerate and stripe width, vSAN could make placement decisions that may use more, less, or even no witnesses or more, or less, hosts than shown in the examples that follow.

Example 1: Failures to Tolerate = 1, Stripe Width = 1

In this first example, the stripe width is set to 1. Therefore, there is no striping per se, simply a single instance of the object. However, the requirements are that we must tolerate a single disk or host failure, so we must instantiate a replica (a RAID-1 mirror of the component). However, a witness is also required in this configuration to avoid a split-brain situation. A split-brain could be when ESXi-02 and ESXi-04 continue to operate, but no longer communicate with each another. Whichever of the hosts can communicate with the witness is the host that has a valid copy of the data in that scenario. Data placement in these configurations may look like the one displayed in the diagram below.

Figure 114: FTT = 1 – RAID-1

The data remains accessible in the event of a host or disk failure. If ESXi-02 has a failure, ESXi-03 and ESXi-04 continue to provide access to the data as a quorum continues to exist. However, if ESXi-02 and ESXi-03 both suffer failures, there is no longer a quorum, so data becomes inaccessible. Note that in this scenario the VM is running (from a compute perspective) on ESXi-01, while the components of the objects are stored on ESXi-02, 03, and 04. The VM can run on any host in the cluster, and vSphere DRS is free to migrate it anywhere when deemed necessary.

Example 2: Failures to Tolerate = 1 and Stripe Width = 2

Turning to another example, this time the stripe width is increased to 2. This means that each component must be striped across two devices at a minimum. However, vSAN may decide to stripe across capacity devices on the same host or across capacity devices on different hosts. The diagram below shows one possible distribution of storage objects.

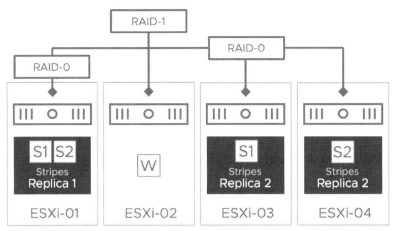

Figure 115: FTT = 1 – SW = 2

As you can see, vSAN in this example has chosen to keep the components for the first stripe (RAID-0) on ESXi-01 but has placed the components for the second stripe across ESXi-03 and ESXi-04. Once again, with failures to tolerate set to 1, we mirror using RAID-1. In this configuration, a witness is also used. Why might a witness be required in this example? Consider the case where ESXi-01 has a failure. This has an impact on both components on ESXi-01. Now we have two components that failed and two components still working on ESXi-02 and ESXi-03. In this case, we still require a witness to attain quorum. Note that this may not always be the case. In some situations, assigning votes to components may negate the need for a witness as discussed previously.

Note that if one component in each of the RAID-0 configurations fails, the data would be inaccessible because both sides of the RAID-1 are impacted. Therefore, a disk failure in ESXi-01 used by one of the stripes and a disk failure in ESXi-02 used by another of the stripes will make the VM inaccessible until the disk faults are rectified. Because a witness contains no data, it cannot help in these situations. Note that this is more than one failure, however, and our policy is set to tolerate only one failure.

Example 3: Failures to Tolerate = 1 and RAID-5

In this last example, the failures to tolerate is set to 1, and RAID-5 is used instead of mirroring. In this example the minimum number of hosts needed is 4, compared to 3 with mirroring.

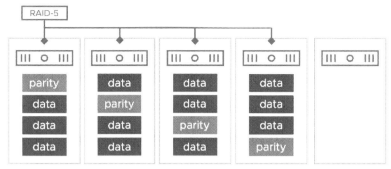

Figure 116: FTT = 1 – RAID-5

One thing to point out is that when it is desired to have the ability to resync data after a failure, an additional host will need to be part of the cluster. For a RAID-5 configured object, this means that the number of hosts required is 5 if you want to be able to repair data after a host failure has occurred. When a single host fails in the example above, the VM will be able to access its disk. And by leveraging parity blocks, vSAN will be able to reconstruct the missing data.

Changing VM Storage Policy On-the-Fly

Being able to change a VM storage policy on-the-fly is a useful aspect of vSAN. This example explains the concept of how a VM storage policy can be changed on-the-fly, and how it changes the layout of a VM without impacting the application or the guest operating system running in the VM.

Consider the following scenario, briefly mentioned earlier in the context of stripe width. A vSphere administrator has deployed a VM on a hybrid vSAN cluster with the default VM storage policy, which is that the VM storage objects should have no disk striping and should tolerate one failure. The layout of the VM disk file would look as follows.

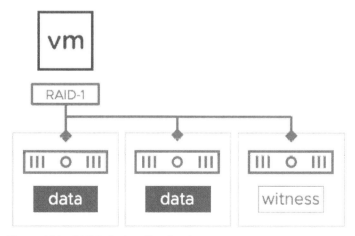

Figure 117: vSAN Default policy data layout

The VM and its associated applications initially appeared to perform satisfactorily with a 100% cache hit rate; however, over time, an increasing number of VMs were added to the hybrid vSAN cluster. The vSphere administrator starts to notice that the VM deployed on vSAN is getting a 90% read cache hit rate. This implies that 10% of reads need to be serviced from magnetic disk/capacity tier. At peak time, this VM is doing 2,000 read operations per second. Therefore, there are 200 reads that need to be serviced from magnetic disk (the 10% of reads that are cache misses). The specifications on the magnetic disks imply that each disk can do 150 IOPS, meaning that a single disk cannot service these additional 200 IOPS. To meet the I/O requirements of the VM, the vSphere administrator correctly decides to create a RAID-0 stripe across two disks.

On vSAN, the vSphere administrator has two options to address this. The first option is to simply modify the VM storage policy currently associated with the VM and add a stripe width requirement to the policy; however, this would change the storage layout of all the other VMs using this same policy. Not just for a single cluster, but potentially for all clusters being managed by the same vCenter server and running VMs using the same policy. This is because policies are defined on a vCenter Server level. This change could lead to a huge amount of rebuild traffic and is not our recommended approach.

We recommend creating a brand-new policy that is identical to the previous policy but has an additional capability for stripe width. This new policy can then be attached to only the VM (and of course its VMDKs) suffering from cache misses. Once the new policy is associated with the VM, vSAN takes care of changing the underlying VM storage layout required to meet the new policy, *while the VM is still running* without the loss of any failure protection. It does this by mirroring the new storage objects with the additional components (in this case additional RAID-0 stripe width) to the original storage objects.

When the new policy is created, it can be associated with the VM and the storage objects in a number of places in the vSphere Client. In fact, policies can be changed at the granularity of individual VM disk objects (e.g., VMDK) if necessary.

After making the change the new components reflecting the new configuration (e.g., a RAID-0 stripe) will enter a state of reconfiguring. This will temporarily build out additional replicas or components, in addition to keeping the original replicas/components, so additional space will be needed on the vSAN datastore to accommodate this on-the-fly change. When the new replicas or components are ready and the configuration is completed, the original replicas/components are discarded.

> **One should keep in mind that making a change like this could lead to rebuilds and generate resync traffic on the vSAN network. For that reason, policy changes should be considered a maintenance task and kept to a minimum during production hours.**

Note that not all policy changes require the creation of new replicas or components. For example, adding an IOPS limit, or reducing the number of failures to tolerate, or reducing space reservation does not require this. However, in many cases, policy changes will trigger the creation of new replicas or components or potentially even trigger a full rebuild of the object. (Table 7 describes which policy setting triggers a rebuild.) Therefore, caution should be used when changing storage policies on the fly, especially if the change may impact many virtual machines. Significant improvements have been made over the years to ensure that rebuild network traffic does not negatively impact VM network traffic, but our advice is to treat large policy changes as a maintenance task, and to implement those changes out of normal production hours.

Your VM storage objects may now reflect the changes in the vSphere Client, for example, a RAID-0 stripe as well as a RAID-1 replica configuration, as shown below.

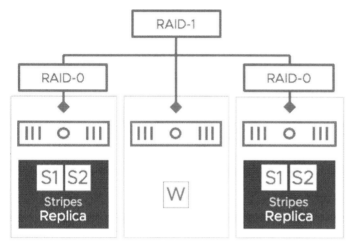

Figure 118: vSAN data layout after change of policy

Compare this to the tasks you may have to perform on many traditional storage arrays to achieve this. It would involve, at the very least, the following:

- The migration of VMs from the original datastore.
- The decommissioning of said LUN/volume.
- The creation of a new LUN with the new storage requirements (different RAID level).
- Possibly the reformatting of the LUN with VMFS in the case of block storage.
- Finally, you must migrate your VMs back to the new datastore.

In the case of vSAN, after the new storage replicas or components have been created and synchronized, the older storage replicas and/or components will be automatically removed. Note that vSAN is capable of striping across disks, disk groups, and hosts when required, as mentioned before. It should also be noted that vSAN can create the new replicas or components without the need to move any data between hosts; in many cases, the new components can be instantiated on the same storage on the same host.

We have not shown that there are, of course, additional witness components that could be created with such a change to the configuration. For a VM to continue to access all its components, a full replica copy of the data must be available and more than 50% of the components (votes) of that object must also be available in the cluster. Therefore, changes to the VM storage policy could result in additional witness components being created, or indeed, in the case of introducing a policy with fewer requirements, there could be fewer witnesses.

You can see the configuration changes taking place in the vSphere UI during this process. Select the vSAN cluster object in the vCenter inventory, then select monitor, vSAN, and finally "resyncing components" in the menu. This will display all components that are currently resyncing/rebuilding. The screenshot below shows the resyncing dashboard view with a resync in progress for a VM where we manually changed the policy from RAID-6 to RAID-1 with SW = 2.

Figure 119: Resync/rebuild activity

The big question which then remains is when exactly is a full rebuild needed when changing a policy and when will vSAN simply create extra components? As you can imagine, a full rebuild of many virtual machines can have an impact on required storage capacity, and potentially also on performance. The following table outlines when a full rebuild is required and when it is not required.

POLICY CHANGE	REBUILD REQUIRED?	COMMENTS
Increasing/decreasing FTT without changing RAID type	No	
Changing the RAID type used	Yes	Also applies when going from RAID-5 to RAID-6 or back.
Increasing/decreasing stripe width	Yes	
Changing object space reservation	Yes	Note, only when changing from 0 to non-zero, or non-zero to 0 is a rebuild required!
Changing read cache reservation	Yes	Applies to hybrid only
Enabling/disabling checksum	No	

Table 7: Impact of policy changes

Summary

This completes the coverage of VM storage policy creation and VM deployments on the vSAN datastore. What you will have noticed is that there are a few behaviors with VM storage policies that might not be intuitive, such as the default policy settings, the fact that failures to tolerate set to 1 is implicitly included in a policy, and that some virtual storage objects implement only some of the policy settings. We are hoping though that this chapter provided you with sufficient confidence to create, apply and edit VM storage policies.

06

vSAN Operations

This chapter covers the common procedures and tasks when monitoring and maintaining a vSAN deployment. It also provides some generic workflows and examples related to day-to-day management often referred to as day-2 management. Management, monitoring, and maintenance of vSAN have changed considerably since the initial version. This chapter will look at how operations have changed with the evolution of vSAN.

Skyline Health

We will begin this chapter with a look at what has become the most valuable tool in an administrator's arsenal when it comes to monitoring vSAN. This is of course Skyline Health, formerly known as vSAN health check. Skyline health is embedded into both vCenter Server and ESXi and is automatically available without any administrative actions required. The vSAN health check immediately provides a complete overview of the current health of a vSAN cluster.

Skyline Health Tests

Possibly the most useful aspect of the health check is the sheer number of tests that it performs on all aspects of the vSAN cluster. Among the range of tests are checks to ensure that all the hardware devices are on the *VMware Compatibility Guide* (VCG) as well as supportability and version checks on the storage controller's driver and firmware versions. It verifies that the network is functioning correctly between all the ESXi hosts that are participating in the vSAN cluster, that the cluster is formed properly, and that the storage devices do not have any errors. This is invaluable when it comes to troubleshooting vSAN issues and can quickly lead administrators to the root cause of an issue. Administrators should always refer to the Skyline health tests to ensure that vSAN is completely healthy before embarking on any management, lifecycle, or maintenance tasks. The next figure, shows a sample of some of the health checks taken from a 7.0U3 vSAN cluster. Enhancements are being added to the health check with each release, so expect a different list of health checks depending on the vSAN version. There are also additional health checks for different use cases and features, such as vSAN stretched cluster, HCI Mesh, etc.

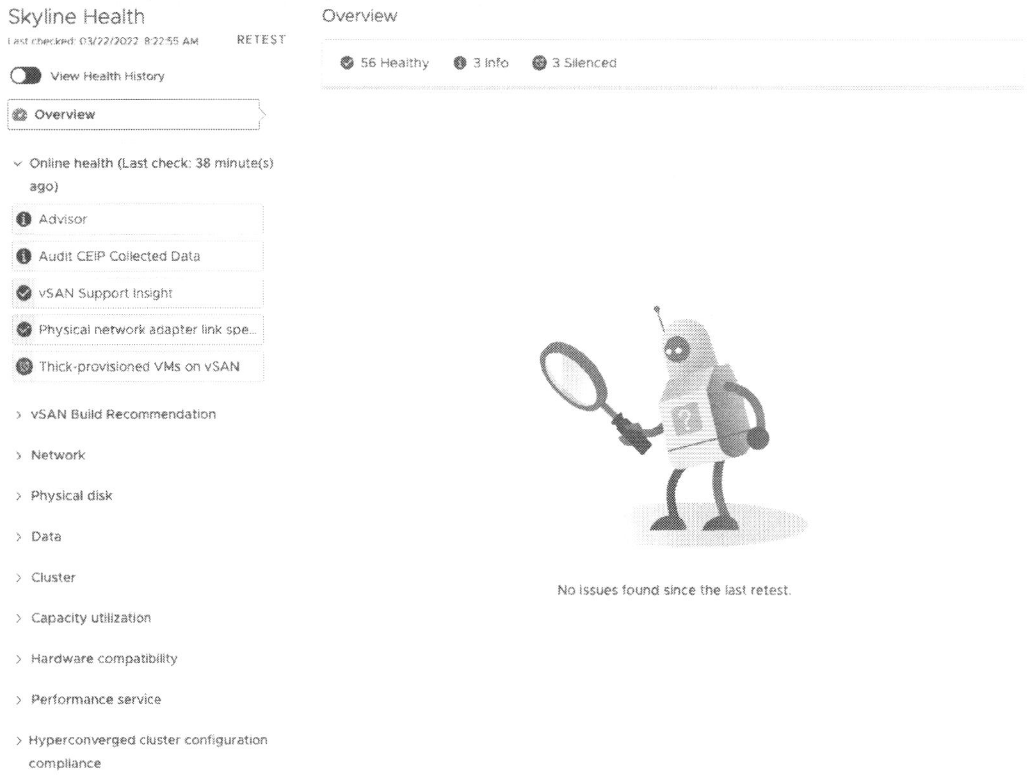

Figure 120: Skyline Health check tests listing

Skyline health for vSAN also includes an alerting/alarm mechanism. This means that if a test fails in the health check, an alarm in vSphere is raised to bring it to the administrator's attention. The other nice feature of the health check tests is that, through the *AskVMware* mechanism, all tests are linked to a VMware knowledgebase article which provides details about the nature of the test, what it means when it fails, what may have caused the error and how you can remediate the situation. To run the health check tests, first, select the vSAN cluster object in the vCenter inventory, then select Monitoring, and then select vSAN followed by Skyline Health. The tests can be re-run at any time by clicking the "Retest" button at the top of the overview section. However, all the checks are run automatically every 60 minutes.

Online Health

Online Health are health checks that can be dynamically updated by VMware. This is extremely useful when new potential issues are identified by VMware and new knowledgebase articles are released. Customers can be proactively informed about these new issues and resolutions before potentially encountering them on their own vSAN clusters. The benefit of this approach is that it can automatically identify if a new knowledgebase article or new update or patch applies to your environment. This saves on time and effort that might otherwise be spent trawling the VMware knowledgebase or vSAN Release Notes. However, the authors would always recommend reviewing the Release Notes before attempting any vSAN or vSphere upgrade to that particular release.

To benefit from the Online health checks, the CEIP (Customer Experience Improvement Program) function must be enabled. VMware's *Customer Experience Improvement Program* ("CEIP") provides information that helps VMware to improve its products and services, fix problems, and advise customers on how best to deploy and use our products. To learn more about CEIP, check out the following online resource: https://vmwa.re/ceip. Enabling CEIP has other benefits which will be covered later.

Customers often ask what kind of data is sent back to VMware when CEIP is enabled. This is described in great detail in the link provided above, but the data collected is primarily to do with configuration information, such as which vSAN features are enabled, as well as some performance data and logs. No actual customer data is being captured, only metadata, or to put another way, only information about data is captured (if that makes sense). The data that is captured is also obfuscated so that even when the configuration is reviewed, no information such as hostnames and VM names are available. There is a way for VMware support engineers to de-obfuscate the names, but this can only be done via customer consent as the customer needs to provide support for a so-called obfuscation map. This map can be found in the vSphere Client under Monitor > vSAN > Support on the vSAN cluster object as demonstrated in the screenshot below.

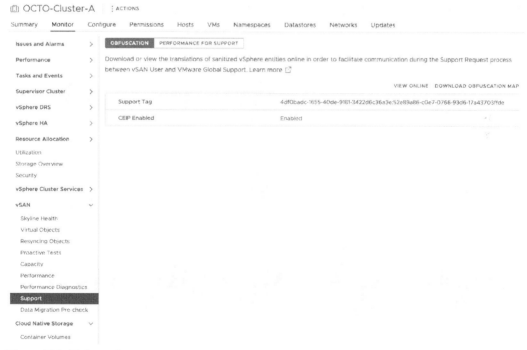

Figure 121: Obfuscation map

We have seen great success for customers, both from a proactive and reactive perspective, when CEIP is enabled in an environment. Please consider taking the step of enabling this very useful feature.

Health History

The health history feature keeps all vSAN Skyline Health data for up to 30 days depending on the vCenter Server database available capacity. This is extremely useful for trying to identify if an issue occurred when the system was not being actively monitored, perhaps overnight or over a weekend. It is also very useful for trying to identify patterns in behavior. For example, an administrator might use the historical health data to see if the same issue happens at the same time every day, or every week, in an attempt to try and root cause a problem.

To view the health history, there is a slider button located on the Skyline Health Overview window called "View Health History". Once enabled, the overview can be examined to see if there have been any issues with any of the other tests over a specific period. By default, it displays the last 24 hours of health data. Administrators can roll back as far as 30 days to view health status history if necessary.

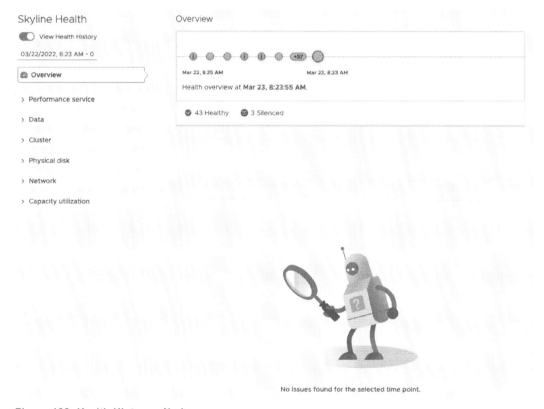

Figure 122. Health History – No issues

In the above example, there has been no issue in the last 24 hours, but if the timeline is expanded to a longer period, some historical issues may be viewed, as shown in the next example.

06 // vSAN Operations

Figure 123: Health History – Issues found

In this example, various warnings and errors have been observed in the past 30 days. Periods with repeated, identical errors are collapsed together for visibility. Click on any of the periods to expand.

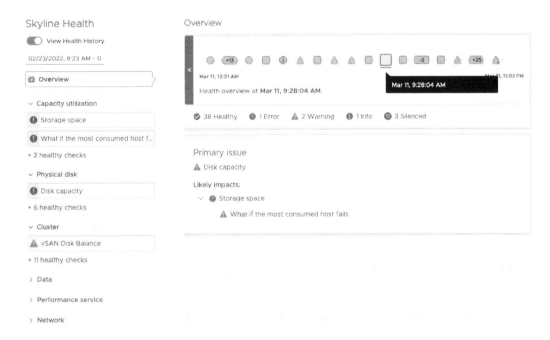

Figure 124: Health History – Disk capacity / Storage space issue

189

Administrators may now drill into the time of the event to see exactly when it occurred, and the type of warnings or errors that were encountered at that time. In this example, after drilling down to the actual time of the error, we see that there were some capacity issues on the cluster.

The health check history is informing the administrator that there were some disk capacity issues. It is also highlighting that if there was a host failure during the disk capacity issue, there may not have been enough capacity left in the cluster to address the storage needs of all workloads deployed on the cluster. This is accurate since this cluster was used to build out some large, thick-provisioned, 100% Object Space Reservation virtual machines for demonstrating policy behavior in chapter 5. After building the VMs, and capturing the necessary information for this book, they were deleted. Therefore, the space issue only occurred temporarily, and the capacity usage returned to a healthy state in the health history view.

Proactive Health Checks

Along with the set of health check tests introduced previously, vSAN health check also provides a set of proactive tests. Typically, one would not run these proactive tests during production. However, these tests can be very useful if you wish to implement a *proof-of-concept* (PoC) with vSAN, or even as part of the initial vSAN 'burn-in' tests to test the functionality of your newly deployed hardware (servers, NICs, storage devices).

These proactive tests can give you peace of mind that everything is working correctly before putting vSAN into production. The proactive tests have changed over the various versions of vSAN. vSAN 6.7 only included the VM Creation Test, while vSAN 6.7U1 includes the VM Creation Test and Network Performance Test. The current vSAN version (7.0U3) includes 3 tests:

- VM Creation Test
- Network Performance Test
- Storage Performance Test

Simply select the test that you wish to run and click the "Run Test" button to begin the test. A popup window is displayed giving you additional information about the test. The next screenshot shows the tests as they appear in the vSphere client. The Last Run Result field displays the time of the last test and whether the test was successful or not.

The actual tests that are run are well described in the vSphere Client. The "VM Creation Test" quickly verifies that virtual machines can be deployed on the vSAN datastore, and once that verification is complete, the sample VMs are removed. The VMs are created with whatever policy is the default policy for the vSAN datastore, and the test reports if the test was successful or not, along with any relevant error messages.

06 // vSAN Operations

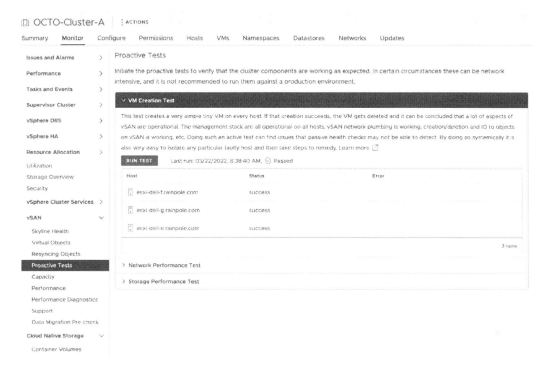

Figure 125: Health check proactive tests

The "Network Performance Test" simply verifies that the network infrastructure can handle a particular throughput of network traffic, and highlights if the network is unable to carry a particular load that is desirable for vSAN. This is especially important when there is a complex network configuration that may involve several hops or routes when vSAN is deployed over L3.

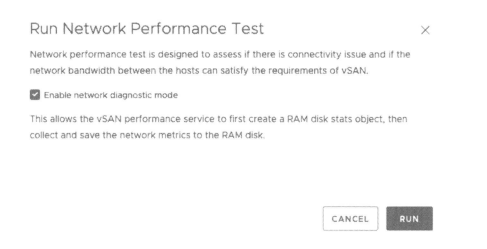

Figure 126: Enable network diagnostic mode

The "Network Performance Test" offers an additional option of including network diagnostics. These diagnostics can be useful in determining whether there is sufficient bandwidth between all the ESXi hosts to support vSAN. The test checks to make sure there is at least 850Mbps between the hosts.

Figure 127: Health check Network Performance Test

Before we leave proactive tests, a short note about a test that no longer exists but which appeared in earlier versions of vSAN – the storage performance test. It was decided that, due to the problematic nature of some of the tests run as part of the storage performance test, VMware would deprecate this test. Now VMware advises customers who wish to run storage performance benchmarks on vSAN to use the HCIbench tool. This HCI benchmarking tool was written specifically with hyperconverged infrastructures in mind and is much more powerful than the built-in proactive storage performance tests. HCIbench is designed to be run as part of a PoC acceptance test and is tightly integrated with other management and operational aspects of vSAN, as we shall see shortly. HCIbench is available from the VMware Fling site; http://flings.vmware.com. This location also includes documentation on how to quickly get started with the tool. Anyone involved in running storage benchmarks on vSAN is recommended to familiarize themselves with this tool going forward.

In vSAN 7.0U3, administrators are redirected to HCIbench from the vSphere Client Storage Performance Test as shown in the next screenshot.

06 // vSAN Operations

Figure 128: Health check Storage Performance Test

Performance Service

The Performance Service can be considered part of the health check. Since the initial release of vSAN, an area that was identified as needing much improvement was the area of monitoring vSAN performance from the vSphere Client. While some information was available in the vSphere Client, such as per-VM performance metrics, there was little information regarding the performance of the vSAN cluster from an overall cluster basis, a per-host basis, and a per disk group basis, or even a per device basis. This information was only attainable via the vSAN observer tool which was not integrated with vSphere in any way. Nor could the vSAN observer provide any historic data; it only ran in real-time mode. With the performance service, metrics such as IOPS, latency, and throughput (and many others) are now immediately available in the vSphere Client.

The performance service is automatically enabled in the recent versions of vSAN. In previous versions, it was disabled, and administrators needed to enable it via the Web Client. The status of this service, and other vSAN services, are visible on the Cluster > Configure > vSAN > Services view in the vSphere client.

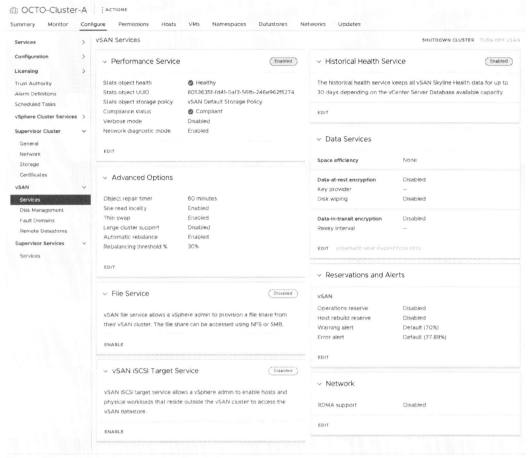

Figure 129: vSAN Performance Service status

A nice feature of the performance service is that it does not put any additional load on the vCenter Server for maintaining metrics. Instead, all metrics are saved on a special VM home object on the vSAN datastore (called the statistics database). This database is created when the performance service is enabled.

Historical performance data views (up to 90 days) as well as the current system status, are now available. The metrics displayed in the UI are calculated as an average performance over a 5-minute interval (roll-up). Since the statistics are stored in a VM home namespace object, commonly referred to as the statsDB, it may use up to a maximum of 255 GB of capacity. This is the reason why performance metrics expire after 90 days. Figure 130 shows the policy for the statistics database using the vSAN default policy once the performance service is enabled. This can be accessed by clicking on the Edit button associated with the Performance Service as shown in Figure 129.

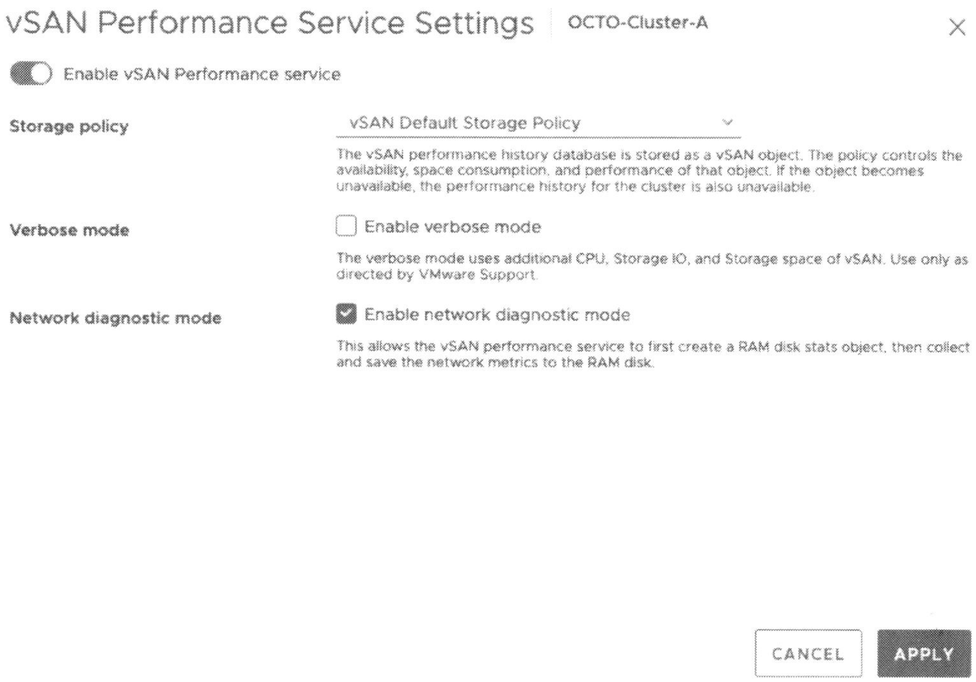

Figure 130: Performance service enabled

Note that the health check also includes several tests to ensure that the performance service is functioning normally. A verbose mode is also available. This gathers additional CPU, storage IO, and storage capacity information and should only be used if VMware Technical Support directs you to do so – this is stated in the UI. Finally, there is a new Network diagnostics mode option, which is disabled by default. If enabled, this allows the vSAN Performance Service to create a RAM disk stats object which can subsequently be used for the collection and storing of network metrics. Typically, this is also only done when a customer is directed to do so by VMware support. The advantage is that it provides more detailed performance data but be aware that it generates a lot more data.

vSAN performance service is convenient and powerful. However, due to the sampling rate of 5-minute intervals, short spikes in I/O may not be observed. Shortly vSAN IOInsight will be discussed where metrics are captured with a high level of granularity (1 second Intervals).

Performance Diagnostics

The Performance Diagnostics, found in Cluster > Monitor > vSAN > Performance Diagnostics, is a feature aimed at helping those running benchmarks to optimize their benchmarks, or optimize their vSAN configuration to reach their expected goals. To use this feature, you must participate in the Customer Experience Improvement Program once again. Obfuscated data from previously executed benchmarks are sent to VMware anonymously, analyzed, and the results are sent back to the Web Client. Performance diagnostics suggest remediation steps on how to achieve a benchmark goal, such as Maximum IOPS, Maximum Throughput, or Minimum Latency, and provides performance graphs so that further investigation can take place.

After selecting the desired benchmark goal, administrators next select a time range that the benchmark ran. When a benchmark such as HCIbench vSAN is run on the vSAN cluster, the time ranges for recent test runs automatically appear in the drop-down for Time Range. So instead of choosing for instance "Last 1 hour", one could have clicked on the drop-down for Time Range and chosen the benchmark that one wished to analyze.

Similarly, if Proactive Tests have been run, administrators can also select this time range for analysis by the vSAN Performance Diagnostics feature. In **Figure 131: Performance diagnostics** the objective was to discover the 'Max Throughput' as part of a proof-of-concept. After selecting the appropriate Time Range (which was the duration of the network performance test) from the dropdown menu, and setting the benchmark goal of Max Throughput, the Performance Diagnostic tool reports that the size of the IOs is too small to achieve the desired goal. This test is not a suitable benchmark for creating a Max Throughput test. The tool highlights that there are several disks in the cluster that were not used during this time, which is not useful for a performance test. Performance benchmarks should be configured to use all disks. Notice the Ask VMware link to a VMware knowledgebase article which provides additional information about the performance goal and how to achieve it.

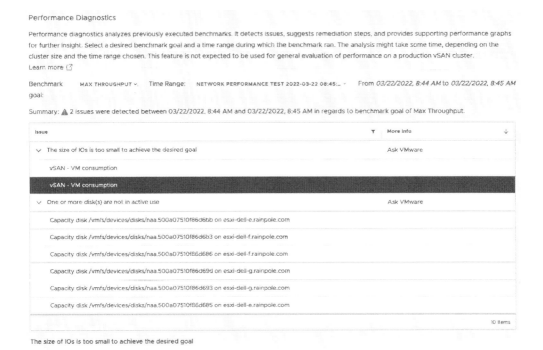

Figure 131: Performance diagnostics

06 // vSAN Operations

As mentioned in the introduction to the Performance diagnostics, this feature is not expected to be used on a production vSAN cluster. Instead, it is intended to be used during a proof-of-concept phase of a vSAN deployment.

Network Diagnostics

Network diagnostics, introduced in vSAN 7.0U2, is another nice feature from a management and monitoring perspective. It allows a vSAN administrator to get access to network diagnostic information. By navigating to an ESXi host in a vSAN cluster, then selecting Monitor > vSAN > Performance > Physical Adapters, there are several new metrics and counters to look at such as Port Drop Rate, RX CRC Error, TX Carrier Errors, and so on. Since vSAN is a distributed system, the network plays a critical role, and having some metrics that are continuously capturing the state of the network will be extremely beneficial for troubleshooting and diagnosis.

Figure 132: Networking Diagnostics

vSAN IOInsight

In vSAN 7.0U1, a new feature called vSAN IOInsight was introduced. The object of this feature was to provide even more insight into the storage I/O characteristics of workloads running on a vSAN cluster. vSAN IOInsight captures and displays I/O sizes, sequential and random I/O as well as 4K alignment. vSAN IOInsight may be run against individual VMs or hosts, or the entire vSAN cluster. It is run for a defined period to capture workload characteristics. The data collection operation can be resource-intensive, but it does gather detailed metrics during this period. The time duration ranges from 1 minute, to 24 hours. The data collection operation may be interrupted by the administrator if necessary.

The performance service needs to be enabled for vSAN IOInsight functionality. The collected data by vSAN IOInsight is stored in the performance service statsDB object. As previously mentioned, the statsDB object is limited in size. Thus, care should be taken if storing multiple data collections from different runs of vSAN IOInsight, running the performance service in verbose mode, or using network diagnostics mode. This may lead to a truncation of available performance metrics.

vSAN IOInsight is ideally suited for scenarios where a problematic host or VM has been identified, and additional data is required to add clarity to findings that have already been observed via performance metrics. Note that vSAN IOInsight is not intended for continual use. As mentioned earlier, vSAN IOInsight aggregates performance data at 1 second intervals, providing greater insight into spikes in I/O activity, something that the Performance Service sampling rate of 5 minutes is not able to provide.

To gather an instance of vSAN IOInsight metrics, navigate to Cluster > Monitor > vSAN > Performance, and then select IOINSIGHT from the list of options. Unless an instance of IOInsight has been previously created, there will be none found initially. Click on the NEW INSTANCE option to create an I/O Insight run. A prompt to select the monitoring target appears; by default, all hosts in the cluster are selected. Alternatively, you can select individual hosts or VMs.

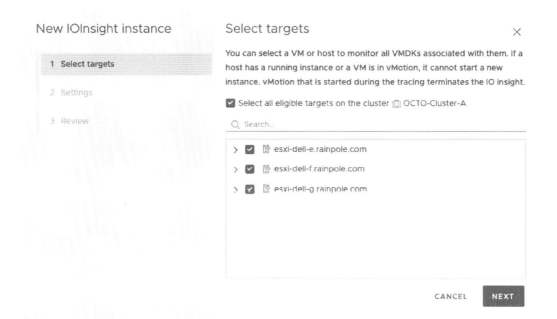

Figure 133: vSAN IOInsight targets

The next step is to provide a name and duration for the instance. Note the warning about monitoring overhead. This should be considered when running I/O Insight on a production system. By default, the duration is 10 minutes, but this can be reduced to 1 minute minimum or left to run for 24 hours maximum. I changed it to 5 minutes for the purpose of this demonstration.

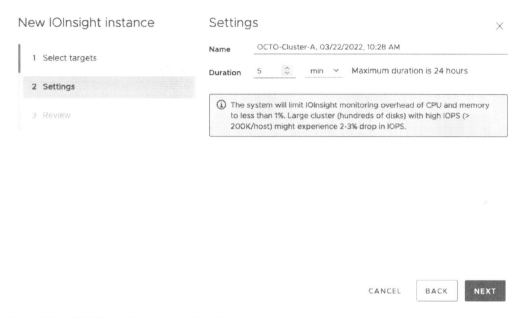

Figure 134: vSAN IOInsight name and duration

After initiating the instance, the new instance now appears in the IOINSIGHT view. It provides a status field that details how much time is remaining until the operation is complete. An administrator can view the metrics from the running instance or can choose to stop the run at any time as well. If an administrator chooses to view the metrics from a running instance, these are updated at 10-seconds intervals. **Figure 135: vSAN IOInsight results** shows some of the storage metrics from a VM's hard disk (VMDK) which resides on a vSAN datastore, as gathered by vSAN IOInsight.

Figure 135: vSAN IOInsight results

Finally, vSAN IOInsight provides administrators with the ability to export the metrics from an instance run. By clicking on the EXPORT RESULT link as shown in the top left-hand corner of Figure 135, a zip file that includes both graph images and raw data in CSV file format is created.

I/O Trip Analyzer

vSAN 7.0U3 builds on the work done with the vSAN IOInsight and introduced a new feature called the I/O Trip Analyzer. This examines the path of a vSAN I/O and provides information about the latency incurred at different stages in the I/O path. This tool complements vSAN IOInsight to provide administrators with additional information when performance troubleshooting, or even getting a better understanding of the I/O path.

I/O Trip Analyzer is a VM centric tool. Thus, to enable I/O Trip Analyzer, navigate to any VM that you wish to query, select the Monitor tab, then vSAN, and then select I/O Trip Analyzer. This will drop you to the I/O Trip Analyzer page, which prompts administrators to click on the "RUN NEW TEST" button. Simply click on this button to launch it. A prompt for the duration of the I/O Trip Analyzer test appears, which defaults to 5 minutes. This can be changed to a maximum of 60 minutes if so desired. Finally, click on the "RUN" button after the time has been chosen. Note that only a single I/O Trip Analyzer test can be run on the cluster at a time. Like vSAN IOInsight, the UI is updated with the amount of time left before the test is complete. Once the test completes, the "VIEW RESULT" button is highlighted, and the latency can be examined.

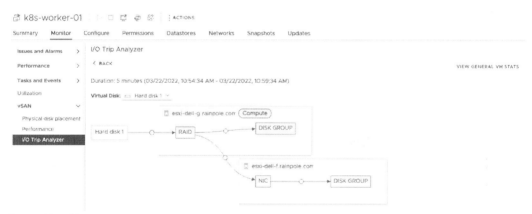

Figure 136: I/O Trip Analyzer results

To see the latency at any point in the I/O path, simply click on one of the dots. This displays the kind of latency introduced at that layer. I/O Trip Analyzer also provides a potential cause for the latency as well as some insights in terms of how you can potentially resolve a latency issue. If a significant amount of latency is introduced, the diagram will highlight it using colors for the respective layer where the latency is introduced.

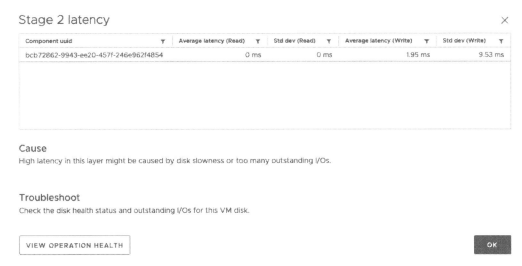

Figure 137: I/O Trip Analyzer latency

Note that there are some limitations to using both vSAN IOInsight, as well as I/O Trip Analyzer. At the time of writing, it is not possible to vMotion a VM that currently has metrics being gathered by vSAN I/O Insight. The vMotion will succeed but data collection will stop and cannot be viewed. The advice from the authors is therefore to override any DRS automation for any VMs that are being traced so that DRS does not interfere with the data collection. The reason for this is that the tracing is happening at the ESXi host level. A user world is created on the host where the VM is running to trace the IO. If the VM is moved to another ESXi host, the user world doesn't know what has happened to the VM and obviously cannot continue to monitor it.

There are also a few limitations regarding I/O Trip Analyzer. At the time of writing, it could not be used with vSAN Stretched Cluster, iSCSI, or Kubernetes Persistent Volumes created via CSI-CNS. These restrictions will most likely be lifted over time.

Now that we have provided an overview of the health check and associated services, let's now turn our attention to some of the more common management tasks an administrator might be faced with when managing vSAN.

Host Management

VMware vSAN has a scale-up and scale-out storage architecture. This means that it is possible to seamlessly scale the cluster by adding extra storage resources to your vSAN cluster. These storage resources can be magnetic disks or flash devices for additional capacity which can be added to existing disk groups in a scale-up approach. It could entail the addition of complete disk groups, including both cache and capacity devices for an alternative scale-up approach. And of course, it could also be a scale-out approach by adding additional hosts to the vSAN cluster. These not only contribute additional compute to the cluster but also additional storage capacity.

06 // vSAN Operations

Those who have been managing vSphere environments for a while will not be surprised that host management with vSAN is extremely simple; adding more resources (either a combination of compute and storage capacity or just storage capacity) can truly be as simple as adding a new disk device to a host or adding a new host to a cluster. Let's look at some of these tasks in more detail.

Adding Hosts to the Cluster

Adding hosts to the vSAN cluster is quite straightforward. Of course, you must ensure that the host meets vSAN requirements or recommendations such as a NIC port (10 GbE being required for all-flash vSAN and highly recommended for hybrid vSAN) and at least one cache tier device and one, or multiple, capacity tier devices if the host is to provide additional storage capacity. A recommendation would be to ensure that the host that is being added to the cluster is as similar as possible to the existing hosts, and uniformly configured, although this may not always be possible. VMware does support non-uniformly configured hosts participating in the same cluster by the way, though uniformly configured hosts are preferred.

Also, pre-configuration steps such as a VMkernel port for vSAN communication should be considered, although these can be done after the host is added to the cluster. After the host has successfully joined the cluster, you should observe the size of the vSAN datastore grow according to the size of the additional capacity devices in the new host. Remember that the flash cache tier device does not add to the capacity of the vSAN datastore. Just for completeness' sake, these are the steps required to add a host to a vSAN cluster using the vSphere Web Client:

1. Right-click the cluster object and click Add Hosts.
2. Fill in the IP address or host name of the server, as shown below.

Figure 138: Adding a host to the cluster

3. Fill in the user account (root typically) and the password.
4. Accept the **SHA1 thumbprint** option.
5. Click **Next** on the host summary screen.
6. Select the license to be used.
7. Enable lockdown mode if needed and click **Next**.
8. Click **Next** in the resource pool section.
9. Click **Finish** to add the host to the cluster.

And that is all that is needed. A vSAN cluster should automatically claim any local storage on the host that was just added and create a disk group. You will learn more about managing disk groups and disks later in this chapter in the disk management section.

Removing Hosts from the Cluster

Should you want to remove a host from a cluster, you must first ensure that the host is placed into maintenance mode. The various options will be discussed in further detail in the next section. After the host has been successfully placed into maintenance mode, you may safely remove it from the vSAN cluster. To remove a host from a cluster using the vSphere client, follow these steps:

1. Right-click the host and click **Enter Maintenance Mode** and select the appropriate vSAN migration option from the screen below and then click **OK**. If the plan is to truly remove this host from the cluster, then a full data migration is the recommended maintenance mode option. If it is a temporary maintenance operation that should last less than 60 minutes, and therefore no rebuild of vSAN objects will be initiated, "Ensure accessibility" (default option) may be chosen.

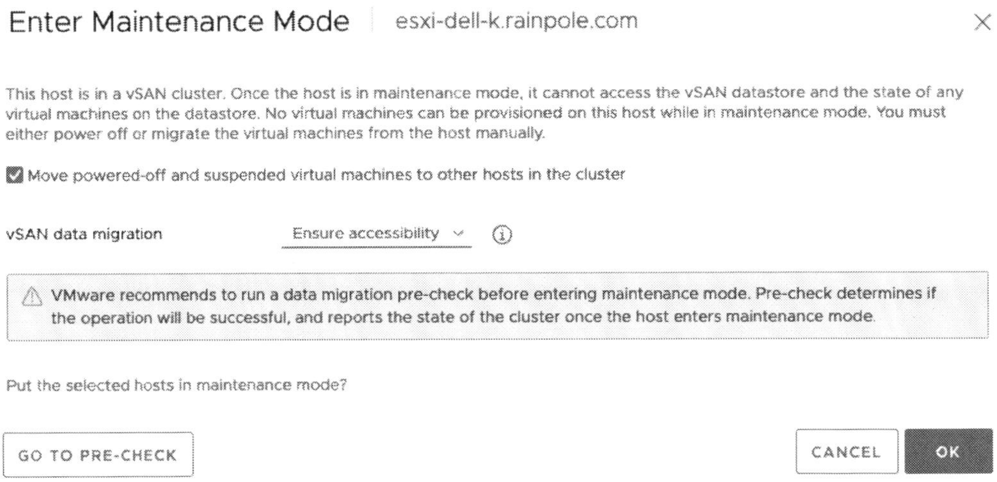

Figure 139: Enter maintenance mode

2. Now all the virtual machines will be migrated (vMotion) to other hosts. If DRS is enabled on the cluster, this will happen automatically. If DRS is not enabled on the cluster, the administrator will have to manually migrate VMs from the host entering maintenance mode for the operation to complete successfully.
3. When migrations are completed, depending on the selected vSAN migration option, vSAN components may also be rebuilt on other hosts in the cluster.
4. When maintenance mode has completed, right-click the host again and select move to option to move the host out of the cluster.
5. If you wish to remove the host from vCenter Server completely, right-click on the host once again, and select remove from inventory. This might be located under all vCenter

actions in earlier versions of vCenter Server.
6. Read the text presented twice and click Yes when you understand the potential impact.

Maintenance Mode

The previous section briefly touched on maintenance mode when removing an ESXi host from a vSAN cluster. With vSAN, maintenance mode includes new functionality that we will elaborate on here. When an ESXi host is placed in maintenance mode, the primary focus is on migrating VM compute resources from that ESXi host to other hosts in the cluster; however, with vSAN, maintenance mode provides you with the option to migrate storage resources as well as compute resources. The vSAN maintenance mode options related to data migration are as follows:

- **Ensure Accessibility**: This option evacuates enough data from the host entering maintenance mode to ensure that all VM storage objects are accessible after the host is taken offline. This is not full data evacuation. Instead, vSAN examines the storage objects that could end up without quorum or data availability when the host is placed into maintenance mode. It then ensures that there are enough components belonging to the object available to achieve quorum and remain accessible. vSAN (or to be more precise the cluster level object manager) will have to successfully reconfigure all objects that would become inaccessible due to a host entering maintenance mode and no longer providing its storage to the vSAN datastore. One example where this could happen is when VMs are configured with "failures to tolerate" set to 0. Another example is when there is already a host with a failure in the cluster, or indeed another host is in maintenance mode. Ensure Accessibility is the default option of the maintenance mode workflow and the recommended option by VMware if the host is going to be in maintenance for a short period of time. If the maintenance time is expected to be reasonably long, administrators should decide if they want to fully evacuate the data from that host to avoid risk to their VMs and data availability. There is one subtle behavior difference to note between the original release of vSAN and later releases. In the first release, when a host was placed in maintenance mode, it continued to contribute storage to the vSAN datastore and components were still accessible. In later releases, this behavior was changed. Now when a host is placed into maintenance mode, it no longer contributes storage to the vSAN datastore, and any components on the datastore are marked as ABSENT.
- **Full Data Migration**: This option is a full data evacuation and essentially creates replacement copies for every piece of data residing on disks on the host being placed into maintenance mode. vSAN does not necessarily copy the data from the host entering maintenance mode; however, it can and will also leverage the hosts holding the replica copy of the object to avoid creating a bottleneck on the host entering maintenance mode. In other words, in an eight-host cluster, when a host is placed in maintenance mode using full data migration, then potentially all eight hosts will contribute to the re-creation of the impacted components. The host does not successfully enter maintenance mode until all affected objects are reconfigured and compliance is ensured when all the component(s) have been placed on different hosts in the cluster. This is the option that VMware

recommends when hosts are being removed from the cluster, or there is a longer-term maintenance operation planned.
- **No Data Migration**: This option does nothing with the storage objects. As the name implies, there is no data migration. It is important to understand that if you have objects that have *number of failures to tolerate* set to 0, you could impact the availability of those objects by choosing this option. There are some other risks associated with this option. For example, if there is some other "unknown" issue or failure in the cluster, or there is another maintenance mode operation in progress that the administrator is not aware of, this maintenance mode option can lead to VM or data unavailability. For this reason, VMware only recommends this option when there is a full cluster shutdown planned (or on the advice of VMware support staff).

Again, just to reiterate an important point made earlier, when a host is placed into maintenance mode, it no longer contributes storage to the vSAN datastore. Any components that reside on the physical storage of the host that is placed into maintenance mode are marked as ABSENT.

Maintenance Mode and Host Locality

vSAN 6.7 introduced support for shared-nothing architectures. This is essentially the deployment of virtual machines which use *failures to tolerate* value of 0 (thus, no protection) in its policy, as well as the ability to specify a feature known as *host locality*. This ensures that the compute and storage for a particular VM are confined to the same host. This was only useful for some next-gen type applications which had their own built-in data protection mechanism, as well as a requirement to keep compute and storage on the same host. Hadoop's HDFS is one such example. When the VMware vSAN team first started to test Hadoop on vSAN, one of the stipulations was that it could only be validated when the compute and storage were co-located on the same host. It since transpired that this was not a hard requirement and was later relaxed. However, as mentioned, there are still some use cases for host locality, especially when the application has its own built-in protection. Many modern applications provide this built-in replication capability, such as NoSQL databases like Cassandra from vendors such as Datastax and S3 Objects Stores from vendors such as Minio and Cloudera.

Note that support for this *host locality* policy setting is only available on special request (RPQ) – it is not generally available. Customers wishing to use such a policy would need to raise a request via their local VMware contacts.

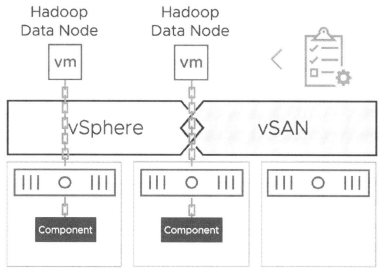

Figure 140: Host locality

There are a number of caveats around host locality which have yet to be ironed out before the feature can be generally available. One such restriction is the use of maintenance mode. Since the VM's compute and storage must reside on the same host, one cannot vMotion the VM or evacuate the data from this host during a maintenance mode operation. Users will have to rely on the built-in application protection mechanism if a host is required to be taken offline for maintenance, etc.

Default Maintenance /Decommission Mode

One other important point is the default maintenance mode setting when a product like vSphere Lifecycle Manager is being used. Lifecycle management refers to the process of installing software, maintaining it through updates and upgrades, and decommissioning it. Certain lifecycle operations require placing hosts into maintenance mode, and even rebooting them depending on the update.

The default maintenance mode (decommission mode) option is set to `ensureAccessibility` but this can be controlled through an advanced setting. The advanced setting is called `vSAN.DefaultHostDecommissionMode` which is set on a per host basis. It allows administrators to set the default maintenance mode to an option other than Ensure Accessibility, as listed in the next table.

Maintenance Mode Option	Description
ensureAccessibility	vSAN data reconfiguration should be performed to ensure storage object accessibility
evacuateAllData	vSAN data reconfiguration should be performed to ensure storage object accessibility
noAction	No special action should take place regarding vSAN data

Table 8: vSAN.DefaultHostDecommissionMode Options

Maintenance Mode for Updates and Patching

It is best to draw a comparison to a regular storage environment first when discussing options for updates and patches. When working on a traditional storage array, updates are typically done in a rolling fashion. If you have two controllers, one will be taken offline and upgraded while the other remains active and handles all the I/O. In this dual controller scenario, you are at risk while performing the upgrade because if the active controller hits a problem during the upgrade of the offline controller, no further I/O can flow and the whole array is offline.

The big difference when working on vSAN as a virtualization administrator is that *you have a bit more flexibility*. Each node in the cluster can be thought of as a storage controller, and even with one node out of the cluster, a second node failure may not impact all VM workloads (depending on the size of the vSAN cluster and the *failures to tolerate* setting of course). Coupled with other vSphere features, such as HA, for instance, you can reduce your level of risk during maintenance operations. The question that a vSphere/vSAN administrator needs to ask themselves is what level of risk they are *willing* to take, and what level of risk they *can* take.

From a vSAN perspective, when it comes to placing a host into maintenance mode, you will need to ask yourself the following questions:

- **Why am I placing my host in maintenance mode?** Am I going to upgrade my hosts and expect them to be unavailable for just a brief period? Am I removing a host from the cluster altogether? This will play a big role in which maintenance mode data migration option you should use.
- **How many hosts do I have?** When using three hosts, the only option you have is Ensure Accessibility or No Data Evacuation because, by default, vSAN always needs three hosts to store objects (two replica components and one witness component) to implement RAID-1 protection. Therefore, with a three-node cluster, you will have to accept some risk by using maintenance mode and run with one copy of the data. There is no way to do a Full Data Evacuation with just 3 nodes. Therefore, VMware makes the recommendation for 4 node vSAN clusters. This allows vSAN to self-heal on failures and continue to provide full protection of VMs during maintenance.

- **How long will the move take?**
    - Is this an all-flash cluster or a hybrid cluster?
    - What types of capacity disks have I used (SAS versus SATA)?
    - How much space has been consumed?
    - How big is my network interconnect? Do I have 25GbE, 10GbE, or 1GbE?
    - How big is my cluster?
- **Do I want to move data from one host to another to maintain availability levels?** Only stored components need to be moved, not the "raw capacity" of the host! That is, if 6 TB of capacity is used out of 8 TB, 6 TB will be moved.
- **Do I just want to ensure data accessibility and take the risk of potential downtime during maintenance?** Only components of those objects at risk will be moved. For example, if only 500 GB out of the 6 TB used capacity is at risk, that 500 GB will be moved.

There is something to say for all maintenance mode data migration options. When you select full data migration, to maintain availability levels, your "maintenance window" will be elongated, as you could be copying terabytes of data over the network from host to host. It could potentially take hours to complete. If your ESXi upgrade (including a host reboot) takes about 20 minutes, is it acceptable to wait hours for the data to be migrated? Or do you take the risk, inform your users about the potential downtime, and do the maintenance operation with a higher level of risk. The benefit is that the maintenance may be completed in a matter of minutes rather than hours. Is it worth the risk? If the maintenance mode takes longer than 1 hour, then you may have components begin to rebuild and resync on other nodes on the cluster, which will consume additional resources. Remember that 60 minutes is when the clomd repair delay timeout expires, and absent components are automatically rebuilt. This timer is tunable, so if you know maintenance is going to take longer than 60 minutes, you could change it to a higher value to avoid the rebuilds taking place.

However, the main risk is if another failure occurs in the cluster during the maintenance window. Then you risk availability to your VMs and your data. One other way to overcome this is to use *failures to tolerate* setting equal to 2, which means that you can do maintenance on one node, and still tolerate another host failing in the cluster at the same time. With erasure coding, customers can implement a RAID-6 configuration that can tolerate two failures. But as seen previously, this does not consume as much capacity as a RAID-1 configuration with FTT=2. RAID-6 requires a minimum of 6 hosts in the cluster.

To be honest, the authors can't give you advice on what the best approach is for your organization. We do strongly feel that for normal software or hardware maintenance tasks that only take a short period of time (of less than 1 hour), it will be acceptable to use the Ensure Accessibility maintenance mode data migration option. You should still, however, discuss *all* approaches with your storage team and look at their procedures. What is the agreed SLA with your business partners and what fits from an operational perspective?

One final point to note on maintenance modes; as was mentioned earlier, it is possible to change the clomd repair delay timeout to be something much larger if you are involved in a maintenance task that is going to take some hours, but you do not want to have any data rebuilding during this maintenance. Approach this with caution, however, since your VMs will be at risk for an extended period. And it is important to remember to put this setting back to the default after maintenance has finished. This is because certain failure scenarios will also use this timeout before rebuilding failed components, so you want this to kick off as soon as possible, and not be delayed. After all, you modified the timer value.

Starting in 6.7U1, a new global "object repair timer delay" setting is now available in the vSphere client should an administrator needs to adjust the timeout before vSAN begins to rebuild components. Previously it had to be set on a host-by-host basis, which was a pain point operationally and could lead to a mix of timeout values across hosts (although vSAN does have a health test to check for that issue occurring). This has already been highlighted in the book; see Advanced Settings in chapter 4, **Figure 49**.

Maintenance Mode and vSphere Lifecycle Manager

VMware Lifecycle Manager (vLCM) uses maintenance mode operations to automatically place hosts in maintenance in a rolling fashion during upgrades. vLCM, by default, uses Ensure Accessibility as the data migration option. This is deemed acceptable as any required components to keep a VM available will still be evacuated from the host entering maintenance mode. Upgrade operations, along with reboot operations, are not expected to exceed the 60-minute timeout associated with the commencement of rebuild activity.

Multiple hosts in Maintenance Mode simultaneously

There are several concerns with placing multiple vSAN nodes into maintenance mode. The first of these is related to available capacity on the vSAN datastore after multiple hosts have been removed. Now, there is indeed a Skyline health check which reports whether the vSAN cluster can fully re-protect all VMs even after a host has left the cluster, either gracefully (maintenance) or non-gracefully (failure). It checks that there is going to be enough capacity on the vSAN datastore should it lose the contributing devices from a single host. Several vSAN administrators have been caught by surprise when placing multiple hosts into maintenance mode because the hosts would happily enter maintenance mode, even when it meant that the vSAN datastore would fill up because of fewer resources being available. vSAN would simply try to re-protect and rebuild as many VMs as possible until there was no space left. This has been improved in 6.7U1 where vSAN will now simulate the data migration required to place a host into maintenance mode. A calculation is now made to determine if the data migration succeeds or fails before it even starts. If it finds that there is not going to be enough space, it will fail the maintenance mode operation immediately, rather than continuing with a 'best-effort' approach. Additional checks now look for other hosts already in maintenance mode, or if there is any resync activity underway.

Maintenance Mode Pre-Check

In the section "Removing Hosts from the Cluster" earlier in this chapter, we saw an example of the popup window (**Figure 139**) which appears when you request a host to be placed into maintenance mode. In the lower left-hand corner of that popup window, the was a "Go to Pre-Check" button. This is the data migration precheck and it will determine if there are any issues, such as object availability, or capacity issues, if the administrator proceeds with the maintenance mode operation.

When the "Go to Pre-Check" button is clicked, the administrator is automatically brought to the Cluster > Monitor > vSAN > Data Migration Pre-Check section in the vSphere UI. From here the administrator can choose which host the pre-check for data migration should be run on (it should be set to the host that was selected for maintenance mode). The other configurable option is the vSAN data migration setting, which is one of "Full data migration", "Ensure accessibility" or "No data migration", all of which have been described earlier in this chapter. This should also be set to whatever was chosen as the data migration option in the maintenance mode window.

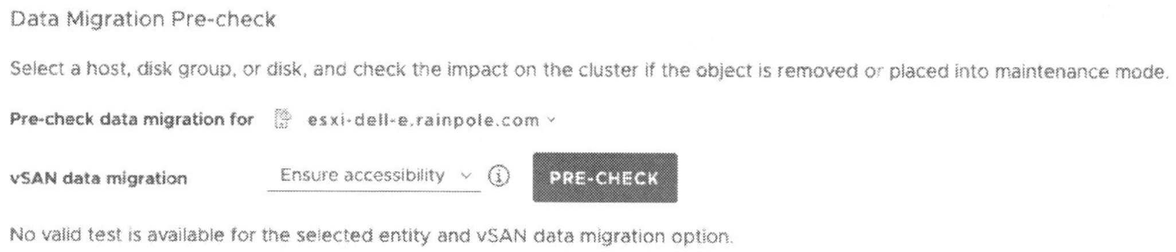

Data Migration Pre-check

Select a host, disk group, or disk, and check the impact on the cluster if the object is removed or placed into maintenance mode.

Pre-check data migration for   esxi-dell-e.rainpole.com

vSAN data migration   Ensure accessibility   **PRE-CHECK**

No valid test is available for the selected entity and vSAN data migration option.

Figure 141: Data Migration Pre-check

Once the "Pre-Check" button is clicked, several tests to check the impact of placing this host into maintenance mode are run. Remember that placing a host into maintenance node, it effectively removes this host from providing any storage capacity to the vSAN cluster. Thus, in a 3-node cluster, every single RAID-1 object will be unprotected and thus displayed as non-compliant. The test result will inform the administrator if the host can be placed in maintenance mode or not and then report on the Objects state, as shown next.

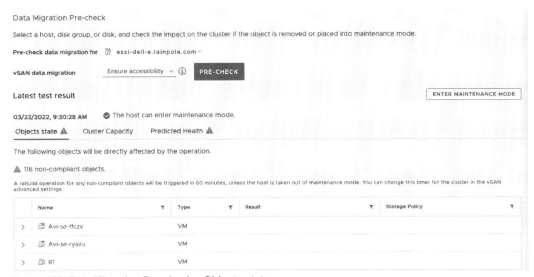

Figure 142: Data Migration Pre-check – Objects state

The precheck also reports on cluster capacity, both before and after the maintenance mode operation. This is useful as on an overloaded cluster, it may not be possible to move all components from the storage on the host that is entering maintenance mode to the remaining hosts in the cluster. This check will highlight such a predicament.

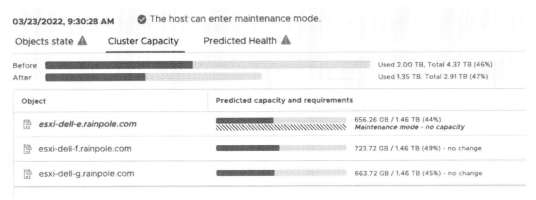

Figure 143: Data Migration Pre-check – Cluster Capacity

Finally, the Data Migration pre-check reports on the impact that the maintenance mode operations will have on the health of the vSAN cluster. Since this is a 3-node vSAN cluster, all RAID-1 objects will be impacted; there is no place to move the components that are currently on the host that is entering into maintenance mode, so all objects will be unprotected and thus non-compliant with their policy.

Figure 144: Data Migration Pre-check – Predicted Health

The Data Migration pre-check is an extremely useful feature to examine the impact of maintenance mode operations and should be used regularly by vSAN administrators to understand what impact taking a host out of the vSAN cluster has on the overall system from an availability, capacity, and health perspective.

Stretched Cluster Site Maintenance

In vSAN Stretched Cluster, there is no way to place a complete site or even a specific fault domain into maintenance mode. Administrators must work at the host granularity, placing each host in a site into maintenance mode individually. Additional manual steps may be required, such as modifying the DRS affinity to ensure that all workloads are failed over to the site that is to remain online and available. Once the workloads have been migrated, administrators can begin placing hosts into maintenance mode with the 'ensure accessibility' option. This option should be used if there is a possibility of VMs using the *failures to tolerate* set to 0. If all VMs protected by the stretched cluster are using *failures to tolerate* > 0, then the 'no data evacuation' option may be used when placing hosts into maintenance mode.

Shutting down a complete cluster

Prior to vSAN 7.0U3, there was no button that would shut down the whole of a vSAN cluster. Administrators had to shut down the cluster on a host-by-host basis. In this case, the advice was to shut down all VMs, and then place each host into maintenance mode using the 'no data evacuation' option. Once each host is in maintenance mode, the individual ESXi hosts can be shut down.

In vSAN 7.0U3, a new cluster shutdown feature was added. This feature enables an administrator to power off all the hosts in a cluster in one step. To trigger a cluster shutdown, right click the cluster object, select vSAN in the drop-down menu, and then select "shutdown cluster". This will launch a window that initiates a shutdown pre-check as shown below. Note that there is a requirement for all VMs to be powered off before the cluster can be shutdown. Some VMs, such as Agent VMs and the vCenter Server VM (if it exists) can be automatically managed. The remaining customer VMs are checked by the shutdown pre-check to make sure they are powered off. As per *VMware knowledgebase article 85594*, any VMs that are not powered off will be identified during the shutdown pre-check and will need to be powered off manually by the administrator. The figure below displays the set of shutdown pre-checks that are run before a cluster can be shut down and highlights the fact that some VMs are still powered on, preventing the shutdown from proceeding.

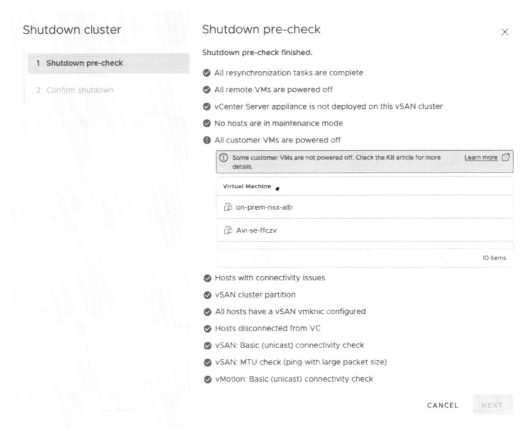

Figure 145: Cluster Shutdown pre-check

Upgrade Considerations

vSAN is integrated with vSphere Lifecycle Manager (vLCM). vLCM understands that it is upgrading a vSAN cluster. Therefore, it will automatically take care of selecting a host in the cluster to upgrade, and place it into maintenance mode using the default setting of 'ensure accessibility'. It then does the upgrading, reboots the host if needed, and once the host has reconnected to vCenter Server and re-joins the cluster, vLCM takes the host out of maintenance mode and lets the 'out of date' components resync. It then selects the next host and repeats the upgrade task in a rolling fashion until all nodes in the cluster are upgraded.

vLCM not only does hypervisor lifecycle management, but also supports firmware lifecycle management as well. In the past, this was a manual process, with administrators needing to download third-party tools along with the appropriate firmware versions to carry out this task on a per host basis. Today, this can be automated through vLCM. There are some prerequisites before administrators can use vLCM to apply firmware updates, such as ensuring that the vSAN cluster is lifecycle managed with a single image. Firmware updates require a special firmware and drivers add-on which is vendor-provided. The add-on contains the firmware packages. Note that VMware does not host these firmware packages in its own online depots. Instead, each vendor hosts their add-ons in their own proprietary depot. Access to the depot is provided through a vCenter plugin, called a "hardware support manager". The appropriate "hardware support manager" must be selected when converting from baseline to image-based lifecycle management, and selecting the appropriate Firmware and Drivers Addon, as shown below.

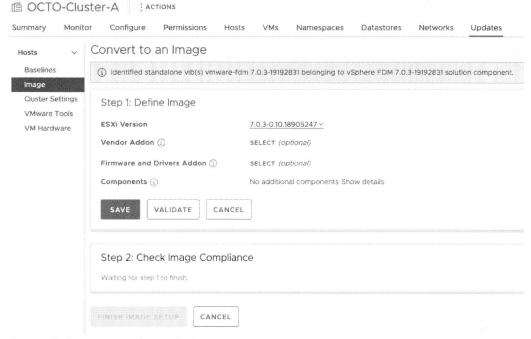

Figure 146: Firmware and Drivers Addon

At the time of writing, there are hardware support managers available for DELL, HPE, Lenovo & Hitachi.

vLCM is also aware of vSAN stretched clusters, 2-node clusters, and fault domain configurations, and can orchestrate the upgrades of those different vSAN configurations.

An important consideration relates to the vSAN *on-disk format*. *VMware knowledgebase article 2145267* provides an excellent overview of the various on-disk formats that vSAN has had with its various releases. Some of the on-disk format changes were minor and did not require a rolling upgrade (for example, the ability to support encryption with vSAN 6.6). However, others required a completely new on-disk format (for example vSAN 6.2 which introduced support for checksum, deduplication, and compression).

The main consideration with the *on-disk format change*, referred to as DFC, is the evacuation of all the data from a host before doing the on-disk changes. The on-disk format is done one disk group at a time. First, the disk group is evacuated to available capacity elsewhere in the cluster. It is then basically removed, recreated with the new disk format, and finally added back into the cluster. This is then repeated throughout the cluster.

You may well ask what happens when there are not enough resources in the cluster to accommodate a full disk group evacuation, especially on two-node or three-node vSAN clusters? In this case, there is an option to do the DFC with 'Allow Reduced Redundancy' where only one copy of the data is available during the DFC. There is a risk with this approach, and it is another reason why VMware recommends an additional host be available in the cluster. Having an additional host in the cluster will mean VMs will be fully protected against a failure occurring in the cluster during this task. As mentioned, not every on-disk format change requires an evacuation to format the disks. The most recent on-disk formats that were made to vSAN did not require one.

Another item that should be highlighted is the change from multicast to unicast for network communication, and how this is handled during the upgrade process. Unicast was introduced with vSAN 6.6. During the upgrade of vSAN from pre-6.6 to 6.6 or later, all nodes continue to communicate using multicast. Therefore, you continue to see multicast settings in place when you examine vSAN networking. However, once the final node in the cluster is upgraded, and joined to the cluster, all nodes automatically flip from multicast communication to unicast communication.

As an example, let's take a vSAN cluster running vSAN 6.2 and is upgraded to vSAN 6.6U1. All nodes switched from multicast to unicast. Assume that a DFC was not initiated, so the hosts continue to have on-disk format version 3. Now assume that another vSAN 6.2 host is added to the cluster. At this point, all hosts will revert to multicast so that they can communicate with this newly added host. So, what role does DFC play here?

Assume now that at the point that all hosts in the original cluster are upgraded from vSAN 6.2 to 6.6U1, a DFC is also initiated which changes the on-disk format from version 3 to version 5. In effect, by upgrading the on-disk format, we prevent the cluster from ever reverting to multicast – it is now permanently unicast. Now repeat the action of adding a vSAN 6.2 host to the cluster. At this point, the 6.2 host cannot join the 6.6U1 cluster. By upgrading the DFC, the cluster is forevermore prevented from reverting to multicast.

One final consideration around upgrading the cluster and changing the cluster communication to unicast is that cluster membership now must be tracked by a completely different mechanism. You will read more about that when you read about vCenter Server later in this chapter.

Disk Management

One of the design goals for vSAN, as already mentioned, is the ability to scale up the storage capacity. This requires the ability to add new disks, replace capacity disks with larger capacity disks, or simply replace failed drives. This next section discusses the procedures involved in doing these tasks in a vSAN environment.

06 // vSAN Operations

Adding a Disk Group

Chapter 2, "vSAN Prerequisites and Requirements," demonstrated how to add a disk group; however, for completeness, here are the steps again. This example shows how to create a disk group on a host-by-host basis. However, administrators can also create disk groups on all hosts simultaneously.

1. Click your vSAN cluster in the left pane.
2. Click the **Configure** tab on the right side.
3. Click **vSAN > Disk Management**.
4. As shown below, one gets a cluster overview of hosts, disk groups, and capacity disks. The hosts and their disk in use are shown, along with health, capacity, and network partition information, which is very useful in determining whether there is a network partition, and which host or hosts are in a different network partition group.

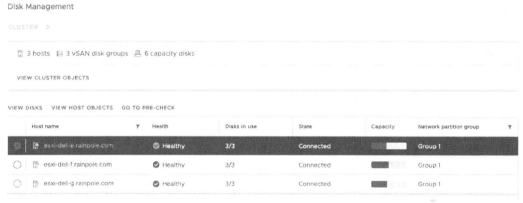

Figure 147: vSAN disk management

5. On selecting a host, an administrator can choose "View Disks", "View Host Objects", or "Go to Pre-Check". This "View Disks" option narrows the focus to the disk group(s) and disks. It informs us about the configuration (in this case All-flash rather than Hybrid) as well as the disk format version, which may change with different vSAN versions. On expanding the table, administrators can see the devices, their health and state, their capacity, their type, and which disk tier (vSAN Cache or vSAN capacity) that they are being used for in the disk group.

Figure 148: vSAN Disk Group details

6. Note that there is now an option to create a new disk group on this host, assuming there are local devices available. By clicking on this text in the UI, a new window is launched which allows administrators to view available local storage devices on the host. Administrators can then select whether to claim a device for the cache tier or the capacity tier. Select "Capacity tier" for all capacity devices and select "Cache tier" for all the cache devices, then click OK.

Now a new disk group is created; this takes seconds. We will talk about the other storage management options throughout the rest of this section.

Removing a Disk Group

Administrators can remove a disk group from vSAN once they have selected the "View Disks". This is one of many tasks available in the drop-down menu that is displayed when the 3 dots in the Disk Group header bar are clicked, as shown below.

06 // vSAN Operations

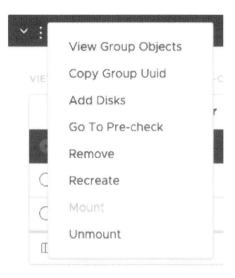

Figure 149: vSAN Disk Group actions

Before the Remove task starts, the administrator is prompted to evacuate the components that are currently in that disk group, as shown in the next figure. vSAN allows administrators to evacuate disk groups without placing the host where the disk group resides into maintenance mode. Another useful feature like what was seen in the Host Maintenance Mode section is that Disk Group Removal also includes a "Pre-Check" option. As before, you can choose "Full data evacuation", Ensure accessibility" and "No data evacuation". An administrator can also go directly to the pre-check option from the drop-down menu list above.

Figure 150: vSAN Disk Group Removal

As you can imagine, this operation of removing a disk group would return the same Object state, Cluster Capacity, and Predicted Health results that were seen earlier with the maintenance mode operation. Since this is a 3 node vSAN cluster, and each node only has a single disk group, removing one of the disk groups is akin to removing a host from the cluster, which is why the results are identical.

Evacuating the VM components from a disk group is not a required step for deleting a disk group, but the authors believe that most administrators would like to move the VM components currently in this disk group to other disk groups in the cluster before deleting it. If you don't do this step, and evacuate the data, you may be left with degraded components that are no longer highly available. vSAN will then need to reconfigure these components when the disk group is deleted. As highlighted many times now, if there is another failure while the objects are degraded, it may lead to data loss.

However, there may be valid reasons for wanting to delete a disk group without first evacuating all the data, and those options are also provided. Just like with ESXi hosts, administrators can choose simply to ensure accessibility, or indeed not to evacuate the data at all.

If you are planning on doing a full data evacuation of a disk group, vSAN will validate first whether sufficient disk space is available within the cluster to do so. When you complete this step, you should be able to remove the disk group.

However, as shown in the pre-check below, an attempt to do a full data migration on a 3-node cluster is simply not possible, as there is nowhere to move the replicated data to.

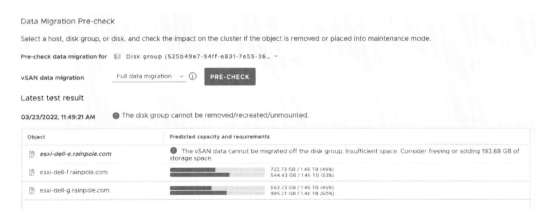

Figure 151: Remove vSAN disk groups

Historically vSAN could be configured in two modes "automatic" mode, or "manual" mode. In a nutshell, this decided how disks were claimed by vSAN. By default, vSAN used to be configured to automatic mode, which meant that if a disk group was removed, vSAN immediately claimed the disks again. Thus, the option to remove a disk group was not presented to the user in automatic mode but was only available in manual mode.

When an administrator needed to remove a disk group, vSAN had to be placed in manual mode for the remove the disk group option to appear. This was done through the vSAN cluster settings.

When the vSAN was placed in manual mode, the remove the disk group option became visible when you select the disk group in the disk management view. Administrators could now proceed with removing the disk group.

Fortunately, this jumping through hoops to remove a disk group from vSAN is no longer necessary since the ability to configure vSAN in automatic and manual mode was deprecated. vSAN no longer automatically claims any disks as of vSAN version 6.7, and administrators have full control over disk group creation and removal.

Adding Disks to the Disk Group

Administrators need to add new disks to disk groups to scale up and increase the capacity of the vSAN datastore. This can easily be done via the vSphere Client. Navigate to the vSAN cluster, select the Configure tab, and then the vSAN > Disk Management section. Expand the host to which you want to add the disk to. Click on the Disk Group actions (3 dots) and select "Add Disks" from the drop-down menu. Remember that vSAN can only consume local, empty disks. Remote disks, such as SAN LUNs, and local disks with partitions, cannot be used and won't be visible.

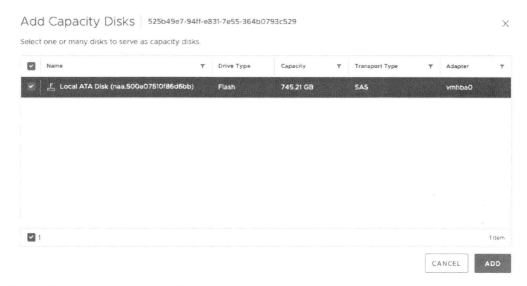

Figure 152: Add Capacity Disks to Disk Group

In this example, we are adding a disk to an already existing disk group. This means that any devices that are added can only be added as capacity devices up to a maximum of 7 per disk group. Similarly, if the device is not a flash device, then it can only be added to a capacity tier on hybrid systems. After clicking ADD, the device is added to the vSAN datastore, and the datastore size is automatically increased.

Removing Disks from the Disk Group

Just like removing disk groups discussed previously, disks can be removed from a disk group in the vSphere Client. Navigate to the Disk Management section of the vSAN cluster, select the host, then click "View Disks" to see the disk group. Expand the disk group to see the individual disks, then click on the disk that you wish to remove. The "Remove Disk" option will become enabled above the list of disks, as shown below. Simply click this "Remove Disk" option to begin the process of removing the disk from the disk group.

Figure 153: Remove a disk from a disk group

In the same way that the administrator is prompted to run a pre-check when the delete disk group option is chosen, administrators are also prompted to pre-check individual disks when a disk is being removed from a disk group. In this 3-node cluster, with only 1 disk group per host and assuming there is sufficient space, vSAN will migrate all the components on the said disk to other disks in the disk group.

Figure 154: Pre-Check: Remove a disk from a disk group

In the example above, the disk has several components residing on it, so much so that there are 277.21GB of data to move. However, it does appear that the remaining disk or disks in the disk group can handle this request. Clicking on the "Remove" button pops up one last warning about evacuating the data.

Figure 155: Remove a disk from a disk group – evacuate warning

Once the "Remove" button is clicked, a percentage of removing progress is displayed so administrators can monitor the activity. Similarly, removal tasks can also be observed in the vSphere UI Recent Tasks view.

Removing Disks with dedupe enabled

There is one important note on the removal of an individual disk from a disk group. If **deduplication and compression is enabled** on the cluster, **it is not possible to remove the disk from a disk group**. The reason for this is that the deduplicated and compressed data, along with the associated hash tables and metadata associated with deduplication and compression, are striped across all the capacity tier disks in the disk group. Therefore, it is not possible to remove a single disk. To remove a single disk from a disk group where deduplication and compression are enabled on the cluster, the entire disk group should be evacuated and then the disk may be replaced. Afterward, the disk group should be recreated.

Removing Disks with Compression Only enabled

As we have already learned from earlier chapters in this book, support for a Compression Only space-efficiency feature was introduced in vSAN 7.0U1. Device failures when using the "compression only" option do not have the same impact when compared to clusters that have both deduplication and compression enabled. This is because a failed capacity device in a cluster using the "compression only" option will only impact that device and not the entire disk group. Similarly, individual disks may be removed from a disk group with Compression Only enabled on the cluster.

Erasing a Disk

In some cases, other features or operating systems may have used magnetic disks and flash devices before vSAN is enabled. In those cases, vSAN will not be able to reuse the devices when the devices still contain partitions or even a file system. Note that this has been done intentionally to prevent the user from selecting the wrong disks. If you want to use a disk that has been previously used, you can wipe the disks manually, either via the command line or from the vSphere

Client.

The Erase Partitions option in the vSphere Client is found by selecting an ESXi host, the selecting Configure > Storage Devices, as shown below.

Storage Devices									
REFRESH ATTACH DETACH RENAME TURN ON LED TURN OFF LED ERASE PARTITIONS MARK AS FLASH DISK MARK AS REMOTE									
Name	LUN	Type	Capacity	Datastore	Operational State	Hardware Acceleration	Drive Type	Transport	
Local DP Enclosure Svc Dev (naa.500056b35af7c1fd)	0	enclosure		Not Consumed	Attached	Not supported	HDD	SAS	
Local ATA Disk (naa.55cd2e404c31e2c7)	0	disk	186.31 GB	vsan-OCT...	Attached	Not supported	Flash	SAS	
Local ATA Disk (naa.55cd2e404c17bc15)	0	disk	372.61 GB	vsan-OCT...	Attached	Not supported	Flash	SAS	
Local ATA Disk (naa.55cd2e404c17bbb4)	0	disk	372.61 GB	vsan-OCT...	Attached	Not supported	Flash	SAS	
Local USB Direct-Access (mpx.vmhba32:C0:T0:L0)	0	disk	14.92 GB	Not Consumed	Attached	Not supported	HDD	Block Adapter	
Local TOSHIBA Disk (naa.5000039756430469)	0	disk	1.09 TB	Not Consumed	Attached	Not supported	HDD	SAS	

Figure 156: Erase partition

It is possible to remove a magnetic disk or a flash device from a disk group through the Command Line Interface (CLI). However, this should be done with absolute care and the authors strongly recommend going through the UI for such operations, as shown on the previous pages.

Similarly, if a disk was previously used for another function and the wish is to now use it for vSAN, its partitions can be erased using the UI as already seen. Alternatively, another method is to use the CLI to wipe a disk. The disk can be erased from the commands line using the `esxcli vsan storage` utility

The above options assume that you have an existing vSAN cluster. Some other less conventional ways are included here in case you do not have a vSAN cluster (i.e. vSAN has been disabled), and thus you do not have the above options available. In those cases, disks can be erased:

- Using the command `partedUtil`, a disk partition management utility that is included with ESXi.
- Booting the host with the `gparted` bootable ISO image.

The `gparted` procedure is straightforward. You can download the ISO image from **http://gparted.org/**, and create a boot CD from it. Then, boot the ESXi host from it. After that, it is simply a matter of deleting all partitions on the appropriate disk and clicking **Apply**.

> **Warning: The tasks involved with wiping a disk are destructive, and it will be nearly impossible to retrieve any data after wiping the disk.**

The `partedUtil` method is slightly more complex because it is a command-line utility. Administrators will need to SSH to the ESXi host that contains the disks that need its partitions erased. The `partedUtil` binary is available and preinstalled on the ESXi host. The following steps are required to wipe a disk using `partedUtil`. If you are not certain which device to wipe, make sure to double-check the device ID using `esxcli storage core device list`:

Step 1: Display the partition table
```
~ # partedUtil get /vmfs/devices/disks/naa.500xxx
24321 255 63 390721968
1 2048 6143 0 0
2 6144 390721934 0 0
```

Step 2: Display partition types
```
~ # partedUtil getptbl /vmfs/devices/disks/naa.500xxx
gpt
24321 255 63 390721968
1 2048 6143 381CFCCC728811E092EE000C2911D0B2 vsan 0
2 6144 390721934 77719A0CA4A011E3A47E000C29745A24 virsto 0
~ #
```

Step 3: Delete the partitions
```
~ # partedUtil delete /vmfs/devices/disks/naa.500xxxxxx 1
~ # partedUtil delete /vmfs/devices/disks/naa.500xxxxxx 2
```

If you are looking for more guidance about the use of `partedUtil`, read the following VMware Knowledge Base (KB) article: 1036609.

Turn on the LED on a Disk

Starting with vSphere 6.0, administrators can blink the LEDs on the front disk drives when using certain storage controllers. Having the ability to identify a drive for replacement becomes very important for vSAN, as clusters can contain tens or even hundreds of disk drives.

You'll find the buttons for turning on and off LEDs when you select a disk drive in the UI, under Host > Configure > Storage Devices, as seen earlier in **Figure 156** when we looked at the "Erase Partitions" option. As you can probably guess, clicking on the "Turn On Led" turns the LED on; clicking on the "Turn Off Led" icon turns the LED off again.

Please note that this may not work for all storage controllers, and for the ones that do work, certain third-party tools may need to be installed. For example, when you are using HPE servers, you should verify that the HP SSA CLI is installed.

vSAN Capacity Monitoring and Management

One major operational aspect of managing storage is being able to view how much space is being consumed on the cluster. vSAN provides a capacity view to give detailed information about space consumption. Navigate to Cluster > Monitor > vSAN > Capacity to see this information.

There are two views available, Capacity Usage and Capacity History. The default view is Capacity Usage, which has several distinct sections, such as Capacity Overview, What If Analysis, and Usage breakdown, as shown next.

Figure 157: vSAN Capacity Overview

Capacity Overview

The Capacity Overview provides a quick glance of the vSAN datastore capacity. Not shown here, but something commonly observed in this view is space that has been reserved for objects, which is shown in a lighter green color in the UI. Also of interest in this view is the **Operations threshold** bar. As has been mentioned several times at this point in the book, vSAN requires some capacity to be able to carry out some of its internal operations. The Operations threshold highlights the amount of space needed by vSAN to handle these sorts of operations. If the used space exceeds the operations threshold, vSAN might not be able to function properly. One other item that might be observed in this view is a bar that represents the Host rebuild threshold. In the event of a host failure, vSAN requires free space to re-protect the data on the failed host. The Host rebuild threshold highlights how much space vSAN requires to tolerate one host failure. If the used space exceeds the host rebuild threshold, vSAN might not successfully re-protect all data from a failed host elsewhere in the cluster.

Operations reserve and Host rebuild reserve

This is probably a good point to introduce two new reservations, operations reserve, and host rebuild reserve. These are configurable from the Cluster > Configure > vSAN > Service page under the Reservations and Alerts section, as shown below.

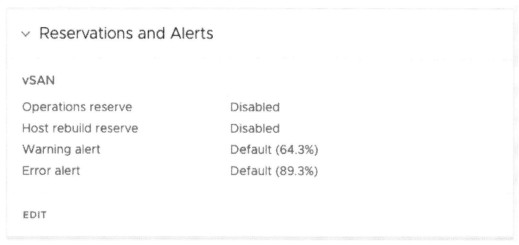

Figure 158: Reservations and Alerts

As per the description in the UI, which is displayed when the Edit button is clicked and the Reservation and Alerts wizard is launched, enabling operations reserve helps ensure that there will be enough space in the vSAN cluster for internal operations to complete successfully. Enabling host rebuild reserve allows vSAN to tolerate one host failure. Another interesting point to note is that when the reservation is enabled and capacity usage reaches the limit, new workloads will not deploy on the vSAN cluster. This gives a vSAN administrator the ability to avoid situations where the vSAN datastore completely fills up. This has been problematic in the past and can be a difficult situation to recover from since vSAN is not able to carry out its own internal housekeeping operations, never mind handle virtual machine workloads.

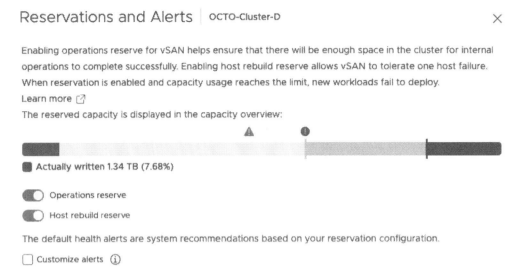

Figure 159: Configure Reservations

Once the Operations reserve and Host rebuild reserve are enabled, the Capacity Overview is now updated to reflect these new reservation settings. Note that Operation reserve can be enabled without needing to enable Host rebuild reserve. However, to enable Host rebuild Reserve, Operational reserve must first be enabled.

Figure 160: Reservations Enabled in Capacity Overview

Note that the reserved capacity feature is not supported on a vSAN stretched cluster, vSAN clusters with fault domains, or vSAN clusters with less than four nodes. You will see a message in the Reservations and Alerts wizard highlighting this limitation.

What if analysis / Thin Provisioning Considerations

There are two very useful features in the What if analysis section of Capacity Usage. The first allows you to see how much effective free space is available if all workloads were provisioned with a particular policy. For example, RAID-1 deployments would require capacity set aside for another replica if the failures to tolerate was set to 1. Capacity would need to be set aside for 2 full replicas if failures to tolerate was set to 2, and similarly, 3 replicas would be needed for failures to tolerate set to 3. By selecting the appropriate policy to match these requirements, the What If analysis can inform the administrator how many workloads can be provisioned with such policies on the vSAN datastore.

Below are two examples of using the What if analysis. The first uses the vSAN Default Storage Policy which uses RAID-1 with failures to tolerate set to 1. The second uses a RAID-5 policy. Note the effective free space for workloads that use those different policies.

What if analysis	
Effective free space (without deduplication and compression)	
With the policy vSAN Default Storage Policy	The effective free space for a new workload would be: 9.16 TB
Oversubscription	
If all thin provisioned VMs and user objects are used at full capacity	Capacity required: 12.48 TB (0.57x) the available capacity 21.82 TB)

Figure 161: What If Analysis – FTT=1, RAID-1 Policy

What if analysis	
Effective free space (without deduplication and compression)	
With the policy R5	The effective free space for a new workload would be: 18.32 TB
Oversubscription	
If all thin provisioned VMs and user objects are used at full capacity	Capacity required: 12.48 TB (0.57x) the available capacity 21.82 TB)

Figure 162: What If Analysis – FTT=1, RAID-5 Policy

One final item to highlight in the What If analysis is the oversubscription option. As you will be aware by now, vSAN provisions all objects as thin provisioned, unless explicitly told to do otherwise via the Object Space Reservation parameter. The advantage to using thin-provisioned objects is that workloads are not consuming any more disk capacity than is completely necessary. It is not uncommon in datacenter environments to see 40% to 60% of unused capacity within the VM. You can imagine that if a VM were thick provisioned, it would drive up the cost, but it would also make vSAN less flexible in terms of placement of components.

Of course, there is an operational aspect to thin provisioning. There is always a chance of filling up a vSAN datastore when you are severely overcommitted and many VMs are claiming new disk capacity. This is not different in an environment where NFS is used, or VMFS with thin provisioned VMs. This oversubscription view informs the administrator about the amount of capacity that would be consumed should the thin provisioned objects grow to the maximum size. This is a useful parameter for administrators to keep an eye on, simply to ensure that workloads don't become capacity constrained at some point in the future.

When certain capacity usage thresholds are reached, vCenter Server will raise an alarm to ensure that the administrator is aware of the potential problem that may arise when not acted upon. By default, this alarm is triggered when the 75% full threshold is exceeded with an exclamation mark (severity warning), and another alarm is raised when 85% is reached (severity critical). (Note that this issue will also raise an alarm in the health check).

Usage breakdown

In the lower part of the Capacity overview section, one can see a breakdown of which objects are consuming space. These are separated into VMs, User objects, and System usage. If the "expand all" text is selected, a breakdown of the different objects and services is displayed, as shown below.

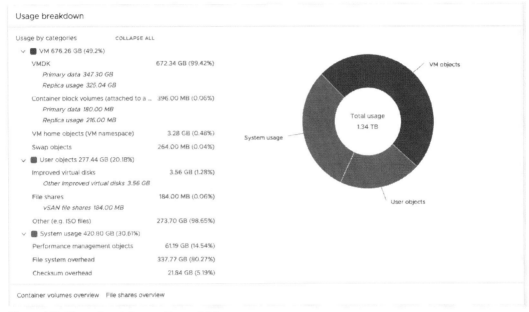

Figure 163: Usage breakdown – Expand All

Under the VM usage breakdown, objects include:
- VM Home namespaces
- VM Swaps
- Virtual Machine Disk Files (includes VMDKs, snapshot delta, linked clones, etc.)
    - The usage is shown as different types such as Primary data and its replica usage
- Snapshot memory
- Container block volumes (typically consumed via the vSphere CSI driver, which will be discussed in more detail shortly)
    - The usage is shown as different types such as Primary data and its replica usage

Also included as part of the breakdown are user objects. These include File Shares created by vSAN File Service. Note that this may also include Container file volumes, which are backed by vSAN File Service.

Finally, the System usage section highlights various vSAN overheads. The thing to note about vSAN overheads is that they may start relatively small but will grow as the datastore is consumed. Therefore, they are displayed here for administrators to monitor. Overheads include:

- Filesystem overhead
- Checksum overhead
- Performance management objects

Finally, there is also a Capacity History which enables administrators to go back in time and review capacity usage charts for a given period (default is 1 day, maximum is 30 days). This feature was introduced in vSAN 6.7U1. From here, you can observe the total capacity, free capacity, and used capacity of the vSAN datastore from the last X number of days (where 30 >= X >=1) or indeed, add their own custom data range. This is a great tool for forecasting the future capacity requirements of the vSAN cluster.

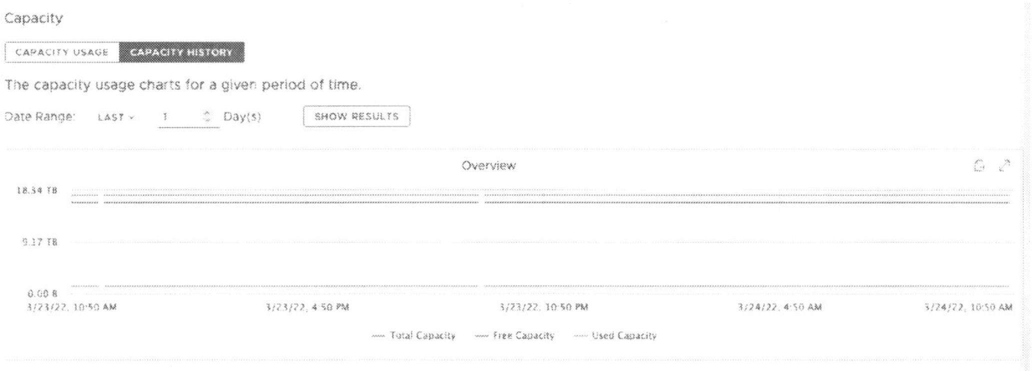

Figure 164: vSAN Capacity History

Disk Full Scenario

You might ask, "What happens when the vSAN datastore gets full?" To answer that question, you should first ask the question, "What happens when an individual magnetic disk fills up?" because this will occur before the vSAN datastore fills up.

Before explaining how vSAN reacts to a scenario where a disk is full, it is worth knowing that vSAN will try to prevent this scenario from happening. vSAN balances capacity across the cluster and can and will move components around, or even break up components, when this can prevent a disk full scenario. Of course, the success of this action is entirely based on the rate at which the VM claims and fills new blocks and at which vSAN can relocate existing components.

It should also be noted that the new reservation options (operations reserve, host rebuild reserve) discussed earlier can be used to mitigate the impact of this situation should it arise, by ensuring that there is enough space set aside to prevent the disk from filling up. However, these reservations are not available to all vSAN configurations as mentioned. It is only available on vSAN clusters that are greater than 3 nodes in size, and cannot be used with vSAN stretched clusters, or with vSAN clusters that use fault domains. So, it is still a possibility in some configurations.

In the event of a disk's reaching full capacity, vSAN pauses (technically called *stun*) the VMs that are trying to write data and require additional new disk space for these writes; those that do not need additional disk space continue to run as normal. Note that vSAN-based VMs are deployed thin by default and that this only applies when new blocks need to be allocated to this thin-provisioned disk.

This is identical to the behavior observed on VMFS when the datastore reaches capacity. When additional disk capacity is made available on the vSAN datastore, the stunned VMs may be resumed via the vSphere Web Client. Administrators should be able to see how much capacity is consumed on a per-disk basis via the Configure > vSAN > Disk Management view and viewing the disks on a per host basis as shown in the next figure.

Figure 165: Monitoring physical disks

UNMAP Support

We should start by explaining what UNMAP does. In a nutshell, UNMAP is a way of reclaiming dead or stranded space on a volume or datastore. For the longest time, UNMAP was associated with reclaiming once used, but no longer used space on a VMFS datastore. When a file was deleted on or migrated from a VMFS, there was no way to inform the storage array that these blocks on the volume are now free. Enter UNMAP. Using this standard SCSI command, hosts could now tell the array to reuse this space, essentially reclaiming space for reuse.

The second variant of this process came about when guest OSes running in VMs could send UNMAP commands to declare that space that they were consuming on their local filesystem (and thus VMDK) was no longer being used, enabling VMDKs to be shrunk in size.

Now when we look at these scenarios in the context of vSAN, the first method isn't relevant. vSAN has full knowledge of who is using space from an object perspective. Thus, if a VM is moved from, or deleted on, the vSAN datastore, vSAN can automatically reclaim and use that space. However, it was not until vSAN 6.7U1 that UNMAP support for guest OS appeared. This is completely automated, so there is not very much to consider from an operational perspective. One caveat to be aware of is that this is not supported by all guest OSes. Typically, it is supported in the later versions of Microsoft Windows and various Linux distributions. Also, note that there could be some performance impact while the UNMAP operation is running.

UNMAP is not enabled by default. It can be configured via the *Ruby vSphere Console* (RVC). The command to enable or disable unmap is as follows, as must be run against a cluster object.

```
> vsan.unmap_support -h
usage: unmap_support [opts] cluster
Manage vSAN cluster on supporting SCSI command 'unmap', by default check current status
   cluster: vSAN cluster to manage
   -e, --enable      Enable unmap support on vSAN cluster
   -d, --disable     Disable unmap support on vSAN cluster
   -h, --help        Show this message
```

There are several caveats and considerations when running UNMAP on vSAN. This includes a reliance on the version of VM Hardware used by the virtual machine. We would urge you to read the official VMware documentation to obtain the full list of requirements when using this feature.

vCenter Management

vCenter server is an important part of most vSphere deployments because it is the main tool used for managing and monitoring the virtual infrastructure. In the past, new features introduced to vSphere often had a dependency on vCenter Server to be available, like vSphere DRS for instance. If vCenter Server was unavailable, that service would also be temporarily unavailable; in the case of vSphere DRS, this meant that no load balancing would occur during this time.

Fortunately, vSAN does not rely on vCenter Server in any shape or form, not even to make configuration changes or to create a new vSAN cluster. Even if vCenter Server goes down, vSAN continues to function, and VMs are not impacted whatsoever when it comes to vSAN functionality. If needed, all management tasks can be done through ESXCLI or RVC, the Ruby vSphere Console that ships with vCenter Server. While there are plans to eventually deprecate RVC in favor of the ESXCLI, at the time of writing, it is still available.

You might wonder at this point why VMware decided to align the vSAN cluster construct with the vSphere HA and DRS construct, especially when there is no direct dependency on vCenter Server and no direct relationship. There are several reasons for this, so let's briefly explain those before looking at a vCenter Server failure scenario.

The main reason for aligning the vSAN cluster construct with the vSphere HA and DRS cluster construct is user experience. Today, when vSAN is configured/enabled, it takes just a handful of clicks in the cluster properties section of the vSphere Client. This is primarily achieved because a compute cluster already is a logical grouping of ESXi hosts.

This not only allows for ease of deployment but also simplifies upgrade workflows and other maintenance tasks that are typically done within the boundaries of a cluster. On top of that, capacity planning and sizing for compute is done at cluster granularity; by aligning these constructs, storage can be sized accordingly.

A final reason is of course availability. vSphere HA is performed at cluster level, and it is only natural to deal with the new per-VM accessibility consideration within the cluster because vSphere HA at the time of writing does not allow you to fail-over VMs between clusters; it can only failover a VM to another host within the same cluster. In other words, life is much easier when vSphere HA, DRS, and vSAN all share the same logical boundary and grouping.

Running vCenter Server on vSAN

A common support question relates to whether VMware supports the vCenter Server that is managing vSAN to run in the vSAN cluster. The concern would be a failure scenario where the access to the vSAN datastore is lost and thus VMs, including vCenter Server, can no longer run. The major concern here is that no vCenter Server (and thus no tools such as RVC) is available to troubleshoot any issues experienced in the vSAN environment. Fortunately, vSAN can be fully managed via ESXCLI commands on the ESXi hosts. So, to answer the initial question, yes, VMware will support customers hosting their vCenter Server on vSAN (as in it is supported), but in the rare event where the vCenter Server is not online and you need to manage or troubleshoot issues with vSAN, the user experience will not be as good. This is a decision that should be given some careful consideration.

vSAN Storage Services

As we have seen many times throughout this book, the vSAN datastore is typically consumed by VMs deployed on the same cluster where vSAN is enabled. However, the vSAN datastore can also be consumed remotely through several different vSAN Storage Services, namely the iSCSI Target Service, vSAN File Service, and HCI Mesh. These services allow vSAN datastores to be consumed from remote clients. In this section, we will look at these storage services in further detail and highlight operations considerations where applicable.

vSAN iSCSI Target Service

This service enables an iSCSI Target on the vSAN Cluster, which then allows remote/external iSCSI initiators to consume storage on the vSAN datastore.

Enable vSAN iSCSI Target Service

Configurable options for the iSCSI Target Service include the default network (VMkernel) for the iSCSI traffic. A storage policy must also be associated with the target, which is then used to create a VM Home Namespace object to store iSCSI metadata. Authentication protocols include CHAP (Challenge Handshake Authentication Protocol), where the target authenticates the initiator, as well as mutual (bi-directional) CHAP, where both the initiator and the target authenticate one another. The final consideration is the TCP port on which the initiator and target communicate. By default, this is port 3260.

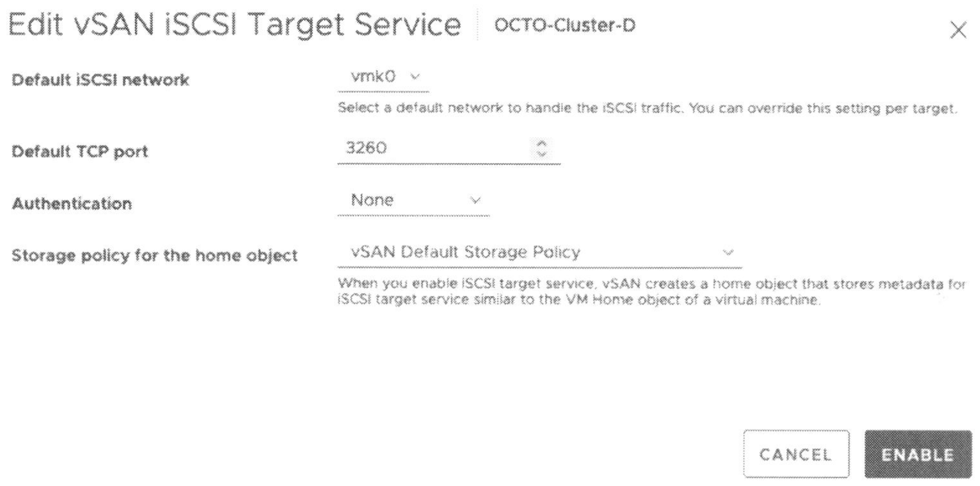

Figure 166: vSAN iSCSI Target Service Setup

Information about the service is now displayed on the Cluster > Configure > vSAN > Services page.

Figure 167: vSAN iSCSI Target Service Enabled

Create a vSAN iSCSI Target

Once the iSCSI Target Service is enabled, a new iSCSI Target Service menu entry appears in Cluster > Configure > vSAN.

iSCSI Targets and Initiator Groups can now be created. Administrators will need to create the target IQN (iSCSI Qualified Name), along with a target alias and a storage policy. If the IQN is left blank, the system will automatically generate one for you. However, a target alias must be supplied, Once again, you may add the TCP port on which the initiator and target communicate. By default, this is port 3260. Other settings include Authentication (CHAP/Mutual CHAP) and the network to use for iSCSI. A network selection is presented since the iSCSI Targets can be configured to use different networks than that defined for the service.

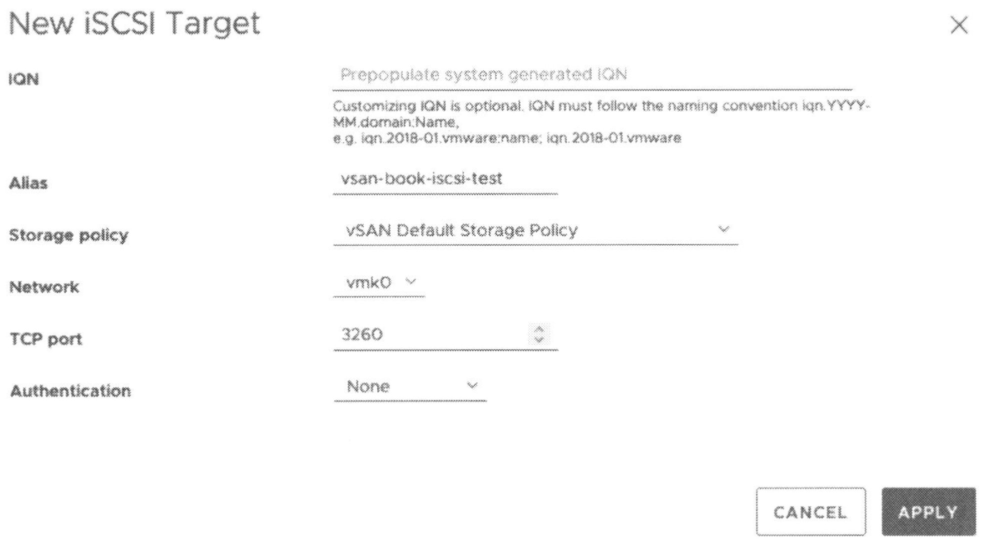

Figure 168: vSAN iSCSI Target Create

Create a vSAN iSCSI LUN

The vSAN iSCSI Target should now be visible in the vSphere client. From here, vSAN iSCSI LUNs can now be created. The main consideration here is to assign a LUN ID.

06 // vSAN Operations

Figure 169: vSAN iSCSI LUN Create

Create a vSAN iSCSI Initiator Group

The final step is to grant access to the target (and any LUNs on the target) to the remote initiators. To do this, the initiators first need to be added to an initiator group. This can be done at various points in the UI. One way is via the iSCSI Target Service. From there, select the Initiator Groups view. Next, under the vSAN iSCSI Initiator Groups, click on Add. This opens a wizard which requests you to provide an initiator group name and add the initiator(s) IQN. The IQN is a specifically formatted identifier, which looks something like iqn.YYYY.MM.domain:name. Note that this IQN comes from the remote initiator; it is not the local vSAN target initiator.

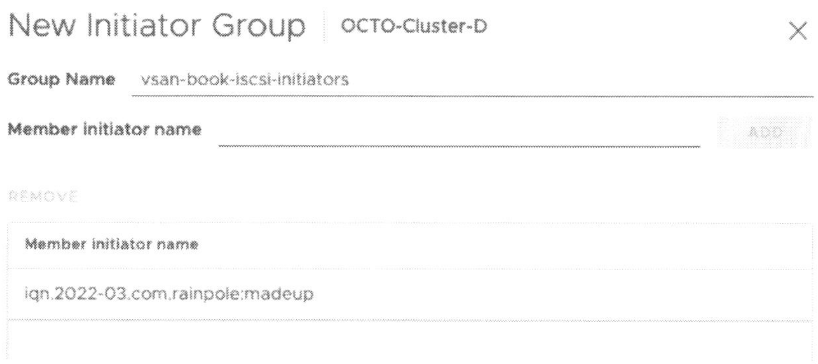

Figure 170: vSAN iSCSI Initiator Create

The initiator group must now be given access to the target. In the Initiator Groups view, under Accessible Targets, click on Add, and add the vSAN iSCSI target created previously. This now completes the step of granting members of the initiator group "vsan-book-iscsi-initiators" access to target "vsan-book-iscsi-test", and thus access to LUN ID 0 which was created on that target.

Note that there are several considerations and limitations around the vSAN iSCSI Target Service. The number one item to highlight is that the vSAN iSCSI target service does not support other vSphere or ESXi clients or initiators. Thus, it is not supported to present these vSAN iSCSI targets and LUNs to other ESXi hosts. In fact, VMware does not support presenting these vSAN iSCSI targets and LUNs to third-party hypervisors either. Other operational considerations include the following:

- L3 Routing between initiators and targets (on the vSAN iSCSI network) is supported
- Jumbo Frames (on the vSAN iSCSI network) is supported
- IPv4 and IPv6 are both supported
- IPsec / IP Security supported (available on ESXi hosts using IPv6 only)
- NIC Teaming configurations (on the vSAN iSCSI network) supported
- iSCSI feature Multiple Connections per Session (MCS) not supported

vSAN iSCSI Target Service and vSAN Stretched Cluster

One final consideration is related to vSAN Stretched Clusters and iSCSI. Let's first describe a little about the iSCSI on vSAN architecture. With the iSCSI implementation on vSAN, there is the concept of a target I/O owner for vSAN iSCSI. The I/O owner is what the iSCSI initiator connects to. However, the I/O owner may be on a completely different vSAN node/host to the actual iSCSI LUN backed by a vSAN VMDK object. This is not a problem for vSAN deployments, as this can be considered akin to a VM's compute residing on one vSAN host and the VM's storage residing on a completely different vSAN host. This 'non-locality' feature of vSAN allows us to do operations like maintenance mode, vMotion, capacity balancing and so on without impacting the performance of the VM. The same is true for the vSAN iSCSI Target Service implementation; an administrator should be able to move the I/O owner to a different host, and even migrate the iSCSI LUNs to different hosts while not impacting iSCSI performance. This enables the vSAN iSCSI implementation to be unaffected by operations such as maintenance mode, balancing tasks, and of course any failures in the cluster.

The key issue however is if the initiator is somewhere on-site A, and the target I/O owner is on site B. In this case, the iSCSI traffic (as well as any vSAN traffic) will need to traverse the inter-site link. In a nutshell, there could be an additional inter-site trip for iSCSI traffic, and this is why VMware did not support iSCSI on vSAN Stretched Clusters for some time. A mechanism to offer some sort of locality between the iSCSI initiator and the target I/O owner was needed. Fortunately, this is now available as described in chapter 4 when the architecture of the vSAN iSCSI Target service was discussed. Administrators can now select which site that the I/O owner should have affinity to, starting with vSAN 7.0U1.

Once the I/O owner has been placed correctly, and the iSCSI initiator does not have to traverse the interconnect to communicate, we can consider the behavior of iSCSI LUNs in a vSAN stretched cluster. A scenario could arise where the I/O owner is residing on one site in the stretched cluster, whilst the actual vSAN object backing the iSCSI LUN (VMDK) could be on the other site. This is not an issue. For write workloads, no matter if it is VM or iSCSI, all the traffic between the iSCSI initiator (which has established connectivity through the I/O owner) and the iSCSI target has to traverse the inter-site link since write data is written to both sites anyway (RAID-1). Thus, writes are not a concern. When it comes to read workloads, the ability to read data from the local site for both iSCSI and VM workloads is available, avoiding the need to traverse the inter-site link. This means that it doesn't matter which site has the I/O owner resides. The real concern is to be able to place the initiator and the I/O owner on the same site, and this functionality is now available.

vSAN File Service

With vSAN 7.0, VMware released a fully integrated File Service feature. Initially, it provided support for NFS v3 and NFS v4.1 protocols but soon followed this up with support for SMB (Server Message Block) protocols v2 & v3 in vSAN 7.0U1. The architectural details of how vSAN File Service is implemented have been covered in detail in chapter 4. In this section, we will look at how to enable vSAN File Service, how to create a file share, and look at any operations considerations associated with these actions.

Enable vSAN File Service

File Service is implemented as a set of File Server "Agent" VMs which are managed by vSphere ESX Agent Manager (EAM). The image that is used to create the file service VMs is an OVF which is downloaded and deployed during the configuration step. This OVF is stored in vCenter along with the File Service configuration. If File Service is disabled and re-enabled, the configuration persists and does not need to be re-added.

File Service is available for configuration on the Cluster > Configure > vSAN > Services page.

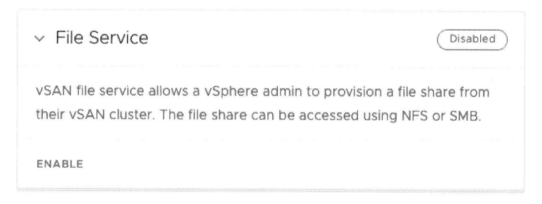

Figure 171: vSAN File Service

Simply click on the "Enable" text to start the configuration process. The introduction screen provides some information about the sorts of information that will be needed during the enabling process. You will need to provide DNS names for each of the file servers. The number of file servers required is dependent on the size of the vSAN cluster, one per node. If the file shares that are created from vSAN File Service need to be integrated with Kerberos Security, additional parameters such as the AD domain and a user account with appropriate privileges are also needed. One final note on this screen – you may notice that the diagram also shows Pods consuming file shares. This is a reference to Kubernetes Read-Write-Many volumes which can be dynamically created through the vSphere CSI driver. This is covered in detail in the Cloud-Native Applications chapter later in this book.

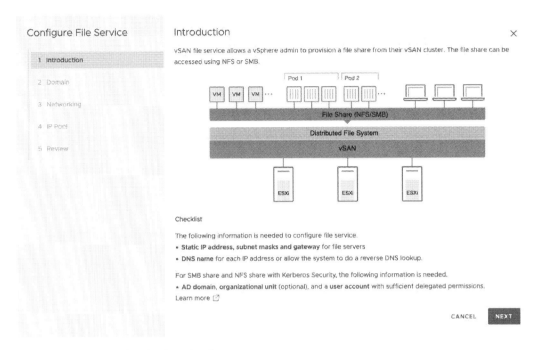

Figure 172: vSAN File Service Introduction

The very first time that File Service is enabled, you are prompted to let the system download the agent OVF from the VMware download site. Since this is a vSAN 7.0U3 system, the OVF is also v7.0.3. You will need to trust the certificate to proceed.

Figure 173: vSAN File Service agent download

On the domain page, a file service domain must be provided. This is used to maintain security and network information about the shares. The DNS server and suffixes are self-explanatory, and the last option relates to Kerberos Security, and when or not you want to enable Active Directory. If the administrator chooses not to enable Active Directory, then SMB file shares cannot be created, only

NFS file shares.

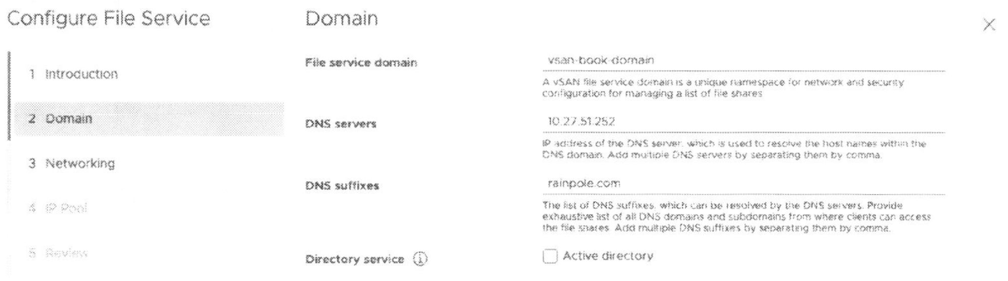

Figure 174: vSAN File Service Domain

After completing the domain configuration (in this example, I did not add Active Directory), the wizard moves to the Networking section. This is looking for a Network port group (selectable from the dropdown list), a Subnet mask, and a gateway.

Figure 175: vSAN File Service Networking

Note the information window above, in blue. It is informing the administrator that the port group needs to have Promiscuous Mode and Forged Transmits enabled. This enables the containers within the agent VMs to communicate successfully over the network.

The next step is to add the IP addresses and DNS names for the agents. There are two very useful tools built into the IP Pool section. The first is "Autofill" which, once the first IP address is added, will consecutively populate the remaining IP addresses. Similarly, there is the "Lookup DNS" tool which will resolve all the IP addresses to the fully qualified domain names (FQDNs). These tools are very useful when configuring File Service on very large vSAN clusters. In the example below, File Service is being enabled on a 4 node vSAN cluster, thus there are 4 agents to populate.

To begin adding the IP pool for the agents, add the first IP address and click on "Autofill". Note, as per the blue information window, the Primary IP address or primary DNS name is used to access the file shares.

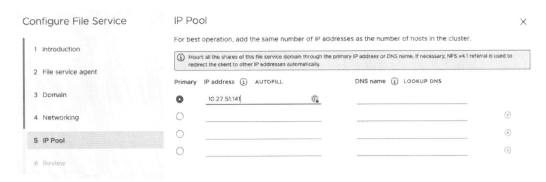

Figure 176: vSAN File Service IP Pool – First IP Address

Once the IP addresses have been populated, click on the "Lookup DNS" to populate all the DNS names.

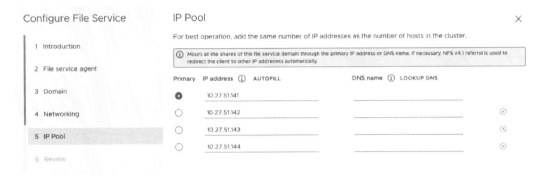

Figure 177: vSAN File Service IP Pool – Autofill

When the IP addresses and DNS names have been successfully populated, as shown below, proceed to the Review screen and validate the configuration.

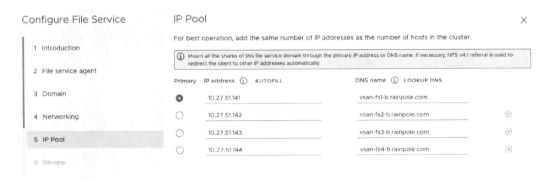

Figure 178: vSAN File Service IP Pool – Lookup DNS

The Review screen should show the status of the OVF download, and report that it is ready for use.

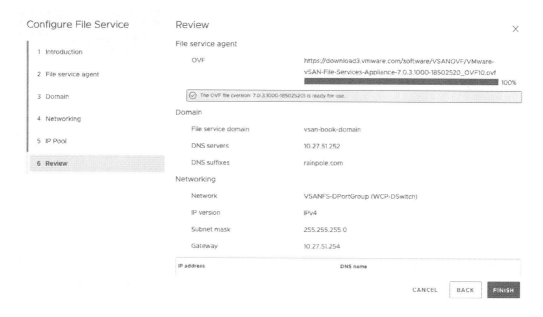

Figure 179: vSAN File Service IP Pool – Review

Assuming the configuration is correct, the "Finish" button will commence the setup. The file service domain is created and the vSAN file service is enabled. The agent VMs are deployed and are visible in the vCenter inventory under the folder ESX Agents. They are names vSAN File Service Node (X) where X is a numeric value, and the NFS servers in each container (one per VM) are started with the IP addresses that were assigned during the vSAN File Service configuration process. If there are no issues encountered, File Service should now appear enabled in the Cluster > Configure > vSAN > Services view, as shown below.

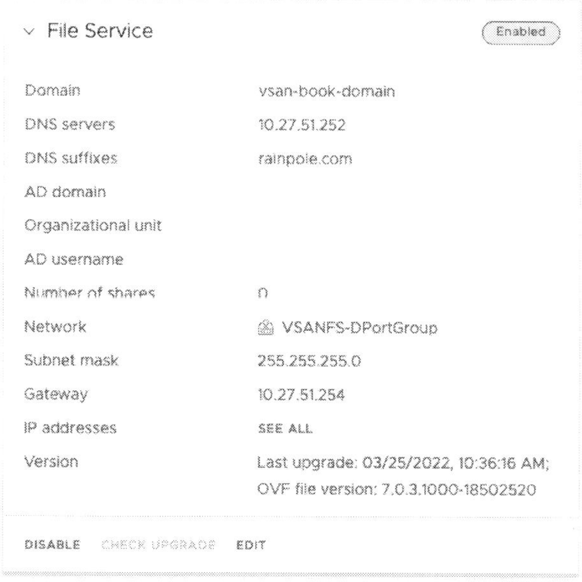

Figure 180: vSAN File Service Enabled

Note that there is no AD information displayed since Active Directory was not selected. The File Service can now be used to create file shares.

Create a vSAN File Service NFS File Share

To create a vSAN file share, navigate to Cluster > Configure > vSAN > File Shares. From here, administrators can create file shares that can be remotely mounted by clients. In the following example, an NFS file share is created. To create a file share, click on the "Add" button. This launches a wizard that prompts for information such as the name of the share, which protocol to use, security mode, storage policy to use for the share (since the file share is backed by a vSAN object), and what quotas, if any, to put in place. A share warning threshold quote and a hard quota can both be configured. Finally, there is the option to add labels to the file share using a key-value format. In the example below, a file share called "vsan-book-file-share" using NFS (supporting both NFS 4.1 and NFS 3 protocols) is being created. There is no option to change the security mode since Active Directory was not enabled, so Kerberos authentication is not available. Lastly, I set the space quotas to 90 GB and 100GB respectively, and added a label of "owner:cormac".

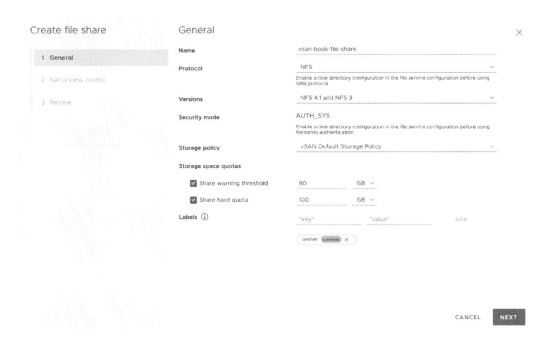

Figure 181: vSAN File Share Creation - NFS

The next window defines the network access controls. There are 3 options available, either no access to the share, allow access from anywhere, or control the clients who can access the share by allowing only certain IP addresses or a range of IP addresses to access the share. The only other options that require administrator consideration is the permission on the volume as well as the root squash option. Permission can be set to No access, read-only or read-write. Root squash means that anyone who attempts to mount the NFS share as user root will have their permissions squashed. In this example, I am specifying that anyone accessing from a particular network range has full access, but anyone from any other network only has read access.

Figure 182: vSAN File Share Network Access Control

The final step is to review the file share configuration, and to click "Finish" to create the share. The file share should now be visible in the File Shares view.

Figure 183: vSAN File Share Created

The NFS share can now be mounted. The *showmount* command shows the exported shares from an NFS server.

```
# showmount -e vsan-fs1-b.rainpole.com
Export list for vsan-fs1-b.rainpole.com:
/vsan-book-file-share 10.27.51.0/24,*

# mkdir /vsan-book

# mount vsan-fs1-b.rainpole.com:/vsan-book-file-share /vsan-book

# cd /vsan-book/

# df -h .
Filesystem                                      Size  Used Avail Use% Mounted on
vsan-fs1-b.rainpole.com:/vsan-book-file-share   100G     0  100G   0% /vsan-book
```

Note the mount path used above. The mount paths for NFS v3 and NFS v4.1 can be obtained by selecting the file share in the vSphere UI and using the "Copy Path" option. It offers path information for both protocols.

Figure 184: vSAN File Share Copy Path

There is a lot of good information on file shares available to an administrator, as you might expect. By clicking on the "details" icon (2nd field of the file share), administrators can glean basic information as shown below. Since the file share is backed by a vSAN block device, physical placement details relating to this object are also available to review. There is also a Performance view so that administrators can see per file share metrics such as IOPS, Throughput and Latency. There also is a snapshot view that provides the ability to take snapshots of the file share. Note that the snapshot feature is probably not of much use to an administrator via the UI, but it can be leveraged by backup partners to take backups of vSAN File Service file shares. Before the snapshot feature was available, the recommendation was to back up the file share from the client which has the share mounted. This ability to take file share snapshots provides an alternate solution.

Modifying vSAN File Service

It is possible to modify the vSAN File Service configuration after it has been enabled. In the example previously, Active Directory was not configured. This means that only NFS file shares could be created, and not SMB. Suppose that there is a need to now use vSAN File Service for both NFS and SMB. Administrators can edit the vSAN File Service configuration, and Enable Active Directory, as shown here. No changes are required to the networking, or the IP pool sections when enabling AD.

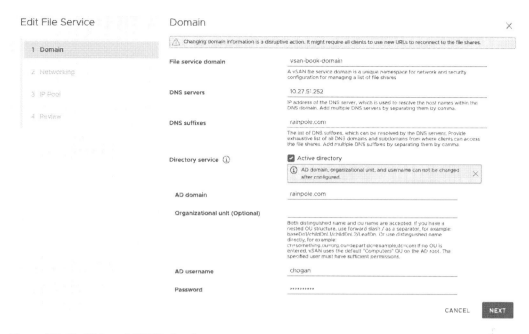

Figure 185: Modifying vSAN File Service

If the operation was successful, the File Service overview in the vSAN Services page should now show AD domain and AD username information.

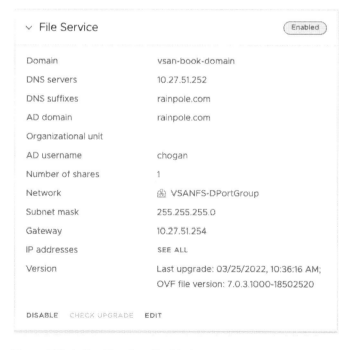

Figure 186: Active Directory Enabled

Create a vSAN File Service SMB File Share

Now that Active Directory is enabled, I have the option to create SMB file shares as well as NFS file shares. SMB shares have some additional options not available to NFS. It allows Protocol Encryption, which encrypts data-in-transit traffic to a share. It also includes an option to do access-based enumeration (ABE). This feature, if enabled, only displays files and folders that a user has permissions to access. If a user does not have the correct permissions, files or folders are hidden from that user when they mount the share. Note that when ABE is enabled, it could impact performance for directories that have lots of files, since all the Access Control Lists (ACLs) will need to be checked to see if the user has permission to view them or not. This consideration is highlighted when ABE is enabled, as shown below. Otherwise, the configuration of an SMB share is very similar to that of an NFS share.

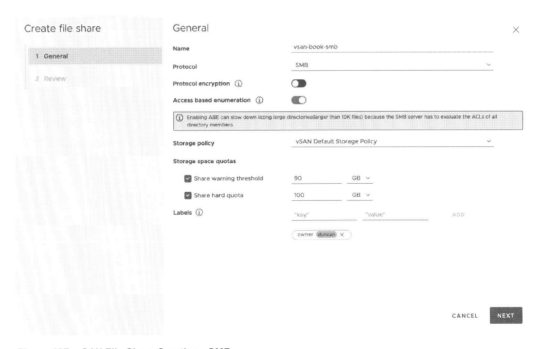

Figure 187: vSAN File Share Creation - SMB

Once the SMB file share has been successfully created, it will appear in the File Share view alongside the NFS file share created previously. Note that as well as having a "Copy Path" option, this also has a "Copy MMC Command" option available. This is a reference to the Microsoft Management Console and allows administrators to view permissions, connections, etc., of shared folders.

06 // vSAN Operations

Figure 188: SMB File Share

Using the "Copy Path", it is a simple matter of going to the Windows host where you want to mount the share and mapping the network drive. Here is an example of mounting the share to a Windows 10 desktop.

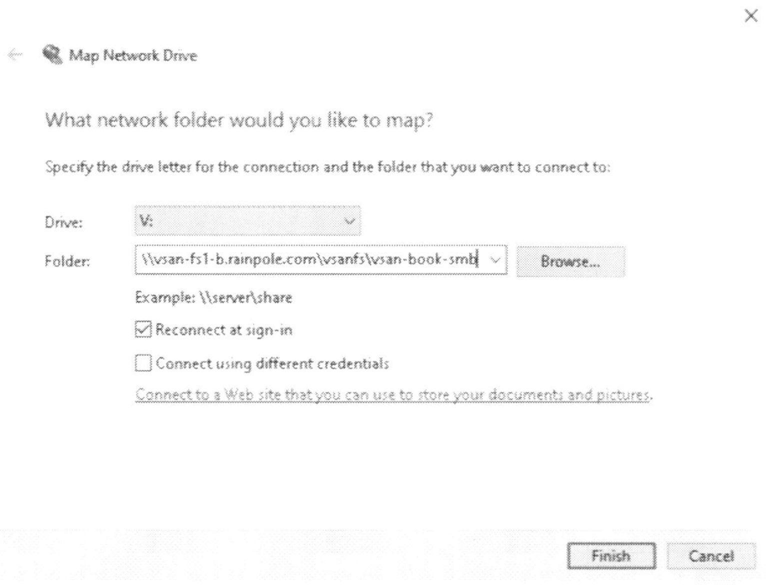

Figure 189: SMB File Share – Map Network Drive using "Copy Path"

Once the drive is mounted, the MMC command can be used to see information about the share. Simply open a Command Prompt on the Windows desktop and run the copied MMC command, as shown here:

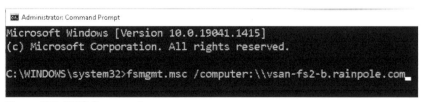

Figure 190: MMC Command

This command will launch the Shared Folders view, and from there you will be able to see who has the share mounted, open files, how long they have been connected, etc.

249

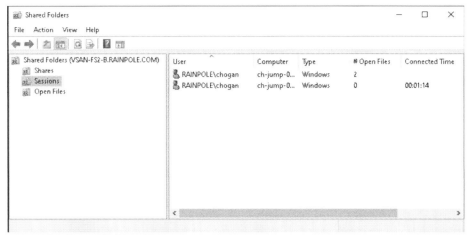

Figure 191: Shared Folders View

vSAN File Service and Maintenance Mode

In chapter 4, the architecture chapter, the behavior of vSAN File Service and Maintenance Mode was discussed. There, it was discussed that when a host is placed into maintenance mode the protocol stack container is restarted on a different agent VM. This means that some agent VMs could end up running 2 (or more even) protocol stack containers. This is all managed by vSAN, and vSAN File Service will rebalance the protocol stack containers when the host exits maintenance mode, placing a single protocol stack container on each agent VM, and the cluster returns to normal. However, there are one or two oddities in relation to the agent VM that might be observed when a node that has been configured with vSAN File Service is placed into maintenance mode. The vSAN File Service agent VM node is powered off but is not migrated. An error is thrown for the "Install agent" task, as shown below. Interestingly, the initiator of the task is EAM, the ESX Agent Manager.

Figure 192: File Service Maintenance Mode Install Agent task error

If the associated event log is examined, we see the reason for the error.

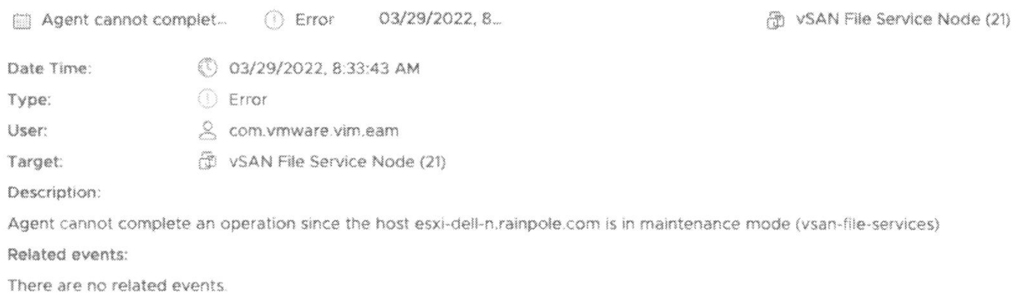

```
Agent cannot complet...    Error     03/29/2022, 8...              vSAN File Service Node (21)

Date Time:        03/29/2022, 8:33:43 AM
Type:             Error
User:             com.vmware.vim.eam
Target:           vSAN File Service Node (21)
Description:
Agent cannot complete an operation since the host esxi-dell-n.rainpole.com is in maintenance mode (vsan-file-services)
Related events:
There are no related events.
```

Figure 193: File Service Maintenance Mode Events

EAM is responsible for maintaining an agent VM on each host in the vSAN cluster, but since one of the hosts has been placed into maintenance mode, it can no longer do this. Thus, the above agent install task error and associated events are expected when placing a vSAN host into maintenance mode that has vSAN File Service is enabled.

You might ask why this behavior is happening. The reason is related to the storage policy that is used by agent VMs. The policy is called "FSVM_Profile_DO_NOT_MODIFY" and has some unique settings. It uses a *failure to tolerate* setting of "No data redundancy with host affinity". This means that there is only one copy of the data, and that data always stays on the same host. Thus, when a host is placed into maintenance mode, the data is not migrated to another host in the cluster. This is also why the agent VM is powered off, and not migrated.

Resetting vSAN File Service

As observed, vSAN File Service downloads, and configures an OVF image. This image is stored on vCenter, and if an administrator needs to disable vSAN File Service, the configuration is retained. This means that if vSAN File Service is re-enabled, the configuration is already in place and most of the fields required for setup are already populated. However, there may be occasions where a new vSAN File Service configuration is required. In that case, the existing OVF images on vCenter will need to be removed. VMware Knowledgebase article 80028 provides detailed instructions on how to do this task.

vSAN File Service Requirements and Limitations

This chapter has already discussed some of the limitations around vSAN File Service, such as the requirement to enable promiscuous mode and forged transmits on the portgroup used by File service for networking. The fact that NFS file shares from vSAN File Service cannot be mounted to ESXi hosts or any other hypervisor was also mentioned. This section attempts to highlight the main requirements and limitations of vSAN File Service that administrators need to consider. Note that these are accurate at the time of writing but will most likely change over time. Check vSAN Release Notes for future releases to see if any of these requirements/limitations have changed.

- Support for 2-node is available since vSAN 7.0 U2
- Enabling vSAN File Service on a cluster with "compute only" nodes is not supported
- NFS v3 and NFS v4.1 protocols are supported since the initial vSAN 7.0 release
- SMB v2.1 and v3 protocols are supported since 7.0 U1
- Active Directory authentication is supported with SMB for 7.0 U1 but note that there can be no spaces in OU names at present
- Kerberos authentication supported with NFS since 7.0 U1
- vSAN File Service on a vSAN stretched cluster is supported since vSAN 7.0 U2
- Data-in-transit encryption is supported starting vSAN 7.0 U2
- UNMAP is supported starting vSAN 7.0 U2
- Mounting NFS file share to hypervisors, including ESXi hosts, is not supported
- The maximum number of shares per cluster is 100 starting vSAN 7.0 U2
- The maximum size of the file share is equal to the maximum available capacity of the vSAN cluster
- The IP addresses assigned to vSAN File Service must be on the same L2 segment
- On standard and distributed (v)Switches, the following settings are enabled on the port group automatically: Forged Transmits, Promiscuous Mode
- For NSX-T, MAC Learning should be enabled on the Segment Profile

vSAN HCI Mesh / Remote vSAN Datastores

vSAN HCI Mesh allows administrators to mount a remote vSAN datastore. The benefit of this feature is that if there is "stranded space" on some vSAN datastores in your datacenter, this can now be consumed by a remote cluster, and that remote cluster can use the datastore for the provisioning of virtual machine workloads.

While the initial release of this feature in vSAN version 7.0U1 required vSAN clusters both locally and remotely, vSAN version 7.0U2 introduced compute-only support. This means that the cluster that is mounting the remote vSAN datastore does not require to be in a vSAN cluster configuration, nor does it require a vSAN license, to mount the vSAN datastore. A vSAN datastore may also be mounted to a single ESXi host. However, that ESXi host does need to be placed in its own cluster in the vCenter inventory before mounting can take place. It also needs to be in the same datacenter as the vSAN cluster in the vCenter inventory.

Mount a Remote vSAN Datastore

The ability to mount a remote datastore is dependent on the fact that the datastore resides in the same datacenter in the vCenter inventory. To mount the remote datastore, navigate to one of the clusters in the datacenter and select Configure > vSAN > Remote Datastores. This should automatically provide a view of the local vSAN datastore, as shown below, if one exists.

06 // vSAN Operations

Figure 194: HCI Mesh Remote Datastores (Local)

By clicking on the "Mount Remote Datastore" option, a list of vSAN datastores belonging to vSAN clusters within the same datacenter is displayed.

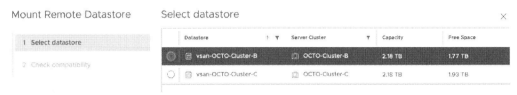

Figure 195: HCI-Mesh Mount Remote Datastore

When the remote datastore is selected as a mount candidate, several compatibility checks are run to ensure that the requirements are met, and none of the limitations around HCI Mesh are exceeded. Figure 196 shows the list of compatibility checks.

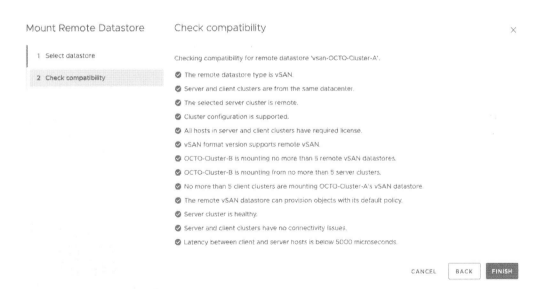

Figure 196: HCI-Mesh Remote Datastore Compatibility Check

There are a significant number of compatibility checks. These ensure that neither the source nor the destinations cluster is a 2-node or vSAN stretched cluster, both of which are currently unsupported with HCI Mesh. It also checks licensing and ensures that none of the mounting limits are exceeded. Also important is ensuring there are low latency, and high bandwidth connections between the local and remote clusters.

253

Once the mount operation completes the Remote Datastores view should now show both the local and remote datastore details.

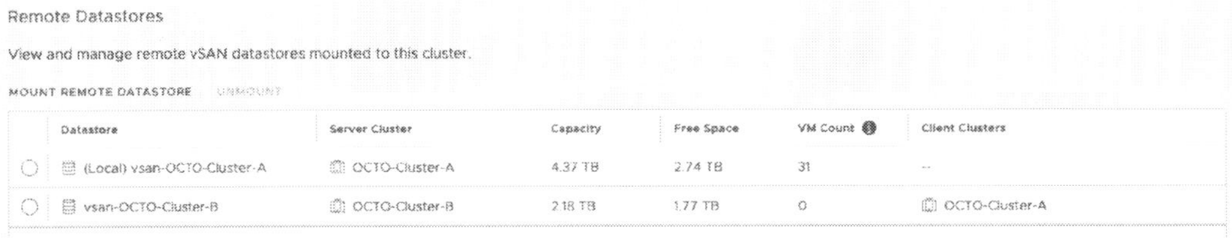

Datastore	Server Cluster	Capacity	Free Space	VM Count	Client Clusters
(Local) vsan-OCTO-Cluster-A	OCTO-Cluster-A	4.37 TB	2.74 TB	31	--
vsan-OCTO-Cluster-B	OCTO-Cluster-B	2.18 TB	1.77 TB	0	OCTO-Cluster-A

Figure 197: HCI-Mesh Local and Remote datastore

Note the VM Count column. The VM Count is only referring to virtual machines owned by the local cluster on the remote vSAN datastore. There could be virtual machines deployed to this datastore by the vSAN cluster that "owns" the vSAN datastore, i.e., its local vSAN cluster, or indeed other remote clusters that are also mounting the datastore. They do not show up in the VM Count. Only VMs created by this cluster appear in this column.

VMs are provisioned on remote datastores in the same way as VMs are provisioned on local datastores. Customers select a storage policy when provisioning a VM, and both local and remote datastores which are compliant with the policy are shown as suitable datastores for the deployment. In the polices chapter earlier in this book, we saw how storage rules could be used to differentiate between multiple vSAN datastores, including those that are encrypted, have deduplication and compression capabilities as well as choosing between hybrid and all-flash vSAN datastores. See the Storage rules section in chapter 5 for further details.

HCI Mesh and vCLS

Some additional operational considerations need to be considered when with working with HCI-Mesh. The first of these relates to the VMware vSphere Cluster Services (vCLS) virtual machines. vCLS is a mechanism that decouples both vSphere DRS and vSphere HA from vCenter Server. vCLS ensures the availability of critical services even when vCenter Server is impacted by a failure.

vCLS is a consideration if the remote vSAN datastore is the only datastore available to a compute cluster. In such a case, vCenter / ESX Agent Manager (EAM) will try to provision the vCLS VMs onto the remote vSAN datastore. The remote vSAN datastore may not be the most optimal datastore – perhaps it is only mounted to the cluster temporarily. In the past administrators had no control over the placement of the vCLS VMs, but starting with vSphere 7.0U3, administrators can now choose which datastore to use for vCLS and prevent it from using the remote vSAN datastore. Navigate to Cluster > Configure > vSphere Cluster Services > Datastore and click on the 'Add' button to choose which datastores to use for vCLS, as shown below.

06 // vSAN Operations

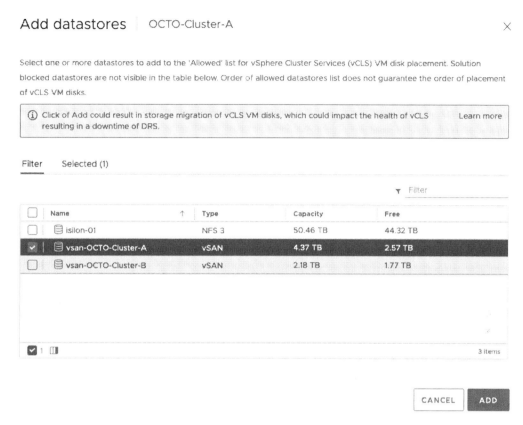

Figure 198: Selecting a vCLS datastore

Similarly, if you are using an HCI Mesh with a single ESXi node in the vSphere cluster, then neither DRS nor HA is relevant. Thus, vCLS can be disabled. This is achieved by enabling a feature called 'Retreat Mode' for vCLS. Refer to VMware knowledgebase article 80472 for details on how to turn on 'Retreat Mode'.

One final consideration for administrators relates to maintenance mode. Administrators should now be cognizant of the fact that a vSAN datastore may be used by both the local cluster as well as remote clusters. Any maintenance mode operation could adversely impact the remote workloads on the shared vSAN datastore, not just the local ones. Actions that impact availability or performance, such as rebuilding and resyncing of objects, will also affect objects belonging to remote workloads. It is something administrators, who so far have only needed to worry about local workloads, will need to consider when doing maintenance on clusters participating in HCI Mesh. This is especially true when doing operations such as taking a complete cluster offline for maintenance.

HCI Mesh Requirements and Limitations

This section attempts to highlight the main requirements and limitations of HCI Mesh. Note that these are accurate at the time of writing, but many may change over time, as updated releases of vSAN appear. Once again, the authors recommend checking the vSAN Release Notes for future releases to see if any of these requirements/limitations have changed or been relaxed.

- HCI Mesh requires vSAN 7.0 Update 1 or later
- HCI Mesh supports "compute only" as of vSAN 7.0U2 (vSAN not required on mounting cluster)
- The vSAN cluster must have the vSAN Enterprise license
- Stretched Clusters and 2-node configurations are not supported
- A vSAN Datastore can be mounted by a maximum of 5 vSAN Client Clusters
- A vSAN cluster can mount a maximum of 5 remote vSAN datastores
- A vSAN Datastore can be mounted by up to 64 vSAN hosts for 7.0 U1, and 128 host for 7.0 U2. This includes the "local hosts" for that vSAN Datastore
- Both the mounting host/cluster and remote cluster need to be managed by the same vCenter Server, and appear in the same Datacenter
- 10Gbps NICs are the minimum required for hosts, but 25Gbps NICs are recommended
- L2 and L3 connectivity are both supported
- RDMA is not supported
- IPv6 needs to be enabled on the hosts
- Network Load Balancing: LACP, Load-based teaming, and active/standby are all supported.
- Network Load Balancing: Dual VMkernel configuration / air-gapped configurations are explicitly not supported
- Data-in-transit encryption is not supported, data-at-rest encryption is supported
- VMs cannot span datastores, in other words, you cannot store the first VMDK on the local vSAN datastore and the second VMDK of the same VM on a remote vSAN datastore
- Remote provisioning (on a mounted remote vSAN datastore) of vSAN File Shares, iSCSI volumes, and/or CNS persistent volumes is not supported
- It is supported to mount an All-Flash Datastore from a Hybrid cluster and the other way around. VM Provisioning can be controlled via SPBM policies to ensure VMs are placed on the correct datastore

Failure Scenarios

We have already discussed some of the failure scenarios in Chapter 4, "Architectural Details," and in Chapter 5, "VM Storage Policy and VM Provisioning". In those chapters, we explained the difference between *absent* components and *degraded* components. From an operational perspective, though, it is good to understand how a capacity device failure, flash device failure, network problem, or host failure impacts your vSAN cluster. Before we discuss them, let's first shortly recap the two different failure states, because they are fundamental to these operational considerations:

- **Absent**: vSAN does not know what has happened to the component that is missing. A typical example of this is when a host has failed; vSAN cannot tell if it is a real failure or simply a reboot. When this happens, vSAN waits for 60 minutes by default before new replica components are created. This is called the CLOM daemon timeout, CLOM being shorthand for Cluster Level Object Manager.

- **Degraded**: vSAN knows what has happened to the component that is missing. A typical example of when this can occur is when an SSD or a magnetic disk has failed, and it is generating SCSI sense codes that allow vSAN to understand that this device has failed and is never recovering. When this happens, vSAN instantly spawns new components to make all impacted objects compliant again with their selected policy.

One other feature that should be mentioned here is the concept of durability components or delta components, first introduced in vSAN 7.0U1. Durability components provide a mechanism to maintain the required availability for vSAN objects (e.g., virtual machines) when components go absent. For example, if a host is placed into maintenance mode, the new "durability components" get created on behalf of the components stored on that host. This then allows all the new VM I/O to be committed to the remaining component, as well as the durability component. Another benefit of durability components is reduced recovery times. Once an absent component comes back online, the contents of the durability component can be merged with the out-of-sync recovered component, reducing resync times considerably.

An additional enhancement was made to durability components in vSAN 7.0U2. In this release, durability components can also be used in situations where a host failure has occurred. If a host has failed in the vSAN cluster, durability components may be created to ensure the specified availability level within the policy is maintained.

Now that you know what the different states are, and understand the concept of durability components, let's look again at the different types of failures, or at least the "most" common and what the impact is. Note that in all the scenarios below, durability components are used to improve both the resync times and provide a higher level of availability to vSAN

Capacity Device Failure

A disk failure is probably the most common failure that can happen in any storage environment, and vSAN is no different. The question, of course, is this: How does vSAN handle disk failure? What if it is doing a write or read to or from that disk after it has failed?

If a read error is returned from a storage component in a RAID-1 configuration, be it a magnetic disk in the case of hybrid configurations or a flash device in the case of all-flash configurations, vSAN checks to see whether a replica component exists and reads from that instead. Every RAID-1 object is created, by default, with *failures to tolerate* set to 1, which means that there are always two identical copies of your object available.

There are two separate scenarios when it comes to read data. The first one is where the problem is recoverable, and the second one is an irrecoverable situation. When the issue is recoverable, the I/O error is reported to the *Distributed Object Manager* (DOM) object owner. A component re-creation takes place to replace the failed one. This new component is synchronized with the help of the functioning/working component or components, and when that is completed, the errored component is deleted. However, if for whatever reason, no replica component exists, vSAN will report an I/O error to the VM. This is an unlikely scenario and something an administrator would have had to create a policy with *failures to tolerate* of 0 specifically set, or there have been multiple failures or maintenance mode operations on the cluster.

Like read errors, write failures are also propagated up to the DOM object owner. The components are marked as degraded, and a component re-creation is initiated. When the component re-creation is completed, the cluster directory (*cluster monitoring, membership, and directory service* [CMMDS] is updated. Note that the cache device (which has no error) continues to service reads for the components on all the other capacity devices in the disk group while this remediation operation is taking place.

As mentioned previously, the vSphere Client provides the ability to monitor how much data is being resynced in the event of a failure. Selecting the vSAN cluster object in the vCenter Server inventory, then selecting Monitor, vSAN, and then "Resyncing Objects" will show this information. It will report on the number of resyncing objects, the bytes left to resync and the estimated time for the resyncing to complete, as shown below.

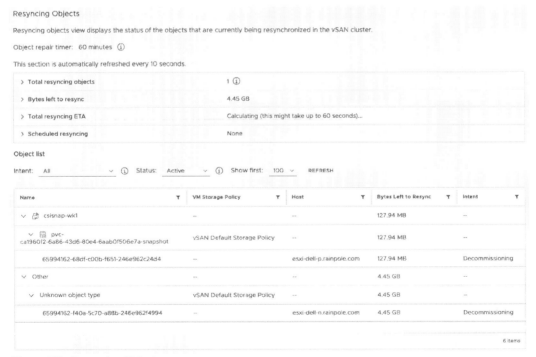

Figure 199: Resyncing Objects

Capacity Device Failure with Erasure Coding

As you have read in chapter 5, "VM Storage Policy and VM Provisioning", vSAN supports different protection mechanisms. As well as the default RAID-1, vSAN supports both RAID-5 and RAID-6.

RAID-5 requires a minimum of 4 hosts in the vSAN cluster since it is implemented as a 3+1, 3 data disks and 1 parity disk. VMs which are configured with a RAID-5 policy can tolerate 1 failure in the cluster. RAID-6 requires a minimum of 6 hosts in the cluster. It is implemented as a 4+2, 4 data disks and 2 parity disks. VMs which are configured with a RAID-5 policy can tolerate 2 failures in the cluster. Note that neither RAID-5 nor RAID-6 employ dedicated parity disks. The parity is striped across all 4 and 6 disks in the configuration respectively. How failures impact VMs with erasure coding is now discussed.

To understand how failures are handled with erasure coding, it is important to understand that it uses Exclusive OR (XOR) operations on the data to calculate the parity. With RAID-5, let's take the example of a single disk failure. If it is simply the parity component of a VM that is impacted, then obviously reads and writes can continue to flow, but there is no protection for the VM until parity is rebuilt elsewhere in the cluster. If it is one of the data components that is impacted, then the missing data blocks are calculated for reads by using the two remaining data components and the XOR parity results. With these pieces of information, the missing data blocks can be re-calculated.

With RAID-6, there is a double parity calculation to allow any VM with this policy setting to tolerate a double failure. If the double failure impacts both parity segments, then that is ok since we still have a full copy of the data. If it impacts 2 data segments, then that is ok since the data can be rebuilt using the remaining data and the parity. If the double failure impacts both a data segment and a parity segment, then this is ok as well as we simply rebuild the missing data blocks using the remaining data blocks and the remaining parity segment.

The advantage of erasure coding versus RAID-1 mirroring is of course space savings. However, performance is a consideration, not just during normal operations which often requires a read-modify-write operation on the data and then a parity calculation + write-parity operation. This performance penalty may become even more pronounced when there is a failure in the cluster. All this should be considered when debating whether RAID-5 or RAID-6 should be chosen over RAID-1.

Capacity Device Failure with Deduplication Enabled

Note that the following discussion does not apply to vSAN clusters that use the Compression Only feature. This discussion relates to having both Deduplication and Compression enabled on the vSAN cluster, since Deduplication can only be enabled with Compression at the time of writing.

Earlier in the book, the act of removing an individual disk from a disk group was discussed. If deduplication and compression are enabled on the cluster, it was highlighted that it is not possible because the deduplicated and compressed data, along with the associated hash tables and metadata associated with deduplication and compression, are striped across all the capacity tier disks in the disk group.

There is a similar caveat when it comes to a capacity device failure when deduplication and compression are enabled. If a single capacity disk in a disk group where deduplication and compression are enabled fails, the entire disk group becomes inaccessible. Rebuild of the disk group contents will start immediately if the failure allows appropriate sense codes to be sent to the system. Once again, the whole of the disk group would need to be deleted, and when the failing disk has been replaced, the disk group should be recreated. vSAN will automatically take care of rebalancing all components across the vSAN cluster and will overtime utilize the newly created disk group. The resync dashboard will show this balancing of components and will have the rebalance task flagged as a rebalance operation rather than a resync/rebuild operation.

Cache Device Failure

What about when the cache device becomes inaccessible? When a cache device becomes inaccessible due to some failure scenario, all the capacity devices backed by that cache device in the same disk group also become inaccessible. A cache device failure is the same as a failure of all the capacity devices bound to the cache device. In essence, when a cache device fails, the whole disk group is degraded. vSAN immediately tries to find another host or disk to start re-protecting the objects impacted by the failure. This scenario is the same no matter if deduplication and compression are enabled on the cluster or not.

Therefore, from an operational and architectural decision, depending on the type of hosts used, it could be beneficial to create multiple smaller disk groups versus a single large disk group because a disk group is considered a failure domain, as shown in the next diagram.

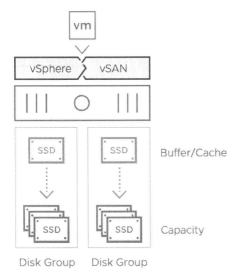

Figure 200: vSAN disk groups

Host Failure

Assuming vSAN VM storage policies have been created with *failures to tolerate* set to at least 1, a host failure in a vSAN cluster is like a host failure in a cluster that has a regular storage device attached. The main difference, of course, is that the vSAN host that has failed contains storage components of objects that will be out of sync when the host returns. However, as we have discussed already, vSAN has a durable components mechanism that replaces missing components for availability purpose, and then speeds up the resync operation against the active components as soon as they re-appear. The active components could reappear for many reasons e.g., a host reboot completing or a host exiting maintenance mode. The durability component concept is shown in the next diagram.

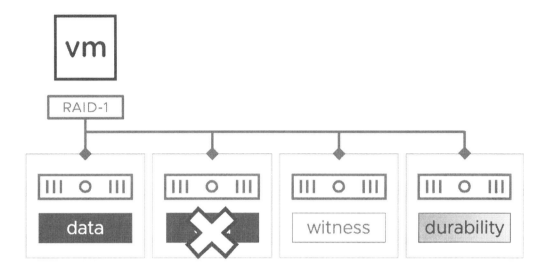

Figure 201: Durability component

In the case of a host failure, after 60 minutes vSAN will start re-creating components because the likelihood of the host returning online is now slim. Most likely this is not a transient failure. When the reconstruction of the storage objects is completed, the cluster directory (CMMDS) is once again updated with the new information about the object. In fact, it is updated at each step of the process, from failure detection, the start of resync, resync progress, and rebuild complete.

Historically, in early releases of vSAN, if the host that originally failed recovers and rejoins the cluster, the object reconstruction status is checked. If object reconstruction has been completed on another node or nodes, no action is taken and the component that was originally ABSENT can now be discarded from the recovered host. If object resynchronization is still in progress, the components of the failed host that have now recovered are also resynched just in case there is an issue with the new object synchronization. When the synchronization of all objects is complete, the components of the original host are discarded, and the more recent copies are utilized. Otherwise, if the new components failed to resync for any reason, the original components on the original host are used.

With the release of vSAN version 6.6, this behavior changed. If a failing component recovers after the CLOMD repair timeout and a new component has already been instantiated and is currently resyncing, vSAN will look at the amount of data remaining for that new component to complete rebuilding and compare it to how long it would take to repair or resync the component that just recovered. vSAN will then choose the component that will complete the quickest and cancel the other rebuild operation. vSAN maintains a bitmap of changed blocks in the event of components of an object being unable to synchronize due to a failure on a host, network, or disk. This allows updates to vSAN objects composed of two or more components to be reconciled after a failure. Let's use a RAID-1 example to explain this. If a host with replica A of object X has been partitioned from the rest of the cluster, the surviving components of X have quorum and data availability, so they continue functioning and serving writes and reads. These surviving components of X are the other replica/mirror and the witness. While A is "absent," all writes performed to X are persistently tracked in a bitmap by vSAN, that is, the bitmap is tracking the regions that are still out of sync. If the partitioned host with replica A comes back and vSAN decides to reintegrate it with the remaining components of object X, the bitmap is used to resynchronize component A.

This behavior changed once again in vSAN versions 7.0U1 and 7.0U2 with the introduction of durability components, as already discussed. New writes are committed to existing components and the newly created durability components. When then the previously failed or missing component recovers and is once again available, the durability component(s) are merged and are subsequently deleted when object resync is complete.

When a host has failed, all VMs that were running on the host at the time of the failure will be restarted by vSphere HA. vSphere HA can restart the VM on any available host in the cluster whether or not it is hosting vSAN components, as demonstrated in the next diagram.

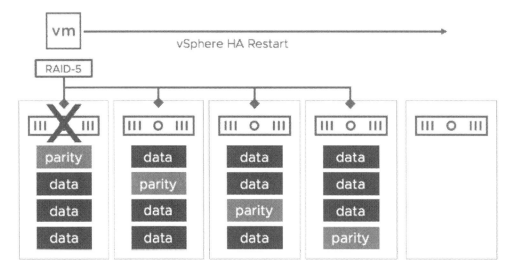

Figure 202: vSAN 1 host failed, HA restart

In the event of an isolation of a host, vSphere HA can and will also restart the impacted VMs. As this is a slightly more complex scenario, let's look at it in more depth.

Network Partition

A vSAN network partition could occur when there is a vSAN network failure. In other words, some hosts can end up on one side of the vSAN cluster, and the remaining hosts on another side. vSAN health checks will surface warnings related to network issues in the event of a partition. There has also been a significant enhancement to Network Diagnostics in the recent version to assist with troubleshooting network issues.

After explaining the host and disk failure scenarios in the previous sections, it is now time to describe how isolations and partitions are handled in a vSAN cluster. Let's look at a typical scenario first and explain what happens during a network partition based on this scenario. In the scenario depicted in the next diagram, vSAN is running a single VM on ESXi-01. This VM has been provisioned using a VM storage policy that has number of failures to tolerate set to 1 using RAID-1.

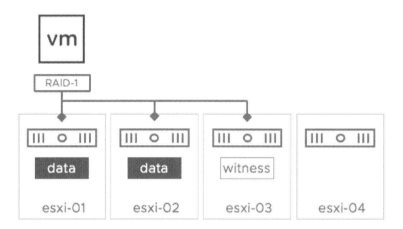

Figure 203: vSAN I/O flow: Failures to tolerate = 1

Because vSAN has the capability to run VMs on hosts that are not holding any active storage components of that VM, this question arises: What happens in the case where the network is isolated? As you can imagine, the vSAN network plays a big role here, made even bigger when you realize that it is also used by vSphere HA for network heart beating. For that reason, as mentioned before, vSAN must be configured before vSphere HA is enabled, so that the vSAN network is used. The following steps describe how vSphere HA and vSAN will react to an isolation event.

- HA will detect there are no network heartbeats received from esxi-01 on the vSAN network.
- HA primary will try to ping the secondary esxi-01.
- HA will declare the secondary esxi-01 is unavailable.
- VMs on esxi-01 will be restarted on one of the other hosts, as shown in the next diagram.
- The vSphere administrator, through the vSphere HA isolation response setting, decides what happens to the original VM on the isolated host. Options are to power off, leave powered on, or disable. We recommend using power off.

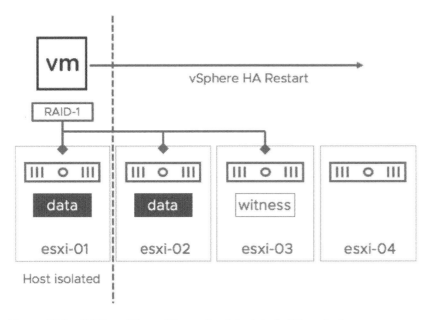

Figure 204: vSAN partition with one host isolated: HA restart

What if something has gone horribly wrong in my network and esxi-01 and esxi-04 end up as part of the same partition? What happens to the VMs then? Well, that is where the witness component comes into play, and how quorum is used to make decisions on what actions to take. The next diagram should make it a bit easier to understand the behavior.

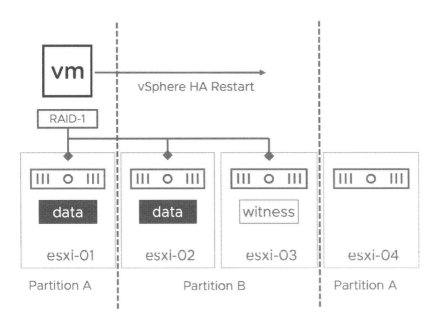

Figure 205: vSAN partition with multiple hosts in a partition

Now this scenario is indeed slightly more complex. There are two partitions, one of which is running the VM with its virtual machine disk (VMDK), and the other partition has a VMDK replica and a witness. Guess what happens? For RAID-1, vSAN uses the witness to see which partition has quorum, and based on that result, one of the two partitions will win. In this case, partition B has more than 50% of the components/votes of this object and therefore is the winner. This means that the VM will be restarted on either esxi-02 or esxi-03 by vSphere HA. Note, however that as this is a partition scenario and not an isolation the isolation response will not be triggered, and as such the VM running on esxi-01 will not be powered off! The VM running on esxi-01 will not be able to access the vSAN datastore however, as it has lost quorum!

> We would like to stress that it is highly recommended to set the isolation response to power off, even though it does not help in the above scenario.

But what if esxi-01 and esxi-04 were isolated, what would happen then? The next diagram will show this, but as expected the result would be very similar to the partition above.

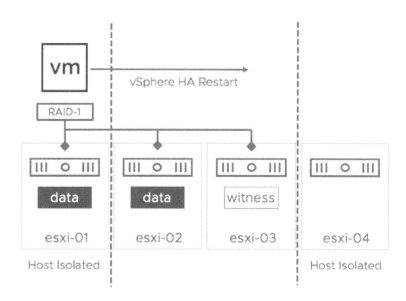

Figure 206: vSAN 2 hosts isolated: HA restart

Remember the rule we discussed earlier?

> "The winner is declared based on the percentage of components available or percentage of votes available within that partition."

If the partition has access to more than 50% of the components or votes (of an object), it has won. For each object, there can be at most one winning partition. This means that when esxi-01 and esxi-04 are isolated, either esxi-02 or esxi-03 can restart the VM because 66% of the components of the RAID-1 object reside within this part of the cluster.

To prevent these scenarios from occurring, it is most definitely recommended to ensure the vSAN network is made highly available through NIC teaming and redundant network switches, as discussed in Chapter 3, "vSAN Installation and Configuration." Note that in the above situation, as these hosts are isolated from the rest of the network, the isolation response will be triggered and the VM running on esxi-01 will be powered off by vSphere HA.

vCenter Server Failure Scenario

What if you would lose the vCenter Server? What will happen to vSAN, and how do you rebuild this environment? Even though vSAN is not dependent on vCenter Server, other components are. If, for instance, vCenter Server fails and a new instance needs to be created from scratch, what is the impact on your vSAN environment?

After you rebuild a new vCenter, you simply recreate a new vSAN-enabled cluster and add the hosts back to the cluster.

Now, vCenter is used by vSAN to keep track of cluster membership since the removal of multicast network traffic back in vSAN 6.6. Because VMware received a considerable amount of feedback from customers to remove the dependency on multicast traffic for membership, a new method was decided upon. This new method uses vCenter to track cluster membership. This introduced the concept of a Configuration Generation number. What this means is that all the ESXi hosts and the vCenter server use this number to track changes in the cluster. If vCenter is unavailable for a certain length of time, once it can communicate to the vSAN cluster once more, it compares its Configuration Generation number with the ESXi hosts. If it is not the same, vCenter Server realizes that changes have taken place since it was last online, so requests an update from all the hosts in the cluster to make sure it is synchronized from a configuration perspective. There is no need for any administrative action here; this is all taken care of automatically. The latest configuration Generation number can be viewed on the ESXi hosts via the command `esxcli vsan cluster get`.

```
[root@esxi-dell-i:~] esxcli vsan cluster get
Cluster Information
   Enabled: true
   Current Local Time: 2018-10-10T14:09:26Z
   Local Node UUID: 5b8d18eb-4fb4-670a-94b7-246e962f4ab0
   Local Node Type: NORMAL
   Local Node State: AGENT
   Local Node Health State: HEALTHY
   Sub-Cluster Master UUID: 5b8d1919-8d9e-2806-dfb3-246e962f4978
   Sub-Cluster Backup UUID: 5b8d190c-5f7c-50d8-bbb8-246e962c23f0
   Sub-Cluster UUID: 52e934f3-5507-d5d8-30fa-9a9b392acc72
   Sub-Cluster Membership Entry Revision: 7
   Sub-Cluster Member Count: 4
   Sub-Cluster Member UUIDs: 5b8d1919-8d9e-2806-dfb3-246e962f4978, 5b8d190c-5f7c-50d8-bbb8-246e962c23f0, 5b8d18f9-941f-f045-7457-246e962f48f8, 5b8d18eb-4fb4-670a-94b7-246e962f4ab0
   Sub-Cluster Member HostNames: esxi-dell-l.rainpole.com, esxi-dell-k.rainpole.com, esxi-dell-j.rainpole.com, esxi-dell-i.rainpole.com
   Sub-Cluster Membership UUID: 2a8f965b-671a-921c-0c8b-246e962f4978
   Unicast Mode Enabled: true
   Maintenance Mode State: OFF
```

```
  Config Generation: e4e74378-49e1-4229-bfe9-b14f675d23e6 10 2018-10-10T12:57:50.947
[root@esxi-dell-i:~]
```

One additional consideration, however, is that the loss of the vCenter Server will also mean the loss of the VM storage policies that the administrator has created. SPBM will not know about the previous VM storage policies and the VMs to which they were attached. vSAN, however, will still know exactly what the administrator had asked for, policy wise, and keep enforcing it. Today, there is no way in the UI to export existing policies, but there is an application programming interface (API) for VM storage policies has been exposed. In fact, using PowerCLI, administrators can export, import, and restore policies very quickly and easily. Refer to the official PowerCLI documentation for more detail on SPBM cmdlets.

Summary

As demonstrated throughout the chapter, vSAN is easy to scale out and up. The vSAN team spent a lot of time making day 2 operations easy for vSphere administrators, especially for those who must also take on the role of the storage administrator. Maintenance modes, disk groups and disk operations are all available through the UI. For those who prefer the command line, ESXCLI is a great alternative to the vSphere Client. For those who prefer PowerShell, VMware has a wide variety of PowerCLI cmdlets also available.

07

Stretched Cluster Use Case

This chapter was developed to provide insights and additional information on a very specific type of vSAN configuration, namely stretched clusters. In this chapter, we will describe some of the design considerations, operational procedures, and failure scenarios that relate to a stretched cluster configuration specifically. But first, why would anyone want a stretched cluster?

Stretched cluster configurations offer the ability to balance VMs between datacenters. The reason for doing so could be anything, be it disaster avoidance or, for instance, site maintenance. All of this can be achieved with no downtime from a VM perspective since compute, storage, and network are available across both sites. On top of that, a stretched cluster also provides the ability to actively load balance resources between locations without any constraints when desired.

What is a Stretched Cluster?

Before we get into it, let's first discuss what defines a vSAN stretched cluster. When we talk about a vSAN stretched cluster, we refer to the configuration that is deployed when the stretched cluster workflow is completed in the vSphere Client. This workflow explicitly leverages a witness host, which can be physical or virtual, and needs to be deployed in a third site. During the workflow, the vSAN cluster is set up across two active/active sites, with (preferably) an identical number of ESXi hosts distributed evenly between the two sites and as stated, a witness host residing at a third site. The data sites are connected via a high bandwidth/low latency network link. The third site hosting the vSAN witness host is connected over a network to both active/active "data" sites. The connectivity between the data sites and the witness site can be via lower bandwidth/higher latency network links. The diagram below shows what this looks like from a logical point of view.

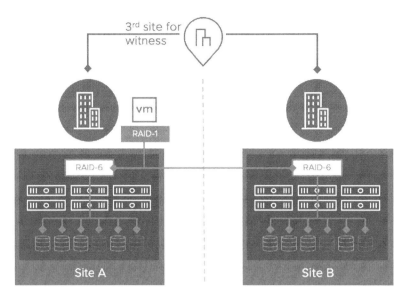

Figure 207: Stretched cluster scenario

Each site is configured as a vSAN fault domain. A maximum of three sites (two data, one witness) is supported in a stretched cluster configuration.

The nomenclature used to describe a vSAN Stretched Cluster configuration is X+Y+Z, where X is the number of ESXi hosts at data site A, Y is the number of ESXi hosts at data site B, and Z is the number of witness hosts at site C. Data sites are where VMs are deployed. The minimum supported configuration is 1+1+1 (3 nodes). Starting with vSAN 7.0 U2 the maximum configuration at the time of writing is 20+20+1 (41 nodes), pre-vSAN 7.0 U2 the maximum configuration was 15+15+1.

In vSAN stretched clusters, there is only one witness host in any configuration. For deployments that manage multiple stretched clusters, each cluster must have its own unique witness host, the shared witness deployment described in chapter 8 is not supported for a stretched cluster configuration at the time of writing. As mentioned before however, this witness host can be a virtual appliance, which does not even require a vSphere or vSAN license and is our preferred method of deployment for the witness.

By default, when a VM is deployed on a vSAN stretched cluster, it is deployed with a RAID-1 configuration. In previous versions of vSAN this was referred to as primary failures to tolerate. Thus, it will have one copy of its data on site A, the second copy of its data on site B, and a witness component placed on the witness host in site C. This configuration is achieved through fault domains. In the event of a complete site failure, there will be a full copy of the VM data as well as greater than 50% of the components available. This will allow the VM to remain available on the vSAN datastore. If the site which fails is the site where the VM is running, then the VM needs to be restarted on the other data site, vSphere HA will handle this task.

Note, however, that vSAN also provides the ability to specify what the level of protection within a site location should be. In previous versions of vSAN, this was referred to as secondary failures to tolerate. But before we dive further into all policy options, let's look at the configuration process first.

Requirements and Constraints

vSAN stretched cluster configurations requires vSphere 6.0.0 Update1 (U1) at a minimum. This implies both vCenter Server 6.0 U1 and ESXi 6.0 U1. This version of vSphere includes vSAN version 6.1. This is the minimum version required for vSAN stretched cluster support. However, we strongly recommend implementing the latest available version of vSAN, which at the time of writing was vSAN 7 Update 3. Especially as vSAN 7.0 Update 3 includes a feature called Stretched Cluster Sites/Witness resilience, which improves the overall availability of the cluster during failures. We will discuss the details of this feature later in this chapter.

From a licensing point of view, vSAN Enterprise is required to create stretched cluster configurations larger than 1+1+1. Yes, that is right, you could theoretically create a 1+1+1 stretched cluster configuration with the vSAN Standard or vSAN Advanced license and not breach the license agreement. Yes, we have customers using this feature in a 1+1+1 configuration!

There are no limitations placed on the edition of vSphere used for vSAN. However, for vSAN Stretched Cluster functionality, vSphere DRS is very desirable. DRS will provide initial placement assistance and can also help with migrating VMs to their correct site when a site recovers after a failure. Otherwise, the administrator will have to manually carry out these tasks. Note that DRS is only available in the Enterprise Plus edition of vSphere.

When it comes to vSAN functionality, VMware supports stretched clusters in both hybrid and all-flash configurations. In terms of on-disk formats, the minimum level of on-disk format required is v2, which comes by default with vSAN 6.0. (vSAN 6.2 comes with v3.) However, to be able to specify what the protection should be within a site (primary and secondary FTT) vSAN 6.6 is required at a minimum, and again vSAN 7.0 U3 is highly recommended.

Both physical ESXi hosts and virtual appliances (nested ESXi host in a VM) are supported for the witness host. VMware is providing a pre-configured witness appliance for those customers who wish to use it. A witness host/VM cannot be shared between multiple vSAN stretched clusters. Also, note that VMware does not support cross hosting of Witness Appliances in a scenario where there are multiple stretched cluster configurations across two locations. That means that you can't run the witness of Stretched Cluster A on Stretched Cluster B when these two clusters are stretched across the same two geographical locations. At all times 3 locations (or more) are required to avoid any circular dependency during failure scenarios.

One thing we would like to point out is that SMP-FT, the new Fault Tolerant VM mechanism introduced in vSphere 6.0, is supported on standard vSAN deployments, but at the time of writing is not supported on stretched cluster deployment at this time, be it vSAN or *vSphere Metro Storage Cluster* (vMSC) based, unless you contain and pin all the SMP-FT VMs to a single location. How to do this is explained later in this chapter. The reason for this is the bandwidth and latency requirements associated with SMP-FT. Pre-vSAN 7.0 Update 1 the use of vSAN iSCSI in a stretched cluster was also not supported, starting with 7.0 U1 however it is fully supported as it is now possible to specify site affinity when creating iSCSI targets. The same applies to vSAN File Service, starting with vSAN 7.0 U2 it is now also supported to configure vSAN File Service on a vSAN stretched cluster.

Lastly, at the time of writing VMware does not support remote mounting (HCI-Mesh) of a vSAN datastore which is stretched across locations.

Now that we have discussed some of the constraints, let's look at the vSAN stretched cluster bandwidth and latency requirements.

Networking and Latency Requirements

When vSAN is deployed in a stretched cluster across multiple sites, certain networking requirements must be adhered to.

- Between data sites both Layer 2 and Layer 3 are supported
    - Layer-2 is recommended for simplicity
- Between the data sites and the witness site Layer 3 is required
    - This is to prevent I/O from being routed through a potentially low bandwidth witness site
- Maximum round trip latency between data sites is 5ms
- Maximum round trip latency between data sites and the witness site is 200ms
- A bandwidth of 10 Gbps between data sites is recommended
- A bandwidth of 100 Mbps between data sites and the witness site is recommended

Networking in any stretched vSphere deployment is always a hot topic. We expect this to be the same for vSAN stretched deployments. VMware has published two documents that hold a lot of detail about network bandwidth calculations and network topology considerations. The above bandwidth recommendations are exactly that, recommendations. Requirements for your environment can be determined by calculating the exact needs as explained in the following two documents.

- vSAN stretched cluster bandwidth sizing guidance - https://vmwa.re/bandwidth
- vSAN stretched cluster guide - https://vmwa.re/stretched

Witness Traffic Separation and Mixed MTU

By default, when using vSAN Stretched Clusters, the Witness VMkernel interface tagged for vSAN traffic must have connectivity with each vSAN data node's VMkernel interface tagged with vSAN traffic. It is also supported to have a dedicated VMkernel interface for stretched cluster configurations, like what is supported for 2-node configurations. This allows for more flexible configurations, but also lowers the risk of having data traffic traverse the witness network. Configuration of the Witness VMkernel interface at the time of writing can be achieved through the command line interface utility esxcli. Below is an example of the command used in our lab to designate the VMkernel interface vmk1 to witness traffic.

```
esxcli vsan network ip add -i vmk1 -T=witness
```

> Note that the vSAN Witness Host will only have a VMkernel interface tagged for "vSAN Traffic". It will not have traffic tagged as "Witness".

One thing to note is that even in the case of witness traffic separation it is still required to have different networks for vSAN traffic as well as witness traffic. Not doing so may lead to multi-homing issues and various warnings in vSAN Skyline Health.

New Concepts in vSAN Stretched Cluster

A common question is how stretched cluster differs from regular fault domains. Fault domains enable what might be termed "rack awareness" where the components of VMs could be distributed amongst multiple hosts in multiple racks. Should a rack failure event occur, the VM would continue to be available. These racks would typically be hosted in the same datacenter, and if there were a datacenter-wide event, fault domains would not be able to assist with VM availability.
A stretched cluster essentially builds on the foundation of fault domains, and now provides what might be termed "datacenter awareness." A vSAN stretched cluster can now provide availability for VMs even if a datacenter, or site, suffers a catastrophic outage. This is achieved primarily through intelligent component placement of VM objects across sites, alongside features such as site preference, read locality, and the witness host.

The witness host must have a connection to both the master vSAN node and the backup vSAN node to join the cluster (the master and backup were discussed previously in Chapter 4, "Architectural Details"). In steady-state operations, the master node resides in the "preferred site"; the backup node resides in the "secondary site."

Note that the witness appliance ships with its own license, so it does not consume any of your vSphere or vSAN licenses. Hence it is our recommendation to always use the appliance over a physical witness host. The Witness Appliance also has a different icon in the vSphere Client than a regular ESXi host, allowing you to easily identify the witness appliance as shown below. This is only the case for the witness appliance, however. A physical appliance will show up in the client as a regular host and also requires a vSphere license!

10.202.25.231

Figure 208: Witness appliance icon

Another added benefit of the witness appliance is the operational aspect of the witness. If for whatever reason maintenance is needed on the physical host, the witness appliance will enable you to do maintenance without disruption when the appliance runs on a vSphere cluster as vSphere provides the ability to migrate the appliance while running. On top of that, in case the witness appliance fails, you also can simply replace the current witness by deploying a new one and initiating the "Change Witness Host" wizard in the Fault Domains section of the UI as shown in the next screenshot. Now, of course, this is also possible when you have a spare physical host, but in our experience, customers do not have unused hardware available for a quick replacement.

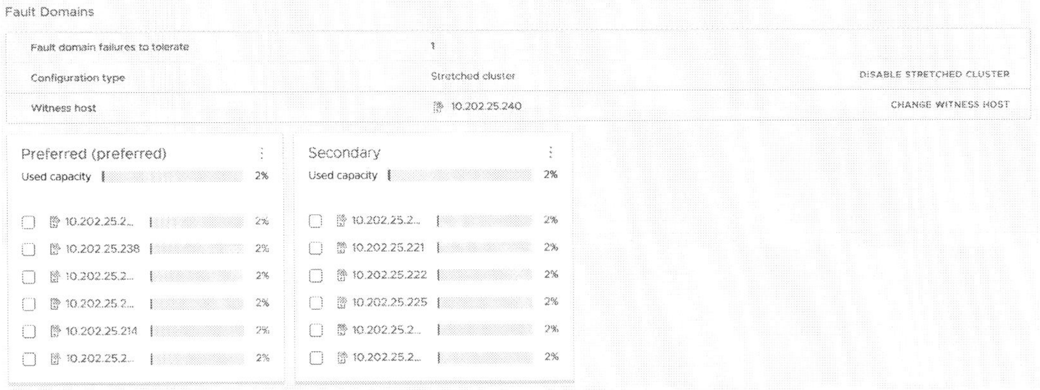

Figure 209: Change witness host

Another new term that will show up during the configuration of a stretched cluster, and was just mentioned, is "preferred site" and "secondary site." The "preferred" site is the site that vSAN wishes to remain running when there is a network partition between the sites and the sites can no longer communicate. One might say that the "preferred site" is the site expected to have the most reliability.

Since VMs can run on any of the two sites, if network connectivity is lost between site 1 and site 2, but both still have connectivity to the witness, the "preferred site" binds itself to the witness and gains ownership over all components. The vSAN components on the preferred site remain active, while the vSAN components on the secondary site are marked instantly as absent as quorum is lost. This also means that, in this situation, any VMs running in the secondary site will need to be restarted in the primary site to be usable and useful again. vSphere HA, when enabled on the stretched cluster, will take care of this automatically for you.

In non-stretched vSAN clusters, a VM's read operations are distributed across all replica copies of the data in the cluster. In the case of a policy setting of *Failures to tolerate* =1, which results in two copies of the data, 50% of the reads will come from replica 1, and 50% will come from replica 2.

Similarly, in the case of a policy setting of *Failures to tolerate* = 2 in non-stretched vSAN clusters, which results in three copies of the data, 33% of the reads will come from replica 1, 33% of the reads will come from replica 2, and 33% will come from replica 3.

However, we wish to avoid this situation with a vSAN stretched cluster, as we do not wish to read data over the inter-site link, which could add unnecessary latency to the I/O and waste precious inter-site link bandwidth. Since vSAN stretched cluster supports a maximum of *Failures to tolerate* = 1, there will be two copies of the data (replica 1 and replica 2). Rather than doing 50% reads from site 1 and 50% reads from site 2 across the site link, the goal is to do 100% of the read IO for any given VM from the local site, wherever possible. In previous versions of vSAN, this was a per host setting. Starting with vSAN 6.7U1, this setting, called Site Read Locality, has been placed into the Advanced options under vSAN > Configure > Services. This makes it extremely simple to set cluster wide, as shown below:

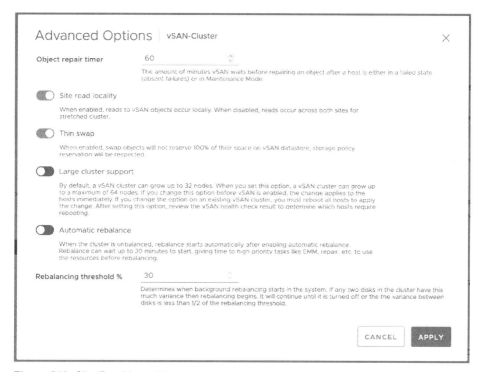

Figure 210: Site Read Locality

The distributed object manager (DOM) in vSAN, is responsible for dealing with read locality. DOM is not only responsible for the creation of storage objects in the vSAN cluster, but it is also responsible for providing distributed data access paths to these objects. There is a single DOM owner per object. There are three roles within DOM: client, owner, and component manager. The DOM owner coordinates access to the object, including reads, locking, and object configuration and reconfiguration. All object changes and writes also go through the owner. In vSAN stretched cluster, an enhancement to the DOM owner of an object means that it will now consider the "fault domain" where the owner runs and will read 100% from the replica that is in the same "fault domain."

There is now another consideration with read locality for *hybrid vSAN configurations*. Administrators should avoid unnecessary vMotion of virtual machines between data sites. Since the read cache blocks are stored on one (local) site, if the VM moves around freely and ends up on the remote site, the cache will be cold on that site after the migration. Now there will be sub-optimal performance until the cache is warmed again. To avoid this situation, soft (should) affinity rules (VM/Host rules) should be used to keep the virtual machine local to the same site/fault domain where possible. Note that this only applies to hybrid configurations, as all-flash configurations do not have a read cache. However, even in the case of an all-flash configuration VM/Host rules could be used to provide more visibility of where a virtual machine is, or was, running at the time of a site failure. When the location where a VM is running is configured is tightly controlled, the impact of a full site failure is much easier to understand. Better said, it provides predictability. We see most customers applying VM/Host rules on all VMs, even when vSAN stretched clustering is enabled on an all-flash configuration.

Witness Failure Resilience

Every installation of a vSAN stretched cluster has a witness host of some sort. As mentioned, this can be a virtual appliance or a physical host. The question that always arises is what about the availability of the witness host, as it plays a crucial role during failure scenarios?

Over the years we have had customers asking if it was supported to enable vSphere Fault Tolerance (FT) on a witness appliance. If they could clone the witness appliance, leave it on standby, and power it on when the "active" witness appliance had failed. If they should back up the witness appliance. The answer to all these questions is no. It is not supported to enable FT on the appliance, it is not supported to backup and recover the appliance, and it is not recommended to clone the appliance either.

Starting with vSAN 7.0 U3 a new feature was introduced around Witness failure resilience. What is this feature exactly? Let's look at the diagram of the stretched cluster again.

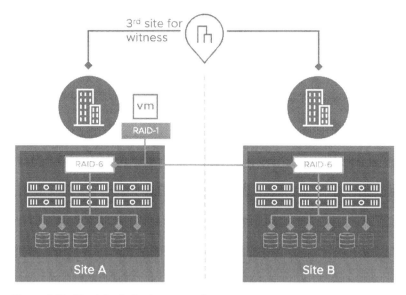

Figure 211: Stretched cluster scenario

In the diagram, we have 3 locations. In the case Site A fails, all VMs will be restarted in Site B. If, however at a later stage the witness is impacted by a failure all VMs running would be inaccessible. Why? Well, it is simple, 2 out of 3 sites have failed and as a result, we have lost quorum. This is where the new witness failure resilience feature comes into play. Starting with vSAN 7.0 U3 when a site has failed, vSAN will recalculate the votes for all objects assuming that the witness will also be impacted by a failure over time. This recalculation of votes can take up to five minutes. If the witness now fails, after the recalculation has been completed, the VMs (running in Site B) will remain running. As votes have been recalculated quorum will not be lost.

In the "full site failure" scenario we will demonstrate what that looks like from a votes perspective by inspecting the objects through RVC.

Configuration of a Stretched Cluster

The installation of a vSAN stretched cluster is almost identical to how fault domains are implemented, with a couple of additional steps. This part of the chapter will walk the reader through a stretched cluster configuration.

Before we get started with the actual configuration of a stretched cluster, we will need to ensure the witness host is installed, configured, and accessible from both data sites. This will most likely involve the addition of static routes to the ESXi hosts and witness appliance, which will be covered shortly. When configuring your vSAN stretched cluster, only data hosts must be in the (vSAN) cluster object in vCenter Server. The witness host must remain outside of the cluster and must not be added to the vSAN cluster.

Note that the witness OVA must be deployed through a vCenter Server. To complete the deployment and configuration of the witness VM, it must be powered on the very first time through vCenter Server as well. The witness OVA is also only supported with standard vSwitch (VSS) deployments.

The deployment of the witness host is pretty much straightforward and like the deployment of most virtual appliances as shown below.

Figure 212: Witness appliance deployment

The only real decision that needs to be made is regarding the expected size of the stretched cluster configuration. There are four options offered. If you expect the number of VMs deployed on the vSAN stretched cluster to be 10 or fewer, select the **Tiny** configuration. If you expect to deploy more than 10 VMs, but less than 500 VMs, then the **Medium** (default option) should be chosen. For more than 500 VMs, choose the **Large** option. Note, there also is an **Extra Large** option, this is should be used when you deploy multiple two-host configurations and connect them all to the shared witness, it is intended to host the witness components of up to 64 clusters, in other words, this option is not intended for a stretched cluster configuration!

Figure 213: Configuration size

Next, the datastore where the witness appliance will need to be stored and the network that will be used for the witness appliance will need to be selected. Note that you will need to specify the destination network for both witness traffic (secondary network) and management traffic.

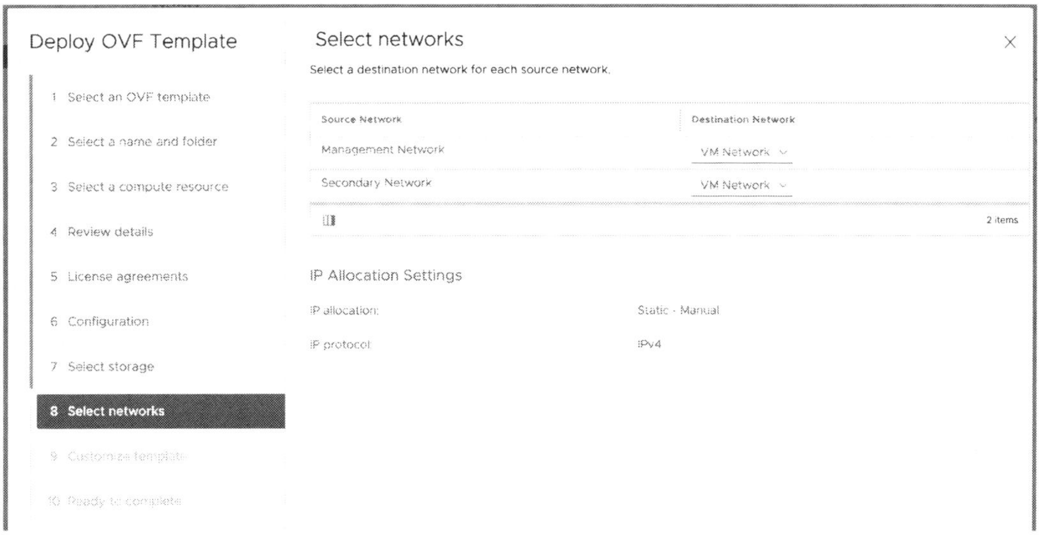

Figure 214: Change of networks

Next, you will have the option to customize the OVF Template by providing networking information, such as IP address and DNS, for the management network. On top of that, the root password for the virtual ESXi host will need to be entered on this screen as shown in the screenshot below.

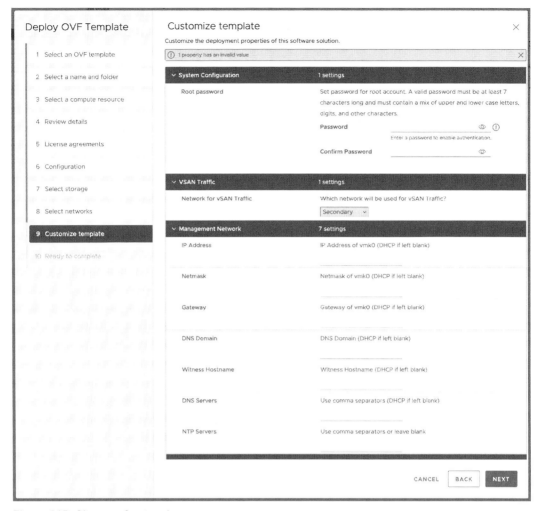

Figure 215: Change of networks

After this has been done and the witness has been deployed it can be added to the vCenter Server inventory where the stretched cluster configuration is deployed as a regular host. But remember not to add it to any type of vSphere or vSAN cluster; it must remain outside the cluster as a stand-alone host. One thing to stress, when you add it to the cluster, make sure the "Virtual SAN Witness" license is selected as demonstrated in the next screenshot.

07 // Stretched Cluster Use Case

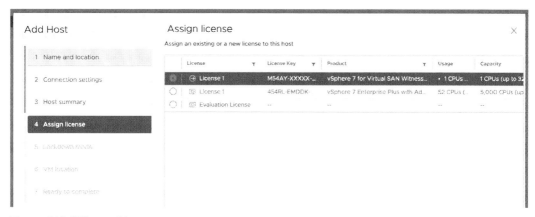

Figure 216: Witness License

Once the witness appliance/nested ESXi host has been added to vCenter, the next step is to configure the vSAN network correctly on the witness. When the witness is selected in the vCenter inventory, navigate to Manage > Networking > Virtual Switches. The witness has two port groups predefined called Management Network and *secondaryPG*. *Do not remove these port groups, as it has a special modification to make the MAC addresses on the network adapters match the nested ESXi MAC addresses.*

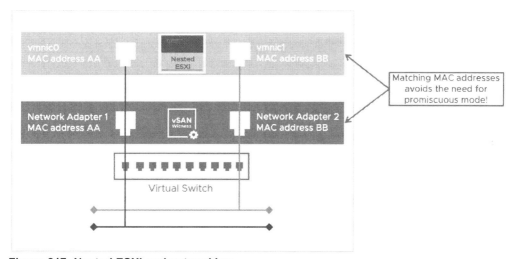

Figure 217: Nested ESXi and networking

Finally, before we can configure the vSAN stretched cluster, we need to ensure that the vSAN network on the hosts residing in the data sites can reach the witness host's vSAN network, and vice-versa. To address this, there are two options:

1. Define a static route
2. Override the default gateway for the vSAN VMkernel adapter

Static routes tell the TCP/IP stack to use a different route to reach a particular network rather than using the default gateway. We can instruct the TCP/IP stack on the data hosts to use a different network route to reach the vSAN network on the witness host rather than via the default gateway, and similarly, we can tell the witness host to use an alternate route to reach the vSAN network on the data hosts rather than via the default gateway.

Note once again that in most situations, the vSAN network is most likely a stretched L2 broadcast domain between the data sites, but L3 is required to reach the vSAN network of the witness appliance. Therefore, static routes are needed between the data hosts and the witness host for the vSAN network but may not be required for the data hosts on different sites to communicate with each other over the vSAN network.

The esxcli commands used to add a static route is:
esxcli network ip route ipv4 add -n <remote network> -g <gateway>

As mentioned, the second option is to override the default gateway and specify a specific gateway for your vSAN environment. This gateway will need to have a route to your witness network. Using this method avoids the need to manually enter routes using the CLI and is preferred for most customers. The screenshot below shows how to override the default gateway.

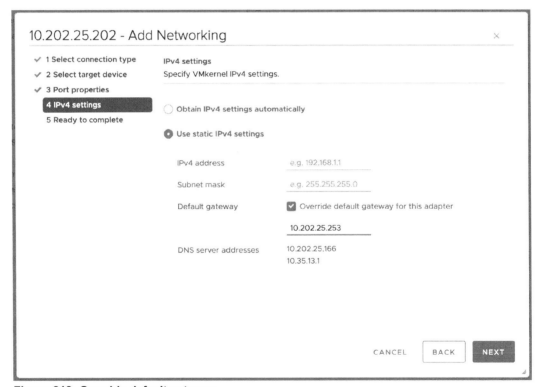

Figure 218: Override default gateway

Lastly, before we create the cluster, we will need to test the network configuration. To do so, we use the vmkping -I <vmk> <ipaddress> command to check that the witness and physical hosts can communicate over the vSAN network. Now that the witness is up and accessible, forming a vSAN stretched cluster takes less than a couple of minutes. The following are the steps that should be followed to install vSAN stretched cluster.

Configure Step 1a: Create a vSAN Stretched Cluster

In this example, there are eight hosts available. Four hosts reside in each site of this stretched cluster. The ninth host is the witness host, it is in its own datacenter and is not added to the cluster, but it has been added as an ESXi host to this vCenter Server. This example is a 4+4+1 deployment, meaning four ESXi hosts at the preferred site, four ESXi hosts at the secondary site and one witness host in a third location.

Depending on how you are configuring your cluster you can decide to either create the stretched cluster during the creation of the vSAN cluster itself or do this after the fact in the fault domain view. Both workflows are similar and so is the result. Functionality like deduplication and compression can also be enabled in a stretched cluster. However, do note that RAID-5/6 can only be configured as protection within a site location (previously referred to as secondary failures to tolerate). We are going to demonstrate how to create a vSAN stretched cluster out of an existing vSAN cluster, simply because we have already shown the configuration of a normal cluster using the Quickstart workflow in chapter 3.

Configure Step 1b: Create Stretch Cluster

If your vSAN cluster has already been formed, it is easy to create a stretched cluster configuration separately. To configure stretched cluster and fault domains when a vSAN cluster already exists, navigate to the cluster object followed by Configure > vSAN > Fault Domains view as shown below, and click on the button "configure" in the stretched cluster section, that begins the stretch cluster configuration.

Figure 219: Start of stretched cluster creating

Depending on whether you create the vSAN cluster as part of the workflow you may need to claim disks as well when the vSAN cluster is set up.

Configure Step 2: Assign Hosts to Sites

At this point, hosts can now be assigned to stretch cluster sites as shown in the figure below. Note that the names have been preassigned. As described earlier, the preferred site is the one that will run VMs if there is a split-brain type scenario in the cluster. In this example,
hosts .201, .202, .206, .207, .220, and .221 will remain in the preferred site, and
hosts .222, .225, .226, ,228, .238, and .239 will be assigned to the secondary site.

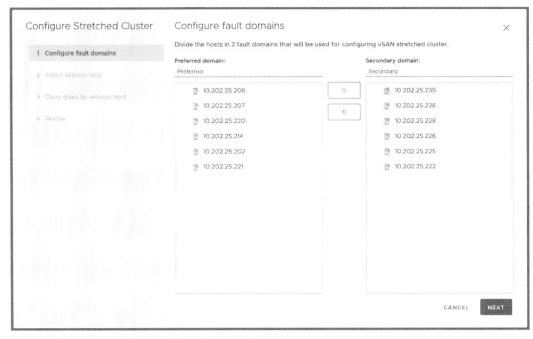

Figure 220: Host selection and site placement

Configure Step 3: Select a Witness Host and Disk Group

The next step is to select the witness host. At this point, host .231 is chosen. Note once again that this host does not reside in the cluster. It is outside of the cluster.

Figure 221: Witness host selection

When the witness is selected, a flash device and a magnetic disk need to be chosen to create a disk group. These are already available in the witness appliance (both are in fact VMDKs under the covers since the appliance is a VM).

07 // Stretched Cluster Use Case

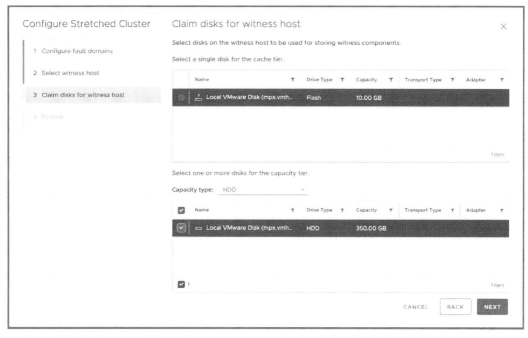

Figure 222: Witness disk claim

Configure Step 4: Verify the Configuration

Verify that the preferred fault domain and the secondary fault domains have the desired hosts, and that the witness host is the desired witness host as shown below, and click **Finish** to complete the configuration.

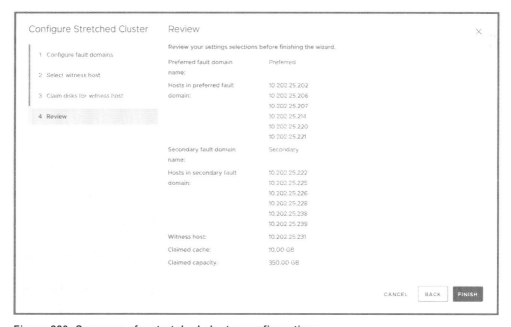

Figure 223: Summary of a stretched cluster configuration

285

When the stretched cluster has completed configuration, which can take several seconds, verify that the fault domain view is as expected.

Configure Step 5: Skyline Health Stretched Cluster

Before doing anything else, use vSAN Skyline Health to ensure that all the stretched cluster health checks have passed. These checks are only visible when the stretched cluster has been configured, and if there are any issues with the configuration, these checks should be of great assistance in locating them.

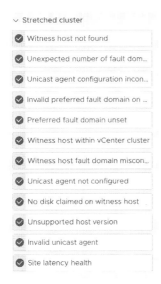

Figure 224: Stretched cluster health

That may seem very easy from a vSAN perspective, but there are some considerations from a vSphere perspective to consider. These are not required, but in most cases recommended to optimize for performance and availability. The vSAN stretched cluster guide outlines all vSphere recommendations in-depth. Since our focus in this book is vSAN, we will not go into that level of detail. Instead, you should refer to the stretched cluster guide mentioned previously in this chapter.

We will however list some of the key recommendations for each of the specific areas:

vSphere DRS:
- Create a Host group per data site, containing each of the hosts of a particular site.
- Create VM groups per site, containing the VMs that should reside in a particular site.
- Create a VM/Host rule to create affinity between the VM and host groups.
- Create a "should" rule for these affinity groups to ensure that during "normal" operations, VMs reside in the correct site, but do have the ability to failover when needed.

This will ensure that VMs will not freely roam around the stretched cluster, maintaining read locality, and performance is not impacted due to rewarming of the cache. It will also help from an operational perspective to provide insights around the impact of a full site failure, and it will allow you to distribute VMs running scale-out services such as Active Directory and DNS across both sites.

Lastly, we want to point out that starting with vSAN 7.0 U2 DRS is **tightly integrated** with vSAN. In previous versions when a failure occurred it could happen that when hosts recovered from the failure that DRS would automatically migrate VMs back to their original location. If a VM is moved, by DRS, to its original location before the resync of its object had completed, vSAN would be unable to read from the local site. Both the vMotion process, as well as the traversing of read I/O could lead to a degradation of performance and a prolonged resynchronization process. Starting with vSAN 7.0 U2, DRS will not migrate VMs of which objects are to be resynced.

Pre-vSAN 7.0 U2 customers would configure DRS to "manual" or "partially automated" during these failure scenarios to avoid the above situation. As a result of the integration between DRS and vSAN, this is no longer needed as DRS knows which objects belong to which VMs and which objects are being replicated!

vSphere HA:
- Enable vSphere HA admission control and set it to use the percentage-based admission control policy and to 50% for both CPU and memory. This means that if there is a full site failure, the remaining site has enough unreserved capacity to power-on all of the VMs.
- Make sure to specify additional isolation addresses, one in each site using the advanced setting `das.isolationAddress0` and `das.isolationAddress1`. The IP address needs to be on the vSAN network. This means that in the event of a site failure, a host in the remaining site can still ping an isolation response IP address when needed on the vSAN network and isolation can be validated, and when needed action can be taken.
- Configure the Isolation Response to "Power off and restart VMs"
- Disable the default isolation address if it can't be used to validate the state of the environment during a partition. Setting the advanced setting `das.usedefaultisolationaddress` to false does this.
- Disable the insufficient heartbeat datastore warnings, as without traditional external storage you will not have any datastores to use as vSAN datastores cannot be used for datastore heartbeating. Setting the advanced setting `das.ignoreInsufficientHbDatastore` to true does this.

These settings will ensure that when a failure occurs, sufficient unreserved resources are available to coordinate the failover and power-on the VMs (admission control). These VMs will be restarted within their respective sites as defined in the VM/host rules. In the case of an isolation event, all necessary precautions have been taken to ensure all the hosts can reach their respective host isolation response IP address(es).

That is not of course where it stops, there is one important aspect of availability in a stretched cluster that we will need to discuss first, and this is policy settings.

Failures To Tolerate Policies

Starting vSAN 6.6 the notion of *Primary* and *Secondary Failures To Tolerate* was introduced. This feature allowed you to specify how objects should be protected within a stretched cluster and also within a site. The current vSphere Client however uses "Site disaster tolerance" and "Failures to tolerate" as shown in the screenshot below.

Figure 225: vSphere Client VM storage policy for a stretched cluster

Let's list all the different options which are available within the vSphere Client for a stretched cluster configuration when defining a policy:

- Site Disaster Tolerance – None – standard cluster
- Site Disaster Tolerance – Host mirroring – 2 node cluster
- Site Disaster Tolerance – Site mirroring – stretched cluster
- Site Disaster Tolerance – None – keep data on preferred (stretched cluster)
- Site Disaster Tolerance – None – keep data on secondary (stretched cluster)
- Site Disaster Tolerance – None – stretched cluster
- Failures to tolerate – No data redundancy
- Failures to tolerate – No data redundancy with host affinity
- Failures to tolerate – 1 Failure – RAID-1
- Failures to tolerate – 1 Failure – RAID-5
- Failures to tolerate – 2 Failure – RAID-1
- Failures to tolerate – 2 Failure – RAID-6
- Failures to tolerate – 3 Failure – RAID-1

The first decision that needs to be made is the *Site Disaster Tolerance*. This is the "*Primary Level of Failures To Tolerate*" and specifies whether objects should be mirrored across locations. Note that this is essentially a RAID-1 mirror. Starting with vSAN 6.6, administrators also have the ability to specify that an object should not be replicated and should only be made available in a specific location i.e., site. You can imagine that this is useful in a scenario where the application is already replicating its data to the other location natively. A good example would be Oracle RAC or Microsoft SQL Always On, or even Microsoft Active Directory for that matter.

Failures to tolerate then specifies how the object within each location then needs to be protected. You could specify that you would like to mirror objects across locations via *Site Disaster Tolerance*

(RAID-1) and have a RAID-5 or RAID-6 configuration within each location. This RAID-5 or RAID-6 configuration would then allow you to survive one (or multiple) host failures in the remaining site after a full site failure has occurred, without losing access to the object. The diagram below shows what this looks like logically.

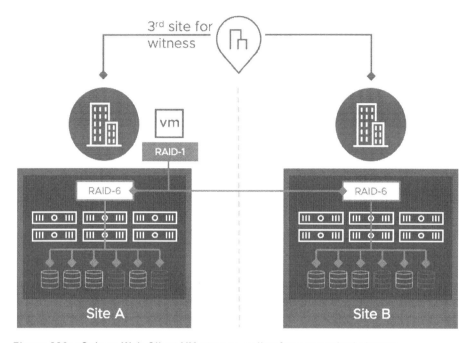

Figure 226: vSphere Web Client VM storage policy for a stretched cluster

The added benefit of local protection within each location is that when a capacity or caching device, disk , or host has failed, data can now be resynced or rebuilt locally. In earlier versions of vSAN stretched cluster, only the top-level RAID-1 configuration existed, and as such only 1 replica existed within each site. Components impacted by a failure would need to be resynced across the network between the two locations in such a configuration. This lengthened the time it would take to protect the component, and as such during that time your data was at risk. In vSAN stretched cluster today, such a situation is mitigated with "in-site protection".

One thing we do want to point out however is that a failure of the witness host is considered a full site failure, meaning that it could take out a full one-third of the available votes for all objects. Any further failures that occur after the witness site has failed could place data at risk if quorum is lost, depending on the number of hosts in the cluster and the selected policy for the object of course. We realize that this can be difficult to grasp, so let's look at the various failure scenarios.

Site Disaster Tolerance Failure Scenarios

There are many different failures that can occur in a datacenter. It is not our goal to describe every single one of them, as that would be a book by itself. In this section, we want to describe some of the failures, and recovery of these failures, which are particular to the stretched cluster configuration. Hopefully, these will give you a better insight into how a stretched cluster works.

In this example, there is a 6+6+1 stretched vSAN deployment. This means that there are six data hosts at site 1, six data hosts at site 2, and a witness host at a third site.

A single VM has been deployed, we selected a policy that dictates that the data needs to be stretched across locations and be protected within each location with RAID-1. When the physical disk placement is examined, we can see that the replicas are placed on the preferred and secondary data site respectively as shown in the Fault Domain column, and the witness component is placed on the witness host and is placed in both the preferred and secondary fault domain as shown below. This ensures that we have a quorum mechanism used for full site failures, as well as host failures within a location.

Physical disk placement

☐ Group components by host placement

Virtual Object Components

Type	Component State	Host	Fault Domain
∨ ⬜ Hard disk 1 (RAID 1)			
Witness	✅ Active	10.202.25.239	Secondary
∨ RAID 1			
Component	✅ Active	10.202.25.202	Preferred
Component	✅ Active	10.202.25.206	Preferred
∨ RAID 1			
Component	✅ Active	10.202.25.238	Secondary
Component	✅ Active	10.202.25.226	Secondary
Witness	✅ Active	10.202.25.231	
Witness	✅ Active	10.202.25.221	Preferred

Figure 227: VM Component placement

The next step is to introduce some failures and examine how vSAN handles such events. Before beginning these tests, please ensure that vSAN Skyline Health is working correctly, and that all vSAN health checks have passed, this will make troubleshooting much easier.

Skyline Health should be referred to regularly during failure scenario testing. Note that alarms are now raised for any health check that fails. Alarms may also be referenced at the cluster level throughout this testing, of course depending on the type of failure being triggered.

07 // Stretched Cluster Use Case

Finally, when the term site is used in the failure scenarios, it implies a full fault domain.

Single data host failure—Secondary site

The first test is to introduce a failure of a host in one of the data sites, either the "preferred" or the "secondary" site. The sample virtual machine deployed for test purposes currently resides on the preferred site and the failure occurs on the secondary site and impacts a "data" component as shown in the next diagram.

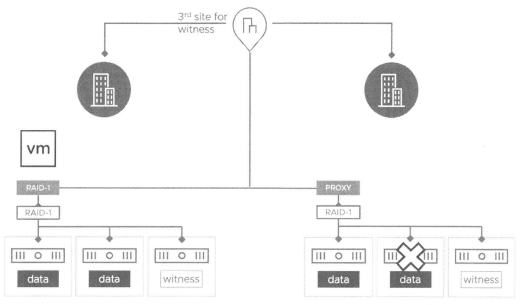

Figure 228: Failure scenario – host failed secondary site

In the first part of this test, the host which holds a component in the secondary site has been rebooted, simulating a temporary outage and loss of a component.

There will be several power and HA events related to the secondary host visible in the vSphere Client. Change to the physical disk place view of the virtual machine. After a few moments, the components that were on the secondary host will go "absent," as shown in the next screenshot. The other thing we should point out is that the VM remains accessible and that vSAN immediately creates a durability component that will be used for write I/O.

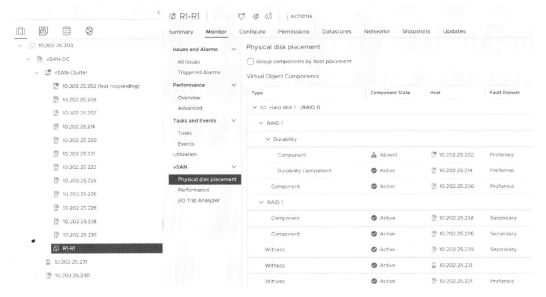

Figure 229: VM Component absent

As mentioned, the virtual machine continues to be accessible. This is because there is a full copy of the data available on the hosts on the preferred site, and there are more than 50% of the votes available. Opening a console to the virtual machine verifies that it is still very much active and functioning. Since the ESXi host which holds the compute of the virtual machine is unaffected by this failure, there is no reason for vSphere HA to act, meaning that the VM is not restarted.

At this point, vSAN Skyline Health can be examined. There will be several failures, as shown in the next figure, since a host in the secondary site is no longer available, as one might expect.

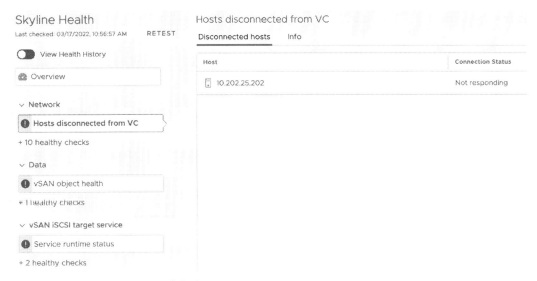

Figure 230: Health check tests failed

When examining these tests in your environment, please note that before starting a new test, it is strongly recommended to wait until the failed host has successfully rejoined the cluster and the resync has been completed. All "failed" health check tests should show OK before another test is started. Also, confirm that there are no "absent" components on the VMs objects and that all components are once again active. Failure to do this could introduce more than one failure in the cluster, and result in the VM being unavailable.

Single data host failure—Preferred site

This next test will not only check vSAN, but will also verify vSphere HA functionality. If each site has multiple hosts and host affinity rules are defined, then a host failure on the primary site will allow vSphere HA to restart the virtual machine on another host on the same site. In this test, the configuration is 6+6+1, but we have not defined any rules, so the virtual machine will be restarted on a random host in the cluster.

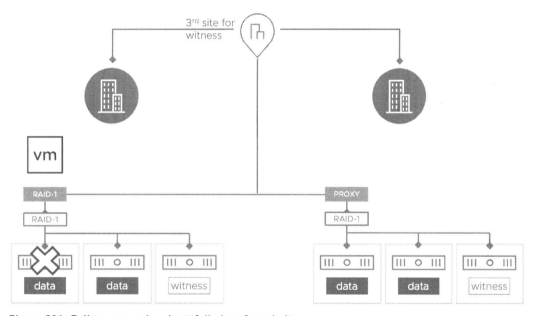

Figure 231: Failure scenario – host failed preferred site

After the failure has occurred in the preferred site there will be a few vSphere HA related events. Like the previous scenario, if there were any components on the host, these will show up as "absent."

Note that these components will be rebuilt fully after 60 minutes automatically by vSAN leveraging the existing durability component and the full remaining full component within the location. However, when desired you can manually trigger the rebuild of these components by clicking "Repair objects immediately" in the vSAN Skyline Health under vSAN Object Health.

Figure 232: Repair objects immediately

Since the host on which the virtual machine's compute resides is no longer available, vSphere HA will restart the virtual machine on another host in the same site. It is important to validate this has happened as it shows that the VM/host affinity rules are correctly configured. It should also be noted that they are configured as "should" rules and not as "must" rules. If "must" rules are configured, then vSphere HA will only be able to restart the virtual machine on hosts that are in the same host group on the same site/fault domain and will not be able to restart the virtual machine on hosts that reside on the other site. "Should" rules will allow vSphere HA to restart the virtual machine on hosts that are not in the same VM/host affinity group, i.e., in the event of a complete site failure.

Information about the restart of the virtual machine can be found in the vSphere Client and in the log file `/var/log/fdm.log` on the ESXi host which is the HA primary. Note that it usually takes between 30-60 seconds before a failover has occurred. If trying to monitor these HA events via the vSphere Client, ensure that you regularly refresh the vSphere client, or you may not see it.

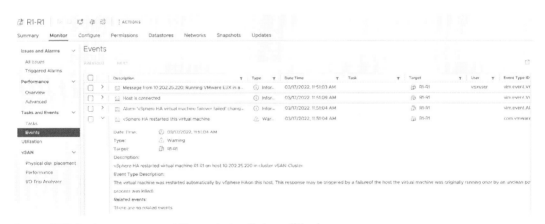

Figure 233: Failure scenario – HA events in vSphere Client

Full Site Failure – Data Site

This next test in essence is very similar to a single host failure, the big difference of course being that in a full site scenario, typically 50% of your cluster resources are now missing. When a full site failure occurs it also will not be possible to rebuild your components, simply because the second fault domain is missing completely as demonstrated in the diagram below.

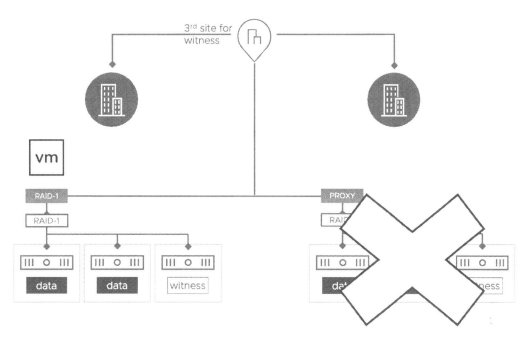

Figure 234: Failure scenario – Full Site Failure

After the failure has occurred in the secondary site, all VMs will automatically be restarted in the preferred location. Do however note that this will only be the case when VM-Host rules were configured as "**should rules**". When "must rules" have been configured vSphere HA will not violate these. For more details on vSphere HA and VM/Host rules please refer to the vSphere 6.7 Clustering Deep Dive book by Frank Denneman, Duncan Epping, and Niels Hagoort.

Previously when a full site failure had occurred and was resolved, vSAN would automatically and instantly start resyncing components. However, vSAN never waited for all of the hosts to recover before starting this process. This in some cases led to a situation where rebuilds and resyncs would occur to only a limited number of hosts. When the additional hosts would return, they would not be leveraged for these rebuilds or resyncs since the components had been rebuilt on the hosts that recovered first. As such, VMware has modified some of the vSAN behavior when a site failure occurs and subsequently recovers. In the event of a site failure, vSAN will now wait for some additional time for "all" hosts to become ready on the failed site before it starts to sync components.

A more pressing issue with recoveries is when virtual machines would fall back to their appropriate site based on VM/Host affinity rules. Now we may have a situation where the VMs are running on their "correct" site but the data on that site has not yet been rebuilt. Essentially, we would be in a situation where all VM I/O must traverse the inter-site link, which may in turn lead to performance issues. Starting with vSAN 7.0 Update 2, DRS understands the state of objects on vSAN. DRS will verify with vSAN the state of the environment, and it will not migrate the VMs back as long the VMs (objects) are healthy again. When the VMs are healthy and the resync has fully completed,

DRS will automatically migrate the VMs back to comply with the specified VM/Host rules (when DRS is configured to Fully Automated that is).

> **vSAN and DRS are tightly integrated starting with vSAN 7.0 U2. As a result, it is no longer needed to change the automation mode of DRS after a failure has occurred.**

The last thing we would like to discuss as part of this failure scenario is the witness failure resilience. We have already briefly discussed it in a previous section, but we now want to show what the immediate impact is of this feature using RVC. As stated, the secondary site has failed completely. We will examine the impact of this failure through RVC, the Ruby vSphere Console on the vCenter Server. This should provide us with a better understanding of the situation and how the witness failure resilience mechanism works. Note that the below output has been truncated for readability reasons. Let's look at the output of RVC for our VM directly after the failure.

```
VM R1-R1:
    [vsanDatastore] 0b013262-0c30-a8c4-a043-005056968de9/R1-R1.vmx
    RAID_1
      RAID_1
        Component: 0b013262-c2da-84c5-1eee-005056968de9 , host: 10.202.25.221
          votes: 1, usage: 0.1 GB, proxy component: false)
        Component: 0b013262-3acf-88c5-a7ff-005056968de9 , host: 10.202.25.201
          votes: 1, usage: 0.1 GB, proxy component: false)
      RAID_1
        Component: 0b013262-a687-8bc5-7d63-005056968de9 , host: 10.202.25.238
          votes: 1, usage: 0.1 GB, proxy component: true)
        Component: 0b013262-3cef-8dc5-9cc1-005056968de9 , host: 10.202.25.236
          votes: 1, usage: 0.1 GB, proxy component: true)
    Witness: 0b013262-4aa2-90c5-9504-005056968de9 , host: 10.202.25.231
      votes: 3, usage: 0.0 GB, proxy component: false)
    Witness: 47123362-c8ae-5aa4-dd53-005056962c93 , host: 10.202.25.214
      votes: 1, usage: 0.0 GB, proxy component: false)
    Witness: 0b013262-5616-95c5-8b52-005056968de9 , host: 10.202.25.228
      votes: 1, usage: 0.0 GB, proxy component: false)
```

As can be seen, the witness component holds 3 votes, the components on the failed site (secondary) hold 3 votes, and the components on the surviving data site (preferred) hold 3 votes. After the full site failure has been detected, the votes are recalculated to ensure that a witness host failure does not impact the availability of the VMs. Below shows the output of RVC once again.

```
VM R1-R1:
    RAID_1
      RAID_1
        Component: 0b013262-c2da-84c5-1eee-005056968de9 , host: 10.202.25.221
          votes: 3, usage: 0.1 GB, proxy component: false)
        Component: 0b013262-3acf-88c5-a7ff-005056968de9 , host: 10.202.25.201
          votes: 3, usage: 0.1 GB, proxy component: false)
      RAID_1
        Component: 0b013262-a687-8bc5-7d63-005056968de9 , host: 10.202.25.238
          votes: 1, usage: 0.1 GB, proxy component: false)
        Component: 0b013262-3cef-8dc5-9cc1-005056968de9 , host: 10.202.25.236
          votes: 1, usage: 0.1 GB, proxy component: false)
    Witness: 0b013262-4aa2-90c5-9504-005056968de9 , host: 10.202.25.231
          votes: 1, usage: 0.0 GB, proxy component: false)
```

```
Witness: 47123362-c8ae-5aa4-dd53-005056962c93 , host: 10.202.25.214
    votes: 3, usage: 0.0 GB, proxy component: false)
```

As can be seen, the votes for the various components have changed, the data site now has 3 votes per component instead of 1, the witness on the witness host went from 3 votes to 1, and on top of that, the witness that is stored in the surviving fault domain now also has 3 votes. Resulting in a situation where quorum would not be lost even if the witness component on the witness host is impacted by a failure. Do note, that the redistribution process of the votes can take up to 5 minutes to complete, depending on the size of the cluster. Nevertheless, a very useful enhancement to vSAN 7.0 Update 3 for stretched cluster configurations.

Witness host failure—Witness site

A common question that is asked is what happens when the witness host has failed. This should have no impact on the run state of the virtual machine since there is still a full copy of the data available and greater than 50% of the votes are also available, but the witness components residing on the witness host should show up as "absent."

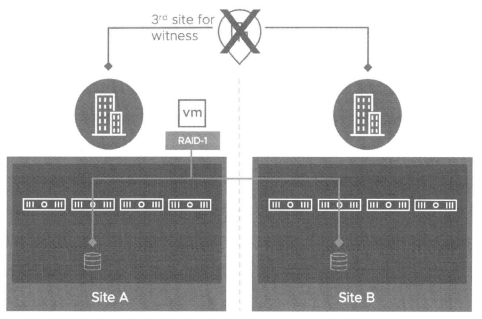

Figure 235: Failure scenario – Witness host failed

In our environment, we've simply powered off the witness host to demonstrate the impact of a failure. After a short period of time, the witness component of the virtual machine appears as "absent" as shown below.

Type	Component State	Host	Fault Domain	Cache Disk
∨ 🗀 Hard disk 1 (RAID 1)				
Witness	✅ Active	🖥 10.202.25.228	Secondary	💾 Local VMware Disk (mpx.vmhba0:C0:T4:L0)
∨ RAID 1				
Component	✅ Active	🖥 10.202.25.202	Preferred	💾 Local VMware Disk (mpx.vmhba0:C0:T4:L0)
Component	✅ Active	🖥 10.202.25.206	Preferred	💾 Local VMware Disk (mpx.vmhba0:C0:T4:L0)
∨ RAID 1				
Component	✅ Active	🖥 10.202.25.238	Secondary	💾 Local VMware Disk (mpx.vmhba0:C0:T4:L0)
Component	✅ Active	🖥 10.202.25.226	Secondary	💾 Local VMware Disk (mpx.vmhba0:C0:T4:L0)
Witness	✅ Active	🖥 10.202.25.221	Preferred	💾 Local VMware Disk (mpx.vmhba0:C0:T4:L0)
Witness	⚠ Absent	🖥 10.202.25.231		52fdb790-2fdc-72dc-a442-e38176adacec

Figure 236: Failure scenario – Witness component absent

However, the virtual machine is unaffected and continues to be available and accessible. The rule for vSAN virtual machine object accessibility is, as we have discussed multiple times now, at least one full copy of the data must be available, and more than 50% of the components that go to make up the object are available. In this scenario both RAID configurations of the data are available, leaving access to the VM intact.

Network failure—Data Site to Data Site

The next failure scenario we want to describe is a site partition. If you are planning on testing this scenario, then we highly recommend ensuring that the host isolation response and host isolation addresses are configured correctly before conducting the tests. At least one of the isolation addresses should be pingable over the vSAN network by each host in the cluster. The environment shown below depicts our configuration and the failure scenario.

07 // Stretched Cluster Use Case

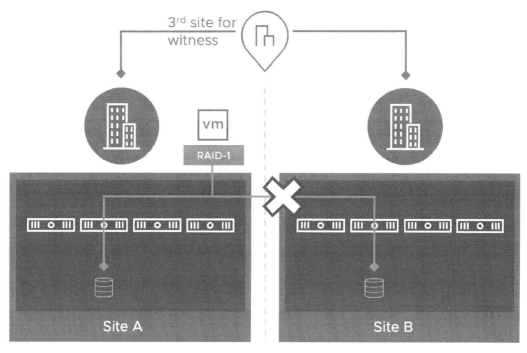

Figure 237: Failure scenario – Network failure

This scenario is special because when the inter-site link has failed, the "preferred" site forms a cluster with the witness, and most components (data components and witness) will be available to this part of the cluster. The secondary site will also form its own cluster, but it will only have a single copy of the data and will not have access to the witness. This results in two components of the virtual machine object getting marked as absent on the secondary site since the host can no longer communicate to the other data site where the other copy of the data resides, nor can it communicate to the witness. This means that the VMs can only run on the preferred site, where most of the components are accessible.

From a vSphere HA perspective, since the host isolation response IP address is on the vSAN network, both data sites should be able to reach the isolation response IP address on their respective sites. Therefore, vSphere HA does not trigger a host isolation response! This means that the VMs that are running in the secondary site, which has lost access to the vSAN datastore, cannot write to disk but are still running from a compute perspective. It should be noted that during the recovery, the host that has lost access to the disk components will instantly kill the impacted VM instances. This does however mean that until the host has recovered, potentially two instances of the same VM can be accessed over the network, of which only one is capable of writing to disk and the other is not.

vSAN 6.2 introduced a mechanism to avoid this situation. This feature will automatically kill the VMs on the secondary site has have lost access to the components on the secondary site. This is to ensure they can be safely restarted on the primary site, and when the link recovers there will not be two instances of the same VM running, not even for a brief second. If you want to disable this behavior, you can set the advanced host setting called *vSAN.AutoTerminateGhostVm* to 0. We, however, recommend leaving this setting configured to the default.

On the preferred site, the impacted VMs that were running on the secondary site, will be almost instantly restarted. On average this restart takes around 30 seconds. After the virtual machine has been restarted on the hosts on the preferred site, use the vSphere client to navigate to Cluster > Monitor > vSAN > Virtual Objects, select the VM you are interested in, and click on View placement details. This should show you that two out of the three components are available, and since there is a full copy of the data and more than 50% of the components are available, the VM is accessible. This is demonstrated in the screenshot below. Note that it is the secondary fault domain that is listed as absent in this case.

Virtual Object Components

Type	Component State	Host	Fault Domain
∨ Hard disk 1 (RAID 1)			
Witness	Active	10.161.155.16	
Component	Absent	10.161.143.8	Secondary
Component	Active	10.161.154.66	Preferred
∨ VM Home (RAID 1)			
Witness	Active	10.161.155.16	
Component	Active	10.161.154.152	Preferred
Component	Absent	10.161.143.8	Secondary
∨ Virtual Machine SWAP Object (RAID 1)			
Witness	Active	10.161.155.16	
Component	Active	10.161.135.132	Preferred
Component	Absent	10.161.152.157	Secondary

Figure 238: Two out of three components available

Impact of multiple failures

As discussed in the policy section, vSAN had two layers of protection in a stretched cluster. The first layer is across sites, the second layer is within sites. One thing however that not many people realize is that to not lose access to an object in a vSAN stretched cluster, more than 50% of the total combined votes for that object **across all locations** need to be available. What does this mean?

Let's look at a scenario where we have a stretched cluster and a virtual machine that is protected with RAID-1 across sites, and RAID-1 within the site.

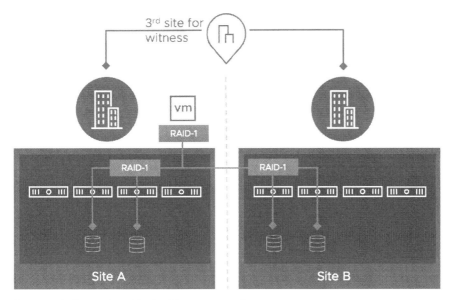

Figure 239: Scenario with dual-layer protection

In the above scenario, we have VM which is running in Site A. This VM is protected across locations and within the locations with both RAID-1. What is important in this case is to understand how the voting mechanism works. Although it is not explicitly shown, both data sites will have a number of votes, so will the witness component for this particular object. Let's examine this through RVC, the Ruby vSphere Console on the vCenter server, so we have a better understanding of the situation. Note that the below output has been truncated for readability reasons.

```
/localhost/VSAN-DC/vms> vsan.vm_object_info 1
Disk backing: [vsanDatastore] 3ddfce5b-a4d5-6e9e-92c1-0200086fa2e6/R1 Stretched.vmdk

    RAID_1
      RAID_1
        Component: 43dfce5b-d117-35ab-ff1a-0200086fa2e6
          votes: 1, usage: 0.0 GB, proxy component: false)
        Component: 43dfce5b-b2e0-36ab-f65e-0200086fa2e6
          votes: 1, usage: 0.0 GB, proxy component: false)
      RAID_1
        Component: 43dfce5b-ffc5-37ab-97a0-0200086fa2e6
          votes: 1, usage: 0.0 GB, proxy component: true)
        Component: 43dfce5b-31c6-38ab-a828-0200086fa2e6
          votes: 1, usage: 0.0 GB, proxy component: true)
    Witness: 43dfce5b-4ea8-39ab-454b-0200086fa2e6
          votes: 3, usage: 0.0 GB, proxy component: false)
    Witness: 43dfce5b-0e4e-3aab-f5b1-0200086fa2e6
          votes: 1, usage: 0.0 GB, proxy component: false)
    Witness: 43dfce5b-3ddc-3aab-ca7b-0200086fa2e6
          votes: 1, usage: 0.0 GB, proxy component: false)
```

In the above situation you see the votes for each of the components, let's list them so that it is easier to digest:

- VM Virtual Disk
    - Witness Site – 3 Votes
        - Witness component – 3 votes
    - Data Site 1 – 3 Votes in total
        - Replica A – 1 Vote
        - Replica B – 1 Vote
        - Witness component – 1 Vote
    - Data Site 2 – 3 Votes in total
        - Replica A – 1 Vote
        - Replica B – 1 Vote
        - Witness component – 1 Vote

This results in a total combined number of votes of 9. For the Witness site that is 3 votes, for Site 1 that is 3 and for Site 2 that is 3. Now if you have the Witness location fail you lose 3 votes. If now Site 1 – Replica A fails and the Witness component, you will end up losing access to the object as 5 out of 9 votes would be missing. Even though the full RAID-1 configuration of Site 2 is still available, the full object becomes unavailable.

You may wonder what this looks like when RAID-5 is used within the location instead of RAID-1. The RVC output, truncated once again, looks as follows.

```
Disk backing: [vsanDatastore] 2fe5ce5b-80b8-d071-59ad-020008b75d27/R1 / R5.vmdk
    DOM Object: 37e5ce5b-6d18-b7f7-f44d-020008b75d27
      RAID_1
        RAID_5
          Component: 37e5ce5b-7982-00f9-0bd4-020008b75d27
            votes: 2, usage: 0.0 GB, proxy component: true)
          Component: 37e5ce5b-d622-03f9-7e3e-020008b75d27
            votes: 1, usage: 0.0 GB, proxy component: true)
          Component: 37e5ce5b-b053-04f9-9aec-020008b75d27
            votes: 1, usage: 0.0 GB, proxy component: true)
          Component: 37e5ce5b-839d-05f9-7dab-020008b75d27
            votes: 1, usage: 0.0 GB, proxy component: true)
        RAID_5
          Component: 37e5ce5b-bafe-06f9-dfb5-020008b75d27
            votes: 1, usage: 0.0 GB, proxy component: false)
          Component: 37e5ce5b-32a3-08f9-a784-020008b75d27
            votes: 1, usage: 0.0 GB, proxy component: false)
          Component: 37e5ce5b-3b93-09f9-cf04-020008b75d27
            votes: 1, usage: 0.0 GB, proxy component: false)
          Component: 37e5ce5b-a159-0af9-a6e1-020008b75d27
            votes: 1, usage: 0.0 GB, proxy component: false)
        Witness: 37e5ce5b-1828-0df9-5c6c-020008b75d27
            votes: 4, usage: 0.0 GB, proxy component: false)
```

The big difference compared to the previous RAID-1 example is the fact that there are now 4 components for each replica (RAID-5 with vSAN is a 3+1 configuration as explained earlier) and there is only a single witness component. The votes are distributed across the components, and are as follows:

- Witness – 4 Votes
- Site A – 5 Votes
- Site B – 4 Votes

In this case, Site A has a component with an extra vote, this is to ensure we have an odd number of votes, allowing us to determine who has quorum when a failure occurs and allows us to handle a full site failure and a host failure within a location while maintaining object availability.

In a previous example failure scenario, we already discussed the witness failure resilience mechanism. This ensures that in the case of a double failure, where first a full site fails and then the witness host fails, the VM and its components are still available. Again, we would like to point out that this mechanism at the time of writing only works for scenarios where all components in a single location are impacted by a failure and after the recalculation of the votes the witness fails. If the witness fails first then, unfortunately, there's no recalculation happening.

Hopefully, the above explanation makes it clear how the voting mechanism works in vSAN stretched clusters and why in certain failure scenarios a restart of the virtual machine may or may not occur.

vSAN File Service

Earlier in this chapter, we mentioned that vSAN File Services is supported on a stretched cluster. Hopefully, everyone remembers the architectural details we shared in chapter 4. We can imagine however that some of those details have slipped, let us provide a brief refresher of what vSAN File Service looks like. Let's look at the diagram we initially shared.

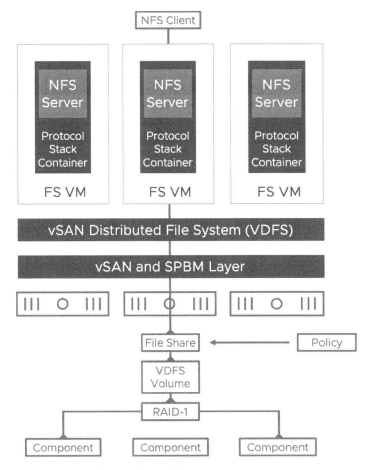

Figure 240: vSAN File Service Architecture

The diagram show the FS VMs and the Protocol Stack Container. As mentioned, when configuring vSAN File Services a range of IP addresses and DNS names needs to be provided. These DNS names and IP addresses are associated with the Protocol Stack Container, as this enabled vSAN File Service to restart the Protocol Stack Container in a different FS VM if a VM is impacted by a failure. Why is all this important?

Well, with a stretched cluster you have two primary locations and a witness location typically. To optimize I/O, it is recommended to try to avoid traversing the network as much as possible. With vSAN File Service however you access a share via a DNS name or an IP address. Depending on where that IP address is located geographically compared to the workload, it could be that access is traversing the ISL. Let's look at a diagram that visualizes this concept.

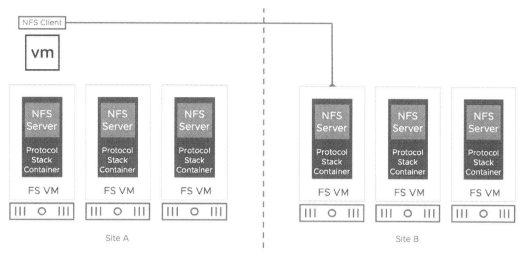

Figure 241: vSAN File Service Stretched

In the diagram above we have a workload running on the first physical host in Site A. It is accessing a file share through a file server that is running on the fourth host, which is in Site B. We can simply get around this by properly configuring vSAN File Service to take the configured fault domains into account. Do note, that this is a manual process, and we highly recommend documenting the DNS names and IP addresses associated with each location.

Let's look at the stretched cluster specific configuration aspects of vSAN File Service and the creation of a file share. First, when deploying vSAN File Service you need to have IP addresses and DNS names equal to the number of protocol stack containers deployed. Recommended is to keep the number of protocol stack containers equal to the number of hosts in a cluster. In other words, if you have an 8+8+1 configuration, you will need a total of 16 IP addresses and 16 DNS names for vSAN File Service, 8 for each location.

In our next screenshot, we show the configuration screen of vSAN File Service where the IP addresses, DNS name, and site affinity can be configured.

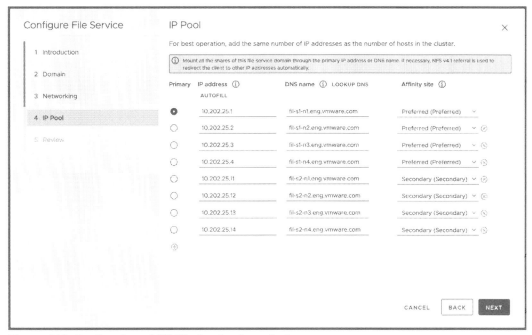

Figure 242: Configuring vSAN File Service Stretched

Site affinity determines in which location a protocol stack container (and its associated IP address and DNS name) *should* reside. Please take notice, we used the word "should", this is a soft affinity rule. Meaning that if all hosts, or VMs, fail on which these file service protocol stack containers are running, it could be that the container is restarted in the opposite location. Again, a soft rule, not a hard rule. However, during normal operations, each of these protocol stack containers will run in the specified location, preferred or secondary.

Of course, that is not the end of the story. You also need to be able to specify for each share with which location it has affinity with. Again, you do this during the creation of the share (or edit it afterward if desired), and this then sets the affinity for the file share to a location. What does this mean? It will ensure that when you connect to file share, one of the file servers in the specified site will be used. Again, this is a *soft rule*, meaning that if none of the file server protocol stack containers are available on that site, you will still be able to use vSAN File Service, just not with the optimized data path you defined. The next screenshot displays how this is represented in the vSphere Client during the creation of the file share. Note, in our example, we demonstrate this capability for NFS 4.1 and 3, but the same concept applies to SMB.

Figure 243: File share creating on a stretched cluster

Last, but not least what about my storage policy? Well, the same applies here as it does to your VM workloads. If you need your file share to be replicated between locations, then you will need to select the policy which specifies the "Site Disaster Tolerance" is "Site Mirroring – stretched cluster". Of course, you can also decide not to replicate the data, but that will result in downtime when the respective site fails.

Operating a Stretched Cluster

We have discussed how to configure a stretched cluster, and how a stretched cluster acts during certain failure scenarios. We have, however, not discussed yet if there are any specific things to consider when it comes to the operational aspects of a stretched cluster. Operating vSAN is discussed in chapter 6, there are however a few exceptions and things to know when it comes to a stretched cluster configuration.

The first concept we want to discuss is Maintenance Mode and Upgrades or Updates. Hopefully, everyone uses vSphere Lifecycle Manager (vLCM) for lifecycle management of their vSphere (and vSAN) hosts. One common question we have received over the years is what customers should do with the witness appliance. Do you upgrade it, or do you simply deploy a new version of the appliance and click on "Change Witness Host" under Fault Domains, displayed in the next screenshot?

Fault Domains

Fault domain failures to tolerate	1	
Configuration type	Stretched cluster	DISABLE STRETCHED CLUSTER
Witness host	10.202.25.231	CHANGE WITNESS HOST

Preferred (preferred)		Secondary	
Used capacity	2%	Used capacity	2%
10.202.25.2...	2%	10.202.25.2...	2%
10.202.25.221	2%	10.202.25.238	2%
10.202.25.2...	2%	10.202.25.2...	2%
10.202.25.2...	2%	10.202.25.222	2%
10.202.25.214	2%	10.202.25.225	2%
10.202.25.2...	2%	10.202.25.2...	2%

Figure 244: Changing witness for a stretched cluster

Before you decide on a strategy, it is good to know that starting with vSAN 7.0 U3 it is now also supported to upgrade the Witness Appliance using vLCM. This greatly simplifies the update, or upgrade process. We do not have a preference when it comes to lifecycle management of the appliance, we have seen customers successfully using either the update as well as the replacement approach. It boils down to what you feel most comfortable with.

When it comes to updating the entire cluster, we recommend using vLCM for all hosts, and preferably integrated with your OEM's firmware management solution. This way both vSphere, as well as the firmware of all components, are at the correct version. Especially for a vSAN cluster, this is extremely important, hence vSAN Skyline Health validates your environment against the most current VMware Compatibility Guide whenever it runs.

The last thing we want to mention is that, at the time of writing, there is no option to place a full site into maintenance at once. Maintenance happens on the host level. If you end up in a situation where a single site needs to be powered off, then all hosts will need to be placed into maintenance mode one by one.

Another thing that is important to realize is that monitoring for disk capacity is slightly different. Although all regular screens still provide useful information, there is one additional section in the UI we would recommend to regular monitor. The screenshot above shows vSAN capacity per fault domain, as well as per host within each fault domain. In an environment where all VMs are replicated between locations, the capacity consumption is typically equal between both locations. However, we have many customers that have workloads that do not need to be replicated between locations, and they leverage VM Storage Policies to specify where the VM needs to be located. In other words, using policies they specify in which fault domain all components of the VM (or file share, etc.) need to be stored. This can then lead to a situation where one fault domain has less free capacity than the other, which is of course useful to know when provisioning decisions are made.

Another aspect of managing a stretched cluster that we want to stress is that the use of standardized VM Storage Policy names is key. We also recommend customers to regularly validate if VMs are associated with the correct policy. Unfortunately, we have witnessed situations where VMs were supposed to be mirrored across locations, but because of an incorrectly assigned policy were not mirrored. In normal situations this is not a problem, however, it is during that unexpected site failure that you typically find out that your business-critical VM was not replicated. You can, for instance, use PowerCLI to create a report of all VMs and their associated policies.

Lastly, VM/Host rules. This is a hot topic in every stretched cluster architectural or operational discussion. Should you create rules and specify in which location a VM should run. We believe that this is desired. It provides you the ability to control where a particular VM runs, and as a result, it will give you a better understanding of what the impact is on IT services and Applications when a (site) failure has occurred.

Summary

A vSAN stretched cluster architecture will allow you to deploy and migrate workloads across two locations without the need for complex storage configurations and operational processes. On top of that, it comes at a relatively low cost that enables most VMware users to deploy this configuration when there are dual datacenter requirements. As with any explicit architecture, there are various design and operational considerations. We would like to refer you to the official VMware documentation and https://core.vmware.com/ as the source of the most updated and accurate information.

08

Two Host vSAN Cluster Use Case

Two host configurations were introduced in vSAN 6.1 and are often used by customers looking to deploy workloads into remote office or branch office locations. Unfortunately, this configuration is often confused with the VMware Remote Office / Branch Office license, which is nothing more than a license key that allows you to run 25 virtual machines across several locations on as many ESXi hosts as needed. In no shape or form is this license key associated with the two-host configuration. It is important to make that distinction before we begin, as it is a question that comes up time and again.

When configuring a two host vSAN cluster it quickly becomes obvious that it is very similar to a stretched cluster configuration. The main difference is that normally a two-host cluster would have both hosts located in the same location, whereas in a stretched cluster configuration, hosts would be located in different locations. Another difference is that it is not uncommon to see a single vCenter Server instance managing numerous two host vSAN clusters. It is not uncommon to see hundreds of two host vSAN clusters registered in the same vCenter Server. The below diagram displays what this could look like from a logical point of view.

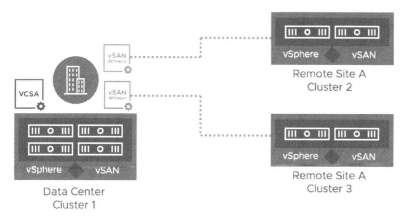

Figure 245: Multiple two host clusters

As mentioned earlier, a two-host configuration closely resembles a stretched cluster configuration when it comes to the setup and implementation. There are however some differences in functionality, and there are some design considerations as well. Before we investigate those, let us first look at how to configure a two host vSAN cluster.

Configuration of a two-host cluster

Configuring a two-host cluster can simply be done through the interface we have seen many times by now at this point in the book. Go to your cluster object and configure vSAN. When you configure vSAN select *Two node vSAN cluster* as depicted below.

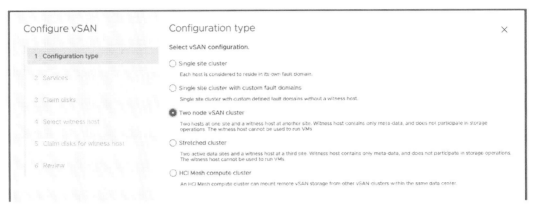

Figure 246: Configuration of a two-host cluster

Next, select all the services which you require. Note that all services are available but note that in a two host vSAN cluster, it can be configured as either hybrid or all-flash. From a product or feature standpoint, there is no limitation. However, with only two hosts, you will not be able to set *failures to tolerate* value greater than 1, nor will you be able to select RAID-5 or RAID-6 for availability, since these erasure coding features require 4 and 6 hosts respectively. What will however limit you is, of course, the vSAN and vSphere license you have procured. In our case, we have an all-flash cluster, but we will not use any of the additional services as we have a vSAN Standard license.

Figure 247: Data services

Next, we will need to claim the devices that will form the vSAN shared datastore. In our case, this is an all-flash configuration so we will select the flash devices for the cache tier and the flash devices for the capacity tier.

In the next step, we are going to select the host that will act as the witness host. In our case, this is the virtual witness appliance, and after that, we will need to claim the disks for this witness host as this witness host will store the witness components for the virtual machines running on the two-host cluster. This again is very similar to the configuration of a stretched cluster. The step missing however is the creation of fault domains (preferred and secondary) and the selection of the host that belongs to these locations. This is because the fault domains are automatically implied; each physical host and the witness are in their own respective fault domain, as we shall see next.

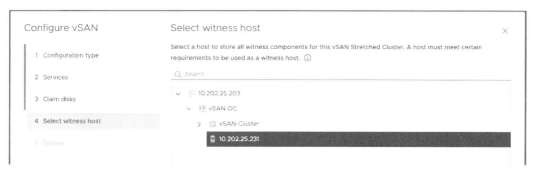

Figure 248: Selecting the witness host

Now we can review the two-node configuration and complete the creation by clicking finish. After we have clicked finish, we can simply examine the configuration in the vSphere Client. One thing that immediately stands out is that even though we did not create fault domains and specified which hosts belong to which fault domain, faults domains have been configured and each of the two hosts is assigned to a fault domain.

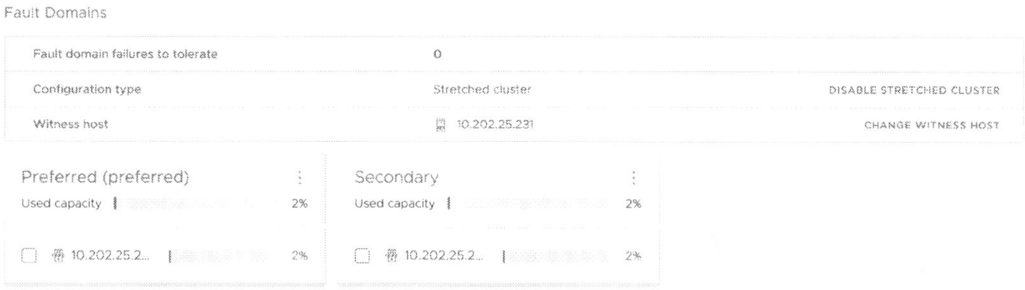

Figure 249: Fault domains in a two-host configuration

That completes the configuration of a two-host cluster. In this case, we have shown a regular two host configuration. There are however a couple of different ways of configuring vSAN 2-host configurations. One way is to use the Quickstart wizard, which is shown in the next screenshot.

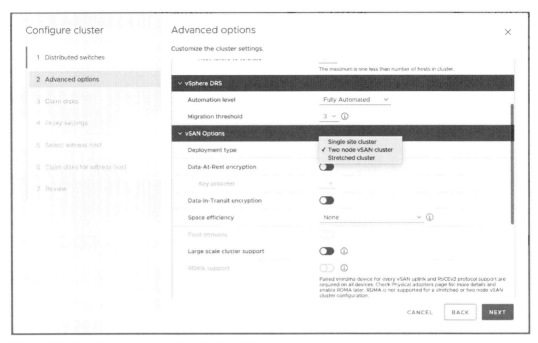

Figure 250: Two-host configuration via QuickStart

What is interesting to know is that when another 2-host cluster is created, the same vSAN Witness Appliance can be selected. This capability, shared witness host, was introduced in vSAN 7.0 U1 and designed for customers with multiple 2-host clusters who want to limit the number of Witness Appliances deployed. There are some limitations and considerations for a shared witness deployment.

First and foremost, the size of the vSAN Witness Appliance determines how many 2-host clusters the witness can be shared. The largest vSAN Witness Appliance can support up to 64 2-host clusters and a maximum of 64.000 components. Typically, the component limit should not be a concern, as this means you can store 1000 witness components per cluster. This means you can run easily over a hundred VMs per 2-host cluster before you hit this limit. We have not seen any customers reaching those numbers in a 2-host cluster yet. Having said that, you could be that one customer that does deploy a large number of VMs, make sure you select the correct witness appliance size and monitor the number of components when you potentially could reach the specific limits. It is possible to monitor the currently assigned number of configurations to your shared witness host. Simply right click the host, click on "vSAN" and click "assign as shared witness host". You will now be presented with a window that shows the currently assigned two-host clusters. You can look at the same information by clicking on the witness appliance and then go to "Monitor", Two Node Clusters". As demonstrated in the next screenshot, you will be presented with a list of clusters, the witness component count, and information like the limits.

Two Node Clusters

Clusters assigned to this witness	2 (out of max 21)
Witness components limit per cluster	1000

ASSIGN TO THIS WITNESS   REASSIGN TO ANOTHER WITNESS

	Cluster Name	▼	Witness Components Count
☐	Cluster B - 2node		7
☐	Cluster A - 2node		0

Figure 251: Two-host Clusters information

In the above screenshot, you can also see the option "Assign to this witness". This option allows you to assign this shared witness to an existing 2-host configuration. This 2-host configuration will already have a witness assigned, but this witness is typically a non-shared witness. Using the "Assign To This Witness" option you can migrate from non-shared to shared, but you can also use this option to replace a currently shared witness appliance with a new shared witness appliance.

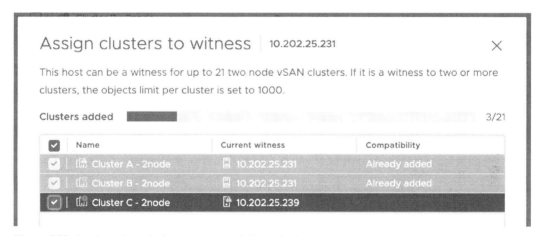

Figure 252: Assign shared witness to an existing cluster

There is another rather unique configuration possible as well. This is a configuration that has started to become more and more popular amongst customers as it lowers the cost of the deployment significantly.

vSAN Direct Connect

When VMware first introduced the two-host cluster option, the immediate request that we heard from customers was to cross-connect the hosts. This is something that customers have done for vMotion for the longest time and doing the same for vSAN with 10 GbE NICs (or higher) without the need for a 10 GbE switch (or higher) would provide the ability to deliver great performance at a relatively low cost. Starting with vSAN 6.5, cross-connecting two-host configurations became fully supported. Please note that this only works with, and only is supported for, two-host clusters.

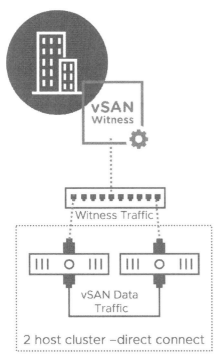

Figure 253: vSAN Direct Connect

As demonstrated in the diagram above, this will require Witness Traffic Separation to be configured for vSAN. We have already described how to do this in the stretched cluster chapter as the same functionality can be leveraged to separate witness traffic from vSAN data traffic for that configuration. If you are considering deploying a two-host configuration with direct connect, please make sure you are familiar with the required *esxcli* command.

Now that we have seen the configuration, and the two-host direct connection option, let's look at requirements, constraints, and two host cluster specific support statements.

Support statements, requirements, and constraints

In a vSAN two host configuration support, requirements and constraints are slightly different than in a stretched cluster configuration. Let's start by listing all requirements and constraints, followed by support statements that are different for two host configurations versus a stretched cluster configuration.

- 500ms maximum latency is tolerated between the two-host cluster and the witness host
- Between data sites both Layer 2 and Layer 3 are supported
    - Layer-2 is recommended for simplicity
- Between the data sites and the witness site Layer 3 is required
    - Prevents I/O from being routed through a potentially low bandwidth witness site
- In the case of multiple locations, multiple witness VMs running in a central location may share the same VLAN
- When only a single VLAN is available per 2-host location, it is supported to tag the Management Network for Witness traffic
- VM Storage Policies can only be configured with *Number of Failures To Tolerate* = 1 and RAID-1 (Mirroring) due to the fact that there are only 2 hosts in the cluster
- Bandwidth between vSAN Hosts hosting VM objects and the Witness Host is dependent on the number of objects residing on vSAN. A standard rule of thumb is 2Mbps for every 1000 components on vSAN. Because vSAN hosts have a maximum number of 9000 components per host, the maximum bandwidth requirement from a 2 Host cluster to the Witness Host supporting it, is 18Mbps
- SMP-FT is supported when using 2 Host configurations in the same physical location. SMP-FT requires appropriate vSphere licensing. The vSAN Witness Appliance managing a 2 Host cluster may not reside on the cluster it is providing quorum for. SMP-FT is not a feature that removes this restriction
- By default, in a two-host configuration and a stretched configuration vSAN only reads from the fault domain in which the VM resides. This is very valuable as it lowers bandwidth requirements. For a two-host cluster, which is located in the same datacenter, this reading from a single host adds no value. The vSAN "*DOMOwnerForceWarmCache*" setting can be configured to force reads across hosts in a 2-host configuration. In vSAN 6.7 U1 this can now be configured in the vSphere Client as shown in Figure 210

One major difference when comparing two host clusters with a stretched cluster however is that, with a two-host configuration, it is supported to cross host the witness appliance when you only have 2 locations via a special support request (RPQ). What does this exactly mean, and what would be the use case for this? Well, the use case for this would be when there are two locations within 500ms RTT latency and both need some form of compute and storage for local services. As shown in the diagram below, each remote location hosts the witness for the other location. This way only two locations are required, instead of 3 normally.

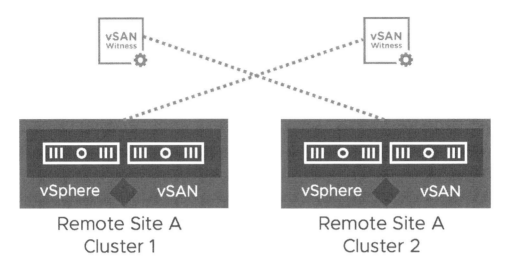

Figure 254: Cross host witness

Although briefly mentioned in the requirements above, we do want to explicitly show two common network architectures for connecting remote locations to a centralized datacenter. In our experience, in almost all cases L3 networking is configured between the central datacenter and the remote location. In some of the cases we have seen multiple networks being available per remote location, and in most cases, we see a single network available. The following diagrams depict these two scenarios.

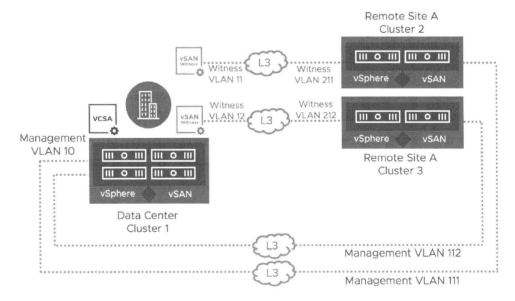

Figure 255: Multiple VLANs per remote location

In the above scenario, per location also two static routes will be required to be defined. One for Management VLAN 10 to the remote location Management VLAN, and one for the witness VLAN to the Witness VLAN. Note that in the case where you have many remote locations, the above scenario does not scale extremely well, and will add a layer of complexity as a result.

Of course, as mentioned, this can be simplified by having a single network to each location that shares both Management as well as Witness traffic. The following diagram depicts this scenario.

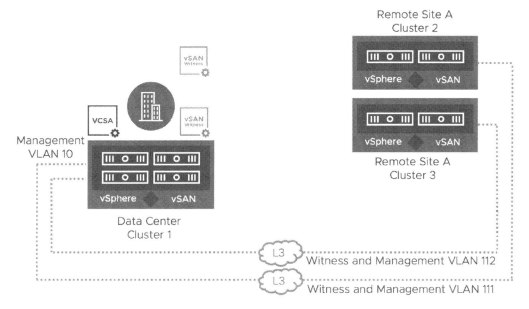

Figure 256: Single VLANs per remote location

Please note that in the case of the above scenario a static route from the management network to the remote location is still required, and the witness appliance will need to be modified so that the management VMkernel interface is also tagged for Witness traffic. Although in the above examples we have shown multiple witness appliances, of course, these architectures are also supported with a shared witness configuration!

Summary

A vSAN two host configuration will allow you to a limited number of VMs in remote locations without the need for complex storage configurations and operational processes. On top of that, these locations can be managed through a centralized vCenter Server instance, lowering operational cost and overhead.

09

Cloud-Native Applications Use Case

When we published edition 3 of the vSAN Book back in 2018, Kubernetes was beginning to gain adoption as an enterprise platform. It was around this time that we also began to see the general availability of Kubernetes service offerings from cloud vendors such as Amazon EKS and Azure Kubernetes Services (AKS). It was at the 2018 KubeCon (Kubernetes Conference) that we also began to hear about plans for the Container Storage Interface (CSI) which eventually was promoted to General Availability in Kubernetes release v1.13 in early 2019. In this chapter, we will explore how vSAN can provide a platform not just for virtual machine workloads, but also for the newer container-based, cloud-native applications. We will show vSAN integration with upstream Kubernetes distributions, as well as vSAN integrations with VMware's own Tanzu branded Kubernetes distributions (which are also upstream but are selective about what is supported – more on this later). This will not be a deep dive into all elements of Kubernetes. Instead, we will focus on those objects in Kubernetes that are relevant to storage, particularly vSAN.

What is a container?

It is not possible to talk about Kubernetes without first describing what a container is. In its simplest form, a container can be considered a very special sort of process, representing an application, that runs in an operating system. I say they are special only because they leverage features such as cgroups and namespaces for limiting and isolating system resources. In the early days of containers, they were often compared to virtual machines, and some very simplistic viewpoints compared them to virtual machines "without the need for an operating system". In some respects, this is correct, but since a container is a process running in an operating system, it does still require an OS. Admittedly, many containers run in the same OS, since again the container is just a process. But the neat thing about containers is portability. Developers could create their container-based app on their laptop, and then deploy it to an on-premises based Kubernetes distribution such as Tanzu Kubernetes, or to a cloud-based Kubernetes distribution, such as Google Kubernetes Engine. While container technology had existed for many years, it was not until Docker (the company) came along and made it very easy for developers to package their containers using Docker (the product) and make them portable, that containers began to gain popularity.

Why Kubernetes?

Now you might be wondering why we need Kubernetes if containers are so great. In a nutshell, Kubernetes allows us to manage containers at scale, or indeed the applications running in containers. The term container "orchestration" is used a lot, but in essence, Kubernetes is a platform that allows us to provision, scale in and out, update and upgrade, and generally, life cycle manage container-based applications. Of course, there is much more to Kubernetes than just containers. Microservices, which is the splitting up of an application into its constituent parts, is another major aspect of Kubernetes. This separation of monolithic application functionality into microservices brings in the concept of Service Mesh, which deals with the partitioning or segmentation of applications at a network and security level. However, Microservices and Service Mesh are beyond the scope of what we wish to discuss in this chapter. Instead, our focus will be on how applications that run in Kubernetes that require persistent storage can leverage vSAN to meet those requirements.

Kubernetes Storage Constructs

Since this book is all about storage, the focus in this section is to highlight just those Kubernetes objects that have some relationship to the underlying storage. We will expand this somewhat to bring in some other Kubernetes objects that are involved in consuming storage, e.g., pods, but suffice to say the scope will not cover every Kubernetes object.

Before delving into the different objects, it is interesting to note that in the early days of containerization, not much thought was given to persistent storage. The feeling was that you would spin up your container, get it to do some units of work, capture the result and then discard the container. The terminology to describe this scenario is "stateless" and for some time, containers were positioned for stateless workloads. Any writes to disk that were needed during this work was done to ephemeral storage. Once the container was discarded, so was the data. However, while there is certainly value in being able to run stateless workloads, people soon realized the value of being able to run "stateful" containerized workloads as well. One pressing concern was the need to persist data in case the container crashed. Thus, a mechanism to provide persistent storage for containers was desired.

Let's now look at the Kubernetes storage objects in some more detail.

Storage Class

As the name implies, this is a way for a Kubernetes cluster administrator to define different "classes" of storage to a developer. Shortly we will see how we can dynamically provision volumes of a particular Storage Class in Kubernetes. Before we do that, let's look at some of the other attributes of a Storage Class.

One of the entries that is placed in a Storage Class manifest is "provisioner". This is probably a good place to introduce the CSI driver, which is essentially what enables Kubernetes to provision persistent volumes on top of different underlying infrastructures, such as vSphere, AWS, Google Cloud, etc. For Kubernetes clusters that are running as a set of virtual machines on vSphere, consuming vSphere datastores for persistent volumes, the provisioner is the vSphere CSI driver, "`csi.vsphere.vmware.com`". This driver is also referred to as the vSphere Container Storage Plug-in, and its purpose is to provision Kubernetes persistent volumes on vSphere storage.

When the provisioner in the Storage Class is set to vSphere CSI driver, a parameter called "`storagepolicyname`" may also be defined. This parameter is used to map a Kubernetes Storage Class to a vSphere Storage Policy. Since vSAN is very much integrated with the Storage Policy-Based Management (SPBM) feature of vSphere, different Kubernetes Storage Classes can be created to reflect different aspects of vSAN storage. This means that any persistent volumes that are created using a particular storage class will be instantiated on the vSAN datastore with the storage policy referenced by "`storagepolicyname`".

Another configurable option is "`allowVolumeExpansion`", which enables the online growth of Persistent Volumes. Note that this feature is only available in CSI driver version 2.2 and later.

One can also specify a "`reclaimPolicy`". This tells Kubernetes what to do with a Persistent Volume after the Persistent Volume Claim has been deleted. By default, the PV is also "Deleted", but the reclaim policy can be set to be "Retained" or "Recycled".

Finally, another optional parameter that one might find in the Storage Class manifest is the filesystem type "`parameters.csi.storage.k8s.io/fstype`". This defines how a persistent volume is formatted. Options for block volumes are "`ext4`", and "`xfs`". Note that "`xfs`" only became available as a format in vSphere CSI driver version 2.3. The only format option available for file volumes is "`nfs4`".

Here is an example of a simple Storage Class containing a vSAN policy for block volumes.

```
kind: StorageClass
apiVersion: storage.k8s.io/v1
metadata:
  name: vsan-sc
provisioner: csi.vsphere.vmware.com
allowVolumeExpansion: true
parameters:
  storagepolicyname: "vSAN Default Storage Policy"
  csi.storage.k8s.io/fstype: "ext4"
```

Compare this to the next example of a simple Storage Class containing a vSAN policy for file volumes. Note the only difference is the setting to "`nfs4`" for "`parameters.csi.storage.k8s.io/fstype`" instead of "`ext4`" used above. Note also that the "`allowVolumeExpansion`" parameter has been omitted from this StorageClass since this is a feature that is only available on block volumes at the time of writing. The feature allows administrators to grow the size of a persistent volume.

```
kind: StorageClass
apiVersion: storage.k8s.io/v1
metadata:
  name: vsan-file-sc
provisioner: csi.vsphere.vmware.com
parameters:
  storagepolicyname: "vSAN Default Storage Policy"
  csi.storage.k8s.io/fstype: nfs4
```

Persistent Volumes

A Persistent Volume, or PV for short, is an allocation of storage resources that can be used by a containerized application to store data. In the case of Kubernetes running on vSphere and using vSAN as a storage platform, persistent volumes map to VMDKs on the vSAN datastore. The VMDK that are instantiated on the vSAN datastore to back a PV are a special virtual disk known as a First Class Disk (FCD) or Improved Virtual Disks (IVD), and enable disk-centric operations outside of the lifecycle of the virtual machine, e.g., snapshot, restore, clone, etc.

Persistent Volumes are not tied to the lifecycle of a pod. They can exist independent of any pod that uses them. Indeed, a pod can be deleted and can be recreated to use the PV without any loss of data from the PV.

Persistent Volumes can be provisioned statically, i.e., created manually outside of Kubernetes and then mapped to a Persistent Volume construct, or they can be provisioned dynamically through a Persistent Volume Claim (PVC).

Persistent Volume Claim

As we have just learned, the way to dynamically create a Persistent Volume (PV) in Kubernetes is through a Persistent Volume Claim (PVC). Let's take a look at some of the attributes that one might find in a PVC manifest when dynamically creating PVCs on vSphere storage, notably vSAN.

One of the first attributes is the "`spec.accessMode`". vSAN supports a number of different access modes for volumes, but the two most common access modes for Kubernetes PVs are read write once (RWO) for block storage and read-write-many (RWX) for file storage. RWO access mode implies that a persistent volume can only be accessed from a single pod. RWX access mode implies that a persistent volume can be accessed from multiple pods. RWX is supported on vSAN through vSAN File Service, available since the 7.0 release. The vSphere CSI driver does not support multi-attach RWX block volumes at the time of writing.

Another attribute of a Persistent Volume Claim manifest is "`spec.resources.requests.storage`" where the size of the Persistent Volume is specified. Other than that, the only important entry is a reference to the Storage Class, which has been described earlier. This maps a request for a volume to a particular storage policy on vSphere, and this in turn guides vSphere to create the volume on the appropriate vSphere datastore.

Here is an example of a simple PVC for a RWO block volume.

```
apiVersion: v1
kind: PersistentVolumeClaim
metadata:
  name: vsan-claim
spec:
  storageClassName: vsan-sc
  accessModes:
    - ReadWriteOnce
  resources:
    requests:
      storage: 2Gi
```

Here is an example of a simple PVC for a RWX file volume. Notice that the only difference between the block and file PVC is the different "`spec.storageClassName`" setting for mounting the volume with a different format, and of course the "`spec.accessmode`" setting.

```
apiVersion: v1
kind: PersistentVolumeClaim
metadata:
  name: vsan-file-claim
spec:
  storageClassName: vsan-file-sc
  accessModes:
    - ReadWriteMany
  resources:
    requests:
      storage: 2Gi
```

Pod

Now that we have successfully learned how to build Kubernetes Persistent Volumes on vSphere datastores such as vSAN, let's look at how an application can consume those volumes. In its simplest form, a pod is a Kubernetes construct comprising of one or more containers. All containers within the pod share storage and network resources. For the purposes of this book, the only aspect of a pod that we are interested in is how it can consume external storage. Thus, the parts of a pod manifest that should be configured are "`spec.volumes`" which references a Persistent Volume Claim (PVC), and "`spec.containers.volumeMounts`" which mounts the volume into the pods. The "`spec.containers.volumeMounts.name`" mounts the volume which matches "`spec.volumes.name`" from the same pod manifest.

Here is an example of a pod with a single *busybox* container that is claiming a Persistent Volume from the PVC "vsan-claim". This container provides a number of Unix utilities in a single executable. Referencing the PVC via "`claimName`" (which was created previously), this creates a request for a 2GB read write once (RWO) block volume matching the Storage Class "`vsan-sc`". Within Kubernetes, this request is sent to the vSphere CSI driver components, which in turn talks to another component in vCenter Server. After applying the various manifest, this should result in a 2GB volume being instantiated on a vSAN datastore. It is created with a configuration that matches the default vSAN storage policy as this is what was placed in the Storage Class. If successful, the volume will be formatted as an "`ext4`" filesystem and mounted onto the folder "`/demo`" in the busybox pod.

```
apiVersion: v1
kind: Pod
metadata:
  name: vsan-block-pod
spec:
  containers:
  - name: busybox
    image: busybox
    volumeMounts:
    - name: block-vol
      mountPath: "/demo"
    command: [ "sleep", "1000000" ]
  volumes:
  - name: block-vol
    persistentVolumeClaim:
      claimName: vsan-claim
```

The following manifest is another example of a pod deployment. However, in this case, we are deploying 2 pods. Both of which will attempt to mount the same read write many (RWX) file volume. The PVC is as described in the "`volume.persistentVolumeClaim.claimName`" attribute. This should request the vSphere CSI driver to instantiate the volume on the vSAN datastore, as well as export it as a vSAN File Share via vSAN File Service. If this is successful, the volume should be mounted onto both pods and accessible in the *busybox* container on the "`/nfsvol`" folder. Referencing the PVC manifest above, this should be a 2GB file share. Note that the next manifest creates 2 pods. Multiple manifests can reside in the same YAML file if they are separated with "---" to indicate a different manifest.

```
apiVersion: v1
kind: Pod
metadata:
  name: file-pod-a
spec:
  containers:
  - name: busybox
    image: busybox
    volumeMounts:
    - name: file-vol
      mountPath: "/nfsvol"
    command: [ "sleep", "1000000" ]
  volumes:
  - name: file-vol
    persistentVolumeClaim:
      claimName: vsan-file-claim

---

apiVersion: v1
kind: Pod
metadata:
  name: file-pod-b
spec:
  containers:
  - name: busybox
    image: busybox
```

```
      volumeMounts:
      - name: file-vol
        mountPath: "/nfsvol"
      command: [ "sleep", "1000000" ]
    volumes:
      - name: file-vol
        persistentVolumeClaim:
          claimName: vsan-file-claim
```

vSphere CSI in action – block volume

To demonstrate the creation of a block PV through a PVC, and then accessing the resulting volume from a pod, I will use a small Kubernetes cluster made up of 1 control plane node and 2 worker nodes. Suffice to say that this Kubernetes cluster is deployed on vSphere infrastructure, and already has the vSphere CSI driver installed.

Let's check the nodes in the cluster. One of the nodes is the control-plane, master, as per the role. The others are the workers. The Kubernetes version that has been deployed to this cluster is v1.23.3.

```
% kubectl get nodes
NAME            STATUS   ROLES                  AGE   VERSION
csisnap-cp0     Ready    control-plane,master   20d   v1.23.3
csisnap-wk0     Ready    <none>                 20d   v1.23.3
csisnap-wk1     Ready    <none>                 20d   v1.23.3
```

Next, we will show the CSI driver components. There is a CSI controller pod, and a CSI node pod for all 3 nodes. We will go into further detail regarding the different CSI components that make up the controller pod shortly. In this version of Kubernetes, which is an upstream, vanilla, Kubernetes, the CSI driver components are placed in the `vmware-system-csi` namespace. Therefore, we need to specify the namespace when querying for pods. Note that vSphere CSI driver version 2.5.x, shown here, has a total of 7 containers in the controller pod. Other, older versions of the vSphere CSI driver may show fewer containers in the controller pod.

```
% kubectl get pods -n vmware-system-csi
NAME                                         READY   STATUS    RESTARTS        AGE
vsphere-csi-controller-5b6dfc6799-lmphc      7/7     Running   7 (11d ago)     19d
vsphere-csi-node-ggkng                       3/3     Running   0               19d
vsphere-csi-node-r6pfh                       3/3     Running   5 (11d ago)     19d
vsphere-csi-node-tsd4r                       3/3     Running   3 (11d ago)     19d
```

To create a sample application, we are going to work in the `default` namespace. Thus, it is not necessary to specify this namespace when we create, query, or delete the objects. Some objects, such as Storage Class and PV, are not namespace scoped, but PVCs and pods are. At present, there are no Storage Classes, PVCs, PVs, or pods on this cluster.

```
% kubectl get pods,pvc,pv,sc
No resources found
```

Next, apply a manifest that contains a Storage Class, a PVC, and a pod. As mentioned, these can all be added to the same file so long as they are separated with "---" on their own line in the file. Thus, a single file can create multiple Kubernetes objects.

```
% kubectl apply -f demo-sc-pvc-pod-rwo.yaml
storageclass.storage.k8s.io/vsan-sc created
persistentvolumeclaim/vsan-claim created
pod/vsan-block-pod created
```

Check if the objects were created successfully. Let's check the Storage Class, the PVC, the PV that should have been created with the PVC, and finally the pod.

```
% kubectl get sc
NAME      PROVISIONER             RECLAIMPOLICY  VOLUMEBINDINGMODE  ALLOWVOLUMEEXPANSION  AGE
vsan-sc   csi.vsphere.vmware.com  Delete         Immediate          true                  12s


% kubectl get pvc
NAME         STATUS  VOLUME          CAPACITY  ACCESS MODES  STORAGECLASS  AGE
vsan-claim   Bound   pvc-e086a59e….  2Gi       RWO           vsan-sc       15s


% kubectl get pv
NAME             CAPACITY  ACCESS MODES  RECLAIM  STATUS  CLAIM       STORAGECLASS  REASON  AGE
pvc-e086a59e…   2Gi       RWO           Delete   Bound   vsan-claim  vsan-sc               16s


% kubectl get pod
NAME            READY  STATUS   RESTARTS  AGE
vsan-block-pod  1/1    Running  0         20s
```

It would appear that all objects have been created successfully. One final check is to open a shell to the pod and check to see if a 2GB volume has been formatted and mounted to the *busybox* container within the Pod. Since the pod only contains a single container, we do not need to explicitly specify the container, but if the pod held more than one container, the container name would need to be also specified on the command line.

```
% kubectl exec -it vsan-block-pod -- sh
/ # df -h
Filesystem              Size      Used  Available  Use%  Mounted on
overlay                 77.7G     12.1G 61.6G      16%   /
tmpfs                   64.0M     0     64.0M      0%    /dev
/dev/sdb                1.9G      6.0M  1.8G       0%    /demo
/dev/sda3               77.7G     12.1G 61.6G      16%   /dev/termination-log
/dev/sda3               77.7G     12.1G 61.6G      16%   /etc/resolv.conf
/dev/sda3               77.7G     12.1G 61.6G      16%   /etc/hostname
/dev/sda3               77.7G     12.1G 61.6G      16%   /etc/hosts
shm                     64.0M     0     64.0M      0%    /dev/shm
tmpfs                   15.5G     12.0K 15.5G      0%
/var/run/secrets/kubernetes.io/serviceaccount
tmpfs                   7.8G      0     7.8G       0%    /proc/acpi
tmpfs                   64.0M     0     64.0M      0%    /proc/kcore
tmpfs                   64.0M     0     64.0M      0%    /proc/keys
tmpfs                   64.0M     0     64.0M      0%    /proc/timer_list
tmpfs                   7.8G      0     7.8G       0%    /proc/scsi
tmpfs                   7.8G      0     7.8G       0%    /sys/firmware
/ # cd /demo
/demo # ls
lost+found
```

```
/demo # mount | grep "/dev/sdb"
/dev/sdb on /demo type ext4 (rw,relatime)
```

A 2GB volume has now been successfully attached (/dev/sdb) as requested by the PVC manifest, formatted as ext4 as requested in the Storage Class manifest, formatted as ext4, and then mounted to /demo as requested in the Pod manifest.

Cloud-Native Storage (CNS) for vSphere Administrators – block volume

One of the primarily goals of VMware when running Kubernetes on vSphere is to provide as much information as possible to the vSphere Administrator. This is to help with monitoring, capacity planning, troubleshooting, etc. To that end, VMware added a Cloud-Native Storage (CNS) section to the vSphere UI to provide this visibility. Please note that the examples below are taken from a vSphere 7.0U3 environment. If you are using a different environment, some of the views and some of the functionality may not be present or may be superseded.

Since a persistent volume has now been created in a Kubernetes cluster running on vSphere and consuming vSAN storage, CNS now displays information about the PV in the vSphere UI. Below is what is visible in the UI for the volume created in the previous steps. The information displayed includes the name of the PV, whether it is a block or file type, any labels associated with the volume, which datastore it is provisioned on, the storage policy used for the volume, whether the storage policy is compliant or not, a volume ID, volume health, which Kubernetes cluster the PV is on (since there can be many Kubernetes clusters running on the same vSphere infrastructure), and then the Capacity Quota of the volume.

Figure 257: Cloud-Native Storage

The second column in the output above contains a "Details" icon. Clicking this icon reveals even more information about the persistent volume, with several different views. The first view is the Basics view, which provides a lot of vSphere specific information about the volume, but of particular interest is the VM which has the volume attached. This VM is, of course, one of the Kubernetes worker nodes. This view also provides the full path to the VMDK object on the vSAN datastore which is backing this persistent volume.

Figure 258: Cloud-Native Storage Basic View

The next view gives additional information about the Kubernetes objects, including the name of the persistent volume claim, the namespace where the PVC was created, and any pods that are currently using the volume. Since we did not specify any labels in the manifests of the PVC, these are not populated. This view is a great way to determine which applications are using which volumes in Kubernetes without having to do manual mappings of Kubernetes objects to vSphere datastore objects.

Figure 259: Cloud-Native Storage Kubernetes Objects View

The next view is of particular interest to vSphere administrators who are also responsible for vSAN storage. It displays the physical placement of the volume. If you recall, we placed a storage policy as a parameter in the Storage Class. The policy chosen at the time was the default storage policy for vSAN, which is a RAID-1 configuration, mirroring the data and using a witness component for quorum. We can now see that the volume has been built using this policy. The three vSAN components are visible below; 2 data components (replicas) and 1 witness component.

09 // Cloud-Native Applications Use Case

Figure 260: Cloud-Native Storage Physical Placement View

The very last view is a performance view, which means you can get visibility into the performance of individual persistent volumes. This is invaluable for a vSphere administrator when developers begin to complain about poorly performing applications and allows vSphere administrators to quickly assess if the poor performance is storage-related.

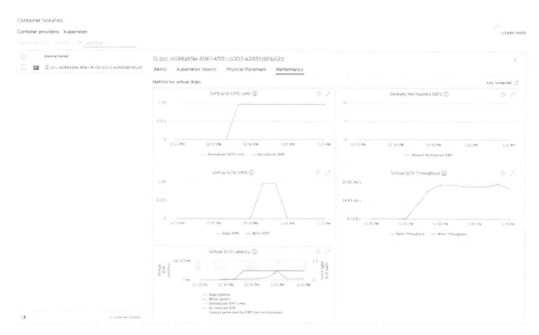

Figure 261: Cloud-Native Storage Performance View

vSphere CSI in action – file volume

In this section, we turn our attention to a read-write-many file volume. As mentioned the vSphere CSI driver has been developed to include the ability to dynamically provision NFS file volumes on vSAN. There is a requirement to have vSAN File Service enabled, however, and the details on how to do this are covered elsewhere in this book. Using standard Kubernetes manifests, requests to create a RWX persistent volume are sent to the vSphere CSI provider. This results in a dynamically provisioned file share that can be mounted into multiple pods simultaneously.

When creating this file volume, the previously created block volume is left in place. Thus, when we query Kubernetes objects for this new file volume, the block volume objects will also be displayed.

Once more, we begin by deploying a manifest that contains the Storage Class, the PVC and the pods that will share the volume, as defined earlier in this chapter. Again, all objects can be defined in a single manifest and separated using the "---" divider. The difference this time is that two pods are created that share access to the same volume.

```
% kubectl apply -f demo-sc-pvc-pod-rwx.yaml
storageclass.storage.k8s.io/vsan-file-sc created
persistentvolumeclaim/vsan-file-claim created
pod/file-pod-a created
pod/file-pod-b created
```

The Storage Class, PVC, PV and pods can be queried as before, but now the outputs report Kubernetes objects for both block and file. Note that the access mode for the new PVC and PV is RWX, read write many.

```
% kubectl get sc
NAME           PROVISIONER   RECLAIMPOLICY   VOLUMEBINDINGMODE   ALLOWVOLUMEEXPANSION   AGE
vsan-file-sc   csi.vsphere…  Delete          Immediate           false                  13s
vsan-sc        csi.vsphere…  Delete          Immediate           true                   74m


% kubectl get pvc
NAME              STATUS   VOLUME          CAPACITY   ACCESS MODES   STORAGECLASS   AGE
vsan-claim        Bound    pvc-e086a59e…   2Gi        RWO            vsan-sc        74m
vsan-file-claim   Bound    pvc-13d1015d…   2Gi        RWX            vsan-file-sc   22s

% kubectl get pv
NAME            CAPACITY   ACCESS   RECLAIM   STATUS   CLAIM             STORAGECLASS   REASON   AGE
pvc-13d1015d…   2Gi        RWX      Delete    Bound    vsan-file-claim   vsan-filesc             24s
pvc-e086a59e…   2Gi        RWO      Delete    Bound    vsan-claim        vsan-sc                 75m

% kubectl get pods
NAME             READY   STATUS    RESTARTS   AGE
file-pod-a       1/1     Running   0          36s
file-pod-b       1/1     Running   0          36s
vsan-block-pod   1/1     Running   0          75m
```

On this occasion, the same volume is mounted to both pods. The following steps will verify that the same volume is mounted on both pods, and that both pods can read and write to the volume. First, exec into pod-a, and create a directory and file on the file volume that is mounted on "`/demonfs`". Then repeat the operation via pod-b.

```
% kubectl exec -it file-pod-a -- sh
/ # df -h
Filesystem         Size      Used   Available   Use%   Mounted on
overlay            77.7G     12.1G  61.6G       16%    /
tmpfs              64.0M     0      64.0M       0%     /dev
```

```
vsan-fs1-b.rainpole.com:/52290524-f5a9-9415-2175-4bfa51e0a6fa
                                2.0G       0     1.9G   0% /demonfs
/dev/sda3                      77.7G   12.1G    61.6G  16% /dev/termination-log
/dev/sda3                      77.7G   12.1G    61.6G  16% /etc/resolv.conf
/dev/sda3                      77.7G   12.1G    61.6G  16% /etc/hostname
/dev/sda3                      77.7G   12.1G    61.6G  16% /etc/hosts
shm                            64.0M       0    64.0M   0% /dev/shm
tmpfs                          15.5G   12.0K    15.5G   0%
/var/run/secrets/kubernetes.io/serviceaccount
tmpfs                           7.8G       0     7.8G   0% /proc/acpi
tmpfs                          64.0M       0    64.0M   0% /proc/kcore
tmpfs                          64.0M       0    64.0M   0% /proc/keys
tmpfs                          64.0M       0    64.0M   0% /proc/timer_list
tmpfs                           7.8G       0     7.8G   0% /proc/scsi
tmpfs                           7.8G       0     7.8G   0% /sys/firmware

/ # cd /demonfs
/demonfs #
/demonfs # mkdir POD1
/demonfs # cd POD1
/demonfs/POD1 # echo "Pod1 was here" >> sharedfile
/demonfs/POD1 # cat sharedfile
Pod1 was here
/demonfs/POD1 # exit

% kubectl exec -it file-pod-b -- sh
/ # df -h
Filesystem                      Size    Used Available Use% Mounted on
overlay                        77.7G   12.1G    61.6G  16% /
tmpfs                          64.0M       0    64.0M   0% /dev
vsan-fs1-b.rainpole.com:/52290524-f5a9-9415-2175-4bfa51e0a6fa
                                2.0G       0     1.9G   0% /demonfs
/dev/sda3                      77.7G   12.1G    61.6G  16% /dev/termination-log
/dev/sda3                      77.7G   12.1G    61.6G  16% /etc/resolv.conf
/dev/sda3                      77.7G   12.1G    61.6G  16% /etc/hostname
/dev/sda3                      77.7G   12.1G    61.6G  16% /etc/hosts
shm                            64.0M       0    64.0M   0% /dev/shm
tmpfs                          15.5G   12.0K    15.5G   0%
/var/run/secrets/kubernetes.io/serviceaccount
tmpfs                           7.8G       0     7.8G   0% /proc/acpi
tmpfs                          64.0M       0    64.0M   0% /proc/kcore
tmpfs                          64.0M       0    64.0M   0% /proc/keys
tmpfs                          64.0M       0    64.0M   0% /proc/timer_list
tmpfs                           7.8G       0     7.8G   0% /proc/scsi
tmpfs                           7.8G       0     7.8G   0% /sys/firmware
/ # cd /demonfs
/demonfs # ls
POD1
/demonfs # cd POD1
/demonfs/POD1 # ls
sharedfile
/demonfs/POD1 # cat sharedfile
Pod1 was here
/demonfs/POD1 # echo "Pod2 was also here" >> sharedfile
/demonfs/POD1 # cat sharedfile
Pod1 was here
Pod2 was also here
/demonfs/POD1 #
```

As viewed above, the files created via pod-a are visible on the same volume from pod-b, and both pods are able to write to the volume. It seems that the read-write-many file share volume is working as expected.

Cloud-Native Storage (CNS) for vSphere Administrators – file volume

File volumes are also visible in the vSphere UI, providing some detailed information about how a vSAN file share is being used by Kubernetes. Much the same information is displayed as seen previously, with the Basics and Physical Placement views providing very similar information. One interesting view is the Kubernetes Objects view. Two pods are now shown sharing the same volume.

Figure 262: Cloud-Native Storage Kubernetes Object View (RWX)

There is also a Performance view as seen with RWO block volumes. The focus of the file volume performance charts is IOPS, Latency, and Throughput.

Before leaving RWX volumes, the Cluster > Configure > vSAN > File Shares view can be visited in the vSphere client UI to check that a vSAN File Share was indeed dynamically created to provide the backing for this Kubernetes volume.

Figure 263: vSAN File Shares – Container File Volume

If the "Details" view is opened by clicking on the icon in the second column, much of the same information observed in the Container Volumes view is also available in this vSAN File Shares view. One thing to note is that there are two types of file shares; one is vSAN File Shares and the other is Container File Volumes. If the view is left at vSAN File Shares, dynamically created file shares which back Kubernetes RWX persistent volumes will not be visible. That is why the type is set to ALL in the previous screenshot, as this will show both vSAN File Shares and Container File Volumes.

vSphere CNS CSI architecture

In this section, the major components of how Kubernetes volumes can be backed by vSphere storage are examined. The vSphere CSI driver has been mentioned a few times, and the CNS component that resides on the vCenter server has also been discussed. We also briefly mentioned first class disks (FCDs) also known as independent virtual disks (IVDs), which are special vSphere storage volumes used to back Kubernetes PVs. We can think of the CNS component in vCenter server as the storage control plane, handling the lifecycle operations of container volumes, e.g., create, delete, etc., as well as other functions around metadata retrieval. It is this volume metadata that enables the vSphere client UI to display such detailed information regarding Kubernetes volumes. With the release of vSphere CSI v2.5, CSI snapshots are also supported. This added an additional sidecar container to the pod to watch for snapshot requests, bringing the total number of containers in the CSI controller to 7 at the time of writing.

To put it simply, in the Kubernetes cluster, the CSI driver is the component that communicates to vSphere and handles the volume create and delete requests, as well as the attach and detach of a volume to a Kubernetes node which is a virtual machine. It communicates with the *kubelet* (Kubernetes agent) for the formatting of the volume, as well as the mounting and unmounting of the volume to a pod running in the Kubernetes node. Another major component of the CSI driver is the CSI syncer. This component is what pushes the Kubernetes metadata regarding the volume to CNS on vCenter server so that it can be displayed in the vSphere client UI.

First, let's look at the pods that are deployed in a vanilla, upstream Kubernetes cluster by the CSI driver. This is using a cluster that has vSphere CSI driver v2.5, released in March 2022. This driver uses the namespace `vmware-system-csi` to deploy its components. The two pods that we see deployed are the vsphere-csi-controller pod and several vsphere-csi-node pods.

```
% kubectl get pods -n vmware-system-csi
NAME                                      READY   STATUS    RESTARTS      AGE
vsphere-csi-controller-7b87c8b9bc-fg8c4   7/7     Running   0             87m
vsphere-csi-node-ggkng                    3/3     Running   0             20d
vsphere-csi-node-r6pfh                    3/3     Running   5 (12d ago)   20d
vsphere-csi-node-tsd4r                    3/3     Running   3 (12d ago)   20d
```

vsphere-csi-controller pod

The vSphere CSI controller pod handles multiple activities when it comes to volume lifecycle management within Kubernetes. First and foremost, it provides the communication from the Kubernetes Cluster API server to the CNS component on vCenter server for volume lifecycle operations and metadata syncing. It listens for Kubernetes events related to volume lifecycle, such as create, delete, attach, detach. This functionality is implemented by several distinct containers within the pod. Let's take a closer look at the containers which make up the vSphere CSI driver in Kubernetes. This is using a cluster that has vSphere CSI driver v2.5, released in March 2022.

```
% kubectl get pod vsphere-csi-controller-7b87c8b9bc-fg8c4 \
-n vmware-system-csi -o jsonpath='{.spec.containers[*].name}'
csi-snapshotter csi-attacher csi-resizer vsphere-csi-controller liveness-probe vsphere-
syncer csi-provisioner
```

As you can see, there are 7 containers (sometimes referred to as sidecars) in the pod. The aim of separating distinct features of the CSI driver into separate sidecar containers means that it simplifies the development and deployment of CSI drivers in general. What follows is a brief description of each container within the vSphere CSI controller pod.

csi-snapshotter

This is a new sidecar container introduced with the vSphere CSI driver v2.5 in March 2022. The purpose of this container is to watch the Kubernetes API server for VolumeSnapshot objects. It works with the snapshot controller which watches for Kubernetes VolumeSnapshotContent objects.

csi-attacher

This container monitors the Kubernetes API server for VolumeAttachment objects. If any are observed, it informs the vsphere-csi-controller that a new volume should be attached to a specified node. Similarly, if it observes that the object is removed, then informs the vsphere-csi-controller that a volume should be detached from a specified node.

csi-resizer

This container was added to the vSphere CSI driver v2.2, which was released around April 2021. This is the component that watches for online volume extend operations.

vsphere-csi-controller

This provides the communication from the Kubernetes Cluster API server to the CNS component on vCenter Server for persistent volume lifecycle operations.

liveness-probe

Monitors the overall health of the vSphere CSI controller pod. The kubelet (agent) that runs on the Kubernetes nodes uses this liveness-probe to determine if a container needs to be restarted. This helps to improve the availability of the vSphere CSI controller pod.

vsphere-syncer

Send metadata information back to the CNS component on vCenter Server so that it can be displayed in the vSphere client UI in the Container Volumes view.

csi-provisioner

Watches the Kubernetes API server for PersistentVolumeClaim objects. If any are observed, it informs the vsphere-csi-controller that a new volume should be created. Similarly, if it observes that the PVC is removed, then it informs the vsphere-csi-controller that the volume should be deleted.

vsphere-csi-node pod

Each node gets its own vsphere-csi-node pod. Within each pod are 3 containers. This output is once again using a cluster that has vSphere CSI driver v2.5, released in March 2022

```
% kubectl get pod vsphere-csi-node-ggkng -n vmware-system-csi -o
jsonpath='{.spec.containers[*].name}'
node-driver-registrar vsphere-csi-node liveness-probe
```

node-driver-registrar

This container establishes communication with the node's kubelet (which can be thought of as the Kubernetes agent that runs on the node). Once established, the kubelet can make volume operation requests, such as mount, unmount, format, etc.

vsphere-csi-node

This container performs volume operations associated with pod access, e.g., operations such as format, mount, unmount.

liveness-probe

Monitors the overall health of the vSphere CSI node pod. The kubelet (agent) that runs on the Kubernetes nodes used this liveness-probe to determine if a container needs to be restarted. This helps to improve the availability of the vSphere CSI node pod.

vSphere with Tanzu Considerations

So far in this chapter, we have been discussing the upstream vSphere CSI driver. This is the vSphere Container storage plug-in that runs in a native Kubernetes cluster, deployed on vSphere infrastructure. For the most part, we can also think of Tanzu Kubernetes Grid (TKG) as an upstream Kubernetes cluster. When referring to TKG here, I am referring to the standalone / multi-cloud version of Kubernetes from VMware which is deployed via the tanzu command line or UI. This distribution is often referred to TKGm, and while not an official name, we can use it here to differentiate it from other Tanzu offerings. The difference between TKGm and upstream Kubernetes is that our Tanzu team selects components from the plethora of open-source products that are available for Kubernetes. The team tests this Kubernetes stack, validates it, then offers

VMware support for customers who purchase it. In other words, the team chooses the CSI drivers for storage, the CNI drivers for networking, various Load Balancers, IAM components for identity management, and so on. Once deployed into production, VMware can now support this Kubernetes platform and your vSphere platform. Thus, what we have read so far about the vSphere Container Storage Plug-in/upstream vSphere CSI driver applies to TKGm, once the Tanzu team has completed their tests, and released it with a TKGm build/version.

But VMware offers more than just TKGm. VMware also offers a product called vSphere with Tanzu. This is important as it does not use the upstream CSI driver at the time of writing. This is because vSphere with Tanzu has the concept of a Supervisor cluster which is deployed when vSphere with Tanzu is enabled on a vSphere cluster. And while workloads can be deployed directly onto the Supervisor cluster using PodVMs, the Supervisor cluster is not considered a general-purpose Kubernetes cluster. General purpose Kubernetes clusters are provisioned using a TKG Service, one of many services available in vSphere with Tanzu. The TKG Service, or TKGS for short, can provision fully formed Kubernetes "guest" or "workload" clusters on vSphere through some simple YAML manifest files which describe the cluster configuration. Using Supervisor Namespaces, a vSphere administrator can allocate a certain amount of vSphere resources to a particular development team. Within these namespaces, development teams can provision their own TKG clusters, but never use more resources than the vSphere administrator has allocated. Teams can then develop and test their own applications, and indeed bring applications to production. The idea is that multiple different development teams can operate in an isolated manner on the same vSphere infrastructure using Supervisor Namespaces via vSphere with Tanzu.

This brings us to the reason why the TKG clusters cannot use the upstream vSphere CSI driver. TKG clusters created by the TKG Service are placed on their own virtual workload networks which are not designed to have access to the management network where vCenter server resides. This means that if the upstream vSphere CSI driver is deployed on a TKGS workload cluster in vSphere with Tanzu, it would be unable to reach the vCenter server, nor would it be able to communicate to its associated CNS component for persistent volume lifecycle management. So how are persistent volumes created in TKGS provisioned clusters you might ask?

The creation of persistent volumes is achieved through a paravirtual CSI (pvCSI) running in the workload clusters that have been provisioned by the TKG Service. This is a modified version of the upstream CSI driver. The reason it is called pvCSI is that it "proxies" requests from the TKG guest cluster to the Supervisor cluster which in turn communicates to vCenter and CNS to create persistent volumes on the appropriate vSphere storage. The Supervisor cluster control plane nodes are multi-homed with one network interface on the vSphere management network and the other network interface on the workload network (the one used by the TKGS workload clusters). In this way, PV operations from TKGS workload clusters are sent to the Supervisor cluster, which in turn sends it onto CNS in vCenter.

Note that the CNS views of the persistent volumes in vSphere with Tanzu reveal this proxying of volumes. For a PV created in a TKGS guest cluster, a vSphere administrator will be able to see the relationship between it and the volume that is created on the Supervisor cluster on its behalf, as well as information about which TKGS guest cluster it was created for.

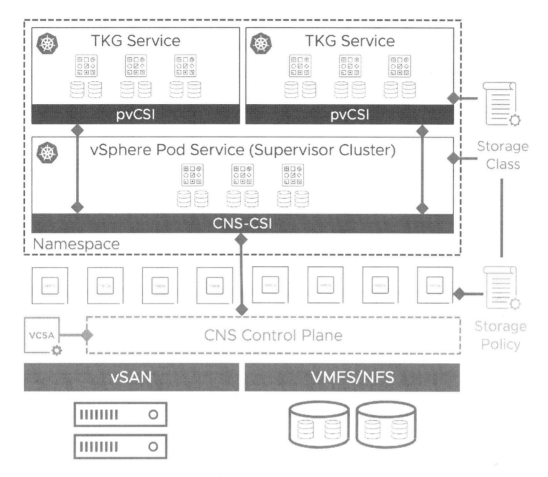

Figure 264: Paravirtual CSI Driver in vSphere with Tanzu

The reason why the pvCSI driver is called out as a consideration is that new CSI features typically get developed for the upstream CSI driver for vanilla Kubernetes distributions before filtering down to vSphere with Tanzu. Examples of this would be the support for read-write-many volumes (RWX) using vSAN File Service, which has been in upstream Kubernetes for some time, but is still not available in vSphere with Tanzu TKGS clusters at the time of writing (April 2022). Similarly, CSI snapshot support was announced in the upstream CSI driver version 2.5 in March 2022, but there will be a lag before the feature appears in TKGS clusters in vSphere with Tanzu.

Thus, it is extremely important to check whether a particular CSI driver capability is specifically available in vSphere with Tanzu, and not to rely on seeing feature support in upstream Kubernetes, then assuming that it is also available in vSphere with Tanzu.

Data Persistence platform (DPp)

VMware continuously enhances vSAN. A primary goal is to build a platform for both container workloads and virtual machine workloads. Data Persistence platform (DPp) is another step on the journey towards enabling "cloud-native" applications to be deployed successfully on vSAN.

Many cloud-native applications implement what is known as a "shared nothing" architecture. These applications do not require shared storage as they are designed with built-in replication/protection features. Thus, we need vSAN to be able to cater for this. At the same time, these applications need to be vSAN and vSphere aware. Applications deployed to DPp have the built-in smarts to understand what action needs to be taken when there is an event on the underlying vSphere infrastructure, e.g., maintenance mode, upgrade, patching, etc.

Since these applications have built-in protection, it implies that vSAN does not need to provide protection at the underlying layer. Therefore, the storage objects for the cloud-native application may be provisioned with no protection. vSAN can hand off storage services to the application if the application already has those capabilities built-in (replication, encryption, erasure-coding, etc.). This means that vSAN does not duplicate these features at the infrastructure layer and avoids consuming more storage capacity than necessary. However, if these features are not available in the application, vSAN may still be leveraged to provide these capabilities.

There is also another deployment option from a storage perspective. To facilitate a high-performance data path for these cloud-native applications, the Data Persistence platform also introduces a new construct for storage called vSAN-Direct. vSAN-Direct allows applications to consume the local storage devices on a vSAN host directly. However, these local storage devices are still under the control of HCI management, so that health, usage, and other pertinent information about the device is bubbled up to the vSphere client. The primary goal here is to allow cloud-native applications to be seamlessly deployed onto vSAN whilst leveraging the native device speed with minimum overhead, but at the same time have those applications understand infrastructure operations such as maintenance mode, upgrades, and indeed host failures. Note that at the time of writing (April 2022), if a decision is reached to use vSAN-Direct for DPp, then the whole of the vSAN cluster must be dedicated to vSAN-Direct. It is not supported to run traditional vSAN workloads and vSAN-Direct workloads side-by-side. As per the official documentation from VMware, "Use vSAN Direct if you are creating a dedicated hardware cluster for the shared nothing cloud-native services".

This is another option if considering the vSAN Data Protection platform for cloud-native applications. You may opt to use DPp without vSAN-Direct and implement vSAN objects with *failures to tolerate* set to 0 since the application is handling the replication. This option is also fully supported but may not deliver on the performance and speed that can be achieved with vSAN-Direct.

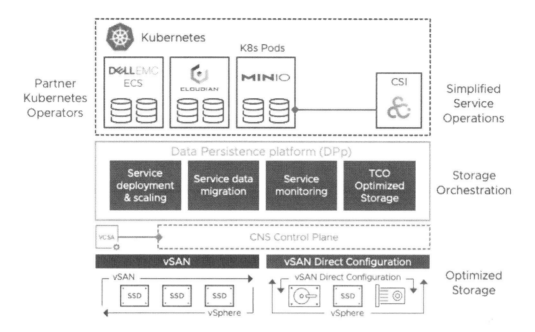

Figure 265: Data Persistence Platform

As mentioned, we have partnered with several cloud-native application vendors who will create bespoke Kubernetes operators that will work with the Data Persistence platform. Partners can then define how their application should behave (e.g., re-shard, evacuate, delete and reschedule Pods, etc.) when a vSphere operation is detected. Partners can also create their own vCenter UI plugins so that operations (e.g., resize, scale in and out) that are specific to their application can be added to vCenter.

DPp Requirements

vSAN Data Persistence platform was first introduced in VMware Cloud Foundation (VCF) 4.2 in early 2021. The reason for requiring VCF was that there are a number of requirements to enable DPp. Obviously, vSAN is a requirement, with or without the vSAN Direct configuration. vSphere with Tanzu is also needed. And since the services are deployed as a set of PodVMs on vSphere with Tanzu, NSX-T is also necessary. This is because one cannot deploy PodVMs without NSX-T providing the necessary network overlays. Thus, while VCF is not a hard and fast requirement for DPp, it does have all the necessary components to enable it. Readers should be cognizant of these requirements before planning to use any partners services provided by Data Persistence platform.

DPp deployment changes

When DPp first released, several services were embedded directly in vSphere. With the release of vSphere 7.0U3, the way in which vSphere administrators install, upgrade, and manage DPp services has changed. Now vSphere administrators need to retrieve the YAML manifests for the partner product to first register the service with vCenter server. After this step is complete, the service can be installed into vCenter, making them available to developers who wish to use the service in Kubernetes workloads.

The partner manifests are available in the following JFROG repository at the time of writing (March 2022): https://vmwaresaas.jfrog.io/. Simply navigate to the appropriate partner folder under `Artifactory > Artifacts > vDPP-Partner-YAML` and select a YAML file to download. The path to the Velero Service is shown below:

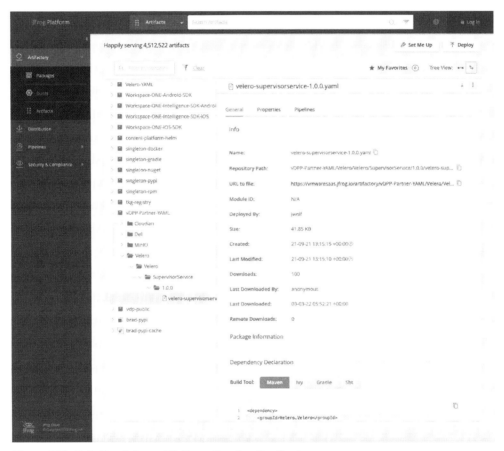

Figure 266: Data Persistence Platform Service Manifests

vSAN Stretched Cluster support

A frequently requested topology on which to deploy a Kubernetes cluster is a vSAN Stretched Cluster. This requires some careful consideration since a vSAN Stretched Cluster has only two availability zones/data sites and Kubernetes always has an odd number of control plane nodes, either 1, 3, 5, or 7. Thus you will always have a situation where one of the vSAN Stretched Cluster sites has more control plane nodes than the other. If the site with the most control plane nodes fails, then the control plane will not be available until vSphere HA has had time to restart the failed nodes on the remaining site and the control plane components such as the Kubernetes key-value store (etcd) has recovered. These are some of the factors that should be considered if you plan to deploy a Kubernetes cluster on vSAN Stretched Cluster. Support for vSAN Stretched Cluster appeared in the official vSAN 7.0U3 release notes in January 2022. However, there was a significant issue uncovered whereby if the data sites partitioned, persistent volume information could be lost from the CNS. When volume metadata is not present in the CNS, you cannot create, delete, or re-schedule pods with CNS volumes since the vSphere CSI Driver must access volume information from CNS to perform these operations. It seems that this issue was addressed in the 7.0U3d release which became available in April 2022. This is vCenter build number 19480866 so ensure you are using this release at a minimum if planning to use vSAN Stretched Cluster topologies for Kubernetes clusters.

The official VMware documentation provides additional guidance such as enabling vSphere HA, DRS, Host and VM Affinity Groups, etc. However, when it comes to PV provisioning, the advice given in the official documentation is that the same storage policy should be used for all node VMs, including the control plane and worker, as well as all Persistent Volumes (PVs). This single, standardized storage policy in vSphere equates to the Kubernetes administrator creating a single, standard Storage Class for all storage objects in the Kubernetes cluster.

The other major limitation at the time of writing (April 2022) is that currently only block based read-write-once (RWO) volumes are supported. There is no support for Kubernetes read-write-many (RWX) vSAN File Service based file volumes in vSAN Stretched Cluster.

Other CSI driver features

Throughout this chapter, several different features of the vSphere CSI driver have been mentioned. Listing every CSI feature is beyond the scope of this book, but a feature that is supported at the time of writing in the vSphere CSI driver is the ability to hot extend block volumes while the pods remain online. CSI snapshots are also supported, which should allow partner backup vendors to be able to take backups of applications that use persistent volumes on Kubernetes running on the vSphere platform. There are also several different topologies that are being investigated for support, such as a single Kubernetes cluster deployed across multiple vSphere clusters, often referred to as a multi-AZ deployment.

This GitHub page, maintained by the vSphere CSI engineering team, is a good starting point for details about vSphere CSI driver versions and supported features: https://github.com/kubernetes-sigs/vsphere-csi-driver

Summary

vSAN lends itself very nicely as a platform for both traditional virtual machine workloads and newer cloud-native workloads. Through the upstream vSphere CSI driver and the pvCSI driver for vSphere with Tanzu, vSAN can be used for block based read-write-once volumes. With upstream Kubernetes, vSAN can also be used for file based read-write-many volumes, but this functionality should also appear in TKGS clusters in vSphere with Tanzu very soon. This does highlight a consideration that many vSphere CSI driver features are first developed for upstream and later implemented in pvCSI. One other significant development in this space is the Data Persistence platform. It allows our partners to create services for the vSphere with Tanzu platform, enabling activities from the underlying vSphere infrastructure to be bubbled up to the application and allowing it to take relevant actions to mitigate any impact. However, as mentioned, there are a considerable number of requirements around using DPp which should be considered.

10

Command Line Tools

This chapter will look at some of the *command line interface* (CLI) tools that are available outside the vSphere client for examining various parts of the vSAN cluster. Some tools are available on the ESXi host, others are available via the vCenter Server command line. The vCenter Server command line tool is called the Ruby vSphere Console, or RVC for short. It should be noted that there is a concerted effort amongst the vSAN engineering teams to move everything to the ESXCLI and deprecate the RVC tool that is available in vCenter Server going forward. However, administrators should familiarize themselves with the ESXCLI toolset, as this may become the de-facto vSAN command line going forward.

CLI vSAN Cluster Commands

There is a namespace in ESXCLI for vSAN. Here, administrators will find several commands for managing and displaying the status of a vSAN cluster. An effort will be made to describe each of the sub-namespaces, but for the most part what the command does is self-explanatory. In places, where it makes sense to do so, sample command outputs will be provided.

esxcli vsan cluster

Using the esxcli vsan cluster commands, you can enable the host on which the command is run to join or leave a cluster, as well as display the current cluster status and members. This can be very helpful in a scenario where vCenter Server is unavailable and a particular host needs to be removed from the vSAN cluster. The restore functionality is not intended for customer invocation and is used by ESXi during the boot process to restore the active cluster configuration from configuration file

```
Usage : esxcli vsan cluster {cmd} [cmd options]
Available Namespaces:
    • preferredfaultdomain - Commands for configuring a preferred fault domain for vSAN.
    • unicastagent - Commands for configuring unicast agents for vSAN.
Available Commands:
    • get - Get information about the vSAN cluster that this host is joined to.
    • join - Join the host to a vSAN cluster.
    • leave - Leave the vSAN cluster the host is currently joined to.
    • new - Create a vSAN cluster with current host joined. A random sub-cluster UUID
      will be generated.
    • restore - Restore the persisted vSAN cluster configuration.
```

In the below example, we can tell that this node has an AGENT role (as discussed in chapter 4, architectural details). It is also a NORMAL node (not a witness host) and it is HEALTHY. The vSAN cluster is a 4-node cluster, as we can see from the member count field, and if you count up the number of members' UUIDs. Finally, it is not in maintenance mode.

```
[/:~] esxcli vsan cluster get
Cluster Information
   Enabled: true
   Current Local Time: 2018-10-15T11:34:42Z
   Local Node UUID: 5982fbaf-2ee1-ccce-4298-246e962f4910
   Local Node Type: NORMAL
   Local Node State: AGENT
   Local Node Health State: HEALTHY
   Sub-Cluster Master UUID: 5982f466-c59d-0e07-aa4e-246e962f4850
   Sub-Cluster Backup UUID: 5b0bddb5-6f43-73a4-4188-246e962f5270
   Sub-Cluster UUID: 52fae366-e94e-db86-c663-3d0af03e5aec
   Sub-Cluster Membership Entry Revision: 11
   Sub-Cluster Member Count: 4
   Sub-Cluster Member UUIDs: 5982f466-c59d-0e07-aa4e-246e962f4850, 5b0bddb5-6f43-73a4-4188-246e962f5270, 5982fbaf-2ee1-ccce-4298-246e962f4910, 5982f42b-e565-196e-bad9-246e962c2408
   Sub-Cluster Membership UUID: a65c755b-be66-f77b-da9d-246e962f4850
   Unicast Mode Enabled: true
   Maintenance Mode State: OFF
   Config Generation: ffb4e877-011b-45b6-b5f6-4c9d7e36a5f7 3 2018-09-07T12:02:16.554
[root@esxi-dell-e:~]
```

esxcli vsan datastore

This command allows administrators to do certain operations on the vSAN datastore. Note the guidance that many of these commands are not expected to be run at the host level, but rather at the cluster level. By default, the vSAN datastore name is vsanDatastore. If you do plan on changing the vsanDatastore name, do this at the cluster level via the vSphere client. It is highly recommended that if you are managing multiple vSAN clusters from the same vCenter Server that the vSAN datastores are given unique, easily identifiable names.

```
Usage : esxcli vsan datastore {cmd} [cmd options]

Available Namespaces:
    • name - Commands for configuring vSAN datastore name.

Available Commands:
    • add - Add a new datastore to the vSAN cluster. This operation is only allowed
      if vSAN is enabled on the host. In general, add should be done at cluster
      level. Across a vSAN cluster vSAN datastores should be in sync.
    • clear - Remove all but the default datastore from the vSAN cluster. This
      operation is only allowed if vSAN is enabled on the host. In general, add
      should be done at cluster level. Across a vSAN cluster vSAN datastores should
      be in sync.
    • list - List datastores in the vSAN cluster.
    • remove - Remove a datastore from the vSAN cluster. This operation is only
      allowed if vSAN is enabled on the host. In general, remove should be done at
      cluster level. Across a vSAN cluster vSAN datastores should be in sync.
```

esxcli vsan debug

This command provides a lot of the functionality that administrators would historically have found in RVC, especially the ability to query the status of objects. However, the command also has options to look at physical disks, and controllers, as well as displaying resync status, disk, disk group evacuations, and individual virtual machine disk status.

```
Usage : esxcli vsan debug {cmd} [cmd options]

Available Namespaces:
    • disk - Debug commands for vSAN physical disks
    • object - Debug commands for vSAN objects
    • resync - Debug commands for vSAN resyncing objects
    • advcfg - Debug commands for vSAN advanced configuration options.
    • controller - Debug commands for vSAN disk controllers
    • evacuation - Debug commands for simulating host, disk or disk group evacuation in
      various modes and their impact on objects in vSAN cluster
    • limit - Debug commands for vSAN limits
    • mob - Debug commands for vSAN Managed Object Browser Service.
    • vmdk - Debug commands for vSAN VMDKs
```

Most of these namespaces only provided a single command, either **list** or **get**. The only namespace that differs is mob, which allows administrators to start and stop the vSAN Managed Object Browser Service.

Again, the output is quite self-explanatory, but what is good to see from this output is the congestion values, and where they might occur. All other aspects as green as well, including operational and space, so quite a useful troubleshooting command to have available for physical disks.

```
[/:~] esxcli vsan debug disk list
UUID: 5288dd4f-dbd2-ce9e-5434-462382eab56c
   Name: mpx.vmhba0:C0:T3:L0
   Owner: localhost.corinternal.com
   Version: 15
   Disk Group: 52ff6833-182e-185b-6ad5-57f220408dbe
   Disk Tier: Capacity
   SSD: true
   In Cmmds: true
   In Vsi: true
   Fault Domain: N/A
   Model: Virtual disk
   Encryption: false
   Compression: false
   Deduplication: false
   Dedup Ratio: N/A
   Overall Health: green
   Metadata Health: green
   Operational Health: green
   Congestion Health:
        State: green
        Congestion Value: 0
```

```
          Congestion Area: none
          All Congestion Fields:
   Space Health:
          State: green
          Capacity: 255.99 GB
          Used: 4.09 GB
          Reserved: 0.34 GB
```

We shall provide one additional example from the debug namespace, and that is looking specifically at an object. In this case, the last field is the object ID. This might be gleaned from the vSphere UI, either in the task view or in an event or log message. You can use the CLI to get further detail on a particular object, as shown here. You can see the health of the object, which policy it is using, the state of its components, and which object on the vSAN datastore the UUID corresponds to. Quite a useful command.

```
[/:~] esxcli vsan debug object list -u c56e4162-501b-3ec8-71b9-00505696fc4c
Object UUID: c56e4162-501b-3ec8-71b9-00505696fc4c
   Version: 15
   Health: healthy
   Owner: localhost.corinternal.com
   Size: 90.00 GB
   Used: 0.01 GB
   Policy:
      stripeWidth: 1
      cacheReservation: 0
      proportionalCapacity: 0
      hostFailuresToTolerate: 1
      forceProvisioning: 0
      spbmProfileId: aa6d5a82-1c88-45da-85d3-3d74b91a5bad
      spbmProfileGenerationNumber: 0
      CSN: 2
      spbmProfileName: vSAN Default Storage Policy
   Configuration:
      RAID_1
         Component: c56e4162-88e4-c9c8-21e5-00505696fc4c
            Component State: ACTIVE,  Address Space(B): 96636764160 (90.00GB),  Disk UUID: 527444a7-a983-c29c-b175-1285111ce26e,  Disk Name: mpx.vmhba0:C0:T1:L0:2
            Votes: 1,  Capacity Used(B): 12582912 (0.01GB),  Physical Capacity Used(B): 4194304 (0.00GB),  Host Name: localhost.corinternal.com
         Component: c56e4162-c814-cdc8-e4e4-00505696fc4c
            Component State: ACTIVE,  Address Space(B): 96636764160 (90.00GB),  Disk UUID: 52084995-949c-5f38-69ab-3bba1e4d1351,  Disk Name: mpx.vmhba0:C0:T3:L0:2
            Votes: 1,  Capacity Used(B): 12582912 (0.01GB),  Physical Capacity Used(B): 4194304 (0.00GB),  Host Name: localhost.corinternal.com
      Witness: c56e4162-1e39-cfc8-4861-00505696fc4c
            Component State: ACTIVE,  Address Space(B): 0 (0.00GB),  Disk UUID: 529d9714-9df1-0042-7893-a3c1a559c20b,  Disk Name: mpx.vmhba0:C0:T1:L0:2
            Votes: 1,  Capacity Used(B): 12582912 (0.01GB),  Physical Capacity Used(B): 4194304 (0.00GB),  Host Name: localhost.corinternal.com
   Type: vdisk
   Path: /vmfs/volumes/vsan:520fedd309237544-5d…42/c…2-bea4-6105-8397-00505696fc4c/vm.vmdk (Exists)
   Group UUID: c36e4162-bea4-6105-8397-00505696fc4c
   Directory Name: N/A
```

esxcli vsan faultdomain

Fault domains were introduced to allow vSAN to be rack, room, or site aware. What this means is that components belonging to objects that are part of the same virtual machine can be placed not just in different hosts, but in different racks. This means that should an entire rack fail (e.g., power failure), there is still a full set of virtual machine components available, so the VM remains accessible.

Probably not a useful command for generic vSAN deployments but could be useful when Rack Awareness or Stretched Cluster has been implemented since both of those require the use of Fault Domains to group multiple hosts into a single fault domain. If you are using any of those features, then you could use this command to determine which hosts are in which fault domain.

For standard vSAN deployments, each host is in its own fault domain, so the command will return a unique fault domain for every host.

```
Usage : esxcli vsan faultdomain {cmd} [cmd options]

Available Commands:
    • get - Get the fault domain name for this host.
    • reset - Reset Host fault domain to default value
    • set - Set the fault domain for this host
```

esxcli vsan health

This is a very useful command to see the overall health of the system.

```
Usage: esxcli vsan health {cmd} [cmd options]

Available Namespaces:
    • cluster - Commands for vSAN Cluster Health
```

As you can see, there is only a single available namespace, cluster.

```
Usage: esxcli vsan health cluster {cmd} [cmd options]

Available Commands:
    • get   Get a specific health check status and its details
    • list - List a cluster wide health check across all types of health checks
```

However, it is also useful as administrators can use it to run individual health checks. For example, if an administrator ran the following command:

```
esxcli vsan health cluster list -w
```

As well as displaying the status of the vSAN health, this command would return the short name of all of the health checks. This short name could now be used to get a specific health check and its details.

In this example, we will look at the status of a single test called vSAN Disk Balance, or in shorthand, diskbalance.

```
[/:~] esxcli vsan health cluster get -t diskbalance
vSAN Disk Balance          yellow

Checks the vSAN disk balance status on all hosts.
Ask VMware:
http://www.vmware.com/esx/support/askvmware/index.php?eventtype=com.vmware.vsan.health.tes
t.diskbalance

Overview
Metric                  Value
--------------------------------
Average Disk Usage      52 %
Maximum Disk Usage      64 %
Maximum Variance        63 %
LM Balance Index        51 %

Disk Balance
Host        Device
----------------------------------------------------
10.10.0.8   Local ATA Disk (naa.500a07510f86d6bf)
10.10.0.6   Local ATA Disk (naa.500a07510f86d6b3)
10.10.0.7   Local ATA Disk (naa.500a07510f86d693)
10.10.0.5   Local ATA Disk (naa.500a07510f86d685)
10.10.0.6   Local ATA Disk (naa.500a07510f86d686)
10.10.0.8   Local ATA Disk (naa.500a07510f86d6bd)
10.10.0.7   Local ATA Disk (naa.500a07510f86d69d)

Rebalance State                 Data To Move (GB)
----------------------------------------------------
Proactive rebalance is needed   48.7432 GB
Proactive rebalance is needed   88.1807 GB
Proactive rebalance is needed    3.8369 GB
Proactive rebalance is needed   52.8838 GB
Proactive rebalance is needed   76.9971 GB
Proactive rebalance is needed   41.1963 GB
Proactive rebalance is needed   73.4268 GB
```

esxcli vsan iscsi

This command allows us to query the configuration and status of iSCSI home namespaces, iSCSI targets and LUNs on vSAN.

```
Usage : esxcli vsan iscsi {cmd} [cmd options]

Available Namespaces:
    initiatorgroup - Commands to manipulate vSAN iSCSI target initiator group
    target - Commands for vSAN iSCSI target configuration
    defaultconfig - Operation for default configuration for vSAN iSCSI Target
    homeobject - Commands for the vSAN iSCSI target home object
    status - Enable or disable iSCSI target support, query status.
```

In the commands that follow, we will first query whether or not the iSCSI service is enabled?

```
[/:~] esxcli vsan iscsi statusget
   Enabled: true
```

Next, we list the initiator groups. This will display the name of the initiator group, what the IQN of the initiator is, and then the IQNs of any targets that have been added to the initiator groups.

```
[/:~] esxcli vsan iscsi initiatorgroup list
Initiator group
   Name: sqlserver-ig
   Initiator list: iqn.1991-05.com.microsoft:sqlserver2016.rainpole.com, iqn.1991-
05.com.microsoft.sqlsrv2.rainpole.com
   Accessible targets:
       Alias: vsan-iscsi-target
       IQN: iqn.1998-01.com.vmware.52f91d3fbdf294d4-805fec05d214a05d
Initiator group
   Name: filserver-ig
   Initiator list: iqn.1991-05.com.microsoft:cor-win-2012.rainpole.com, iqn.1991-
05.com.microsoft:win2012-dc-b.rainpole.com
   Accessible targets:
       Alias: vsan-iscsi-target
       IQN: iqn.1998-01.com.vmware.52f91d3fbdf294d4-805fec05d214a05d
```

Now that we have seen things from the initiator side, let us turn our attention to the target side. Here we can list the target information, and correlate these to any that have been added to the initiator group shown above. Unfortunately, due to the length of the command output, it is not easy to display, but hopefully, you can see the relevant detail.

```
[/:~] esxcli vsan iscsi target list
Alias
----------------
vsan-iscsi-target
tgt-for-sql

iSCSI Qualified Name (IQN)
----------------------------------------------------
iqn.1998-01.com.vmware.52f91d3fbdf294d4-805fec05d214a05d
iqn.1998-01.com.vmware.5261586411b1be81-3b5333f32fec6960

Interface  Port  Authentication type   LUNs
---------  ----  -------------------   ----
vmk3       3260  No-Authentication     2
vmk3       3260  No-Authentication     2

Is Compliant  UUID
------------  ------------------------
true          c52a675a-49f4-ca24-c6be-246e962c2408
true          2a9e695a-c2af-a8a6-5a68-246e962f5270

I/O Owner UUID
5982f466-c59d-0e07-aa4e-246e962f4850
5982f466-c59d-0e07-aa4e-246e962f4850
```

The last example we have for iSCSI is to display which LUNs have been mapped to which target. From the output above, we have seen several targets listed. Here we can list the LUN information and correlate any LUNs that have been mapped to a particular target shown above. Again, the way the command is displayed doesn't easily lend it to being reproduced in an easily readable format for the book, but hopefully, you can see that this target has 2 LUNs mapped.

```
[/:~] esxcli vsan iscsi target lun list -t tgt-for-sql
ID  Alias        Size
--  -----------  ----------
 0  sqldb-lun    153600 MiB
 1  witness-sql    5120 MiB

UUID
------------------------------------
21a0695a-ff8e-676f-9db6-246e962f5270
f5a2695a-c010-9e5c-3fc2-246e962c2408

Is Compliant  Status
------------  ------
true          online
true          online
```

esxcli vsan maintenancemode

`maintenancemode` is an interesting command option. You might think this would allow you to enter and exit maintenance, but it doesn't. All this option allows you to do is to cancel an in-progress vSAN maintenance mode operation. This could still prove very useful, though, especially when you have decided to place a host in maintenance mode and selected the Full Data Migration option and want to stop this data migration process (which can take a very long time) and instead use the Ensure Access option.

```
Usage : esxcli vsan maintenancemode {cmd} [cmd options]

Available Commands:
        • cancel - Cancel an in-progress vSAN maintenance mode operation.
```

This command does not allow you to enter or exit maintenance mode. Note that you can place a node in maintenance mode leveraging `esxcli system maintenanceMode set -e true -m noAction` where "-m" specifies the data evacuation option, and if components need to be moved from the host entering maintenance mode or not.

esxcli vsan network

This command will display details about the VMkernel interface used for the vSAN network by this host.

```
Usage : esxcli vsan network {cmd} [cmd options]

Available Namespaces:
    • ip - Commands for configuring IP network for vSAN.
    • ipv4 - Compatibility alias for "ip"
    • security - Commands for configuring vSAN network security settings

Available Commands:
    • clear - Clear the vSAN network configuration.
    • list - List the network configuration currently in use by vSAN.
    • remove - Remove an interface from the vSAN network configuration.
    • restore - Restore the persisted vSAN network configuration.
```

In this example, it can clearly be seen that vSAN is using vmk2. Note also that there is a considerable amount of multicast information included here. This is historic information, and if you are using a version of vSAN that is later than 6.6, most likely this information is unused. However, there is a corner case scenario where a cluster may revert from multicast to unicast, and therefore the information is still displayed.

```
[/:~] esxcli vsan network list
Interface
   VmkNic Name: vmk2
   IP Protocol: IP
   Interface UUID: f9d6025a-0177-fcd1-3c38-246e962f4910
   Agent Group Multicast Address: 224.2.3.4
   Agent Group IPv6 Multicast Address: ff19::2:3:4
   Agent Group Multicast Port: 23451
   Master Group Multicast Address: 224.1.2.3
   Master Group IPv6 Multicast Address: ff19::1:2:3
   Master Group Multicast Port: 12345
   Host Unicast Channel Bound Port: 12321
   Data-in-Transit Encryption Key Exchange Port: 0
   Multicast TTL: 5
   Traffic Type: vsan
```

Should you still be using multicast, then the Agent Group Multicast Port corresponds to the *CMMDS* port that is opened on the ESXi firewall when vSAN is enabled. The first IP address, 224.2.3.4 is used for the master/backup communication, whereas the second address, 224.1.2.3, is used for the agents. `esxcli vsan network list` is a useful command to view the network configuration and status should a network partition occur.

esxcli vsan policy

This command allows you to query, clear and set the default policy of the vSAN datastore. However, as has been mentioned a few times already in this book, we would strongly recommend not changing the default policy, but instead creating a new policy, and setting that as the default on the vSAN datastore.

```
Usage : esxcli vsan policy {cmd} [cmd options]

Available Commands:
    • cleardefault - Clear default vSAN storage policy values.
    • getdefault   - Get default vSAN storage policy values.
    • setdefault   - Set default vSAN storage policy values.
```

Here is the output querying the default policy which has not been modified in any way.

```
[/:~] esxcli vsan policy getdefault
Policy Class   Policy Value
------------   -------------------------------------------------------
cluster        (("hostFailuresToTolerate" i1))
vdisk          (("hostFailuresToTolerate" i1))
vmnamespace    (("hostFailuresToTolerate" i1))
vmswap         (("hostFailuresToTolerate" i1) ("forceProvisioning" i1))
vmem           (("hostFailuresToTolerate" i1) ("forceProvisioning" i1))
```

Here we can see the different VM storage objects that make up a VM deployed on a vSAN datastore, and we can also see the default policy values. Although the policy value is called host failures to tolerate, it actually is the equivalent to the failures to tolerate in the vSphere client. All the objects will tolerate at least one failure in the cluster and remain persistent. The class vdisk refers to VM disk objects (VMDKs). It also covers snapshot deltas. The class vmnamespace is the VM home namespace where the configuration files, metadata files, and log files belonging to the VM are stored. The vmswap policy class is, of course, the VM swap. One final note for vmswap is that it also has a forceProvisioning value. This means that even if there are not enough resources in the vSAN cluster to meet the requirement to provision both VM swap replicas to meet the failures to tolerate requirement, vSAN will still provision the VM with a single VM swap instance. The final entry is vmem. This is the snapshot memory object when a snapshot is taken of a VM, and there is a request to also snapshot memory.

These policy settings, and the reasons for using them, are explained in detail in chapter 5, Storage Policy Based Management.

If you do want to change the default policy to something other than these settings, there is a considerable amount of information in the help file about each of the policies. The command to set a default policy is as follows:

```
# esxcli vsan policy setdefault <-p|--policy> <-c|--policy-class>
```

However, as stated earlier, VMware recommends avoiding configuring policies from the ESXi host. This is because you would have to repeat all of the steps on each of the hosts in the cluster. This is time-consuming, tedious, and prone to user error. The preferred method to modify policies is via the vSphere web client, or if that is not possible, via RVC, the Ruby vSphere Console.

Of course, we did not cover all of the possible policy settings in the default, but you can certainly include any of the supported policy settings in the default policy if you wish. Take care with changing the default policy. Setting unrealistic default values for failures to tolerate or flash read cache reservation in the case of hybrid vSAN, for example, may lead to the inability to provision any VMs. Using the help output from the `esxcli vsan policy setdefault` command, further details are provided about the policy settings that are displayed here for your information:

- `cacheReservation`: Flash capacity reserved as read cache for the storage object. This setting is only applicable on hybrid configurations; it is not used on all-flash configurations since these configurations do not have a read cache. It is specified as a percentage of the logical size of the object. To be used only for addressing read performance issues. Other objects cannot use reserved flash capacity. Unreserved flash is shared fairly among all objects. It is specified in parts per million. Default value: 0, Maximum value: 1000000.
- `forceProvisioning`: If this option is yes, the object will be provisioned even if the requirements specified in the storage policy cannot be satisfied by the resources currently available in the cluster. vSAN will try to bring the object into compliance if and when resources become available. Default value: No.
- `hostFailuresToTolerate`: Defines the number of hosts, disk, or network failures a storage object can tolerate. For n failures tolerated, $n+1$ copies of the object are created, and $2n + 1$ hosts contributing storage are required. Default value: 1, Maximum value: 3.
- `stripeWidth`: The number of capacity drives across which each replica of storage object is striped. A value higher than 1 may result in better performance (e.g., on hybrid systems when flash read cache misses need to get serviced from magnetic disk), but there is no guarantee that performance will improve with an increased `stripeWidth`. Default value: 1, Maximum value: 12.
- `proportionalCapacity`: Percentage of the logical size of the storage object that will be reserved (similar in some respects to thick provisioning) upon VM provisioning. The rest of the storage object is thin provisioned. Default value: 0%, Maximum value: 100%.
- `iopsLimit`: This setting defines the upper normalized IOPS limit for a disk. The IO rate on a disk is measured and if the rate exceeds the IOPS limit, IO will be delayed to keep it under the limit. If the value is set to 0, there is no limit. Default value: 0.
- `replicaPreference`: This setting is used to select RAID-5 or RAID-6 over the default RAID-1/mirror configurations for objects. If a replication method of capacity is chosen over performance (which is the default), and the number of failures to tolerate is set to 1, then RAID-5 is implemented. If a replication method of capacity is chosen and the number of failures to tolerate is set to 2, then RAID-6 is implemented. Note that capacity is only effective when the number of failures to tolerate is set to 1 or 2. Default value: Performance.

The other argument that needs to be included with the `setdefault` command is the `-c|--policy-class` option. This is the vSAN policy class whose default value is being set. The options are `cluster, vdisk, vmnamespace, vmswap`—one of which must be specified in the command.

Lastly, a word about `cluster`, which is one of the policy class options, but is not a VM storage object like `vmnamespace, vdisk,` or `vmswap`. This option is used as a catchall for any objects deployed on a vSAN datastore that are not part of a VM's storage objects.

esxcli vsan resync

The bandwidth and throttle commands can be used to get to first examine whether the resync bandwidth is too large for the cluster, and is possibly impacting workloads, and if it is, to throttle the bandwidth.

```
Usage : esxcli vsan resync {cmd} [cmd options]

Available Namespaces:
    •   bandwidth - Commands for vSAN resync bandwidth
    •   throttle - Commands for vSAN resync throttling
```

Outputs are displayed in Megabits per second (Mbps). However, considering the number of changes that have been made to the Quality of Service around VM traffic and resync traffic, modifying these parameters should hopefully be a last resort in the later versions of vSAN.

esxcli vsan storage

This command looks at all aspects of vSAN storage, from disk group configurations, to adding and removing storage devices to/from disk groups.

```
Usage : esxcli vsan storage {cmd} [cmd options]

Available Namespaces:
    •   automode - Commands for configuring vSAN storage auto claim mode.
    •   diskgroup - Commands for configuring vSAN diskgroups
    •   tag - Commands to add/remove tags for vSAN storage

Available Commands:
    •   add - Add physical disk for vSAN usage.
    •   list - List vSAN storage configuration.
    •   remove - Remove physical disks from vSAN disk groups.
```

The first thing to mention is that the **automode** option has been deprecated since vSAN 6.7. Even though it still appears in this list of namespaces, it doesn't do anything in later releases of vSAN.

To display the capacity tier and cache tier devices that have been claimed and are in use by vSAN from a particular ESXi host, you may use the `list` option. In this configuration, which is an all-flash configuration, SSDs are used for the capacity tier devices and the cache tier. All devices have a `true` flag against the field `Used by this host`, indicating that they have been claimed by vSAN and the `Is SSD` field indicates the type of device (true for flash devices), as shown in the next example.

```
[/:~] esxcli vsan storage list
mpx.vmhba0:C0:T2:L0
   Device: mpx.vmhba0:C0:T2:L0
   Display Name: mpx.vmhba0:C0:T2:L0
   Is SSD: true
   VSAN UUID: 52102e40-918b-9330-7094-c8dcf9081d78
   VSAN Disk Group UUID: 52ff6833-182e-185b-6ad5-57f220408dbe
```

```
   VSAN Disk Group Name: mpx.vmhba0:C0:T4:L0
   Used by this host: true
   In CMMDS: true
   On-disk format version: 15
   Deduplication: false
   Compression: false
   Checksum: 13422673169603001360
   Checksum OK: true
   Is Capacity Tier: true
   Encryption Metadata Checksum OK: true
   Encryption: false
   DiskKeyLoaded: false
   Is Mounted: true
   Creation Time: Fri Mar 11 10:53:46 2022

mpx.vmhba0:C0:T1:L0
   Device: mpx.vmhba0:C0:T1:L0
   Display Name: mpx.vmhba0:C0:T1:L0
   Is SSD: true
   VSAN UUID: 523ef61d-6fa2-5ad0-9033-b03ece895fc1
   VSAN Disk Group UUID: 52ff6833-182e-185b-6ad5-57f220408dbe
   VSAN Disk Group Name: mpx.vmhba0:C0:T4:L0
   Used by this host: true
   In CMMDS: true
   On-disk format version: 15
   Deduplication: false
   Compression: false
   Checksum: 13143089809506123510
   Checksum OK: true
   Is Capacity Tier: true
   Encryption Metadata Checksum OK: true
   Encryption: false
   DiskKeyLoaded: false
   Is Mounted: true
   Creation Time: Fri Mar 11 10:53:46 2022
```

To use ESXCLI to *add* new disks to a disk group on vSAN, you can use the `add` option. There is a different option to choose depending on whether the disk is a magnetic disk or an SSD (`-d|--disks` or `-s|--ssd`, respectively). Note that only disks that are empty and have no partition information can be added to vSAN.

There is also a `remove` option that allows you to remove magnetic disks and SSDs from disk groups on vSAN. It should go without saying that you need to be very careful with this command and removing disks from a disk group on vSAN should be considered a maintenance task. The `remove` option removes all the partition information (and thus all vSAN information) from the disk supplied as an argument to the command. Note that when a cache tier device is removed from a disk group, the whole disk group becomes unavailable. With the `remove` option administrators do have the option to specify which evacuation mode to use, for example, administrators can choose to evacuate all of the data from a disk before it is removed. Use the `-m|--evacuation-mode=<str>` to specify the desired option. Values can be `ensureObjectAccessibility`, `evacuateAllData` or `noAction`. The default is `noAction`.

If you have disks that were once used by vSAN and you now want to repurpose these disks for some other use (Virtual Machine File System [VMFS], Raw Device Mappings [RDM], or in the case of SSDs, vFRC [vSphere Flash Read Cache]), you can use the `remove` option to clean up any vSAN partition information left behind on the disk.

Additional useful commands for looking at disks and controllers include the following:
- `esxcli storage core adapter list`: Displays the driver and adapter description, which can be useful to check that your adapter is on the hardware compatibility list (HCL)
- `esxcfg-info -s | grep "==+SCSI Interface" -A 18`: Displays lots of information, but most importantly shows the queue depth of the device, which is very important for performance
- `esxcli storage core device smart get -d XXX`: Displays SMART statistics about your drive (where XXX would be the device ID), especially SSDs. Very useful command to display Wear-Leveling information, and overall health of your SSD
- `esxcli storage core device stats get`: Displays overall disk statistics

The **diskgroup** namespace options allows for the mounting and unmounting of disk groups. It really isn't a configuration option with this limited set of commands.

It is probably not immediately clear what the **tag** namespace does. This command has a single tag supported, and tags devices as `CapacityFlash` devices so that they can be used for capacity devices in an all-flash vSAN configuration.

esxcli vsan trace

This command allows you to configure where vSAN trace files are stored, how much trace log to retain, when to rotate them and if they should also be redirected to syslog.

```
Usage : esxcli vsan trace {cmd} [cmd options]

Available Commands:
    • get - Get the vSAN tracing configuration.
    • set - Configure vSAN trace. Please note: This command is not thread safe.

Usage: esxcli vsan trace set [cmd options]

Description:
    • set - Configure vSAN trace. Please note: This command is not thread safe.

Cmd options:
    • -l|--logtosyslog=<bool> - Boolean value to enable or disable logging urgent
      traces to syslog.
    • -f|--numfiles=<long> - Log file rotation for vSAN trace files.
    • -p|--path=<str> - Path to store vSAN trace files.
    • -r|--reset=<bool> - When set to true, reset defaults for vSAN trace files.
    • -s|--size=<long> - Maximum size of vSAN trace files in MB.
```

To see what the current trace settings are, you can use the **get** option.

```
[/:~] esxcli vsan trace get
   VSAN Traces Directory:/vsantraces
   Number Of Files To Rotate: 8
   Maximum Trace File Size: 45 MB
   Log Urgent Traces To Syslog: true
```

Additional Non-ESXCLI Commands for vSAN

In addition to the esxcli vsan namespace commands, there are a few additional CLI commands found on an ESXi host that may prove useful for monitoring and troubleshooting.

vsantop

`vsantop` is a relative new command. Most of you are probably familiar with `esxtop`, and as expected vsantop provides performance details of vSAN on a host level. The tool works very similar to esxtop. You can use the the "?" character for help, add and remove fields using "fF", change the order using "oO" and select entities via "E". When you run vsantop you get presented with the following.

```
[root@localhost:~] vsantop
 8:49:26am  | entity type: host-domclient
    nodeId   iops throughput latyAvg latStd    ioCount congestion      oio     iopsRead
throughput
622b0a3e-d      1       8128     176    129          8          0        1        18128
```

As mentioned, "E" can be used to look at various entities, and there is a significant amount of detail provided by vsantop, below you find the list of entities that can be inspected.

```
Current Entity type: host-domclient

   1: cache-disk                2: capacity-disk            3: clom-disk-stats
   4: clom-host-stats           5: cluster                  6: cluster-domclient
   7: cluster-domcompmgr        8: cmmds                    9: cmmds-net
  10: cmmds-workloadstats      11: ddh-disk-stats          12: disk-group
  13: dom-per-proxy-owner      14: dom-proxy-owner         15: dom-world-cpu
  16: host                     17: host-cpu              * 18: host-domclient
  19: host-domcompmgr          20: host-domowner           21: host-memory-heap
  22: host-memory-slab         23: host-vsansparse         24: lsom-world-cpu
  25: nfs-client-vol           26: object                  27: statsdb
  28: system-mem               29: virtual-disk            30: virtual-machine
  31: vmdk-vsansparse          32: vsan-cluster-capacity   33: vsan-distribution
  34: vsan-host-net            35: vsan-iscsi-host         36: vsan-iscsi-lun
  37: vsan-iscsi-target        38: vsan-pnic-net           39: vsan-vnic-net
  40: vscsi
```

The question arises, what should you be monitoring with vsantop, and the answer is simple, nothing. This tool is not intended for day-to-day operations. It should only be used during performance troubleshooting, and only in the situation where the required data can't be found via the vSphere Client.

osfs-ls

`osfs-ls` is more of a troubleshooting command than anything else. It is useful for displaying the contents of the vSAN datastore. The command is not in your search path but can be found in the location shown in the example output below. In this command, we are listing the contents of a VM folder on the vSAN datastore. This can prove useful if the datastore file view is not working correctly from the vSphere client, or it is reporting inaccurate information for some reason or other:

```
[/:~] cd /vmfs/volumes/vsanDatastore/
[/:~] /usr/lib/vmware/osfs/bin/osfs-ls Win7-desktop-orig
.fbb.sf
.fdc.sf
.pbc.sf
.sbc.sf
.vh.sf
.pb2.sf
.sdd.sf
Win7-desktop-orig-12402f4a.hlog
.ccd15e5b-6fbf-bded-5998-246e962f4850.lck
Win7-desktop-orig.vmdk
.34d65e5b-b6e4-880e-2b0e-246e962f4850.lck
Win7-desktop-orig-000001.vmdk
Win7-desktop-orig.nvram
Win7-desktop-orig.vmsd
Win7-desktop-orig-Snapshot2.vmsn
vmware-2.log
vmware-1.log
vmware.log
Win7-desktop-orig-aux.xml
Win7-desktop-orig.vmtx
.6c1f5f5b-7a02-2935-5f1d-246e962f4910.lck
Win7-desktop-orig_1.vmdk
```

cmmds-tool

`cmmds-tool` is another useful troubleshooting command from the ESXi host and can be used to display lots of vSAN information. It can be used to display information such as configuration, metadata, and state about the cluster, hosts in the cluster, and VM storage objects. Many other high-level diagnostic tools leverage information obtained via `cmmds-tool`. As you can imagine, it has a number of options, which you can see by just running the command.

The `find` option may be the most useful, especially when you want to discover information about the actual storage objects backing a VM. You can, for instance, see what the health is of a specific object. In the below example, we want to find additional information about a DOM object represented by UUID `6cd65e5b-1701-509f-8455-246e962f4910`. As you can see, the output below is not the most human-friendly, as is possibly only useful when you need to work on vSAN from an ESXi host. Otherwise, ESXCLI or RVC is the recommended CLI tool of choice as the command outputs are far more readable.

```
[root@esx1-dell-e:~] cmmds-tool find -u 6cd65e5b-1701-509f-8455-246e962f4910
owner=5982fbaf-2ee1-ccce-4298-246e962f4910(Health Healthy) uuid=6cd65e5b-1701-509f-8455-
246e962f4910 type=DOM_OBJECT rev=44 minHostVer=3  [content = (("Configuration" (("CSN" 140)
("SCSN" 116) ("addressSpace" 1273804165120) ("scrubStartTime" 1+1532941932544878)
("objectVersion" i6) ("highestDiskVersion" i6) ("muxGroup" 119882313540193 64) ("groupUuid"
6cd65e5b-1701-509f-8455-246e962f4910) ("compositeUuid" 6cd65e5b-1701-509f-8455-
246e962f4910) ("objClass" i2)) ("RAID_1" (("scope" i3)) ("Component" (("capacity" (10
1273804165120)) ("addressSpace" 1273804165120) ("componentState" 15) ("componentStateTS"
11534418256) ("faultDomainId" 5982f42b-e565-196e-bad9-246e962c2408) ("lastScrubbedOffset"
1289406976) ("subFaultDomainId" 5982f42b-e565-196e-bad9-246e962c2408) ("objClass" i2))
```

```
6cd65e5b-7520-df9f-f0e3-246e962f4910 52aec246-7e55-5da6-5015-3ffe33ab7e49) ("Component"
(("capacity" (10 1273804165120)) ("addressSpace" 1273804165120) ("componentState" 15)
("componentStateTS" 11539110545) ("faultDomainId" 5982fbaf-2ee1-ccce-4298-246e962f4910)
("lastScrubbedOffset" 1289406976) ("subFaultDomainId" 5982fbaf-2ee1-ccce-4298-
246e962f4910) ("objClass" i2)) 90f6bc5b-c661-cc13-6583-246e962f4910 52286aa4-cb8d-de09-
1577-ba9c10ee31a9)) ("Witness" (("componentState" 15) ("componentStateTS" 11534418256)
("isWitness" i1) ("faultDomainId" 5b0bddb5-6f43-73a4-4188-246e962f5270)
("subFaultDomainId" 5b0bddb5-6f43-73a4-4188-246e962f5270)) 6cd65e5b-d8fd-df9f-47aa-
246e962f4910 520269eb-83be-ffbd-c3c9-a980742ee434))], errorStr=(null)
owner=5982fbaf-2ee1-ccce-4298-246e962f4910(Health: Healthy) uuid=6cd65e5b-1701-509f-8455-
246e962f4910 type=DOM_NAME rev=30 minHostVer=0  [content = ("30julytest2" UUID_NULL)],
errorStr=(null)

owner=5982fbaf-2ee1-ccce-4298-246e962f4910(Health: Healthy) uuid=6cd65e5b-1701-509f-8455-
246e962f4910 type=POLICY rev=30 minHostVer=3  [content = (("stripeWidth" i1)
("cacheReservation" i0) ("proportionalCapacity" (i0 i100)) ("hostFailuresToTolerate" i1)
("forceProvisioning" i0) ("spbmProfileId" "aa6d5a82-1c88-45da-85d3-3d74b91a5bad")
("spbmProfileGenerationNumber" l+0) ("CSN" 140) ("SCSN" 116) ("spbmProfileName" "vSAN
Default Storage Policy"))], errorStr=(null)

owner=5982fbaf-2ee1-ccce-4298-246e962f4910(Health: Healthy) uuid=6cd65e5b-1701-509f-8455-
246e962f4910 type=CONFIG_STATUS rev=37 minHostVer=3  [content = (("state" i7) ("CSN" 140)
("SCSN" 116))], errorStr=(null)
```

There are, of course, many other options available to this command that can run. For example, a `-o <owner>` will display information about all objects of which `<owner>` is the owner. This can be a considerable amount of output.

Type is another option and can be specified with a `-t` option. From the preceding output, types such as `DISK`, `HEALTH_STATUS`, `DISK_USAGE`, and `DISK_STATUS` can be displayed. Other types include `DOM_OBJECT`, `DOM_NAME`, `POLICY`, `CONFIG_STATUS`, `HA_METADATA`, `HOSTNAME`, and so on. Below example shows a list of hostnames taken from a 4-node cluster:

```
[/:~] cmmds-tool find -t HOSTNAME

owner=5982f466-c59d-0e07-aa4e-246e962f4850(Health: Healthy) uuid=5982f466-c59d-0e07-aa4e-
246e962f4850 type=HOSTNAME rev=0 minHostVer=0  [content = ("esxi-dell-g.rainpole.com")],
errorStr=(null)

owner=5982f3ab-2ff0-fd4d-17f5-246e962f5270(Health: Unhealthy) uuid=5982f3ab-2ff0-fd4d-
17f5-246e962f5270 type=HOSTNAME rev=0 minHostVer=0  [content = ("esxi-dell-
f.rainpole.com")], errorStr=(null)

owner=5982f42b-e565-196e-bad9-246e962c2408(Health: Healthy) uuid=5982f42b-e565-196e-bad9-
246e962c2408 type=HOSTNAME rev=0 minHostVer=0  [content = ("esxi-dell-h.rainpole.com")],
errorStr=(null)

owner=5982fbaf-2ee1-ccce-4298-246e962f4910(Health: Healthy) uuid=5982fbaf-2ee1-ccce-4298-
246e962f4910 type=HOSTNAME rev=0 minHostVer=0  [content = ("esxi-dell-e.rainpole.com")],
errorStr=(null)
```

As you can see, this very powerful command enables you to do a lot of investigation and troubleshooting from an ESXi host. Again, exercise caution when using this command. Alternatively, use only under the guidance of VMware support staff if you have concerns.

vdq

The `vdq` command serves two purposes and is really a great troubleshooting tool to have on the ESXi host. The first option to this command tells you whether disks on your ESXi host are eligible for vSAN, and if not, what the reason is for the disk being ineligible.

The second option to this command is that once vSAN has been enabled, you can use the command to display disk mapping information, which is essentially which SSD or flash devices and magnetic disks are grouped together in a disk group.

Let's first run the option to query all disks for eligibility for vSAN use. Example 9.16 is from a host that already has vSAN enabled:

```
[/:~] vdq -q
[
   {
      "Name"            : "naa.624a9370d4d78052ea564a7e00011138",
      "VSANUUID"        : "",
      "State"           : "Ineligible for use by VSAN",
      "Reason"          : "Has partitions",
      "IsSSD"           : "1",
"IsCapacityFlash": "0",
      "IsPDL"           : "0",
      "Size(MB)"        : "512000",
   "FormatType"    : "512n",
   "IsVsanDirectDisk" : "0"
   },
   {
      "Name"            : "naa.624a9370d4d78052ea564a7e00011139",
      "VSANUUID"        : "",
      "State"           : "Ineligible for use by VSAN",
      "Reason"          : "Has partitions",
      "IsSSD"           : "1",
"IsCapacityFlash": "0",
      "IsPDL"           : "0",
      "Size(MB)"        : "512000",
   "FormatType"    : "512n",
   "IsVsanDirectDisk" : "0"
   },
   {
      "Name"            : "naa.624a9370d4d78052ea564a7e0001113c",
      "VSANUUID"        : "",
      "State"           : "Ineligible for use by VSAN",
      "Reason"          : "Has partitions",
      "IsSSD"           : "1",
"IsCapacityFlash": "0",
      "IsPDL"           : "0",
      "Size(MB)"        : "2097152",
   "FormatType"    : "512n",
   "IsVsanDirectDisk" : "0"
   },
```

The second useful option to the command is to dump out the vSAN disk mappings; in other words, which flash devices and/or which magnetic disks are in a disk group. The next example shows a sample output (which includes the `-H` option to make it more human readable):

```
[/:~] vdq -i -H
Mappings:
   DiskMapping[0]:
            SSD:  naa.5001e820026415f0
             MD:  naa.500a07510f86d6bb
             MD:  naa.500a07510f86d685
```

This command shows the SSD relationship to capacity devices, whether they are flash devices in the case of all-flash configurations or magnetic disks in the case of hybrid configurations. Note that even if these are flash devices, they are shown as MD (magnetic disks) in this output, the `IsCapacityFlash` field would need to be examined to see if these are flash devices (e.g., SSD) or not. This is very useful if you want to find out the disk group layout on a particular host from the command line. This command will quickly tell you which magnetic disks are fronted by which SSDs, especially when you have multiple disk groups defined on an ESXi host.

Although some of the commands shown in this section may prove useful to examine and monitor vSAN on an ESXi host basis, administrators ideally need something whereby they can examine the whole cluster. VMware recognized this very early on in the development of vSAN, and so introduced extensions to the RVC to allow a cluster-wide view of vSAN. The next topic delves into RVC.

Ruby vSphere Console (RVC) Commands

The previous section looked at ESXi host-centric commands for vSAN. These might be of some use when troubleshooting vSAN, but with large clusters, administrators may find themselves having to run the same set of commands repeatedly on the different hosts in the cluster. In this next section, we cover a tool that enables you to take a cluster-centric view of vSAN called the Ruby vSphere Console (RVC). RVC is also included in the VMware vCenter Server Appliance (VCSA). As mentioned in the introduction, RVC is a programmable interface that allows administrators to query the status of vCenter Server, clusters, hosts, storage, and networking. For vSAN, there are quite a number of programmable extensions to display a considerable amount of information that you need to know about a vSAN cluster. This section covers those vSAN extensions in RVC.

RVC provides a significant set of very useful commands that enable the monitoring, management, and troubleshooting of vSAN from the CLI.

You can connect RVC to any vCenter Server. On the vCenter Server, you log in via Secure Shell (SSH) and run `rvc <user>@<vc-ip>`. In our lab we leverage root to login to SSH and then use administrator@vsphere.local to login to RVC. This looks as follows:

```
root@localhost [ ~ ]# rvc administrator@vsphere.local@localhost
[DEPRECATION] This gem has been renamed to optimist and will no longer be supported.
Please switch to optimist as soon as possible.
Install the "ffi" gem for better tab completion.
WARNING: Nokogiri was built against LibXML version 2.9.8, but has dynamically loaded
2.9.11
```

```
password:
0 /
1 localhost/
>
```

After you log in, you will see a virtual file system, with the vCenter Server instance at the root. You can now begin to use navigation commands such as **cd** and **ls**, as well as tab-completion to navigate the file system. The structure of the file system mimics the inventory items tree views that you find in the vSphere client. Therefore, you can run `cd <vCenter Server>`, followed by `cd <datacenter>`. You can use ~ to refer to your current datacenter, and all clusters are in the "`computers`" folder under your datacenter. Note that when you navigate to a `folder/directory`, the contents are listed with numeric values. These numeric values may also be used as shortcuts. For example, in the vCenter Server shown in the output below there is only one datacenter, and it has a numeric value of 0 associated with it. We can then `cd` to 0, instead of typing out the full name of the datacenter. RVC also provides tab completion of commands.

```
> ls
0 /
1 vcsa-06/
> cd 1
/vcsa-06> ls
0 CH-Datacenter (datacenter)
/vcsa-06> cd CH-Datacenter/
/vcsa-06/CH-Datacenter> ls
0 storage/
1 computers [host]/
2 networks [network]/
3 datastores [datastore]/
4 vms [vm]/
/vcsa-06/CH-Datacenter> cd 1
/vcsa-06/CH-Datacenter/computers> ls
0 CH-Cluster (cluster): cpu 153 GHz, memory 381 GB
/vcsa-06/CH-Datacenter/computers> cd CH-Cluster/
/vcsa-06/CH-Datacenter/computers/CH-Cluster>
```

The full list of commands, at the time of writing, is shown here. However, as mentioned in the introduction, RVC may be deprecated in favor of ESXCLI, so this list of commands, as well as their functionality, is subject to change in future releases.

The names of the commands describe pretty well what the command is used for. However, a few examples from some of the more popular commands are shown later for your information.

```
vsan.apply_license_to_cluster
vsan.bmc_info_get
vsan.bmc_info_set
vsan.check_limits
vsan.check_state
vsan.clear_disks_cache
vsan.cluster_change_autoclaim
vsan.cluster_info
vsan.cluster_set_default_policy
vsan.cmmds_find
vsan.debug.
vsan.disable_vsan_on_cluster
vsan.disk_object_info
```

```
vsan.disks_info
vsan.disks_stats
vsan.enable_vsan_on_cluster
vsan.enter_maintenance_mode
vsan.fix_renamed_vms
vsan.health.
vsan.host_claim_disks_differently
vsan.host_consume_disks
vsan.host_evacuate_data
vsan.host_exit_evacuation
vsan.host_info
vsan.host_wipe_non_vsan_disk
vsan.host_wipe_vsan_disks
vsan.iscsi_target.
vsan.lldpnetmap
vsan.login_iso_depot
vsan.obj_status_report
vsan.object_info
vsan.object_reconfigure
vsan.observer
vsan.observer_process_statsfile
vsan.ondisk_upgrade
vsan.perf.
vsan.proactive_rebalance
vsan.proactive_rebalance_info
vsan.purge_inaccessible_vswp_objects
vsan.reapply_vsan_vmknic_config
vsan.recover_spbm
vsan.resync_dashboard
vsan.scrubber_info
vsan.stretchedcluster.
vsan.support_information
vsan.unmap_status
vsan.upgrade_status
vsan.v2_ondisk_upgrade
vsan.vm_object_info
vsan.vm_perf_stats
vsan.vmdk_stats
vsan.whatif_host_failures
```

To make this output easier to display, for certain commands we have separated out each of the columns and displayed them individually.

The output of vsan.check_limits

This command takes a cluster as an argument. It displays the limits on the cluster, on a per host as-is. These limits include network limits as well as disk limits, not just from a capacity perspective but also from a component perspective.

```
> vsan.check_limits /vcsa-06/CH-Datacenter/computers/CH-Cluster
+---------------+---------------+-----------------------------------------+
| Host          | RDT           | Disks                                   |
+---------------+---------------+-----------------------------------------+
| 10.202.25.207 | Assocs: 24/   | Components: 5/3500                      |
|               | Sockets: 15/  | mpx.vmhba0:C0:T2:L0: 1% Components: 2/47661 |
|               | Clients: 1    | mpx.vmhba0:C0:T4:L0: 0% Components: 0/0 |
|               | Owners: 4     | mpx.vmhba0:C0:T3:L0: 1% Components: 2/47661 |
|               |               | mpx.vmhba0:C0:T1:L0: 1% Components: 1/47661 |
| 10.202.25.226 | Assocs: 7/    | Components: 5/3500                      |
|               | Sockets: 7/   | mpx.vmhba0:C0:T1:L0: 1% Components: 2/47661 |
|               | Clients: 0    | mpx.vmhba0:C0:T3:L0: 1% Components: 1/47661 |
|               | Owners: 1     | mpx.vmhba0:C0:T4:L0: 0% Components: 0/0 |
|               |               | mpx.vmhba0:C0:T2:L0: 1% Components: 2/47661 |
| 10.202.25.228 | Assocs: 10/   | Components: 6/3500                      |
|               | Sockets: 9/   | mpx.vmhba0:C0:T1:L0: 1% Components: 3/47661 |
|               | Clients: 0    | mpx.vmhba0:C0:T3:L0: 1% Components: 2/47661 |
|               | Owners: 1     | mpx.vmhba0:C0:T4:L0: 0% Components: 0/0 |
|               |               | mpx.vmhba0:C0:T2:L0: 1% Components: 1/47661 |
| 10.202.25.222 | Assocs: 8/    | Components: 4/3500                      |
|               | Sockets: 5/   | mpx.vmhba0:C0:T3:L0: 1% Components: 1/47661 |
|               | Clients: 0    | mpx.vmhba0:C0:T1:L0: 1% Components: 1/47661 |
|               | Owners: 3     | mpx.vmhba0:C0:T4:L0: 0% Components: 0/0 |
|               |               | mpx.vmhba0:C0:T2:L0: 1% Components: 2/47661 |
| 10.202.25.225 | Assocs: 8/    | Components: 6/3500                      |
|               | Sockets: 8/   | mpx.vmhba0:C0:T2:L0: 1% Components: 2/47661 |
|               | Clients: 0    | mpx.vmhba0:C0:T4:L0: 0% Components: 0/0 |
|               | Owners: 1     | mpx.vmhba0:C0:T3:L0: 1% Components: 2/47661 |
|               |               | mpx.vmhba0:C0:T1:L0: 1% Components: 2/47661 |
| 10.202.25.221 | Assocs: 19/   | Components: 6/3500                      |
|               | Sockets: 12/  | mpx.vmhba0:C0:T1:L0: 1% Components: 2/47661 |
|               | Clients: 0    | mpx.vmhba0:C0:T2:L0: 1% Components: 2/47661 |
|               | Owners: 4     | mpx.vmhba0:C0:T3:L0: 1% Components: 2/47661 |
|               |               | mpx.vmhba0:C0:T4:L0: 0% Components: 0/0 |
+---------------+---------------+-----------------------------------------+
```

The output of vsan.host_info

This command can be used to display specific host information. It provides information about what the role of the host is (master, backup, agent), what its UUID is, and what the other member UUIDs are (so you can see how many hosts are in the cluster) and of course information about networking and storage. It displays the adapter and IP address that the host is using to join the vSAN network, and which devices have been claimed for both the cache tier and capacity tier.

```
> vsan.host_info /vcsa-06/CH-Datacenter/computers/CH-Cluster/hosts/esxi-dell-
e.rainpole.com/
Product: VMware ESXi 7.0.3 build-19193900
vSAN enabled: yes
Cluster info:
  Cluster role: master
  Cluster UUID: 520fedd3-0923-7544-5d87-aa9a75af2642
  Node UUID: 622b0a3e-d1ab-2aa0-f1a9-005056968de9
  Member UUIDs: ["622b0a3e-d1ab-2aa0-f1a9-005056968de9", "622b0a41-5417-aec9-4875-
00505696fc4c", "622b0a44-990a-bec6-ed1b-00505696fe2b", "622b0a3d-9bc9-96c5-4e84-
005056967241", "622b0a3e-ca8c-91a0-ed69-005056963c2d", "622b0a3d-9738-7636-a15a-
005056962c93"] (6)
Node evacuated: no
Storage info:
  Auto claim: no
  Disk Mappings:
    Cache Tier: Local VMware Disk (mpx.vmhba0:C0:T4:L0) - 50 GB, v15
    Capacity Tier: Local VMware Disk (mpx.vmhba0:C0:T3:L0) - 256 GB, v15
    Capacity Tier: Local VMware Disk (mpx.vmhba0:C0:T2:L0) - 256 GB, v15
    Capacity Tier: Local VMware Disk (mpx.vmhba0:C0:T1:L0) - 256 GB, v15
FaultDomainInfo:
  Not configured
NetworkInfo:
  Adapter: vmk0 (10.202.25.207)
Data efficiency enabled: no
Encryption enabled: no
```

Output of vsan.disks_info

This is a useful RVC command to display whether or not is free or in use, and if it is in use, who is using it. It takes a hostname as an argument.

```
> vsan.disks_info /vcsa-06/CH-Datacenter/computers/CH-Cluster/hosts/esxi-dell-
f.rainpole.com/
Disks on host 10.202.25.207:
```

DisplayName	isSSD	Size	State
Local VMware Disk (mpx.vmhba0:C0:T4:L0) VMware Virtual disk	SSD	50 GB	inUse vSAN Format Version: v15
Local VMware Disk (mpx.vmhba0:C0:T3:L0) VMware Virtual disk	SSD	256 GB	inUse vSAN Format Version: v15
Local VMware Disk (mpx.vmhba0:C0:T2:L0) VMware Virtual disk	SSD	256 GB	inUse vSAN Format Version: v15
Local VMware Disk (mpx.vmhba0:C0:T1:L0) VMware Virtual disk	SSD	256 GB	inUse vSAN Format Version: v15

Those are just a few sample commands, but as you can tell there are a lot of additional commands that you can run with RVC. Use the -h option on any commands to get more information on how to use it.

Summary

As you can see, an extensive suite of tools is available for managing and monitoring a vSAN deployment. With this extensive suite of CLI tools, administrators can drill down into the lowest levels of vSAN behavior.

The End

You have made it to the end of the book. Hopefully, you now have a good idea of how vSAN works and what vSAN can provide for your workloads in a VMware-based infrastructure.

We have tried to simplify some of the concepts to make them easier to understand. However, we acknowledge that some concepts can still be difficult to grasp. We hope that after reading this book everyone is confident enough to design, install, configure, manage, monitor, and even troubleshoot vSAN based hyperconverged infrastructures.

If there are any questions, please do not hesitate to reach out to either of the authors via Twitter or LinkedIn. We will do our best to answer your questions. Another option we would like to recommend for vSAN related questions is the VMware VMTN Community Forum. It is monitored by dozens of vSAN experts, and answers to questions are typically provided within hours. (https://vmwa.re/vsanvmtn)

Thanks for reading,

Cormac and Duncan

Made in the USA
Coppell, TX
09 May 2022